MW00965364

"At this point in history one cannot help but commend the efforts of Keorapetse Kgositsile and Mothobi Mutloatse for putting into book form the writings of Comrade Z Pallo Jordan, who undoubtedly ranks among the sharpest minds in the intellectual history of the African National Congress (ANC) and indeed our country.

"In many ways this book is strikingly apt for the current historical period. For one thing, it is being published at a time when the current phase of the historical process is astride two separate but conceptually inter-linking periods … the apartheid and the post-apartheid stages. In consequence the book gives the reader a historical continuum, surfacing Jordan's and by extension the ANC's core thinking on the anti-apartheid struggle as well as the novel paradigms that emerged on the heels of the demise of apartheid as the country underwent the process of reconstruction and development. Comrade Jordan's reflections illuminate our understanding of this historical process with the rare clarity of mind for which he is reputed."

FORMER PRESIDENT KGALEMA MOTLANTHE

"Over the many years of exile and the twenty-four years since our return ekhaya I have followed his writings eagerly and I have sometimes been lost in the intricacies of his phenomenal arguments about the history and culture of South Africa.

"He is the arch that has exerted pressure to support the building of our nation. The driving force of his arguments sometimes grates against the grain, even antagonises because his search for truth is unyielding and can beggar the very persuasion that ought to inform public commentary.

"I shudder to think how he has been able to maintain the intellectual equanimity during all the decades of what he would, of course, being Pallo Jordan call his 'Faustian pact', causing all and sundry to rush to their dictionaries to refresh their understanding of this allusion."

BARBARA MASEKELA, AMBASSADOR

"This book is a tribute to Pallo's outstanding contribution to our struggle for freedom, to thought leadership and to standing up not only for what is right but also against that which is wrong, regardless of the consequences. It makes an important contribution to the telling of the South African story through the voice and thoughts of one of South Africa's freedom fighters – Z Pallo Jordan, a person I have been privileged to work with and know over many decades, and who helped forge our young democracy."

GIL MARCUS, FORMER GOVERNOR OF THE SOUTH AFRICAN RESERVE BANK

Letters to My Comrades

Interventions & Excursions

Z Pallo Jordan

COMPILED BY
Keorapetse Kgositsile
& Mothobi Mutloatse

*In association with
African Lives Series*

This book is number 8 in the African Lives Series, an independent writing and publishing initiative that aims to contribute to a post-colonial intellectual history of South Africa. The series editor is Prof. Andre Odendaal.

First published by Jacana Media (Pty) Ltd in 2017

10 Orange Street
Sunnyside
Auckland Park 2092
South Africa
+2711 628 3200
www.jacana.co.za

ISBN 978-1-4314-2486-3

Cover design by Shawn Paikin
Cover image © Helen Kritzler
Set in Ehrhardt 11/15.5pt
Printed and bound by ABC Press, Cape Town
Job no. 003070

See a complete list of Jacana titles at www.jacana.co.za

Contents

Acknowledgements

National liberation, according to Amilcar Cabral,
is necessarily an act of culture.

Cabral's proverb was, and still continues to be, the inspiration behind this compilation of Z Pallo Jordan's intellectual and literary thoughts spanning 40 years.

Thank you, *mhlekazi* Jordan, most graciously – for having allowed Professor Willie Keorapetse Kgositsile (your eternal friend) and me to enjoy the rare honour of assembling your creative expressions into this single volume.

Colin Bundy should be commended for invaluable contributions as consulting editor. We also wish to bow our heads to comrades Barbara Masekela, Gil Marcus and former president Kgalema Motlanthe for their passionate tributes to their compatriot during these difficult episodes of our democracy amid the vexing question: *Quo vadis?*

Grateful thanks are also due to the National Arts Council for supporting the initial stages of compilation; and also the to the Mutloatse Arts Heritage support team, especially Nthabiseng Mhlongo, not forgetting the library staff at Times Media.

The publishers also wish to acknowledge and thank all the publishers of the numerous journals, newspapers and magazines in which the writings of Z Pallo Jordan appeared.

Re a leboga go menagane, compatriots – Mothobi Mutloatse, publisher, Mutloatse Arts Heritage Trust: www.mutloatse.com

Introduction

Zweledinga Pallo Jordan was born in May 1942, the second of four children – two girls, one of whom was adopted, and two boys. Some of the most captivating pages in the autobiography by his mother, Phyllis Ntantala,[1] are those recalling the family's life in Cape Town in the 1940s and 1950s. The family moved to Cape Town in 1946 when his father, A.C. Jordan, was appointed to a lectureship at the University of Cape Town (UCT). In November of that year A.C. (known to his familiars as Joe) bought a plot of land in Fleur Road, Lincoln Estate, in the suburb of Crawford, and built the family home there.

The Jordans were the only African family in Lincoln Estate, a racially mixed, predominantly Coloured working-class area. The children attended local schools where 'they all did well', Phyllis noted matter-of-factly: *Pallo proceeded from an Anglican primary to complete his Senior Certificate at Athlone High School.* His parents had previously avoided Athlone High School as they disapproved of its principal as a 'collaborator': he belonged to a conservative teachers' association, formed when Non-European Unity Movement (NEUM) teachers seized control of the older Teachers' League of South Africa. Both Phyllis and Joe had cut their political teeth in the teachers' movement in the Orange Free State and later the Cape African Teachers' Association; his closeness to I.B. Tabata (his 'best friend' according to Phyllis) made their commitment to the TLSA a given. Phyllis was a member of half-a-dozen left-wing groups, all affiliated to Tabata's NEUM.

Politically active she was through these years, but for the first time while her children were growing up, Phyllis did not go to work but stayed at home, until she returned to her studies in 1957 to take the Diploma in Native Administration (taught by Jack Simons) at UCT. And so Pallo entered his teens during years when her children – on return from school – 'were always with me, in the kitchen, in the living-room, in their bedroom, out in the yard, doing things together'. They learned to paint, and to cook: as they grew up, the Jordan children were 'exposed to a world of books, music and progressive ideas ... [they] lived in a world of ideas, in an intellectual atmosphere'. They went to classical music concerts, shows and plays, ballet and the open-air productions at Maynardville; at home, fortnightly family evening recitals and Sunday music evenings were regular events.

During dinner hours, the family was 'always together, sharing the day's experiences. We talked, discussed, asked questions, had questions answered. This was our happy hour.' There were other hours of happiness: the Jordans held parties which were 'a magnet': school friends attended, so did the older children's white friends from UCT, together with 'nieces, nephews and their cousins'; even the 'street-corner boys' of the neighbourhood swarmed to these events, required only to 'dress up clean and tidy' – in return for which 'they saw that no riff-raff came to our parties'!

It is impossible to read these evocative passages without relating them to Pallo Jordan's later life. His family background and socialisation must have shaped him profoundly: as political actor and office-holder, as thinker and writer, as a culturally confident and cosmopolitan South African intellectual. Unsurprisingly, given their parentage, Pallo and his elder sister Nandi were precocious political activists – 'distributing leaflets and going to political rallies' formed part of their childhood. Pallo was prevented from registering as a student at UCT by the 1959 Extension of University Education Act (an Orwellian title for legislation that segregated higher education) but he had library rights there while upgrading his Senior Certificate to A-levels.

At UCT, he began drifting away from the NEUM through association with the Modern Youth Society, central to the UCT student left although set up as an off-campus society. At their gatherings he met Denis Goldberg, Alex and Blanche La Guma, Amy Rietstein-Thornton, George Peake and others. He became part of the UCT student left – 'well known on Freedom Square and among the Modern Youth Society group', said Phyllis; he mixed with Hillel Ticktin, Fikile Bam, Basil February, James April, Welsh Makanda, Dawn Levy, Archie Mafeje, *Frank van der Horst, the Schimmings from Namibia* – and others (the 'usual political suspects', he recalls with a chuckle).[2] In 1960, in the tense days following the Sharpeville massacre, Pallo and others heard that the march on Parliament, led by Philip Kgosana, was approaching Mowbray and dashed from campus to join it.

The events of 1960 proved to be a watershed for many political opponents of apartheid. Sharpeville itself, but especially the State of Emergency, nation-wide detentions and the banning of the ANC and PAC, precipitated a decision by many to leave South Africa, often on exit permits which foreclosed any prospects of return. The Jordan family was one that followed this route. A.C., having accepted an academic invitation from the University of California, left South Africa illegally through Bechuanaland (now Botswana) and Tanganyika; Phyllis and the children followed, initially to Hull, on the Yorkshire coast in England; and in 1963 A.C. accepted an appointment at the University of Wisconsin, to help set up an African Studies Program.

Pallo and his brother Lindi enrolled as students at the University of Wisconsin, in Madison. Phyllis recalls that they enjoyed their classes; Pallo was 'in great demand among the progressive student groups' who were keen to learn about the situation in South Africa. He wrote for the student newspaper, and in 1964 moved to an apartment in Mifflin Street, home to many of the student left. American politics in the mid-1960s were highly charged and confrontational. Radical students supported voter registration drives in the segregated South, challenged segregation with sit-ins and protests, and celebrated the passage of the Civil Rights Act of 1964 and Voting Rights Act of 1965. From 1964 student opposition to America's war in Vietnam escalated – and the campuses at Wisconsin, Madison and Berkeley in California were at the centre of anti-war protests and mobilisation. The young Jordan flung himself into sit-ins, vigils, marches and protests – and his activities earned him the disapproving scrutiny of the American security and immigration services. Early in 1967 (by which time Pallo had moved to the New School for Social Research in New York, hoping to read for a master's in Economics, History and Philosophy) a court hearing confirmed the order from Immigration expelling him from the United States.

He returned to England, staying initially with Mazisi Raymond Kunene in London. Ever since his days on the UCT campus, and throughout the American years, Jordan's political affiliation had gravitated away from the NEUM sympathies of his parents towards support for the ANC. In London, this political orientation took practical form. He did voluntary work in the ANC offices in Charlotte Street; but also sustained his international political commitments. In 1968, he supported the students' movement in Paris and joined the Camden Vietnam Solidarity Campaign, part of the British Vietnam Solidarity Campaign led by Tariq Ali. At the end of August 1968, his political thinking was severely jolted when the Soviet invasion of Czechoslovakia was supported not only by the South African Communist Party (SACP) but also by its ally in exile, the ANC. It was a watershed moment – 'it shook me radically', he recalled recently – and in consequence Pallo effectively withdrew from his ANC activities. He remained 'out of the fold' for the next four years, never actually breaking with the movement but scaling down his involvement in it.[3]

By 1972 Jordan was grappling with the question of what his primary political role would be: a revolutionary in the abstract, or a participant in actual struggle? His decision in favour of the latter ushered him back into the ANC fold. In 1975 he was working in the London office again; by the time of the Soweto Uprising he was a full-time employee of the movement, working alongside Frene Ginwala, Moeletsi Mbeki, Gill Marcus and others. In 1975 Jordan also joined Mayibuye, a London-based anti-apartheid cultural group formed by Barry Feinberg and Ronnie Kasrils, with John Matshikiza and others. His participation in the ANC-agitprop group provides a glimpse of his unusual stance within the ANC at the time. Kasrils describes Pallo in 1975 as 'a fiercely independent thinker, with a razor-sharp mind and memory, and a waspish temperament'. His sharp criticisms of the Soviet Union made him 'politically unconventional in ANC circles'; some simply dismissed him as a 'Trotskyist'. A debate ensued about whether he should be allowed to join Mayibuye. Kasrils supported his membership, because what mattered 'was his loyalty to the ANC' and not whether he accepted 'the Moscow line'.[4]

Kasrils and Jordan became friends, despite their strongly opposing views on the Communist Party: 'He was a delightful companion on our trips and I soon came to refer to him affectionately as "Zee Pee",' writes Kasrils. Pallo's willingness to overlook doctrinal differences when it came to individuals remained a distinctive feature of his role within the ANC, in exile and upon return to South Africa. His relationship with Joe Slovo is a case in point. The pair were intellectually close in London in the mid-1970s; worked alongside each other in Angola and Zambia; and after 1990 in South Africa their friendship survived substantial and public disagreements [Documents 9, 14].[5]

In 1976 Oliver Tambo sought a meeting with Jordan in London. A friend of his parents, Tambo had been impressed by Pallo's work in starting, with others, a small publication directed mainly at South African students studying abroad. The intention (Jordan told Luli Callinicos) was 'to find ways and means of linking up with the home fountains', attracting 'and then perhaps drawing them into ANC structures, hopefully being able to use them as a jumping off point for building networks inside the country'.[6] Given the Soweto Uprising, Tambo was impressed by the prescience of this initiative and recruited Pallo to serve on the propaganda portfolio of the ANC, and posted him to Luanda in April 1977, to revive Radio Freedom. Radio Freedom became 'a formidable operation', broadcasting out of Angola and Tanzania.[7] In later years, Ethiopia and Madagascar were added as transmission points. In 1979 Jordan returned to London, to lead the 'Year of the Spear' campaign around the centenary of the Battle of Isandhlwana – the first internal mass publicity campaign mounted by the ANC.

Both in London and in Lusaka, Jordan worked in the Department of Information and Propaganda (later Publicity), or DIP. The DIP developed a reputation as the intellectual heart of the movement: it harnessed the energies of Frene Ginwala and Gill Marcus in London, and in Lusaka gave scope to a group of young intellectuals of the Soweto generation – Mandla Langa, Joel Netshitenzhe, Zinjiva Nkondo and others. After a period of internal tensions and reconstruction, the DIP bedded down in the early 1980s with Thabo Mbeki as its director and Pallo Jordan as head of its research function, a position he held from late 1979 until 1988. He worked in Lusaka, London and in Maputo, collaborating with Ruth First in the Centre for Southern African Studies at Eduardo Mondlane University.

The DIP was a natural political home for Pallo Jordan. It made room for his dedication to ideas and the written word, and also welcomed his commitment to the cause of liberation. It provided him with the room to innovate and experiment. Radio Freedom, for example, was not just a technical challenge but a political opportunity: 'We recognised' (he said later) 'that radio was a very important medium; what we said was that radio offers the movement the rare opportunity of *holding a virtual mass meeting* inside the country at least once a day, if you did it right.' Similarly, he insisted on the value of propaganda in different registers. While Radio Freedom was overtly the voice of the ANC, there were also more subtle ways of conveying the message. There was a valuable space for persuasion that could 'be occupied in various ways ... [like] 'T-shirts, stickers, bumper stickers, the poster, various items of clothing, buttons and all these are propaganda media'. These media did not necessarily use ANC slogans, but their message was 'consonant with the ANC', such as T-shirts saying 'The people shall govern'.[8]

In 1982, Jordan considered how the DIP might be most effective, formulating a set of precise guidelines as to how the ANC should use propaganda and information. It should cultivate its image as 'the chief mobiliser, unifier and vanguard of the liberation struggle', but had to be careful not to relegate the masses to the 'role of onlookers'. 'The people' would be their own liberators, agents of change. Jordan also emphasised the need to shape a very specific public image of the ANC. This would embrace the idea that the movement was 'a living and growing organism born out of the struggles of the oppressed people'; as such it was 'both the product of history and the maker of history'. The ANC should avoid the tendency to project itself as 'the brainchild of a handful of patriotic geniuses' even while it recognised the role played by its founders and 'all those individual men and women who have helped shape and mould the ANC into what it is today'.[9] This was an internal document, designed to shape practice; but the guidelines resonate with Jordan's insistence on a dialectic approach even to something as straightforward as the movement's public image.

In June 1985 the ANC held a national consultative conference – its first since Morogoro in 1969 – at Kabwe, in Zambia. The conference was partly an attempt by the ANC to take stock of momentous political developments inside South Africa, and partly to restore unity and legitimacy within the exiled movement. An essential backdrop to the conference was that events in South Africa indicated a tilt in the balance of forces. Internal opposition – by trade unions, by the United Democratic Front (linking youth and student organisations, urban 'civics', and women's movements, and unmistakably pro-ANC in its leanings), and by swirling popular anger during the Vaal Triangle uprising of 1984 – could only be contained by successive States of Emergency and a militarised policing response.

The other precipitant of Kabwe was the need to restore morale after some exceptionally difficult years for the ANC and its armed wing, MK. The difficulties stemmed, firstly, from military pressures by the South African Defence Force and security agencies: these included raids and attacks; the sponsorship of rebel movements in Mozambique and Angola; and, in March 1984, the Nkomati Accord signed by South Africa and Mozambique, which significantly weakened the ANC presence in Mozambique and Swaziland. Problems arose, secondly, in the form of internal tensions: the discovery of South African spies among senior MK operatives in Angola; a security crackdown by the movement's National Intelligence and Security Department (NAT) that combined paranoia, rumour and abuse of power; and, in response, mutinies by several hundred MK soldiers in Angolan camps just before and after the Nkomati Accord.

Pallo Jordan experienced both sets of pressures at first hand, and acutely. He was across the desk from Ruth First, on 17 August 1982, when she opened the letter bomb sent by the state agent Craig Williamson. She died instantly; Jordan suffered multiple injuries which left him deaf in one ear; his eyesight was saved by the wraparound dark glasses that he habitually wore. He was hospitalised for an extended period. He moved back to Lusaka, where he became a victim of the ANC's vicious security crackdown. He was detained for six weeks in 1983 by Mbokodo ('the grinding stone' – NAT's grim soubriquet). His detention followed unguarded disparagement of the strong-handed security agency: 'I had criticised the methods they used and they came to get me,' he told a reporter years later. His detention and questioning were ended by the personal intervention of MK seniors Hani, Kasrils and Slovo.

Although many of Tambo's generation retained their positions in the National Executive Committee (NEC) elected at Kabwe, there was also a partial changing of the guard. This was partly through the election of some younger members: Pallo Jordan, at 43, became one of a younger cohort elected to the NEC. More significantly, after Kabwe, the administration of the *Politico- Military Council (PMC)* and National Working Committee – responsible for the day-to-day direction of MK and ANC – passed primarily into the hands of a younger leadership generation, people in their forties and fifties. The most influential of these were Joe Slovo, Mac Maharaj, Chris Hani, Thabo Mbeki, Joe Nhlanhla, Cassius Make, Josiah Jele and Sizakele Sigxashe. *Pallo Jordan was appointed Administrative Secretary of the NEC, working alongside Ruth Mompathi in the Office of the Secretary-General. Alfred Nzo.* Tambo valued Jordan's intellectual and strategic abilities, and after Kabwe he charged him with several important tasks. One of these was uncompleted. The Kabwe conference had failed to revisit the *ANC's Strategy and Tactics* document approved at Morogoro; and Jordan was appointed to chair a subcommittee to begin this task. The group failed to report, and in October 1989 Jordan acknowledged that it had been 'overtaken by events'.[10]

A second post-Kabwe assignment was the 'Submission on the Question of Negotiations', an internal ANC policy paper mainly written by Pallo. Mark Gevisser felt that Jordan's stance on negotiations in this paper was 'negative and suspicious', even 'archaic': a view that owed much to the fact that while Jordan was 'theorizing about negotiations, Mbeki was out there, doing it'.[11] This is an unconvincing reading of the Submission: the document is pragmatic, alert to potential dangers, and essentially an exercise in realpolitik.[12] It begins by insisting that 'Talks with the enemy are, in and of themselves, not harmful. If negotiations are viewed as yet one more terrain of struggle ... we have no reason to shun them ... we will enter into talks as a means of pursuing our political objectives.' It outlined certain preconditions for talks (which became very familiar in the next few years): unbanning of the movement, release of political prisoners, lifting of the State of Emergency, cessation of all political trials, and repeal of politically repressive laws. Importantly, the paper warned that 'When we reach the conference table, we should have our own set of concrete constitutional proposals (not merely the Freedom Charter) otherwise we will be forced to react to the other side's proposals'. At its core, the Submission might be summarised as warning that 'If we're going to talk, we'd better be prepared; negotiations don't mean surrendering political objectives in advance'.

In parallel with the Submission was another paper by Jordan, circulated to members of the NEC in July 1985 by Tambo, with a note describing it as 'the paper on "Constitutional Models" which (Comrade Pallo) has been working on' **[Document 4]**. It is historically a significant paper, making a forceful and explicit case for a Bill of Rights and for multiparty democracy in a post-apartheid South Africa. It dismisses the 'sad misconception' that had taken root in the National Liberation Movement that radical social transformation was only possible under one-party rule. It proved a key document in the formulation by the ANC of its constitutional future. Strikingly (given his critique of Jordan on negotiations) Gevisser judged that Jordan's report 'was path-breaking and warrants him accolades at least equal to Mbeki for true vanguardism: his proposal would set the scene for nothing less than the ANC's embrace of an open society'.

Between Kabwe and 1990, Jordan was a key figure in ANC policy debates; as administrative secretary to the NEC, he was continuously involved in paperwork between meetings and discussions during them; and he seemed at times positively fizzing with ideas, producing a string of closely argued papers delivered in-house, at conferences and seminars, or submitted for publication **[Documents 2, 3, 5, 6, 7, 8]**. He travelled to conferences in Zimbabwe, Tanzania, the United States, Britain and the Soviet Union; he was a member of the ANC delegations that met South African businessmen in Zambia (in 1985), the National African Federated Chamber of Commerce (NAFCOC) in Lusaka (1986), the IDASA delegation of Afrikaner intellectuals at Dakar (1987), and at IDASA's second gathering, in Paris (1989), a group of home-based South African journalists and activists. All this and much else: it is difficult to imagine that Jordan was ever more intellectually and politically engaged than during these years.

In June 1990, Jordan returned to South Africa after nearly three decades in exile. He soon made his mark, both within political debates on the left, and as a public face of the ANC. In January 1990, Joe Slovo published *Has Socialism Failed?* – and the article was hotly debated not only by members of the SACP but more broadly. Jordan's response **[Document 9]**, published later that year, was a key intervention in these debates, reflecting his distinctive position as a socialist, a Marxist, but critical of the SACP. In his capacity as director of Information for the ANC, Jordan became a prominent spokesperson for the movement across the media, popular with journalists for his quotability, valued by his party for his articulacy and authority. The high profile of this role must have been a factor when, at the 48th National Conference of the ANC, in Durban in mid-1991, Jordan was elected to the NEC by a remarkable 86.8 per cent of the 5000 delegates – only Chris Hani, Thabo Mbeki, Joe Slovo and 'Terror' Lekota polled ahead of him.

It was within the NEC that Jordan's spiky presence, strongly held views, and willingness to challenge apparent consensus were perhaps most evident. NEC meetings in the early 1990s were frequently lengthy, hotly contested, and sometimes fractious. This is unsurprising. The stakes were high, the cards were new, and the rules of the game seemed constantly to shift. Among topics that were frequently debated were the purpose and conduct of negotiations; their relationship to mass action; how the movement should respond to its adversaries; and what options were possible within the prevailing balance of forces. Mandela, chairing these meetings, took notes during the exchanges – and these make clear that Jordan was a forceful critic. In an NEC meeting in June 1992, for example, Jordan argued that there was 'no commonality between ourselves and the regime' and that the destination of negotiations was the transfer of power to the people. He was countered by Slovo, and others, who argued that it was impossible to win people's power in CODESA, and that there must be 'principled compromises'. Mandela, in his concluding remarks the next day, noted 'general criticisms of negotiations', and named Pallo. It may well have been he that Mandela had in mind when he noted (as a 'general observation') the 'temptation to be more militant than their own comrades'![13]

Five months later, in a 'stormy meeting' of the NEC, Jordan *and a few others* objected vehemently to elements of Slovo's 'Perspective on Negotiations' document. Jordan had written, just before this meeting, that Slovo's tendency to make negotiations sound 'as if we were discussing a difficult marriage' was 'not only misleading but dangerous'; that negotiations were not aimed 'at composing differences' but at the 'liquidation of one of the antagonists as a factor in politics'.[14] His was a minority position. The NEC endorsed Slovo's approach – which had indeed underpinned the Record of Understanding signed by the government and the ANC in September 1992.

In August 1993, another NEC meeting was described by Kader Asmal as 'one of the most difficult, heated and painful meetings' that the ANC leadership had in a century of struggle. The issue was whether or not the Motsuenyane report into human rights abuses by the ANC in exile should be published. Some present sought to justify the abuses with the argument that they took place during a war with a vicious enemy; that the cause remained just. 'This line of reasoning prompted Pallo Jordan to stand up and say: "Comrades, I've learnt something very interesting today. There is such a thing as regime torture and there is ANC torture; and regime torture is bad and ANC torture is good. Thank you for enlightening me."'[15] For good measure he reminded his comrades of regimes that had used torture elsewhere – 'Torquemada used torture to save your soul! In Lubyanka the KGB employed torture to instruct you in the dialectic!' – and urged them, as democrats, to oppose and eschew torture. The upshot was that the Motsuenyane report was made public, and the ANC subsequently made a submission to the Truth and Reconciliation Commission.

By 1994, negotiations had succeeded, and Jordan's reservations had been overridden. The process had ensured significant restructuring of the political sphere and broad continuity of the economic sphere. The political settlement was fairly radical; the economic deal relatively conservative. Jordan must have been acutely aware of this at the time, and by 1997 wrote ruefully of the 'distasteful concessions to the old order' involved in the negotiated settlement [**Document 15**]. Along with other party loyalists, however, he campaigned energetically in the run-up to elections; his standing in the party confirmed by his place in the top 5 of the party list. He was appointed as Minister of Posts, Telecommunications and Broadcasting (and took some pride in what he achieved in that post, establishing it as a ministry 'that was going to be important for South Africa in the future, especially in the 21st century').[16] But his work as minister lasted just less than two years: in April 1996 he was dropped from the Cabinet by Mandela. Jordan was never going to be a yes-man as Cabinet colleague, and a series of disagreements with the President led to his dismissal. A well-informed journalist detailed some of these: Jordan opposed proposals that the Constitution's Chapter of Rights be watered down to facilitate the fight against crime; he refused to accept the 'hands-on' relationship with the South African Broadcasting Corporation (SABC) that Mandela advocated, citing the institution's autonomy; and the precipitant for his sacking was his opposition to Mandela's 'Indian Option'.[17] Mandela, borrowing from practice in the Indian National Congress, had sought to approach the ANC's national conference with a slate of candidates to put before delegates: Jordan resisted it strenuously in an NEC meeting as undemocratic. Mandela was unimpressed.

His ousting from Cabinet lasted only a couple of months. The withdrawal of the National Party from the Government of National Unity forced a reshuffle, and however much the younger man irked Mandela, it was virtually impossible to ignore the combination of Jordan's abilities and his popularity in the party. (In 1994, Jordan's re-election to the NEC by conference delegates saw him second in the poll, behind Bantu Holomisa – who was later another casualty of Mandela's disapproval.) Jordan was now allocated the Ministry of Environmental Affairs and Tourism; he held this post until the 1999 election, after which he was dropped from the Cabinet by the new President, Thabo Mbeki. In 2004, he was reinstated, and served for a full five-year term as Minister of Arts and Culture. The portfolio suited his talents and interests: for a minister who took pride in writing his own speeches, events celebrating art, heritage, libraries, literature, music, museums and the like were an opportunity to speak eloquently about things that mattered to him.[18] In 2009, however, Jordan – who had been tipped in the media to be appointed to a more senior post – was among those culled by the new President, Jacob Zuma.

This in-out Cabinet career hardly matched Jordan's abilities or his popularity in the party of government (he consistently polled in the top handful of those elected to the NEC); but accurately reflected that he was at times unpredictable, inconveniently independent-minded, willing to criticise colleagues, and with a deserved reputation for not suffering gladly the intellectual limitations of others. That he was left outside the fold for five years by Mbeki is not surprising: Xolela Mangcu remarked in 1999 that expecting Mbeki to appoint Jordan was like expecting Bill Clinton to appoint Jesse Jackson! His periods in and out of office also shaped what he wrote and published (the documents in this collection had to be chosen from a much larger body of work). He could obviously be more expansive, and more forthright, when not head of a government department. Susan Booysen, writing in 2011, included Jordan (with Frene Ginwala, Jay Naidoo, Ben Turok and Desmond Tutu) as ANC 'big names' no longer dependent on networks of party approval who had 'increasingly dared to break silences on misdirected ANC actions'.[19] This is fair comment.

In Pallo Jordan's case, his most obvious dissidence was his opposition to the ANC's plans for a media tribunal and the details of the Protection of State Information Bill. Fifteen years earlier, he told an interviewer that his views on the press were well known: 'I stand for the untrammelled freedom of the press. I don't question the right of the press to say what they say or to write what they write, to criticise government ... It's their democratic and constitutional right to do so.'[20] In 2012, Jordan represented Ben Turok – who had walked out without voting on the controversial Protection of State Information Bill and who was summoned to a disciplinary hearing – attacking the charges and the bill. The charges against Turok were dropped. But Jordan was also critical of the movement that had been his political home for so long at a more theoretical, and more profound, level. In November 2008, he spoke at the University of Johannesburg **[Document 29]** and argued that the problems confronting the ANC were rooted in its past failures to deal adequately with issues of public morality and its refusal to ask basic questions about the ways in which class interests and political goals intersected. There had been significant social change since 1994 – such as the emergence of 'a well to do upper middle class and capitalist class ensconced in the state and in business' – but the ANC had failed, wilfully, to consider the political implications of such issues.

In 2012, in the immediate aftermath of the Marikana shootings, Jordan took this analysis pointedly further **[Document 33]**. The killings had highlighted the contradictions of transition, a settlement midwived by 'both mass pressure and elite accommodation', so that the property relations of the old South Africa were replicated in the new. In a historically resonant question, he asked whether Marikana was for the ANC what the 18th Brumaire had been for the French and the Kronstadt rebellion for the Russian revolutions, the moment of truth. In 2014, Jordan added his voice to those affronted by the presidential excesses at the Nkandla homestead: Zuma could not 'evade moral responsibility', he wrote.[21]

A few months later, Jordan's world imploded. In August 2014, the *Sunday Times* ran a story demonstrating that the title 'Doctor' routinely attached to Pallo Jordan's name was unmerited: no PhD had ever been awarded. Jordan immediately apologised – and resigned from the public offices he held, as a member of the NEC and a Member of Parliament. It is disquieting even to imagine the humiliation suffered by a proud and sensitive man. There is a touch of Chekhov in the tale: the deeply personal tragedy of a man who had long insisted on the importance of probity in public life brought low by the revelation of his fraudulent title; and the pathos in that his sin appears to have been vanity rather than greed or gain. Even the source of the misattribution is dramatic: when *Africa Confidential* reported the assassination of Ruth First, they noted that 'social scientist Dr Pallo Jordan' had been injured by the blast. Other media repeated this. Jordan let it ride, and the belief that he had a doctorate developed its own momentum.[22] When asked, a few years later, by an American political scientist where he had gained his doctorate, Jordan grinned and said, '*Africa Confidential* bestowed it on me.' But the joke was not explored: and the academic honorific continued to be used.

In terms of this collection, the irony is profound. The pieces selected for publication (and there could have been many more) reveal a sustained intellectual curiosity, the ability to call on wide reading, a sophisticated use of theory and – at times – a robust polemical edge. There are many academics with doctorates who have written less, and less impressively, than Jordan has. Steven Friedman is one of South Africa's leading public intellectuals, and on his Facebook page at the time he paid this tribute to another. There was no doubt, he wrote, that Pallo Jordan was 'one of our outstanding intellectuals ... that he is extremely well read, has a passion for ideas ... and that if he had chosen to enter academic life, his impact would have been immense'.

In many ways the articles in this collection, by Jordan the writer, reflect aspects and characteristics of Jordan the politician. It could scarcely have been otherwise, so intertwined were his roles as ANC intellectual and as ANC activist and office-holder. In these pages one meets a student of Marxist writings: not only the 'approved' classic texts by Marx and Lenin, but Luxemburg, Lunacharsky, Trotsky, Kautsky, Bukharin, Bahro, Djilas and others [**Documents 8, 9, 10**] and their application [**Documents 13, 15**]. One encounters, too, a democratic socialist: hostile to the Soviet model of socialism, steadfast in his support for political pluralism and democratic principles, willing to defend these positions even when it involved criticising the movement that he championed for half a century. Ever-present is the student of South African society and its history [**Documents 2, 3, 7, 15, 19, 25**]. And there is the internationalist: unlike most South African commentators, Jordan is genuinely interested in the history and politics of other societies. As a young man in London, he belonged to 'a hundred and one study groups' studying revolutionary movements across the world – 'I had to keep reading'.[23] And when Padraig O'Malley interviewed Jordan, about South African politics, his answers ranged across Northern Ireland, Cyprus, Malaya and India (where divided societies were a consequence of British colonialism); links between the French Secret Services and the Corsican syndicates in Marseilles during the Algerian war (to illustrate aspects of crime in transitional South Africa); the Battle of Stalingrad and its aftermath (in an elegant analogy to the balance of forces in South Africa after 1990) – and so on. **[And see Documents 23, 24, 28, 35, 37, 38, 39]**

These identities – socialist, democrat, scholar, internationalist – combined to produce a distinctive politician and a singular intellectual. Jordan's political constancy and courage won him respect across the ANC and beyond. When he was first dropped from Mandela's Cabinet, a colleague told Gaye Davis: 'Pallo brings to the ANC integrity and pluck. He will stand up and say what others don't have the guts to say.' His intellectual acuity and influence won him a considerable reputation, again both within and beyond the national liberation movement. An American diplomat (whose views were made public by WikiLeaks!) called Jordan 'one of the ANC's sharpest minds … an introspective and critical thinker'. The writings in this collection cover forty years. They demonstrate a sharp-elbowed politician of conviction *and* a sharp-minded writer; his contribution to South African public life in the democratic era is unmatched.

ENDNOTES

1   Phyllis Ntantala, *A Life's Mosaic* (Mayibuye Centre, UWC & David Philip, 1992).

2   Interview with Pallo Jordan, 31 March 2017.

3   Ibid.

4   Ronnie Kasrils, *Armed and Dangerous: From Undercover Struggle to Freedom*, 4th edition (Jacana Media, 2013), p. 80.

5   Their relationship is charted in Alan Wieder, *Ruth First and Joe Slovo in the*

War against Apartheid (Monthly Review Press, 2013), pp. 192, 204, 215–17, 302–4, 324–5 *et passim*.

6 Luli Callinicos, *Oliver Tambo: Beyond the Engeli Mountains* (David Philip, 2004), p. 383.

7 Mark Gevisser, *Thabo Mbeki: The Dream Deferred* (Jonathan Ball, 2007), p. 421.

8 Callinicos, *Oliver Tambo*, pp. 383–4.

9 Quoted in Rushil Ranchod, *A Kind of Magic: The Political Marketing of the ANC* (Jacana Media, 2013), p. 21.

10 Hugh Macmillan, *The Lusaka Years: The ANC in Exile in Zambia* (Jacana Media, 2013), p. 194.

11 Gevisser, *Thabo Mbeki*, pp. 533, 535.

12 The full text of the Submission is in Gail Gerhart and Clive Glaser, *From Protest to Challenge*, vol. 6 (Indiana University Press, 2010), pp. 589–92.

13 Nelson Mandela Personal Papers, Notes and Notebooks Collection, Series NMPP 2009/8, Folder 3, Notebook 6, Meeting of NEC, 8–9 June 1992.

14 Timothy Sisk, *Democratization in South Africa* (Princeton, 1995), pp. 221–2.

15 Kader Asmal and Adrian Hadland, *Politics in My Blood* (Jacana Media, 2011), pp. 172–4.

16 Interview with Padraig O'Malley, 17 May 1996, *The Heart of Hope: South Africa's Transition from Apartheid to Democracy*, Padraig O'Malley Archives, www.nelsonmandela.org/omalley/.

17 Gaye Davis, 'Crossing Madiba cost Jordan his job', *Mail & Guardian*, 4 April 1994.

18 See http://www.dac.gov.za/p-jordan.

19 Susan Booysen, *The African National Congress and the Regeneration of Political Power* (Wits University Press, 2011), p. 22.

20 Interview with Padraig O'Malley, 25 October 1995, *The Heart of Hope*.

21 Pallo Jordan, 'ANC must display moral courage', *Business Day*, 27 March 2014.

22 Terry Bell, '"Dr" Pallo Jordan: Why I did it', *City Press*, 24 August 2014.

23 Interview with Pallo Jordan.

The Documents

The documents in this volume represent only a portion of Pallo Jordan's writings. They were selected from a total of over 170 separate items: discussion papers, letters to editors, newspaper columns, longer articles, published chapters, and speeches and lectures. This is a prolific output for one who has also held a series of organisational and public offices for four decades. They are clustered for the most part around several themes: the history of the national liberation struggle; the 'national question' with particular reference to South Africa; Marxist theory and theorists, with an emphasis on 'left opposition' (or anti-Stalinist) writings; issues around race and racism, and issues around media and communication. The documents below could have organised in at least three ways: by theme, or by type (published/unpublished, newspaper columns, speeches, etc.), or chronologically. Although a case could be made for each of these, the organising principle chosen for this book is chronological. This has the benefit of demonstrating the development of Jordan's thought over time (and perhaps also illustrating something of the difference between writing from exile, while engaged in debates over transition, and while holding office). It also permits the juxtaposition of items indicating the range and breadth of Jordan's interests; and it demonstrates his response to specific issues at particular historical moments: the process of negotiations, the Arab Spring, the breakaway from the ANC of COPE, and the Marikana shootings.

Each of the documents is introduced by a brief descriptive comment, in some cases alerting the reader to its significance or context.

ONE

Although Jordan had written for a number of student journals as a young man, this is the earliest publication of the writings available for selection. Jordan locates Moses Kotane's political career in 'the interaction between the national and socialist movements' of the South African liberation struggle. Jordan's critical stance towards the South African Communist Party does not surface in the review, which provides a succinct and respectful summary of Bunting's book, concluding with some brief criticisms – essentially that the book fails to give much individuality to its subject. (Sechaba was the official organ of the ANC, launched in 1967.)

A review of Brian Bunting, *Moses Kotane: South African Revolutionary*

(Inkululeko Publications, 1975), in *Sechaba*, volume 10, 1ˢᵗ quarter, 1976, pp. 61–3.

Moses Kotane turned seventy on August 9th of last year. For fifty-two of those years he has occupied a leading role in the South African liberation struggle. It is a fitting tribute to this indomitable freedom fighter that this year saw the publication of his biography.

In 1905, the year Kotane was born, the last embers of the African resistance to conquest were finally extinguished in the Bambatha Rebellion which was crushed in 1906, bringing to a close a long and bitter chapter of South African history. The defeat of Bambatha inaugurated a new era in South Africa. White colonizer and Black colonized no longer confronted each other as two distinct societies but were inexorably drawn into a common society linked by innumerable bonds to an international economic system. 1905 also opened a new chapter in world history. Imperial Japan had dealt Tsarist Russia a crushing blow at Port Arthur, signalling the twilight of the myth of white superiority and European world hegemony. Its immediate effect was the 1905 Revolution, the 'dress rehearsal' for the great October revolution which gave birth to the first socialist state. The little village where Kotane was born knew almost nothing of these momentous events which were to shape and determine the destiny of one of its native sons.

Bunting's biography of Kotane (Moses Kotane: South African Revolutionary. Inkululeko Publications) picks up the story of his life in a small village in the northern Transvaal, follows the young man on his travels, which take him to White-owned farms, the mines and finally to the bustling heartland of industrial South Africa, the Reef. It was here, at the age of twenty-three, that Kotane became politically conscious and joined the African National Congress. His thirst for political knowledge and understanding was not satisfied by the bombastic speeches he heard from ANC platforms at the time and his search led him to the Communist Party. He joined the ranks of the CP endowed with two assets which were to be a source of strength over the years: his keen and questioning mind and a sense of discipline imparted to him by the strict Protestant upbringing he had received from his parents. In the space of ten years he rose from an untutored recruit to the General Secretaryship of the CP, a position he has held ever since.

Kotane's political career spans five decades of our national liberation struggle and is characterised by the interaction between the national and socialist movements. It is a story rich in both conflict and harmony, acrimonious internecine arguments and mutual enrichment through an ideological cross fertilization. Bunting tries to convey the spirit in which these events were played out by the numerous quotations from contemporary journals and the main protagonists in them. He recounts all the major debates which have preoccupied the movement ever since 1918. Kotane played a seminal role in all of these since he entered politics, and his contribution to them has often been crucial in the options the movement has chosen.

When Kotane joined the ANC and the CP in 1928, important changes were afoot in both organisations. James Gumede the newly elected ANC president had adopted a militant anti-imperialist platform and was seeking an alliance with the left. The CP had revised its perspective on revolution and South Africa and adopted the national liberation of African people as its foremost goal. Both organisations were keen to develop closer links with each other. To the detriment of both, this projected alliance was wrecked by the old guard of the ANC leadership who feared both the radical nationalism espoused by Gumede and the CP's advocacy of socialism. It took years of patient work by Kotane and his comrades to rebuild this unity, as often as not, by going over the heads of the conservatives and appealing directly to the masses. Their efforts finally bore fruit in the post war years when a new generation of militant nationalists came into the leadership of the ANC.

The trade union struggles of the thirties, the war against fascism and the upsurge of anti-colonial movements in the post war years infused new blood into the liberation movement and helped to broaden its vision. Four trends dominate this period: the resurgence of militant nationalism; the tendency towards greater unity of all the oppressed national groups; the growth of internationalism and the integration of communism into the mainstream of the national liberation movement. These new trends were tested in the heat of the struggle during the campaigns of 1950 and 1952 and were finally given programmatic expression in the Kliptown conference which adopted the Freedom Charter. As most people are familiar with the course of events after this historic convocation I shall not burden this review with the details.

However, a vital area of this history, which has been hidden from public view until now, is the founding and development of the Communist underground after the Suppression of Communism Act. Reasons of security still shroud the details, but the little light Bunting sheds on it gives us some idea of the tenacious efforts that contributed to the first public statements in 1960. This section of the book contains valuable lessons from which all sections of the movement could benefit. By the time the ANC was banned, the alliance that Gumede and the CP had tried to build thirty years earlier had come into full flower. The conservative victory in 1930 had proved but a temporary setback. The jointly shared trials and tribulations of struggle, the patient work of militants in the teeth of often stubborn resistance, produced a solidarity firmly implanted among the oppressed peoples. Moses Kotane's contribution to this achievement is outstanding.

It is a basic premise of revolutionary historiography that the struggle for human liberation in reality has assumed many forms. Before we can judge any struggle either positively or negatively, we must first decipher its essential aspects which may lie hidden behind its surface features. Those struggles which extend the area of human freedom and possibilities are part of the liberatory process. Those that restrict freedom and circumscribe human possibilities, even though radical in appearance, are essentially reactionary. It is this premise that governs the distinction revolutionaries draw between repressive and liberatory violence; between repressive and liberatory nationalism. It is in this light that one must judge the white workers' struggles which culminated in the 1922 Miner's Strike. Despite the revolutionary rhetoric of its leaders, the workers defence squads and action councils these threw up, the main thrust of these struggles was the defence of privileges obtained at the expense of Black workers, and in the case of the 1922 Strike, to debar them from certain occupations. By their struggles the white workers had forced upon the political representatives of capital, both foreign and South African, the recognition that it was not possible to govern without their cooperation. After the 1924 general elections they extended such cooperation in return for higher wages, job protection and supervisory authority over the Black workers.

Side by side with the white workers' movement had grown the national movements of the oppressed led by western educated intellectuals, small businessmen and professionals. The character of the national movements was in large measure determined by the ambivalence of the oppressed communities and the political elite within them. This elite were the protégés of British imperialism which had sponsored them as a counter weight to the traditional leaders during the nineteenth century. After the destruction of traditional society, both the colonial government and the local white regime began to perceive them as the chief threat to white domination. All the racially discriminating clauses in South Africa's land laws and the constitution were aimed primarily at retarding the development of this class and to prevent it from consolidating its position either in the economy or in the body politic. It was from this privileged stratum that the mass of urban Blacks learnt the skills of modern political organisation which gave rise to an independent Black workers' movement. The left wing of the white workers movement imparted socialism to this Black workers movement. Moses Kotane, in his person, merges these two currents of the liberation movement in South Africa. During the 1920s the Black working class was as yet an untutored mass undergoing its initiation at the mills, mines and forges of capitalism. Though it had acquired enough strength to be a serious force in the political arena, it was not strong enough to give leadership to the national movement. In the fifty years which have elapsed since 1922 it has acquired the political knowledge and skill to do so. We can with confidence predict that this class will be the decisive factor in the liberation of South Africa and that it will leave its imprint on the future society.

Though Bunting's work is commendable it has its faults, one of which I shall touch on briefly. Large chunks of Kotane's life are treated in the most cursory fashion. We are told nothing of his term at the Lenin School though this must have been a profoundly formative experience; Moses Kotane courts, marries, has two sons, divorces, courts again and remarries – this is covered in two paragraphs? We are given no idea how he spends his time between committee meetings, public speaking engagements and conferences. Indeed, his only leisure seems to be football! Even that, merely as a spectator! As a result, even though the authors' informants repeatedly assure us of Kotane's personal warmth and humanity, the received image is that of a no-nonsense professional revolutionary. Surely, even the best revolutionaries do not live by politics alone.

Z. Pallo Jordan

TWO

*This is a review of two books and an article by left-wing academics, all of which discussed aspects of the early 1980s, especially the policy shifts under P.W. Botha's presidency. Jordan welcomes their 'withering critique of the liberal illusions' in many accounts of Botha as 'reformist'. He shows how the approaches of Saul and Gelb and Wolpe converge in arguing that Botha's 'Total Strategy' was an attempt to resolve internal contradictions, but is critical of their 'economism': the assumption of a direct causal relationship between changes in the economy and the regime's political tactics. He endorses Nolutshungu's view that meaningful and substantive change was an unlikely outcome, given the gap between white interests and black aspirations: schemes of 'elite accommodation' had limited leverage as they demanded that the black petty bourgeoisie acquiesce in their continued subordination. Jordan's focus in this review on the black middle class anticipates his own sustained engagement with the topic – see **Documents 3 and 7**.*

Black Middle Class – Eleventh-hour counter insurgency or acquiescence in continued domination?

Review of John Saul and Stephen Gelb, *The Crisis in South Africa* (Monthly Review Press, London 1981); Sam C. Nolutshungu, *Changing South Africa – Political Considerations* (Manchester University Press, 1982); Harold Wolpe: 'Apartheid's Deepening Crisis' (in *Marxism Today*, January 1983). In *Sechaba*, May 1983, pp. 23–28.

Reading much of what is currently being written about South Africa, one is overwhelmed by a sense of déjà vu. Many of the themes one hears repeated with such dogmatic assurance today are anything but new. Most, if not all, are hackneyed restatements of tunes one heard sung in the late 1940s, the 1950s and even the 1960s. then, as today, commentators were drawing unwarranted conclusions about the imminence of dramatic political changes, based on a rudimentary examination of changes in the economic sphere.

Today, as in the past, we are told that South African capitalism has developed to an extent that it no longer requires racism and national oppression, which served it so well during the earlier period of primitive accumulation. Consequently, the wielders of political power are revising their own racist policies and adopting pragmatic principles to accommodate the overriding needs of the economy. Spokesmen of monopoly capital, at home and abroad, mouth praise songs to Botha as a courageous leader who has dared to violate some of the most sacred racial taboos of Afrikaner nationalism and is initiating changes that run counter to everything his party has stood for over the past forty years.

The image of the racist ruling circles as initiators of change has been peddled by rightists, liberals, and, paradoxically, even by leftists. Right wing and liberal commentators are almost invariably fulsome in their praise of Botha the 'reformer'. Commentators on the left, on the other hand, while accepting the liberal myth of Botha's reformism, tend to hedge their remarks with what can only be called carping criticism, pointing to this or that shortcoming in the programme of 'reform'. At the end of the day, both groups agree that substantial changes, which require everyone to reassess the situation, are afoot.

One does not find it surprising that right-wingers and liberals portray Botha and his regime as reformers. Both desperately wish that this was in fact true. The fervour with which they advocate his case betrays their own ill-concealed fears of mass revolutionary upsurge. More difficult to explain is the adherence to this viewpoint of writers on the left. One suspects that despite their political views many such commentators lack confidence in the capacity of the oppressed black masses to liberate themselves.

DEFINING THE RULING CLASS

It is very tempting to see the South African ruling class as an agency of change. Indeed, some writers on the left have even had recourse to Marx's description of the bourgeoisie as a revolutionary class to explain the unfamiliar goings-on in Pretoria. Historical precedent also appears to endorse this conception when one recalls South Africa's bourgeois 'revolution from above'. The works under review all address themselves to the question of change and present a withering critique of the liberal illusions that have been fomented by the bourgeois press, both in South Africa and the outside world.

Saul and Gelb are Canadian scholars active in the solidarity movement in that country. Their short but stimulating monograph was produced under the auspices of that movement. Of the two, John Saul is internationally the better known. An old stalwart of the cause of the

African revolution, he has authored a number of works on African affairs, has taught for many years in Tanzania, and has recently completed a term as lecturer at the Mozambique Institute for Marxism.

Sam Nolutshungu is a South African scholar now working in Britain, where he has been resident since his release from a term of detention under the notorious 90 days clause of the Sabotage Act in the mid-sixties. A committed anti-imperialist fighter and opponent of racism, he has produced a number of studies on Southern Africa, and serves on the editorial board of the Journal of African Marxists.

Harold Wolpe is a long-standing member of the ANC, and the veteran of numerous campaigns. He presently works in Britain, where he has won recognition as one of the most original South African Marxist scholars for his extensive writings on the South African state.

In short, what we have here are works by academicians all of whom are committed to the cause of liberation, and have, in their various ways and in different capacities, made their contribution to that cause.

A Crisis of Profundity

The main thrust of Saul and Gelb's argument is that the South African racist regime is passing through an 'organic crisis'. This is a term they have borrowed from the writings of Antonio Gramsci, the founder of Italian Communism. It is intended to convey the idea of a crisis of such profundity that in order to survive it the incumbent ruling class has to construct a whole new set of policies and programmes. This crisis, they argue, had been precipitated by the internal dynamics of South African monopoly capitalism. These have led on the one hand to the emergence of an Afrikaner monopolist class with class aims and objectives similar to those of the other, non-Afrikaner fraction of monopoly capital. On the other hand, the development of capitalism has created a new economic climate in which South African capital needs new internal and external markets for its growing secondary industry, especially in durable consumer goods. However, these internal contradictions are unfolding in a context of pressures from the masses, and have consequently thrown the whole system into a deep crisis which the ruling class will not be able to resolve except by so restructuring social relations that a new 'historical bloc', representing a new political consensus, emerges. It is in these terms also that they interpret the regime's 'total strategy', which they insist must not be seen as a hastily cobbled together attempt to shore up the rickety structures of apartheid.

How Can Change Come About?

Sam Nolutshungu addresses himself, it would appear, to much of the writing that has come out of the Southern Africa Programme at Yale University in the U.S.A. He himself spent a few years there as a research fellow, and his book bears the stamp of that academic setting. Unfortunately, he has allowed this to affect his style, which is so academically stilted as to render him virtually unreadable. His work which is otherwise a valuable contribution to an ongoing debate, is thus inaccessible to precisely the millions who form its subject matter.

Nolutshungu takes issue with the much touted argument that peaceful change in South Africa is both a desirable and realizable political objective, which could, if pursued, result in the abolition of racial oppression. He, quite correctly, says that no one rejects peaceful change. The question is and will continue to be: 'is it a realistic option?'

Change, Nolutshungu argues, that is both meaningful and substantive will not come from the South African ruling class because of the particular institutional constraints within which both these must operate. To implement any change, the state must have the support of the majority of the Whites, who will want guarantees that such change will not threaten their real or perceived interests. Whether or not the dominant monopoly capitalist class desires and is pressing for change is not the question. In exchange for political and social backing from the other classes of Whites, the monopolists have given them certain privileges and prerogatives which in practice amount to a veto power over measures they find unacceptable. At the same time there is a yawning gulf between the aspirations of all sections of the Black community and the 'reforms' contemplated by the ruling class. Except for a very tight circle of paid functionaries – Bantustan 'leaders', administrators, and their urban counterparts in the community councils – no Blacks are committed to collaboration with the regime.

Resistance to oppression has on the other hand been kept alive despite massive and brutal repression. Resistance leads inexorably to armed confrontation, not because the liberation movement is bloodthirsty, but because the overturning of the institutions of national oppression requires more than the substitution of Black for White faces in the centre of political power.

> '... whether it is mobilised in nationalist or in socialist terms it entails
> repossession and dispossession, the seizure of material assets ...' (p. 67)

Violence, the midwife of the new social order, is therefore the necessary means of coercion to be wielded by the oppressed majority against the ruling minority to make it submit to the popular will. Efforts on the part of the regime and its imperialist allies to co-opt a section of the Black middle strata are eleventh-hour counter-insurgency measures rather than substantive attempts to deracialise the system.

APARTHEID – REFORMIST POSTURE

Wolpe's contribution to the debate is a relatively short article published in the January issue of Marxism Today, the theoretical journal of the British Communist Party. In spite of its brevity this is an article that bears close study because its author packs a great many ideas and arguments into a few pages.

According to Wolpe, the crucial question is not whether or not the changes being undertaken by the racists are real, but rather why they are being introduced at all. This answer to this consists of two parts.

South African monopoly capitalism, he contends, is experiencing a period of readjustment characterised by the transition from labour to capital intensive methods of production. This coincides with the convergence of the Afrikaner monopoly capitalist class with other fractions of white monopoly capital, which has made it possible for the state to adopt a more sophisticated policy, replacing that of blanket repression, with regard to the black urban working and petty bourgeoisie classes. Simultaneously with these changes in the ruling class, the system as a whole is faced with an increasingly effective challenge from below in the shape of mass struggles complemented by and co-ordinated with armed struggle to overthrow apartheid. It is these pressures that have forced the regime to evolve its 'Total Strategy', as a means of resolving the internal contradictions thrown up by capitalist development while holding the line against mass insurgency.

The 'reformist posture' of the regime should not, however, be dismissed out of hand because it inadvertently does reflect an aspect of reality. One of the unintended consequences of the 'new dispensation' is that the regime has opened up new arenas of political struggle that the liberation movement had lost, for example the trade union front. It is our task, therefore, to take account of these developments rather than ignore them as unimportant.

'TOTAL STRATEGY'

There are large areas of agreement between the work of Saul and Gelb, on the one hand, and Wolpe on the other. They stress that there are real material forces underlying the reform rhetoric of the regime. They seem to agree also about the relationship between these forces and the 'Total Strategy', which, they underline, is not merely a hastily thrown together concoction, but a well reasoned defensive strategy. This strategy, they say, has three elements – co-optation of sections of the Black petty bourgeoisie through opportunities to expand and accumulate some wealth; dispersal and containment of the black urban working class by stabilising one portion (the Section 10 exemptees) while bludgeoning the other portion either into migrancy or marginalisation in the Bantustans; direct incorporation of the monopolists into the state apparatus while strengthening the executive at the expense of other branches of the state.

WHO ARE THE BLACK PETIT-BOURGEOISIE?

A reader who is familiar with the history of South Africa during the 20th century will have one great difficulty with these views; who exactly is this black petty bourgeoisie which apparently is being encouraged not to stake out its claim for a share in the spoils of exploitation? In conventional usage the term conjures up images of small property owners, shopkeepers, members of the professions and so on. Except for a handful of Indian merchants, it is hard to find a stratum of blacks which conforms to this image.

True, individual Blacks have over the decades been allowed to glean a few pickings left over by white capital – in the urban townships, in the Bantustans – but the precarious, hand-to-mouth existence of these businessmen can hardly be termed encouragement from the regime. When one examines more closely the impact of both racist legislation – the land acts, the much amended franchise laws, the group areas acts, etc. – and the unequal competition of well endowed white monopoly capital on this stratum of the black community, the picture that emerges is one of systematic grinding down and ruination. To take some typical statistics: since the passage of the Group Areas Act in 1951, 830 Indian traders in Natal lost their licenses to trade, 2 226 in Transvaal, 943 in the Cape. African urban traders still have to renew their licenses annually and the numbers of coloured traders are so small as to be of no consequence.

When we leave the arena of broad generalisation and concretely analyse this so-called black petty-bourgeoisie, we find that the majority are poorly trained teachers and nurses. Controlling little productive property, this stratum of Blacks has one marketable commodity that marks it out from the working class – professional skills. True, in recent years one or two individual Blacks have been brought in on to the board of directors of the Anglo-American Corporation. But surely such measures are more degrading than the rankest forms of tokenism. Neither Saul and Gelb nor Wolpe can make out a convincing case for their co-optation thesis.

Thinly Disguised Economism

In the opinion of this reviewer, their enthusiasm for a materialist explanation behind Botha's reformist posturing has tempted them into a thinly disguised economism that assumes a direct causal relationship between the shifts they detect in the economy and the regime's changing political tactics. This blinds them also to the essentially reactive nature of the many of the measures the regime has adopted in recent years.

To take one example, the recommendations of the Wiehahn Commission were not so much an initiative taken by the regime in response to the needs of monopoly capital as a rearguard action in the hard-fought class battles of the early and mid seventies. Often, spontaneous working class action at the point of production had rendered dysfunctional the whole panoply of repressive laws that the regime had employed to dispense the trade union movement of the 1950s. Wiehahn was the means the regime devised to come to terms with these new realities, and an attempt to contain the rediscovered strength of the working class. Judged from this perspective, much that the ruling class and the racist state propose and have already implemented are an attempt to keep pace with an extremely fluid situation, in which they can no longer take their opponents for granted.

Saul and Gelb, and, to a lesser extent, Wolpe, also have the annoying habit of misconstruing the ruling class's wishful thinking and find sounding rhetoric as reality. Invariably, all the quotes about 'giving them (black middle strata) a stake in society' are from ruling class sources. Though elements of the black petty bourgeoisie are stigmatised as a potential fifth column, or likely defectors from the broad liberation alliance, they are rarely allowed to speak for themselves. Rather these motives are imputed to them on the basis of the ruling class's half-baked schemes and ill-conceived scenarios. These are grave shortcoming in analysts writing in the Marxian tradition, which insists on concrete analysis. Nolutshungu handles this question more satisfactorily by adopting precisely this approach. Recognising the distance between pious hopes and the lived reality of white domination experienced by the black petty bourgeoisie and worker alike, he concludes that ruling class schemes of 'elite accommodation' have little prospect of success, because, in the last instance, they demand acquiescence in continued domination.

CENTRALITY OF THE NATIONAL QUESTION

All the authors under review agree that a broadly based national movement embracing different classes is indispensable in the South African context. The seminal role the black working class will play in a South African revolution is equally recognised and accepted.

None of them, however, seems to grasp the centrality of the national question to the revolutionary struggle. Throughout their work, Saul and Gelb employ a term fraught with severe limitations – 'racial capitalism' – to describe the South African social reformation. Nolutshungu is keenly aware of the colonialist origins of the institutions of national oppression, but their role as instruments of the domination of monopoly capital seems to elude him. The terminological inadequacies of Saul and Gelb lead them into speculations about the relative weight of the various class forces that constitute the ANC, while Nolutshungu tends to treat the multi-class nature of the liberation movement as unproblematic. The tendency to regard the sense of national grievance in a purely instrumentalist light on the part of Saul and Gelb betrays a very shallow conception of the relationship between the national and class aspects of the liberation struggle.

Most of the above is generally accepted in the ranks of our movement, but I would suggest that this is no cause for complacency. Much of the confusion found amongst our friends in the international community is probably attributable to the imprecise terms our movement's discourse is usually couched in. Though we all employ the formulation, 'colonialism of a special type', how many have really bothered to define it? Have we examined all its possible permutations? Is there only one way to interpret this, or are there several? What implications does this formulation have for the question of class leadership over the liberation movement as a whole? All these are questions we must ask and find answers to, because in the last instance, it is only the South African liberation movement that can definitively resolve all these issues.

THREE

This is an impressive piece of original research, yoked to the practical and political question of how the African petty bourgeoisie was likely to respond politically to the national liberation movement. Jordan characterises the National African Federated Chamber of Commerce (NAFCOC) as 'the selfconscious instrument of an aspirant stratum', and charts the organisation's shifting tactics and rhetoric since its formation. He describes how NAFCOC was affected by the Soweto Uprising and militant trade union struggles, moving from abject, deferential political flabbiness to a more assertive posture. As a result, it was no longer 'cap-in-hand petitioner' but 'perhaps the most avidly courted organisation' in the country. For Jordan the clear lesson of the case study was that 'pandering to petty bourgeois sensibilities' would not win the allegiance of the class to national liberation; rather, the ANC stood to gain when militant mass struggles made it possible 'to draw the petty bourgeoisie into its train'.

The African Petty Bourgeoisie:
A case study of NAFCOC 1964–84

Paper prepared by Z. Pallo Jordan for the ANC Economists' Unit
Weekend Workshop Seminar Lusaka May 1984, published in series
ANC Occasional Research Papers (1984)

*'In so far as millions of families live under economic conditions
of existence that separate their mode of life, their interests and
their culture from those of other classes, and put them in hostile
opposition to the latter, they form a class.'* (Karl Marx. The 18th
Brumaire of Louis Bonaparte. Moscow: 1977, p 106)

*'... we are just like the Afrikaners in wanting 100%
ethnic development of our business. Sanlam and Federale
Volksbeleggings were 100% Afrikaner, so why should we want
the same?'* (Mr H Majola, Managing Director of Black Chain
Supermarkets. As quoted in *Financial Mail*, 9/12/83.)

INTRODUCTION

Since the publication of Nimrod Mkele's article, 'The Emergent African
Middle Class' by Harry Oppenheimer's *Optima* (Vol. 10, No. 4, 1960),
it became generally accepted that despite the differentials in lifestyle, life
chances and incomes separating the African petty bourgeoisie from the
majority of the black working people, the commonly shared burden of
national oppression would ultimately make for a united front of all black
classes against white domination. As Mkele, quoting Monica Hunter,
argued:

'While distinctions in wealth and education have become real among Africans and exert a powerful influence, 'There is no sharp cleavage between classes ... The cleavage between Bantu and European ... overshadows economic differences within the Bantu community itself.' Thus, Africans, suffering as they do from disabilities common to all classes, translate their struggle for status and personal recognition not into class terms which would cut across colour lines but into a struggle for the recognition of all Africans ... The African middle class has no stake in the country and sees its salvation in making common cause with the masses with whom it shares common disabilities.'

Few, if any, analysts within our movement until very recently questioned this view. Indeed, it can be said that this view is one of the corner-stones of ANC strategy which emphasises the maximum unity of the various classes and strata in the black community against white domination. We have moreover argued that it is not merely national sentiment that cements such alliance but that it is grounded in material reality – a shared interest in the overthrow of the oppressive racist regime.

Thus Joe Slovo, in his 'South Africa – No Middle Road' (in *Southern Africa: The New Politics of Revolution*), states:

'In the case of the black middle strata, however, class mobility cannot proceed beyond a certain point; and again, this point is defined in race rather than in economic terms. Objectively speaking, therefore, the immediate fate of the black middle section is linked much more with that of the black workers and peasants than with their equivalents across the colour line.'

Similarly, a reviewer in *Sechaba* of May 1983 dismisses the possibilities of 'elite accommodation' on the grounds that the disabilities of the African petty bourgeoisie will inevitably impel them to seek more radical solutions. This conventional wisdom has recently come under the sceptical scrutiny of a handful of analysts, both within the ranks of our movement and amongst our supporters. Such scepticism has in part been occasioned by the role assigned to the African petty bourgeoisie in the South African ruling class's counter-revolutionary strategies and the designs of imperialism to subvert our revolution.

A number of these commentators have remarked unfavourably on the growth of a highly visible, though as yet small, African petty bourgeoisie, embracing the urban commercial sector, the professionals and a sprinkling of potential black business executives in the employ of Transnational corporations. The vanguard, as it were, of the petty bourgeoisie is NAFCOC – the National African Federated Chambers of Commerce – a well organised national network of African business people.

As the self-conscious instrument of an aspirant stratum, NAFCOC strives to bring its ideological influence to bear on the African community. It is able to draw into its activities such diverse personalities as Dr Nthato Motlana to its left and Bantustan leaders like Buthelezi on its right. It has launched projects to mobilise the savings of the African community – The African Bank and Sentry Assurance of South Africa; has sought to harness the economic power of the Africans as consumers to build its own economic strength; and publishes three very glossy magazines directed at its constituency, through which it conducts a dialogue mapping out new strategies and reviewing its own progress. NAFCOC and the section of the African community it represents are by no means a negligible force on the political landscape. Through its organisation the petty bourgeoisie controls its own independent assets plus a very articulate constituency. A myriad of [sic] subterranean channels affords it access to all layers of the black community. Thus, despite its actual size, it wields an influence far out of proportion to its numbers.

Some writers have, rightly, also been concerned about the possibilities of an alliance between this stratum and the bureaucratic caste being groomed in the Bantustans. It is evident that this circle of paid functionaries of apartheid are using the little power they have been delegated as a means of accumulation. 'Toussaint', writing in the *African Communist* (No. 64. 1st Quarter 1976), in a more pessimistic assessment of the petty bourgeoisie warns:

'But the growth of this black bourgeoise (sic) brings into being a group of *willing and indeed anxious* (my emphasis) to operate within the Bantustan establishment and from there – it is hoped – stake a claim to lead the nation ...'

Similar fears have been expressed in other quarters – Wolpe (*Marxism Today*, January 1983) Saul and Gelb ('Crisis in S.A.'. *MR Press*, 1981); O'Meara, to name but a few.

The spokesmen of monopoly capital have also generously contributed their own views, scenarios and schemes to the debate. Thus, Etheredge, a former President of the Chamber of Mines, in an address to NAFCOC's 17th Annual Conference remarked:

'The mass of the working population, the blacks, were entangled in a web of laws wich restricted their mobility, which was the very heart of the free market system and controlled them in so many ways that it was totally wrong to suggest that they lived in a capitalistic state, when they in fact lived under socialism.'

Apart from the sheer hypocrisy of a spokesman from the Chamber of Mines, the one institution responsible for the creation of the labour coercive system that has become the hallmark of capitalism in South Africa, one must admire the gall of this arch-capitalist in labelling this very system socialist! Etheredge then goes further to complain that:

'... since the Carlton Conference, the dismantling of legislative constraints has not proceeded far enough to leave South Africa firmly in the saddle of free enterprise.'

and is quoted as having proposed:

'... that the legislation at national, provincial and local level which inhibited the growth of free enterprise should be the subject of a ... committee composed of senior civil servants, law advisers, academics and business leaders of every race. They should not only review legislation but also prepare amendments which could be placed before Parliament. In particular laws which hurt the newcomer to the business world should be rewritten.'

The monopolists have their own ideas of the role the African petty bourgeoisie should play in South Africa. With their immense wealth and total control over the means of cultural production, they are assiduously cultivating it as an alternative to the revolutionary liberation movement.

The consensus that previously characterised our movement on the African petty bourgeoisie has all but broken down. The emergence of differing views is indicative of the need for a re-examination of the assumption – that so many of us take for granted – on which our strategy is based. If, as we claim, movement theory, programmes, strategy and tactics are grounded in science, then they can be tested by critical evaluation. If found wanting, they will have to be recast in conformity with our new findings.

My intentions in this paper are to provoke thought on a subject that touches key aspects of our strategy. I approach the topic in the spirit of a curious social scientist. The findings I arrive at may be proved correct or incorrect. But then, science advances precisely by the raising of questions and the courage to seek answers.

MULTI-CLASS COALITION

'... Every class alliance of the popular masses (the 'people') involves a series of real contradictions which have to be taken seriously into consideration and resolved correctly ...' (Nicos Poulantzas, *Classes and Contemporary Capitalism*. London, 1979)

It is generally accepted in our movement that the ANC is a multi-class coalition made up of a number of class forces. Since the adoption of the document: *ANC Strategies and Tactics* at the Morogoro Conference of 1969, all ANC statements and documents have underlined that within this multi-class alliance the working class is the leading force. These formulations have now become generally accepted in the ANC and by its allies. Though they are not explicitly stated, this particular definition of the multi-class coalition suggests a number of assumptions. Briefly, these may be said to be: (a) Though united in their common objective, the overthrow of white domination, the different classes read different meanings and interpretations into common programmes and political slogans. (b) Being motivated by differing, and sometimes contradictory, class aims, the various classes making up the alliance differ also in their commitment to radical change – i.e. some are more consistently revolutionary than others. (c) This being the case, one class within the collation will emerge as the hegemonic, or leading, force. This in turn suggests that the liberation movement is itself a site for class struggle in which the interests of one or other class will emerge predominant.

This study seeks to lay bare these implicit assumptions and subject to critical scrutiny one specific stratum within the African community – the commercial petty bourgeoisie. I shall focus on the most articulate and best organised fraction of the stratum, NAFCOC, in the hope that a survey of its activities since it came into being will offer us some clues about the options the various classes are likely to choose in the period ahead.

Defining our terms

Before we proceed it is necessary that we first define exactly whom we are referring to. The classical Marxian definition of the petty bourgeoisie bases itself on the place this stratum occupies within the relations of production. It is distinguished by:

- Small scale productive or commercial property; and or
- Control over marketable professional skills;
- Typically the same agent is both the owner of *his* means of production and the direct producer;
- If and where they employ hired labour the scale is typically small, seasonal or intermittent, being more an extension of, rather than a substitute for, their own labour.

Like all definitions this is a very broad generalization which does not necessarily characterise any particular petty bourgeoisie. In each particular country or region petty bourgeoisie will have its own specificity, shaped by history. Thus is can be said, in general, that the European petty bourgeoisie belongs to the simple commodity mode of production, which was historically the form of transition from feudalism to capitalism. Yet, despite this, it is equally true that this stratum has displayed a remarkable resilience and a capacity to survive into the era of monopoly capitalism. The outstanding examples are the artisan bakers found in France, Central Europe and even some of the East European Socialist countries.

In general, we may also characterise the petty bourgeoisie as a transitional stratum, that recruits its ranks from the two major classes. This is the stratum into which the upwardly mobile proletarian first rises; this is the stratum into which the bankrupted bourgeois is first driven down.

In capitalist social formations, the petty bourgeoisie property owners are overwhelmed by a sense of contingency, caused by the cyclical fluctuations of the capitalist economy. The precariousness of their existence marks the political attitudes of the petty bourgeoisie, hence they prefer stability to the uncertainties of change.

The petty commodity producer, artisan and businessman, works in isolation from others of his stratum, who are perceived as competitors in the market place. Individual effort and initiative determines the life of the petty bourgeois. Hence he tends to be individualistic. Fear of change and individualism tend toward political conservatism.

In the literature of Marxism the petty bourgeoisie is typically referred to as a vacillating stratum. More often than not, this structure splits into fractions in the face of a political crisis. One section will side with the forces of revolution, while another sides with reaction and yet a third will attempt a precarious balancing act between the two extremes. This indecisiveness, like petty bourgeoisie conservatism, has a basis in reality.

Being an intermediate stratum, which draws from both the bourgeoisie and the proletariat, the petty bourgeoisie has interests in common with both major classes. As property owners they share a common interest with the bourgeoisie but as direct producers they also have points in common with the proletariat. Moods, ideas, movements and trends within the two major classes inevitably produce resonances within the petty bourgeoisie. This is the material basis of its oscillation between reaction and revolution.

No other forms of radicalism have been as severely castigated as those of the petty bourgeoisie in the Marxian tradition. This would seem to indicate that though it is preferable to reaction, petty bourgeois radicalism is itself problematic. As an intermediate stratum, the petty bourgeoisie seeks to maintain its position between the two major contenders – possibly even offers itself as mediator. It usually expects the state to perform the role of an arbiter, rather than be what it in reality is, a partisan instrument for class domination. The radical petty bourgeois thus either opts for a corporatist view of socialism – like the British Fabians – or adopts an ultra-radical 'leftism', impatient with reality.

South Africa's African Petty Bourgeoisie

When examining the African petty bourgeoisie in our country, the general characteristics outlined above can guide us, but we must be wary of the peculiarities that mark out this petty bourgeoisie from others. The features we can most readily isolate are:

i) Unlike the classical European petty bourgeoisie (and for that matter the white South African petty bourgeoisie), the African petty bourgeoisie was called into being by capitalist development during the epoch of imperialism.

ii) This stratum is specifically composed of upwardly mobile individuals, drawn from the proletariat, the traditional and modern peasantry. None of its recruits derive from declassed bourgeoisie.

Historically, the African petty bourgeoisie came into existence as the stepchild of British colonial policy in South Africa. In both the Cape and Natal imperialist policy-makers, during the 19th century, encouraged the growth of a stratum of petty commodity producers on the land, both as a means of transforming the traditional African peasant into a consumer of British goods and as a means of undermining the authority of the traditional rulers who led the military opposition to colonialism.

It was South African industrialisation, which has its origins in mining, that definitively laid the basis for a racially exclusive path of capitalist development. As Meillasoux remarks:

'... the discovery and bringing into production of the gold mines at the end of the 19th century considerably increased the demand for labour and cheap food. The subsequent industrialization, which did not cease to grow, required a more numerous workforce, and regular and abundant supplies of labour became the dominant concern of all successive South African regimes. It was to meet this double need that an entire system was introduced to prevent the Africans obtaining a profitable living from their land ...' (Claude Meillasoux, *Apartheid, Poverty and Malnutrition.* FOA, Rome, 1982, p.20).

The only area of capitalist economy in which Africans were allowed to gain an insecure foothold for accumulation during the late 19th century was commercial agriculture. Beginning in 1880 this was savagely attacked by the colonial state in its drive to create a mass labour force. The crowning event in this process was the Native Land Bill, initiated by Hertzog and the whites-only parliament in 1912. In an amazing show of unanimity the bill practically sailed through parliament and became law in June 1913.

The transformation of South African agriculture from pre-capitalist to capitalist has been described as conforming to the 'Prussian road' of capitalist development. This entailed the transformation of the pre-capitalist economy on the land through the actions of the landlords. The instrument employed for this transformation was the 1913 Land Act.

'... it was outside these colonial land structures that the category of African farmers able to compete with white farmers on the internal market had been able to emerge. And it was specifically at this category of black peasants, owners or renters of their land, that the 1913 (Land) Act was directed. By forbidding the acquisition of Africans of new land in areas declared white, the Act put an abrupt halt to the formation of this class of independent peasants.' (Meillasoux. *Op cit.* p.22).

Excluded from the land and from industry by racist laws, the African petty bourgeoisie survived by entering the professions. It was from this stratum of professionally trained Africans that the commercial bourgeoisie emerged when stable urban African communities grew up after the Second World War. In order to prosper, this commercial petty bourgeoisie was forced to explore and discover those areas where white commercial capital was either unable or unwilling to go. Its existential situation is typically a rearguard action, fought to hold back encroachments on its living space by either the state or white capital. Ironically, it was racist legislation that for a long time afforded this stratum a tenuous foothold in the segregated African townships where it could accumulate some capital.

During the 1920s and '30s, the Nationalist-Labour Pact government representing the alliance between white 'national' capital and the white labour aristocracy, intensified the assault on the economic foundations of the African petty bourgeois economy. The African artisan stratum, excluded from practising their trades in the central business districts by Stallardism, were now extruded also from factory employment by the 'civilise' (read, white) labour policy. Driven out of skilled employment, they had to submit to the most humiliating terms, being officially classified as unskilled while in fact performing skilled work. The growth of factory production in South Africa, coupled with the importation of cheap boots from Britain, squeezed the shoemakers and cobblers out of business. By the end of the 1920s, 0.1% of the African male population were classified as traders, artisans or hawkers. In areas like the OFS, a provincial ordinance legally forbade Africans from becoming traders.

The Natives Administration Act of 1927, which extended the principles of the Shepstonian Natal Code to the rest of the country, finally placed the seal on the direction of state policy.

The state-appointed pseudo-traditional bureaucracy was drawn into a formal client/patron arrangement with the capitalist state, with certain powers of labour impressment and coercion delegated to it. The ruling class hereby indicated that it was dispensing with the services of the petty bourgeoisie whom it perceived as, at best, irrelevant; at worst, as a potential threat.

The tables that follow give an indication of the growth and distribution of the African petty bourgeoisie and salariat from the mid-1930s to the mid-1970s.

Table 1

	1936	1946
Civil servant	103	249
Local auth/office/clerk	31	78
Advocate barrister	-	13
Attorney's clerk	-	5
Artist/sculptor	4	12
Attorney/law agent	7	5
Author/editor/journalist	10	10
Chemist	-	19
Clergyman/priest	2 429	2 697
Laboratory assistant	-	74
Librarian	-	31
Physician	7	33
Social worker	7	69
Teacher	8 204	14 002
Translator/interpreter	263	289
Variety artist/actor/etc	2	24
Other professionals	-	555

Distribution of African Professionals and Salaried Personnel

Based on Table CXLVII in *Report of the Fagan Commission on Native Laws*, U. G. 28 1948

Table 2(A)

	White	African	Coloured	Asian
Working proprietors	5 695	16	164	419
Salaried staff	25 138	89	28	167
Wage earners	117 221	211 047	46 689	15 981
Self-employed at home	194	4	189	20

Based on:

'Racial Composition of Working Proprietors, Salaried Staffs and Wage Earners in Private Manufacturing Industry, 1942–1943', in Hellman: *Handbook of Race Relations in South Africa.*

Table 2(B)

	White		African		Coloured		Asian	
	M	**F**	**M**	**F**	**M**	**F**	**M**	**F**
Managers & proprietors	18 561	1 509	818	16	380	71	5 889	166
Bookkeepers	4 764	3 062	6	1	26	18	196	3
Clerks	36 040	11 183	1 756	1	310	40	1 094	15
Typists	71	14 497	8	15	1	15	4	1
Shop assistants	14 932	15 427	1 950	126	1 067	251	5 232	181
Hawkers	992	33	1 636	83	2 065	172	3 137	339

Based on: *Occupational Census*, 1936, in U. G. 11/12, 1942

Table 3

	1960	1970
Engineers	19	80
Technicians	225	560
Doctors & dentists	104	120
Nurses and midwives	13 916	27 800
Medical auxiliaries	103	720
Architects and quantity surveyors	2	2
Physical scientists	1	60
Teachers	23 458	43 960
Jurists	35	40
Surveyors	11	100
Working proprietors	6 202	9 720

African Professionals, Salaried Employees and Business People, 1960–1970
Based on: *Official Year Book of the Republic of South Africa*, 1975, p 481

Table 4

	1936	1946	1960	1970
Teachers	8 204	14 002	28 350	43 960
Nurses & midwives	3 203	3 865	13 916	27 800
Working proprietors			6 202	9 720
Clergymen & priests	2 429	2 697		7 320
Doctors & dentists	7	33	109	120
Lawyers & jurists	7	18	35	40

Growth in Numbers of African Professionals, Salaried Employees and Businessmen

Table 5

	White		African		Coloured		Asian	
	M	F	M	F	M	F	M	F
Physical scientist	2 900	230	60				20	
Science technician	1 630	490	380	60	60	10	110	
Architect/town planner	3 420	110			10		20	
Engineer	14 890	60	80		10		50	
Surveyor	2 750	860	100		10			
Draughtsman	7 480	60	20		1 000		100	
Engineering technician	6 200	10	40		40			
Aircraft/ships' officer	1 610	270						
Life scientist	1 500	640	40		10			
Life science technician	1 880	870	40	20	30	10	30	
Doctor/vet/ dentist	8 310	25 070	100	20	70	40	470	60
Nurse/ midwife/aux	1 190	3 860	2 020	25 780	210	5 640	100	860
Medical auxiliary	4 650	370	560	160	110	110	140	50

	White		African		Coloured		Asian	
	M	**F**	**M**	**F**	**M**	**F**	**M**	**F**
Other medical worker	1 780	170	6 340	1 560	80	60	90	20
Accountant	7 550	100			30		60	
Jurist	5 850	33 730	40		20		40	
Teacher	22 770	900	17 080	26 880	7 480	8 870	4 430	1910
Clergyman/ nun/monk	5 530	9 920	7 320	780	620	60	220	10
Other professional/ technical worker	22 780		2 980	840	780	420	850	50

Distribution of Professional and Salaried Employees by Race and Sex
From Table 4, Chapter 31, *Yearbook*, 1975.

COMMENTARY ON TABLES

Table 1 indicates the growth in absolute numbers of professional and salaried employees amongst the Africans in the period 1936 to 1946. By far the largest numbers are to be found in the categories of teachers and clergymen, indicating that these were the two most favoured avenues for upward mobility.

Table 2(a) gives us the distribution of the South African working population by race. As is clear, the numbers of self-employed Africans and working African proprietors were miniscule at this time. Blacks are overwhelmingly represented in the category of wage earners.

Table 2(b) breaks down the categories of self-employed, salaried staff and working proprietors by race. It is evident from this that the majority of African traders at this time are in fact hawkers (almost double the number of working proprietors). Amongst the blacks it is only in the Asian group that proprietors outstrip hawkers. An interesting sidelight is that the number of Asian women hawkers is almost double that of proprietors. More than likely these are women working on behalf of family businesses.

Tables 3 and 4 are self-explanatory.

In the last table, Distribution by Race and Sex, we may note the concentration of black women in three professions: teaching, nursing and the church. This is particularly striking for Asian women and African women. The professions are obviously overwhelmingly dominated by white men; it is only in teaching and nursing that the figures for white women outstrip those for men.

It is readily evident from the foregoing figures that, in spite of severe restrictions and every conceivable legal device to destroy it, the African petty bourgeoisie has grown steadily. Associated with this growth is the greater visibility and assertiveness of this stratum. This peaked during the 1950s, occasioning a new onslaught by the state. Having grown in numbers and in self-confidence the urban African petty bourgeoisie responded to this attack with self-mobilisation, leading to the founding of the National African Chamber of Commerce (NACOC) in 1964.

How We View the Petty Bourgeoisie

Within our broad movement it is specifically the wing inspired by Marxism that has concerned itself with dissecting the role of the petty bourgeoisie. Broadly speaking, two apparently contradictory approaches have emerged within our ranks with regard to this structure.

The first approach may be summarised as: The national liberation movement, being a broad alliance of class forces, must at all times strive to retain the allegiance of these diverse forces until the immediate goal, national emancipation, has been secured. It is therefore imperative that it finds ways to accommodate the sensibilities of the petty bourgeoisie, lest, by precipitate actions, we drive it into the arms of reaction. This position was very cogently set out in a statement issued by the Central Committee of the SACP during the first quarter of 1980. The relevant portion reads:

> 'Of course, it is clear what the regime's intentions are: to tempt as many of them as possible into collaboration through these limited economic 'concessions'. But we must not assist this process by adopting positions which will help push them right into the enemy's lap.' (Foreword to 'People's Power', *The African Communist*, No. 80)

The second approach, a newer trend, argues that although the national liberation movement correctly seeks to forge a multi-class coalition, embracing workers, peasants and the petty bourgeoisie, it cannot be inferred from the petty bourgeoisie's oppressed status that it will necessarily assumer a posture oppositional to the regime. The main protagonists of this line of argument within our movement are Harold Wolpe and Dan O'Meara. Wolpe argued along these lines in his paper, 'The African Petit-Bourgeoisie'. Published in 1976. In Wolpe's own words:

> 'Thus it cannot be assumed that within a given conjuncture the interests of any of the groups or classes which are subject to a structure of oppression and exploitation will be represented in the course of the struggle, in terms of the complete destruction of that structure. This means, more concretely, that the interests and consequently the political involvement of each class and class fraction within the black population can only be determined through an analysis of the concrete economic, political and ideological conditions in the social formation.' (Wolpe, 1976)

In support of this view, Wolpe and O'Meara argue that the African petty bourgeoisie is being assiduously wooed by the big monopolists; is dependent on state and white capital; and consequently, may well have other options, including that of collaboration, to choose. Superficially these two views of the petty bourgeoisie seem incompatible, but it is my contention that this conceals a fundamental congruence in the conclusions they both lead to. Unless the proponents of these two approaches argue that the African petty bourgeoisie is insignificant (which they do not) the only logical conclusion one can draw from their approaches is that special consideration be given to the particular interests of the African petty bourgeoisie, in order to retain its allegiance to the broad liberation front. Such special consideration is in one instance spelt out: either that the movement moderate its social ambitions and not pose options that are too radical for petty bourgeoisie tastes, or that the movement maintain a tight rein on the exploited classes in order to contain their radicalism within bounds acceptable to the petty bourgeoisie. In other words, the limited social radicalism of the petty bourgeoisie should define the ceiling of the movement's immediate programme. It is not my intention to take issue with these views here. Rather, I intend, by a survey of the history of the organised African petty bourgeoisie, to test the accuracy of these assessments.

NACOC – 1964 TO 1969

Eric Hobsbawm has remarked that one of the ironies of bourgeois society is that it is the working class alone which self-consciously and unequivocally organises itself along class lines. The other classes usually disguise the particular interest they represent under titles, slogans and declared objectives of a general, social character – claiming to represent the general interest. Thus the organisations of the petty bourgeoisie are typically, professional associations, which pose as apolitical and are ostensibly solely interested in pursuance of professional excellence, the better to serve the community at large.

The African petty bourgeoisie was no exception to this general rule; its earliest organisations were indeed for professionals – teachers, ministers of religion, nurses – reflecting the relative weight of these amongst the stratum. The first overt attempts to organise African businessmen were undertaken during the Presidency of Josiah Gumede by the NEC of the ANC. Owing to the brevity of Gumede's term of office, these efforts bore no fruit. It was only after the Second World War, when the urban African community had grown in leaps and bounds, that a serious effort was made to establish a permanent organisation of African traders. This was the Johannesburg African Chamber of Commerce, inspired by Paul Mosaka and others. The JACOC held its first meeting in 1953 with the express aim of defending the rights of African traders in the urban areas. The rapid growth of the numbers of African-owned businesses in Johannesburg swelled the numbers of the organisation. By 1958 there were some 1683 licensed business premises in the townships of Johannesburg. A sizeable portion of these belonged to the JACOC. Though not very vocal, the JACOC participated in the African Leaders Conference of December 1960 and its leadership was present at the All-in Conference at Maritzburg in March 1961. Paul Mosaka was subsequently charged, together with Mandela and others, for inciting the 1961 Stay-at-Home strike.

It was the passage f the Bantu Self-Government Act and the tabling of the Bantu Laws Amendment Bill in 1963 that stirred JACOC into action. Under its leadership a national conference was convened in April 1964, bringing together African businessmen from various parts of South Africa to found the National African Chamber of Commerce (NACOC).

NACOC came into existence at a time when the regime was bent on the ethnic fragmentation of the African community and had just launched an all-out repressive campaign to destroy the forces of the democratic opposition. 1964, the year of its inauguration, coincides with the Rivonia convictions which mark the commencement of a period of enforced quiescence. The political context of its birth left its mark on both the character and style of the movement.

The objectives of the 1963 Bantu Laws Amendment Act were to drive African business permanently out of the urban areas. The terms of the law vested power to licence African enterprises in the Minister of Bantu Administration and Development (BAD). At the beginning of the year the BAD circularised all local authorities to the effect that:

- No Africans were henceforth to be permitted to trade outside the townships.
- No new trading licences were to be granted to Africans.
- Existing African traders were to be confined to retailing provisions and groceries only. Holders of licences to conduct other forms of business were to be encouraged to move to the Bantustans on the expiry of their current licences.
- Only exemptees under Section 10 of the Urban Areas Act would be eligible for licences.
- An African licensee would be permitted to operate only one business. No partnerships, companies or combinations were to be permitted.
- The local authorities would henceforth erect all business premises in the townships and lease them to eligible African traders.
- All service sector enterprises in the townships, including the liquor stores, hotels, restaurants and cinemas were to be owned and controlled

by the local authorities. Such enterprises as were already in the hands of Africans were to be encouraged to relocate to the Bantustans.

The leadership of NACOC tried to petition the regime to relax the provisions of the circular. After a deputation of 44 NACOC executive members interviewed the Minister of BAD, it was agreed that some of the more stringent regulations would be temporarily suspended, provided that the African business community accepted the principle of relocating in the Bantustans. In its first conflict with the regime NACOC was forced to compromise on the principle in return for a promise of dubious value.

Between 1964 and 1969 NACOC became one of the few African interlocutors with the regime body of responsible businessmen. NACOC was allowed to enter into almost annual discussions with the regime. The regime, too, was grateful for this narrow aperture affording it a view into an otherwise hostile urban African community. NACOC was, of course, speaking from a position of extreme weakness in its dealings with the regime. At successive meetings from 1965, the regime warned that dialogue with an entity such as NACOC was itself a violation of policy, because the regime recognised 9 separated African ethnic communities and the very notion of an African 'national' organisation was anathema to it. NACOC was able to ride out these objections until 1968 when at their last meeting of the decade the Minister of BAD made it known that unless NACOC changed its form and fragmented itself into separate Zulu, Xhosa, Sotho, etc. chambers of commerce, he could no longer enter into discussions with them.

This was a challenge that struck at the most fundamental principles underlying the organisation and submission to the BAD's terms would have seriously diluted the only strength NACOC possessed, its national constituency. To avoid the Scylla of head-on confrontation with the regime, and the Charybdis of fragmentation, NACOC hit on the stratagem of transforming itself into a federation of regional chambers of commerce. Consequently, in 1969, NACOC became NAFCOC – National African Federated Chambers of Commerce, covering 15 regions.

Two conclusions may be drawn from this episode:

i. The leadership of the commercial petty bourgeoisie is committed to the non-ethnic character of its organisation, both as a matter of principle and as a source of strength in dealings with the other strata and classes; and

ii. the leadership of the commercial petty bourgeoisie defines its interests as transcending ethnic affiliations and derived from a common class situation in the context of an economically united South Africa.

Though from its own perspective, this first round could be considered a stand-off, with neither side able to claim an outright victory, NAFCOC failed to achieve its immediate objective, keeping the door of dialogue with the regime at least ajar.

NAFCOC During its First Decade

The 1970s may be periodised into three segments:

- The pre-1973 period – which witnessed the emergence of the Black Consciousness ideology amongst university youth;
- The 1973–76 period, characterised by the re-emergence of the mass movement inaugurated by the massive working class struggles in Namibia and Natal;
- The post-Soweto period, characterised by the consolidation of the mass movement and renewal of armed struggle under the leadership of the ANC.

NAFCOC entered the '70s smarting from the blows the petty bourgeoisie had been forced to endure during the previous decade. It now sought to ride the racist tiger by becoming more accommodative to its Bantustan policy. As early as 1969 it was becoming clear that this would be the dominant trend. A memorandum submitted to the Minister of BAD in 1969 implicitly accepted Bantustanisation though arguing for greater flexibility in the application of policy.

'... it must be pointed out that Bantu businessmen, having business establishments in the urban areas, are not permitted to open new business concerns in the homelands, without being compelled to close down their older establishments.'

And in some later document:

'... Black firms or traders (should) be allowed to establish themselves where conditions are favourable and not necessarily within their own ethnic group ...'
(*African Perspectives on South Africa*, Cape Town, 1978, p. 151)

The chief complaint of the organised section of the African petty bourgeoisie became that the regime and its agents were in fact not living up to the spirit of 'separate development'. NAFCOC seemed bent on holding the regime to its promises and forcing it to translate rhetoric into reality. This was specifically true of NAFCOC's critique of the Bantu Investment Corporation (BIC) established in 1959 ostensibly to 'promote and encourage industrial and other concerns among Bantu persons in the Bantu territories.'

In practice, of course, BIC was an extremely selective agency. Its real purpose was to provide an easily manipulated source of patronage through which the regime could cultivate and groom a collaboration layer from amongst the petty bourgeoisie, who, in return for financial sponsorship, would agree to operate the administrative and repressive machinery of the Bantustans. According to its Director, one Dr Adendorff, by the end of 1970 the BIC had granted 959 loans to African entrepreneurs. Of these, 798 were original loans. The fund so disbursed had contributed towards the establishment of 680 commercial enterprises, 100 service sector enterprises (garages, petrol stations) and 18 industrial enterprises. The BIC itself had erected 282 business premises which it was leasing out to entrepreneurs.

BIC figures, like those of the BAD, are deliberately deceptive. One year later, in July 1971, the same Dr Adendorff revealed that the 959 loans the BIC had granted, in fact constituted a mere 16% of the number of applications it had processed (*Sunday Tribune*, 9.7.71). It also later emerged that the BIC was also being discriminatory in favour of white business at the expense of its ostensible clients. In 1974, Dr Adendorff announced that the BIC had disbursed R77 million in loans between 1959 and 1974. Of this sum:

- R14 million had gone to African business
- R20 million had gone toward BIC projects
- R43 million had gone to white-owned enterprises.

(*Rand Daily Mail*, 7.9.1974)

To add insult to injury the terms under which whites and blacks received loan were also differential. While white borrowers were offered loans of up to 60% of their capital investment, at rates of 2.5%, payable over ten years, Africans were offered no such terms, and interest rates were invariably 6½%. The tax concessions offered white investors were withheld from Africans and there were allegations of rampant corruption. But NAFCOC couched its complaints in the most deferential terms:

'… the interests of Bantu businessmen would be better served if some of the directors of the corporations were drawn from the Bantu people as well. Not only would this give the corporation the character of a Bantu organisation, but it would open the way for the eventual takeover of the corporation by the Bantu people themselves.'
(*African Perspectives on South Africa*, Cape Town, 1978, p. 152)

Needless to say, such appeals fell on deaf ears. The furthest the regime was prepared to go was to co-opt a handful of Bantustan politicians, without voting rights, on to the board of the BIC. NAFCOC, however, kept returning to the theme of a flexible application of the Bantustan policy. Sam Motsuenyane, President since 1968, tried to make a strong case for it in a presidential address to NAFCOC's 8th national conference in May 1972.

'The idea of separateness is, to my mind, of much less importance than that of development. The economic development of our territories is the most urgent common factor which ought to bind us together in our struggle to uplift ourselves. If the most developed areas of the world, like Western

Europe, perceive and feel the need for a European Common Market to
sustain and expand their economies, how much more fitting and necessary
is this concept for our poverty-stricken and undeveloped territories?'
(*African Perspectives on South Africa*, Cape Town, p. 149)

Motsuenyane's plea, however, was to lead to conflict not merely with
the regime but also with its delegated agents in the Bantustans, whose
power derived from their control over local patronage. As they moved
towards so-called independence, the Bantustan leaders exerted pressure
on 'their' petty bourgeoisie to dissociate from NAFCOC – a 'South
African' organisation.

While attempting to bend the Bantustan policy to its own purposes,
NAFCOC also sought to jump on the Black Consciousness bandwagon.
In 1969 Motsuenyane launched a 'Buy HOME Week' to encourage
township shoppers to spend their monies in the townships. 'Economic
nationalism' was, however, a non-starter in a context where township
traders charged higher prices than downtown supermarkets. Both these
trends in NAFCOC tactics met with very little success.

But underneath the surface calm of South Africa, there were forces
at work conspiring to change radically the entire political complexion
of the country and region. The first signs were the massive strikes in
Durban during 1973.

NAFCOC WETS ITS FEET

The period commencing 1973 saw the unprecedented growth of the mass
movement which had been forced into dormancy by the repression of the
sixties. The strikes in Durban were opening salvoes of this movement.
Close on its heels the collapse of Portuguese colonialism excited rising
expectations in the entire region.

Southern Africa once again became the focus of international
attention as the imperialist powers sought ways to secure their interests.
It was within this context that both within and outside South Africa
the voices of liberal capitalism were heard warning that if capitalism in
South Africa was to survive, it would have to dissociate itself from overt
racism.

For a decade the organised section of the urban African petty bourgeoisie had steered a very cautious path, distinguished by a pragmatic assessment of the actual power relations in South Africa throughout the 1960s. the racist state during that time appeared to wield almost unlimited power, unrestrained by either the loyal opposition or the extra-parliamentary movement. When conditions began to thaw NAFCOC took its first hesitant steps to delink itself from the Bantustan policy and began to assert the rights of its constituency more forcefully. Motsuenyane signalled this change of direction in August 1973 when he declared:

> 'The idea of black temporariness in the so-called white areas ... is quite absurd and ridiculous when viewed against the stark actualities of our South African situation. I am inclined to share ... the opinion ... that the unscrambling of the mixture of race location, built up over many years, seems impossible both physically and economically ...'
> (*African Perspectives*, p. 71)

This repudiation of the ideology of 'separate development' was, however, not total. We can note however that NAFCOC shifts the grounds of its legitimating rhetoric and begins to appeal to the authority of laissez-faire, now increasingly espoused by spokesmen of the ruling class and, to a lesser extent, the state. Thus the resolutions of the NAFCOC conference of 1974, embodied in a memorandum to the minister of BAD and submitted on NAFCOC's behalf by Chief Gatsha Buthelezi, are an interesting mix of both. While on the one hand calling for the abolition of the restrictions on African ownership, business activities, etc., it justifies these in terms of raising capital to develop the 'Bantu homelands'. As if taking advantage of precisely this ambivalence, when the regime responded to NAFCOC's demands, its response too was couched in terms upholding the Bantustan policy. After the meeting with the Bantustan leaders the regime announced its intention to remove the restrictions imposed on African business in terms of its 1963 provisions and to concede some measure of home-ownership to those Africans who could afford it through long term leasehold agreements. This latter 'concession' however was conditional upon the aspirant homebuyers first acquiring homeland citizenship certificates. Pretoria still held to its old positions and intended using 'concessions' as an inducement to accept them.

Spokesmen for NAFCOC were not slow in seizing their opportunity to exploit the fears of the rulers. A middle stratum, enjoying the fruits of capitalism together with its white colleagues would be a factor for stability. Mr Richard Maponya, a leading member and prominent Soweto 'tycoon', said (in so many words) to a conference on the Reef. Lifting the restrictions on African business was not only sound economics but was also dictated by the self-interest of the rulers. But the hopes raised by the apparent retreat from the regime's 1963 position proved to be premature. In May 1976, under pressure from white commercial interests, the state published a special notice withdrawing most of these concessions. One month later South Africa erupted in a nationwide uprising which rendered all these issues obsolete.

THE SOWETO UPRISING AND BEYOND

The uprising inaugurated by the Soweto events of June 16th 1976, is recognised by friend and foe alike as a watershed in the recent political history of our country. Every class and class fraction, in both the people's and the enemy camp, was touched by these events and there was a clear realisation on both sides that things could never return to the status quo ante.

Though the urban African petty bourgeoisie played little or no role in the uprising, it has undoubtedly been the chief beneficiary of the mass struggles of that year. The first clear sign of this was a meeting between representatives of NAFCOC and the Minister of BAD on 20th August 1976. After consistently refusing to meet NAFCOC since 1968, Dr Koornhof found time to meet its representatives in the midst of a profound crisis. Since then, every quarter in the ruling class, with the exception of the diehard racists of the far right, has courted the African petty bourgeoisie with a view to somehow using it as a bugger against pressures from below. In this changed situation, where it can apparently reap where it has sown, the petty bourgeoisie is discovering untapped

reserves of courage and is adopting a firmer stand both in its relations
with the regime and other class factions of white capital who seek either
to co-opt or emasculate it. Guided solely by its perceived interests as
a distinct socio-economic stratum, the petty bourgeoisie has displayed
a surprising vigour and tenacity in its activities. Though it has not
discarded its 'moderate' demeanour, NAFCOC is on record demanding
the dismantling of key aspects of the apartheid structure – in the fields
of land ownership, the franchise, education and business opportunities.
The irony in all this is that it is the rhetoric of the state and big business
that has afforded NAFCOC the opportunity to do so without fear of
being branded 'subversive'. What has occasioned this rhetoric on the
part of the state and capital are the mass struggles that dominate the post-
Soweto period.

Paradoxically, the appearance of these new options for white capital
has cast NAFCOC into an ambiguous situation. Its decisive class interests
dictate opposition to apartheid, but it pragmatically recognised that at the
moment it is unable to compete on the open market with white capital.
The only tactical advantage the African petty bourgeoisie possesses, is its
virtual monopoly over the African townships – by virtue of apartheid.
NAFCOC has been careful not to throw away this competition. The
regime, in its turn, hopes to exploit this ambivalence in order to redirect
petty bourgeois ambitions into limits it finds acceptable.

After the June 16th uprising forced open Koornhof's door, the BAD
has displayed a remarkable willingness to accommodate some of the
more pressing demands of the African petty bourgeoisie. The homeland
certificate requirements were dropped and the Deputy Minister of BAD
undertook to meet NAFCOC annually for talks, in effect recognising
NAFCOC as the authentic representative of the urban African petty
bourgeoisie. This proved to be the major breakthrough. After the 1977
NAFCOC-BAD talks further concessions were announced, including
the lifting of restrictions on various forms of business activity; an
increase in the size of trading sites; a promise to review the prohibition
against industrial activities in the urban areas. It was during this session
that the regime announced that it was considering a form of land tenure,
'short of freehold' for Africans in the urban areas. The upshot was the

Bantu (Urban Areas) Amendment Act of 1978, providing for the 99 year leasehold scheme for Section 10 exemptees outside the Western Cape. After the 1978 meeting, further concessions enabled African businesses to employ white managerial skills and open supermarkets. Pleas that the Bantu Administration boards surrender their monopoly on liquor stores, cinemas, hotels and restaurants as yet went unheeded, but promises were made to look into the matter. The relaxation of the constraints imposed on African business led to a sudden spurt in growth. From 1 223 licensed business enterprises in Soweto for 1977, the comparable figure in 1980 was 1 585. A NAFCOC survey n 1980 also found that in the Southern Transvaal there were 1000 potential African industrialists, looking for ways to promote their products. The membership of NAFCOC also grew commensurately, by 1980 it numbered 10 000 individual members, spread over 97 local chambers of commerce. (Figures from *Hansard*, 2Q. Col 58.197. 5Q.Col 315.1980; *Race Relations Survey*, 1981).

NAFCOC's leadership had exploited the new situation with a tactical acumen that invites admiration. As in the past they challenged the state to translate rhetoric into reality, arguing that the surest means of protecting the system of private enterprise is to open it up to all South Africans. The highly capitalised white commercial sector has not been slow in taking advantage of NAFCOC's new policy. The Associated Chambers of Commerce (ASSOCOM), representing the British fraction of white commerce, vocally supports NAFCOC's call for an end to racial barriers to African commerce, as do a number of the leading capitalists. Though this has strengthened NAFCOC's hand in dealings with the regime, it has also resulted in the first schism of its ranks.

UNITY AND CONFLICT WITH WHITE CAPITAL

On December 9th 1983, the *Financial Mail* commented: '… most of the black spending power – currently estimated at R650 million a year – has gone to the Johannesburg Central Business District. Because choice on the Soweto doorstep has been limited.' Once again the regime lifted restrictions enabling African traders to set up supermarkets in the townships the white commercial sector could no longer afford to be complacent about the threat of African competition. Highly capitalised white companies, however, saw an opportunity to cash in on this lucrative market through black/white partnerships that were now permitted in terms of the 1978 'concessions'. NAFCOC had originally been one of the chief proponents of such partnerships, but after 1981 it changed its mind and now appears wary of the idea.

In theory there were two ways in which relations between white and black capital could be arranged. One option was that of partnerships which might entail the black partner being emasculated. With their monopoly over business skills based on years of racial privilege, a black company with a white junior partner would become overly dependent on its white partner's managerial skills and connections, effectively reducing the African partner to a mere front for white interests. The second option would entail the African commercial sector seeking assistance of white capital in the shape of loans and managerial skills where necessary, thus preparing the ground for a class alliance across colour lines based on their common stake in the capitalist economy.

NAFCOC prefers the latter course and has bent its efforts towards pursuing it. However, as compared to the white commercial sector, NAFCOC is a shoestring operation. Huge financial inducements finally breached the defences of the organisation in late 1983 when three prominent Soweto 'tycoons' entered into a 51/49 partnership with Metcash, a leading wholesale firm, to found Afrimet. The 'Afrimet affair', as it has become known, sparked a major row in NAFCOC, culminating in the expulsion of the three and a call on NAFCOC members to boycott the company. Explaining their decision to exclude these former luminaries, Motsuenyane explained:

'First, it is NAFCOC's policy, since 1978, to discourage black/white partnerships in the retail trade. This also includes wholesale companies. The reasons underlying this policy are as follows:
- Black businessmen are not allowed to trade in white areas in terms of the Group Areas Act as well as the Black Urban Areas Act
- Black/white partnerships in retailing pose a threat and represent unfair competition for developing black business which was legally supressed until only six days ago …

- A black/white partnership with a management contract that is not carefully structured will often run into the danger of *apportioning greater power and control to the white partner even if share capital suggests a black majority such as in the case of Afrimet.'* (*African Business and Chamber of Commerce Review*. May 1983).

While the outcome of the affair is far from certain it does demonstrate a tenacious will to protect the budding autonomy of the African petty bourgeoisie on the part of NAFCOC. The project of capturing the African market is being pursued through the Black Chain Ltd, a supermarket and wholesale firm established under the auspices of NAFCOC. Thus far it has erected one supermarket at Jabulani and there are plans to build others. The Black Chain is putting all its eggs in the basket of an expanding African consumer marker. According to a recent study done at Stellenbosch University the spending power of Africans should equal that of whites by 1985. (*African Business and Chamber of Commerce Review*, May 1983).

To what extent the Black Chain will be able to tap this potential remains to be seen. The firm has already provoked the ire of the smaller Soweto traders who correctly perceive it as a threat to their business. NAFCOC has thus far managed to assuage these fears by offering to extend wholesale facilities to these Soweto traders and inviting them to buy shares in the Black Chain. While it was able to contain this particular storm, it is indicative of the latent sources of intra-petty-bourgeois friction between NAFCOC and the less well-endowed urban-African traders, white big business has not abandoned its pursuit of the African petty bourgeoisie, indeed each rebuff appears to have fuelled its ardour in the courtship. NAFCOC conferences are graced by the likes of Dennis Etheredge, former President of the Chamber of Mines; Theo Wassenaar of SANLAM; A.M. Rosholt, Chairman of Barlow Rand and others. Six monopolies have become associate members – the constitution restricts full membership to blacks – and its president has become the token African *par excellence* in monopolist circles. Sam Motsuenyane now sits on the boards of at least three big companies: Anglo-American, A.E.C.I. and Permanent Life Assurance. By the good graces of the University

of the Witwatersrand, of which Harry Oppenheimer is Chancellor, he
is now Dr Samuel Motsuenyane, the first African ever to receive this
honour from a white University! Imperialist countries have also entered
the race with all manner of inducements. In June 1983 Motsuenyane
revealed NAFCOC links with the British Embassy in Pretoria, the
possibilities of assistance from US Aid Agency and financial assistance
from the Konrad Adenauer Foundation of the FRG. (*African Business*,
June 1983).

At present the USSALEP is handled by NAFCOC as are a number
of other programmes aimed at assisting African businessmen to
acquire American business skills and imbibe US political attitudes. As
Eagleburger announced on June 23rd 1983:

> 'We are tangibly backing the things we believe in. By strengthening
> the educational standards of the black population, by enhancing the
> organizational ability of labour and by expanding the business base of the
> black community we are engaged in institution building for change away
> from apartheid while encouraging the alternative to it.' (*Washington
> Line*, 24th June 1983. USIS Lusaka)

Within the space of seven years the fortunes of NAFCOC and the urban
African petty bourgeoisie have changed dramatically. From the cap-in-
hand petitioner, humbly seeking an audience with the powers-that-be
during the early seventies, NAFCOC has become perhaps the most
avidly courted organisation in South Africa. The ruling circles in South
Africa and amongst its imperialist allies are anxious to determine which
options the African petty bourgeoisie will choose and, if possible, to be
a factor in their reckoning.

This paper set out to answer two questions that are implicit in the
assessments of the African petty bourgeoisie prevalent to our movement,
viz:

- Does the movement have to accommodate the sectional interests of
  the petty bourgeoisie lest radical policies drive it into the arms of the
  enemy?
- Will the commonly shared disabilities as an oppressed people in the

last instance be the principal determinant of the petty bourgeoisie's behaviour?

I would tentatively suggest that the answer to both these questions can be discovered by analysing the shifting political positions adopted by the organised section of this stratum since 1963. We can draw four conclusions from the foregoing survey in this respect.

- That NAFCOC, as representative of the African petty bourgeoisie, was at its most abject and deferential during the period of induced political quiescence. Indecisive and weak when left to its own devices, it was keen to reach any sort of accommodation with the regime, even at the expense of compromising the very objectives it was set up to pursue.

- NAFCOC, despite its indecision and political flabbiness, remained committed to the ideal of a non-ethnic African identity, or a concept of its class interest that transcends ethnic boundaries. It employed every conceivable ploy to preserve this in the face of unremitting pressure from the regime.

- The organised petty bourgeoisie began to discover its political courage only when the mass movement, led by the African working class, displayed signs of revival. It was in the context of the post 1973 struggles that it began to assume a posture critical of the regime and its policies.

- NAFCOC became assertive, even of its own sectional petty bourgeois interests, only in the wake of the mass struggles of the post-Soweto period. It was precisely as a result or at least a by-product of these struggles that it was able to recoup the losses the African petty bourgeoisie had suffered during the sixties. It is also clear that it is the mass working class struggles, coordinated and combined with the armed liberation struggle that have occasioned the courtship of the African petty bourgeoisie by various fractions of both the local and metropolitan ruling classes, thus affording it marginal leverage in its dealing with the regime.

These conclusions point in one direction. That far from the radicalism of the mass movement alienating or terrifying the petty bourgeoisie, it has in fact paid it handsome dividends. The assertiveness of the proletarian strata in the class struggles of recent years have in fact secured for the petty bourgeoisie, which was distinguished by its inertia, prerogatives it was unable to wrest from the state relying on its own puny forces. The changed political chemistry of South Africa in the 1980s, precipitated by militant mass struggles, has catalysed a situation which favours the African petty bourgeoisie and which it would like to exploit for sectional ends.

I would therefore suggest that the experience of past 20 years indicates that it is not by pandering to petty bourgeois sensibilities that the movement will retain their allegiance. It is only when the mass movement, under the leadership of the black working class, gives a bold lead that it will be able to draw the petty bourgeoisie into its train.

BIBLIOGRAPHY

African Business and Chamber of Commerce Review. (Monthly Organ of NAFCOC.) African Business Publications, Johannesburg. Issues: Jan–Dec. 1983.

Kuper, Leo. An African Bourgeoisie. Yale, 1965.

Meillasoux, Claude. Apartheid, Poverty and Malnutrition. F.A.O. Rome, 1982.

Slovo, Joe. South Africa – No Middle Road. In Davidson, Slovo, Wilkerson, Southern Africa: The New Politics of Revolution. Harmondsworth. 1976.

South African Institute of Race Relations. Survey of Race Relations. (Annual 1963/1983)

The African Communist. Quarterly Journal of the SACP. No.80. Inkululeko Publications. London.

Van der Merwe, Charton, Kotze & Magnuson, African Perspectives on South Africa. Speeches, 1978.

Wolpe, Harold. The Changing Class Structure of South Africa. The African Petit Bourgeoisie. Dept. of Sociology, University of Essex. November 1976.

FOUR

In July 1985 Oliver Tambo wrote to members of the ANC NEC, 'I have asked Comrade Pallo to circulate to NEC members the paper on 'Constitutional Models' which he has been working on.' The 'new face of counter-revolution' of the title is analysed in a survey of the various political models being promoted by verligte and liberal political scientists linked to the regime: consociationism, confederalism, federalism and a conservative version of pluralist democracy. Jordan provides a forensic account of S.P. Huntingdon's advice to South Africa's rulers; analyses the convergence of thinking of the Progressive Federal Party and Buthlezi's Inkatha; and locates all of these within the context of a general crisis for white minority rule. To counter these approaches, the ANC must link universal suffrage to the demand for a unitary state. It must also pronounce in favour of political pluralism – multiple political parties and a role for opposition – dispelling the 'sad misconception' that radical social transformation was possible only under one-party rule. It should also champion a Bill of Rights, an 'extensive and comprehensive exposition of the rights and liberties South Africans would enjoy under an ANC government'. This paper was crucial in defining the ANC's constitutional negotiating stance and must rank as one of the most significant pieces ever penned by Jordan.

The New Face of Counter-revolution: A briefing paper

Since the demise of Vorster's premiership, the air has been thick with rumours and speculations about the possibilities of some dramatic breakthrough in South Africa. Every manner of political pundit, from the savants to the charlatans, has seen fit to add his/her two cents worth to the endless reams of paper that have been devoted to this enterprise. The South African newspaper-reading public and that of the western world have been inundated with learned and half-baked commentaries, singing the praises of Botha the 'courageous reformer', who has dared to tamper with the most sacred taboos of Afrikanerdom, in his search for a peaceful solution to South Africa's problems.

What is surprising about these predictions and speculations is the regularity with which they are refurbished and rehashed in different forms. And, on each occasion they are paraded before the public as refreshingly new. In fact this has occurred so frequently over the past eight years that one has continuously to remind oneself that the latest prediction is in fact old hat, only slightly retouched to take account of more recent developments.

We do not intend to give the impression that there are no changes afoot in South Africa, nor do we argue that the balance of political forces, inside the country and in the region, remains static. Indeed, the very outpouring of speculative writings and premature predictions is a sign of the extreme fluidity of the situation. That South Africa and the entire region are in motion is undoubtedly true. Where we differ with the would-be-political-clairvoyants is in identifying the source of this motion.

There are, broadly speaking, three schools of political thought that have pronounced on 'reform' in South Africa. These could be classed as liberal (English and Afrikaner 'verligte') on the right; and two divergent trends on the left – one of which dismisses these changes as cosmetic while the other traces them to profound structural and ideological pressures within the South African capitalist system.

The spectrum of liberal analysis, on the right, is in fact quite broad, ranging from the undisguised arguments of economic self-interest advanced by spokesmen of big business, to the more sophisticated word spinners of various political scientists. Despite their differing emphasis, these various shades of liberal opinion find a common denominator in the central theme that the system of apartheid, as it operates at present, is untenable and should be scrapped, sooner rather than later. However, this system, as conceived and discussed by these liberal commentators, is abstracted from its material foundations, and they treat it as if it exists as a 'pure' phenomenon – the ideology and practice of the National Party. Traditionally South African liberal scholarship has regarded apartheid as some form of political savage survival, foisted upon the otherwise rational capitalist system by the backward frontier mentality of past generations of white South African politicians. Consistent with this view, the English liberal analysts claim that the capitalist system, left to its own devices would through its imperative to generate the maximum profit, have swept away racial prejudice and the other irrationalities of racism long ago. The task facing South Africa and its people today, so they argue, is to create the space for capitalism to assert its essential rationality, which will in due course, bring about a non-racial society governed by the pursuit of individual profit. Moreover, the liberal claim such a course synchronises well with the economic self-interest of the majority of Whites, who though they are apprehensive about change, will be more amenable to it once they recognise its unmistakeable economic benefits. South Africans, they say, should know from their own experience that state interference with and manipulation of the market forces can only have disastrous consequences. Such interference is in point of fact the record of the racists. Unfettered laissez faire capitalism, with an absolute minimum state intervention, is the ideal. So runs the English liberal argument. (Cf: Michael O'Dowd; Workshop on Socio-Economic and Constitutional Alternatives for South Africa, Aug. 1978.; Harry Oppenheimer; 'Prospects for Change in Southern Africa' Oct 1977; 'Towards Equal Opportunity in South Africa' March 1979).

Parenthetically, it is ironic that this line of argument finds a sympathetic echo in the writings of one commentator on the left, Phineas Malinga, a contributor to the 'African Communist' 1st Quarter 1983. Malinga, essentially agrees with the liberals' reasoning since he too contends that racism/apartheid has acted as a fetter on economic growth and was imposed by backward farmers, pursuing some anti-modern pipe-dream. Malinga however parts company with the liberals because of his support of the national liberation movement. We would argue that his support is grafted onto fundamentally flawed analytical roots. It does not flow logically from his line of reasoning. This is a political trend within our movement which unfortunately has not been subjected to rigorous criticism and hence continues to survive.

The contribution of the verligte Afrikaner analysts has not been as sanguine about the supposed virtues of the capitalist system. Rather than seeking a solution solely through the untrammelled effect of economic forces, they have devoted most of their effort to the political sphere. This consists mainly of political model-building, derived from the experience of various European states. These models, these academics allege, are best suited to the solution of South Africa's problems, because, so they claim, it can only result in the total subordination of the rights of the minorities to the overwhelming numerical preponderance of the Africans. Some have even argued that it could result in domination of specific ethnic communities amongst the Africans. Consociationism, confederalism and federalism are the devices being proffered by the liberal wing of the Afrikaaner [sic] academia. Within the constraints of such a 'pluralist' model, some are quite prepared to accept the principle of one person, one vote. These views have been taken up, with differing degrees of enthusiasm, by other political currents outside 'verligte' Afrikaanerdom [sic] – the PFP, the leaders of the Coloured Labour Party, Gatsha Buthelezi and other Bantustan leaders. Though the English and the Afrikaaner [sic] liberals approach the subject of change from differing perspectives, we may note a fundamental area of agreement between them. Both evince a concern to carry over into the future crucial areas of White privilege and control. That they focus on the economic (in the case of the English) and on the political (in the case of the Afrikaaner [sic]) is probably explained by the relative weight of these two segments of the White community in each of these spheres. Recognition of the convergence of these apparently contradictory perspectives also explains the acceptance of 'verligte' prescriptions by the political representatives of English liberalism – the PFP.

Given the political promises from which they move, the liberals (both English and Afrikaaner [sic]) criticise Botha for not moving fast enough for his own good. They explain the tardiness of the regime in terms of strictures placed on Botha by his unenlightened political constituency and a certain unwillingness on his part to grasp the nettle of consistent reform for fear of provoking a backlash. This assessment is not purely negative. It is in itself a prescription for action which proposes that on the one hand Botha must allay the fears of potential backlashers by explaining how reform coincides with their self-interest, while on the other hand taking more determined action so as to pre-empt revolution from below. Pressures for this latter course, they argue, will be most effective from those quarters who stand to benefit directly from the rationalisation of the capitalist system, the leaders of big business and commerce. Hence the Urban Foundation and related bodies. External pressure can be effective if it has a demonstrative impact through 'constructive engagement' (which, lest we forget, is a concept coined not by Chester Crocker or Reagan, but by the liberal economist Merle Lipton. Cf: 'African Affairs', January 1979; 'South African Labour Bulletin', October 1976).

Commentators on the left, within and outside the national liberation movement, generally accept that the Botha regime is embarked upon a programme to change the face of racial domination in South Africa.

The disagreements that there are centre on both the extent and the significance of those changes. There are at the one extreme, those who contend that the changes envisaged are a thinly veiled exercise in mass deception (cosmetic changes). At the opposite extreme there are others who argue that these changes mark actual shifts and realignments within the ruling capitalist class. We would associate ourselves with a view that lies somewhere between these two extremes and takes account of both the elements of deception and the material forces militating for change.

The arguments of the cosmetic change school are a useful corrective of the illusions being sown by the liberal, but we feel they bend the stick too far (in his 'Ruth First Memorial Lecture', Maputo, August 1984. Cf: Sechaba, February 1985) in which he suggests that little or nothing has changed in terms of the life chances of all Africans across the board. His approach takes no account of the growing opportunities (which had either never existed before or had been abolished by the regime) for capital accumulation afforded African businessmen since the 99 year leasehold rights provisions, the lifting of restrictions on partnerships and manufacturing activities in the urban areas. To be sure, these measures affect only a tiny minority of the urban African population. But the political and social weight of this segment must not and cannot be assessed purely on the basis of its numbers.

Their opposite numbers contend that the measures already undertaken by Botha and all the talk about reform reflect the shifting locus of power within the economy. They point to the evident rise and domination of the economy by powerful monopolites and conglomerates; the transition from labour intensive to more capital intensive systems of production; the failure of various aspects of the regime's internal policies, which have precipitated a crisis that necessitates the creation of a new dominant block, led by the monopolists.

These factors, they argue, combined with the impact of the liberation struggle, especially the mass upsurge that characterises the late 1970s and the 1980s, have forced the ruling class to seek new options. The question, these commentators say, is not whether or not the reforms being undertaken are deceptive or real, but rather why they are being introduced at all. Implicit in the manner they pose the question: is the suggestion that some deeper underlying causes must be sought to explain the actions of the regime (for the views summarised here of: Sechaba', May and June 1983. 'The Rise of the Military in South Africa' by A.W. Parts I and II; 'Marxism Today', January 1983. 'Apartheid's Deepening Crisis' by Harold Wolpe.)

In review, published in Sechaba, May 1983, I argued that there is a degree of economism in the line of reasoning of these commentators, in that they assume a direct casual [causal?] link between the trends they identify in the economic sphere and the developments in the political. It was then and continues to be my considered opinion that 'Reform', talk of reform and all the reformist political model-building we are witnessing, are eleventh hour counter-insurgency ploys, designed to snatch White domination (as distinct from apartheid) from the jaws of defeat.

This survey is intended as a briefing, in the first instance for our NEC, on the various political models being proffered by the liberal and verligte political scientists linked to the regime or other fractions of the South African ruling class. We shall be examining the notions of 'consociationism', 'confederalism', 'federalism' and 'pluralist democracy' as propounded by these ideologists. We shall specifically examine the proposals put forward in the Buthelezi Commission, because it was the most comprehensive plan of this nature to be placed before the South African public. But before we do this we want to locate these ideas within the context of a general theory of reform to which the think thanks that have given them birth subscribe. Through these means we hope to demonstrate:

- the essentially counter-revolutionary character of the models that have been placed before us; while
- briefing the members of the NEC about the core ideas underpinning these models; and
- proposing strategic options, within the framework of our general strategy, to counter these manoeuvres.

THE THEORIES OF COUNTER-REVOLUTIONARY REFORM

The most explicit exposition of the theory that informs the strategic thinking of the South African ruling class came from a strange quarter: the ivied walls of Harvard University in the USA. The author is one Samuel P. Huntingdon, a professor of Political Science who achieved international notoriety at the height of the Vietnam War, when he and a number of his colleagues at Harvard, MIT, Michigan State and other prestigious universities designed the counter-insurgency strategy of the Johnson Administration. This was a period during which the think tank, inspired by Kennedy's vision of the 'new frontier', came into vogue. When US social scientists began to conceive of themselves as 'social engineers' who could manipulate human beings and entire societies in very much the same manner as their counterparts in the natural sciences manipulated chemicals and other inanimate matter. Huntingdon himself has an impeccable US ruling class pedigree, daring back to the American Revolution of 1776, and has a long record of service in the cause of that class.

In a lecture to strategists at RAU published as an article in 'Politikon' – South African Journal of Political Science, based at the University of Pretoria, Huntingdon draws an analogy between present day South African and a number of Latin American countries. He proceeds to recommend the strategy of Bismarck, the 'white revolutionary' as appropriate for South Africa. The role played by Bismarck in the unification of Germany through 'the revolution from above' is well known and need not detain us. There is however one seminal point which needs to be made in this connection. The success of Bismarckian strategy owed much to the epoch in which it was employed. During the 1860s capitalism in Germany was a progressive historical force, on the ascendant. Though confronted by an emergent working class, ... this class was as yet too weak and politically immature to pose an effective challenge. Bismarck succeeded in making the feudalist/capitalist compact work because he could mobilise the support of the petty bourgeoisie on the platform of social order and defence of property at a time when the working class was not yet a serious contender for power. We shall return later to examine how well Huntingdon's analogy fits present day South Africa.

Huntingdon's basic argument is that revolutionary violence does not have to be successful to yield results. Provided it creates sufficient tensions to cause divisions among the ruling class, it can seriously compromise the dominant class's capacity to crush it. He continues, '... fundamental change in South Africa appears to be waiting for its Lenin.' He hastens to warn that this statement should not be read as approbation, but rather as an urging that as 'intense attention' be paid in current South Africa to the strategy and tactics of reform as that 'which Lenin devoted to the strategy and tactics of revolution.'

The reform process, according to Huntingdon, will be affected by six factors, which he enumerates as:

- Political leadership,
- Strategy and tactics,
- Timing,
- Power and its use,
- Issue selection and sequence,
- Divide and reform.

Political leadership

Huntingdon conceives of reform as a three-cornered fight, in which the reformer/s face both the advocates of the status quo and the revolutionaries. In order to succeed the reformer/s must divide and confuse his opponents. He must assume a 'moderate' posture, apparently rejecting both extremes.

Strategy and tactics

The most promising approach is a combination of Fabian strategy (slow incremental changes) with Blitskrieg tactics (executed with a lightning speed).

Timing

Counter elites (like the national liberation movement), he argues, make their maximum demands when they are at their weakest and when they are at their strongest. The optimum moment, therefore, to engage them in constructive negotiations is during the interim growth phase. Such engagement will have the effect of offering the inducements of acquiring power, but at a moment when they too realise they cannot enjoy it on their own terms. Reform, therefore, should be introduced from positions of relative strength, when the incumbent government can still dictate the terms.

Power
'It is not inconceivable that narrowing the scope of political participation may be indispensable to eventually broadening that participation. The route from limited uni-racial democracy to a broader multi-racial democracy could run through some form of autocracy.'

(This is why some of us felt the movement's approach with regard to the slogans to place before the White community during the anti-Tri-Racial parliament campaign was misplaced. Read in this context, there is no contradiction between the growing power of the executive at the expense of the White parliament for Whites if they accept Botha's reform package. In short, for White reform to live White supremacy must die!)

Repression and reform proceed hand in hand, because effective repression enhances the appeal of reform to radical by raising the costs of engaging in revolutionary activity; at the same time it reassures the far right that the government is in control of the situation. 'The government that is too weak to monopolize counter-revolutionary repression is also too weak to inaugurate counter-revolutionary reform.'

Issue selection and sequence
This is essentially a matter of tactics. Selecting those issues which place the reformer/s in the best position to throw their opponents on the left and on the right in disarray, and resolving those issues with a speed and in a sequence that does not allow them time to marshal effective opposition.

Divide and reform
To be successful a reformer/s must enlist some measure of support from the disadvantaged (in our case, the Blacks) therefore fragmentation and leadership rivalries initially are to its advantage. Later on, it is equally

conceivable that a reformer government will require a strong and legitimate Black leadership to negotiate with. A leadership that will be able to induce its followers to accept and support meaningful agreements.

This exposition by Huntingdon gives us some idea of how the long range strategists and ideologists of the ruling class conceptualise what they are doing. We may argue or disagree about the extent to which it conforms to Botha's strategy, but we can all agree that the tactics outlined here have a familiar ring.

We propose that both the regime's manoeuvres and the proposals we are about to examine should be placed against the backdrop of Huntingdon's ideas. On one thing we must absolutely agree, and on this Huntingdon is quite clear, the purpose of reform is to pre-empt revolutionary change – its essence is counter-revolution!

Samuel P. Huntingdon, like most ideologists of the ruling class, ever actually wishes to examine the merits of demerits of the alternatives posed by those who wish to make revolutionary changes. He adopts the pose of a disinterested outsider, who views the entire panorama with keen, objective eyes, unclouded by the mists of partisanship. Reactionaries, conservatives, reformers and revolutionaries, in the eyes of this 'objective' scholar, all are merely elites, each seeking to re-order or order society according to its own design.

Huntingdon's inability (or unwillingness) to deal seriously with the real problems and the forces militating for social change is not merely a function of his bad faith (though he has an abundance of this too). It is rather his prior commitment to the existing social order that prevents him from examining its assumptions and addressing the criticisms voiced by its opponents. As he says, he is quite explicitly for reform of the system, and is opposed to revolution. It thus follows that there are certain core institutions of the old order he wishes to preserve. The hollowness of his 'objectivity' and his claims to 'value free science' are exposed at precisely this point. They conceal partisanship for particular interests and a commitment to certain values. When examining the claims of ruling class theorists, therefore, we must at each point delve beneath the appearance of their objectivity to uncover the real motives.

THE THEORISTS OF PLURALISM

Pluralism has come into vogue in bourgeois political philosophy and theory as an additional means of explaining the persistence of all manner of conflicts that plague capitalist societies. It is in a way a departure from classical liberal democratic theory which was centred on the individual in that it seeks to elevate larger social units to the same or even higher status within its theory. The argument of the pluralists is that classical liberal theory was incomplete in that it concentrated on the individual. Over and above the individual, the pluralists say, individuals coalesce into groups in pursuit of their common interests, and since these groups are the social units that give sustenance to the individual and often provide the immediate sub-soil for his existence, they should be given recognition, on a par with or above the individual.

The federal structure of the United States has often been quoted as an example of the genius of pluralism at work. American political scientists claim that the federal structure 'promotes both effectiveness and liberty in which separate politics are united within an overarching framework in such a way … that all maintain their fundamental integrity.' If the separate states are regarded as representative of local interest, the US can be seen as a pluralist model. Historically, the federal structure was devised to accommodate and reconcile the peculiar features of the fourteen colonies that revolted against British domination, some being slave-owning, and others not. Federalism sought to place each of the states, irrespective of their size or economic importance, on an equal footing. Theoretically, each state has the right to secede from the Union. In practice, however, where there is a conflict between state and federal law, the federal law is supreme. Despite this, each state enjoys a large degree of autonomy over a number of areas. The most conservative and reactionary elements of US society have traditionally been the fiercest advocates of state rights vis a vis the federal authorities, as a means of preserving backward and reactionary institutions. Thus, for example, during the 1950s the states of the Deep South invoked the doctrine of state's rights to preserve overt racism in their legislature, judiciary, administration and all areas of public life. In the 1970s and '80s the same arguments have been employed to uphold fundamentalist Christian teachings in opposition to Darwinian theory, to suppress the rights of women, etc. Because all states are equal, no one state had the right to impose its views on another. The pockets of backwardness thus always have refuge from whence they can wage their struggle to hold back the march of history. Federalism can thus be employed to exercise a vote on necessary reforms and progressive measures.

The proponents of pluralism contend that their models recognise the inevitability of conflicting claims on the body politic by the various clusters of power and communities that make up society. If all power were vested in the central authority, this would tend to emasculate the weaker units and collectivities who cannot muster power at the centre; on the other hand, a large degree of autonomy at local levels will enable these weaker units to make their voices heard. This line of argument is taken a stage further by one particular school, that of 'consociationism', who claim that other models result in minorities being swamped by majorities and it is therefore necessary to counter-balance the numerical preponderance of the majority with the entrenched rights of minorities.

Both federalism and consociationism have begun to assume importance in South African politics. The ruling National Party claims to be experimenting with a consociational model with its 'tri-racial' parliament, Buthelezi's Inkatha has adopted it through sponsorships of the Buthelezi Commission, and the opposition PFP advocates federalism in preference to the unitary state. We now proceed to examine both federalism and consociationism as propounded by its chief advocates. We shall not be addressing ourselves to the 'tri-racial' parliament except in drawing comparisons with other models. We shall address the plan being proffered outside the regime by ostensibly oppositional elements.

The Progressive Federal Party (PFP)

Early in 1975, the 'young Turks' in the United Party broke with it and constituted themselves as the Reform Party in February 1975. The split precipitated the collapse of the UP, which disintegrated into a number of smaller parties. Pressure from big business, especially Oppenheimer's Anglo-American Corporation (AAC) resulted in formation of a ginger group, led by Kowie Marais, to unite the opposition parties. In July

1975 the Reform Party merged with the Progressive Party to form the Progressive Reform Party. In September 1977 the members of the United Party Rump, gathered around Kowie Marais, joined the PRP to become the Progressive Federal Party (PFP).

The transition from Progressive Party to Progressive Federal Party marked more than just a gathering-in of the parliamentary opposition to the Nats. It entailed both a shift in the long-standing policies of the White parliamentary opposition and a change in the political chemistry of White politics.

From 1973–77 Gordon H. Waddel, Oppenheimer's former son-in-law, had been treasurer of the Progressive Party. He is largely credited with placing the party on a firm financial footing. We may note also during these years a continuous interchange of personnel between the directorate of AAC and the top layers of the Progressive Party. These include Waddel himself; Dr. Zac de Beer; Alex Borraine; Douglas Hoffe, Bobby Godsell and others. The party had been linked to Oppenheimer since its inception in 1959, during the 1970s it became the party of English speaking monopoly capitalism – with its base in AAC, but increasingly also in other large corporations. Thus, for example, Waddel could claim by 1977 that 40% of the party's funds came from 'major donors' (read: big business). The changing fortunes of the party are reflected also in the tensions that overtook the UP and the defections from it to the Progs.

The explanation of the tensions in the UP can be found in the events of the preceding years. After a decade of almost total quiescence, in 1973 the system of repressive labour control began to break down. In that year, 70 000 African workers went on strike; the next year, 1974, 38 961 workers went on strike; in 1975 the figure was 12 451; 1976 saw the Soweto Uprisings. Monopoly capital, by now emerging as the dominant force in the South African economy faced a dilemma. At a time when it stood poised to make a number of structural changes, go in for a period of massive retooling and extend its tentacles into its 'natural' African market, it was faced with a serious challenge at home and the collapse of the unholy alliance of racist states in Southern Africa. Until then, most elements in the capitalist political parties had been content to support the ruling Nats, though making the occasional critical noises. Their attitude then was grounded in material advantages and it was to change when these seemed to come under threat. The policies pursued by the Nats had provided the optimum conditions for the growth of the monopolies. Massive political repression had virtually destroyed the Black trade unions and liberation movement. Economic policy had favoured the large aggregates of capital over the small businessman, domestic tranquillity created an investment haven for the foreign investor. The mid-seventies marked dramatic change in all that and it became obvious to the more far-sighted amongst the monopolists that things could never return to the conditions of the mid-sixties. New policies were needed and the English-speaking fraction of monopoly capital sought these in the Progs.

The defections from the rump of the UP represented real shifts of alignment within the capitalist class. At the same time the Progs were called upon to pay a price for the adherence of these new recruits. This came in the shape of the Slabbert Commission, to draw up new constitutional proposals for the PFP's platform. The Commission commenced work in 1977 and its report was adopted in November 1978. This was the first attempt to reformulate the PFP's policy since the Molteno Commission of the 1960s. the Slabbert Report departed from the premises of the Molteno Report in a number of crucial areas and spoke unambiguously of the protection of capitalist interests unadorned by phrases such as 'western civilization' that appear in the earlier version. It explicitly dropped the notion of the unitary state and adopted federalism.

The changes in the PFP's political programme coincide with other developments. Since its inception as the Progressive Party, the PFP had sought to mediate between the White establishment and the Black community. During the early 1960s a number of Coloured political figures had affiliated to it. They included Rev. Alan Hendrickse, David Curry and Sonny Leon, all of whom became prominent leaders of the Labour Party after the Prohibition of Political Interference Act was passed. During the 1970s, the Progs under Colin Eglin had made it a practice to consult with Bantustan leaders and invite those to their party congresses. Their most avid interlocutor amongst the Bantustan leaders proved to be Gatsha Buthelezi. In August 1978 Eglin, Swart, Buthelezi and Dr. Bhengu met and issued a joint statement to the effect that enough common ground existed between Inkatha and the PFP to provide the basis for negotiating a new constitutional framework for South Africa. The two parties to the statement agreed to continue their dialogue through a formalised liaison committee comprising members drawn from each organisation. These developments mark the drawing closer of the Inkatha leadership and the PFP, not only in matters of tactical negotiations, but also in prescriptions to resolve the problems confronting South Africa.

THE BUTHELEZI COMMISSION

Federalism was first mooted as a possible means of resolving the problems of South African by Gatsha in 1974 on the occasion of an address to the South African Institute of Race Relations. Amongst other ideas floated by Gatsha on this occasion was that:

'Change should revolve on allowing each and every group to maintain its identity through new constitutional and political arrangements.'

He goes further along this line of reasoning to posit that there might emerge:

'Three types of states ... in a federal republic or common wealth:
- States in which the interests of an African ethnic group are paramount;
- States in which the interests of White people are paramount;
- Special or federal areas which are multi-ethnic in character in which no particular group interests are designated.'

(All quotations taken for Hoernle Memorial Lecture, January 1974, Delivered at the University of Cape Town by Mangosuthu G. Buthelezi.)

The ideas in this address were allowed to lie fallow for the next four to five years only to be taken up with greater vigour in the late 1970s. One of the factors motivating Gatsha to revive his federalist notions was the publication of the Lombard Report, prepared by Dr. J.A. Lombard under the auspices of the Natal Sugar Association. Lombard had been commissioned by the sugar growers to look into 'Alternatives to the Consolidation of Kwazulu (Natal)' by an anxious body of plantation owners, some of whom feared they may lose their lands to the Bantustan. Lombard published his report in 1980. That same year, in October

1980, Gatsha commissioned his own report by setting up the Buthelezi Commission to investigate a regional constitutional dispensation for the Natal region, including KwaZulu. He invited representatives of big business (AAC, SA Federated Chamber of Industry, the Institute of Bankers, SA Canegrowers Association, etc.), professional bodies, Bantustan institutions (the KwaZulu Development Corporation and Inkatha were both prominent), internationally known academics with experience of South Africa and especially Natal (these included Heribert Adam, Lawrence Schlemmer, Arendt Lijphart, Herman Giliomee) and political parties (the PFP, the New Rupublic Party both participated, the National Party turned down the invitation). He also invited the ANC.

The academics were the central figures in the conduct of both the spadework for the commission and in giving it its theoretical underpinnings. Lawrence Schlemmer of the University of Natal carried out and supervised the greater part of the empirical research, Heribert Adam and Arendt Lijphart provided the political theory. Adam taught in Natal for a number of years before migrating to Canada. He has authored a number of influential books on South Africa, including 'South Africa: Sociological Perspectives' (1970), 'Modernizing Racial Domination' (1973), 'Ethnic Power Mobilized' (with Herman; Giliomee, 1979). Arendt Lijphart is a professor of Political Science at the University of California (San Diego) and was formerly at Leiden in the Netherlands. He is amongst the chief theorisers of 'consociationism', a topic on which he delivered a paper at a conference sponsored by the South African Institute of International Affairs, held at Rustenburg during 1978.

The thrust of Adam and Lijphart's argument may be summarised as:

- The exclusion of the Black majority from the body politic deprives the South African regime of legitimacy and it is the source of instability which could raise the price of continued racial domination to unacceptable levels;
- However, because of the level of White control over the economy, technology, the political apparatus and means of violence, revolutionary overthrow of the regime is an unrealistic project;
- A stalemate is the best the liberation movement can achieve, if it

won't accept that, the level of White resistance will be such that all it will inherit would be a pile of ashes;

- The second-best option is therefore the only rational choice, this amounts to power-sharing in a mutually negotiated consociational arrangement.

We pass over the silence the assumptions underlying this argument for the time being but shall return to them later. Both authors have not shifted their ground since and Adam has repeated his argument in a number of different ways over the past five years.

Consociationism is one of a number of pluralist models which is currently being touted as a solution or constitutional model for South Africa. As defined by Lijphart: 'the opposite of consociational democracy is majoritarian democracy.' ... 'Federalism can be viewed as a consociational device, and consociation can be interpreted as a special form of federalism.'

Lijphart goes on to define consociation in terms of four principles:
- government by a grand coalition of the political leaders of all significant segments of a plural society;
- mutual or minority vote: designed to protect the vital interests of minorities;
- proportionality as the principle for political representation, civil service appointments; allocation of public funds;
- a high degree of autonomy for each segment in the running of its own affairs: according to Lijphart, '(I)t complements the grand coalition principle – on all issues of common interest, the decisions are made jointly by the segments' leaders, but on all other issues decision-making is left to each segment.'

The similarities between the above and the terms of reference of the Botha Tri-racial constitution are striking.

As if to demonstrate the veracity of Lijphart's contention that federalism is a form of consociation, in 1979, Van Zyl Slabbert and David Welsh put forward a federalist plan for South Africa based on the Slabbert Commission Report. The key recommendations of their proposals were:

A federal government with non-racial representation of all politically salient groups in a federal executive; universal suffrage on the basis of proportional representations;

A minority vote;

A bill of rights to guarantee the rights of individuals; the desegregation of all civil service, police and military appointments to be replaced by a system of proportional distribution of key posts.

The Slabbert/Welsh proposals differed from those of Botha's new constitution only in that they included Africans, but the underlying principles are in many respects the same. These proposals form the core of the PFP's thinking on constitutional matters. What is of interest to underline here is that the PFP embraced the principle of universal suffrage when it dropped its earlier insistence on a qualified franchise (in reality, the old Cape 'Liberal' franchise).

Heribert Adams, the other theorist of the Buthelezi Commission, has argued that the 'second best' option will present itself at a time when the Whites are seeking compromise. The sine qua non, for such a situation, he argues, is the break-up of the Afrikaaner [sic] bloc. Only when the solidarity of the 'volk' has been fissured, and each of its strata is looking out for its own best interest will it be realistic to expect them to seek a compromise. He thus views Black political struggle as effective only if it assists the process of disintegration of Afrikaaner [sic] unity. To his reckoning, the recommendations of the Buthelezi Commission, which he assisted in framing, will become relevant at that moment. What then are these recommendations?

The Commission confined itself to the Natal region, which was its original brief, but its recommendations must be read as relating to the country as a whole. It based its findings on empirical research, much of it opinion polls and attitudinal surveys, which the authors claim give an accurate reflection of the political opinions of a representative sample of South Africans. Its recommendations in the political sphere were:

- a geographically based federal system which would avail the whites of the opportunity to defend their 'minority rights' and it it [sic] specifically designated a consociational model as having this merit.

- a regional structure of KwaZulu-Natal government under a consociational agreement which would comprise of:
  - An Executive – made up of equal numbers of Africans and Whites plus Coloured and Indians;
  - A Legislature – elected from all groups on the basis of universal suffrage, with proportional representation, subject to a guaranteed minimum representation for each group;
  - A Bill of Rights to safeguard individual rights;
  - A minority vote – to protect the rights of minorities;
  - The Removal of all racial controls of labour, the acquisition of land and other immovable property, entry into commerce or industry.

The commission justified its recommendations in terms of what its opinion polls and attitudinal surveys revealed. The principal ones it claimed were:

That 90% of the Whites rejected universal suffrage and the comparable figure amongst Indians and Coloureds was 60%;

A majority of Whites favoured the extension of the franchise of Coloured and Indians;

White fears of African majority rule were a constraint on reform which most Whites otherwise favoured.

Adam put forward a number of proposals which he said would be necessary to ensure the implementation of the Commission's recommendations.

These were:
- Freedom of political association across colour lines (i.e. abolition of the Prohibition of Political Interferences Act);
- An Amnesty for all political prisoners and exiles on the condition that they denounce violence and extra-constitutional methods;
- Proportional revenue-sharing and affirmative action programmes to offset the disparities between groups.

COMMENT AND CRITIQUE

We have thus far refrained from commenting on the actual content of the proposals made and proffered by the PFP and the Buthelezi

Commission. In this section we shall dissect these and point up their counter-revolutionary essence. We shall also be making some suggestions about how our movement should respond.

As said at the beginning of this paper, the constitutional model-building must be seen in the context of general crisis of the racist regime and the system of White domination in South Africa occasioned by the ANC-led liberation struggle. As such all the exercise of this nature has a single objective. Because the models being proffered come from different quarters, representing specific interests within the ruling monopoly capitalist class, they lay emphasis on different aspects and approach the solutions from differing perspectives. There is nonetheless a unifying theme that links them all – the preservation of White privilege and the dilution of the revolutionary programme of the people. All the schemes that have been placed before our country from a reformist perspective thus form parts of a single continuum which unites Gatsha on its 'left' with Botha on its right.

We noted parenthetically in relation to the PFP that it dropped the qualified franchise in 1978. By taking up the federal model it could achieve the same objective, which is to weight the political process in favour of the White minority. Thus though the appearance is that the PFP has taken a step forward, the reality is that it is marking time. This is the pattern right through the spectrum, except for the obvious ones like Botha's which excludes Africans.

Coming specifically to the Buthelezi Commission, it must be seen in the context of the association between Gatsha, the Inkatha leadership and the forces within the monopoly capitalist class represented by the PFP. It is no coincidence that it comes after the Lombard Report. Through both these, fractions of monopoly capital who wished to broaden the constitutional debate initiated by Botha with his 'new dispensation' hoped to make their own input. What both Botha's 'new dispensation' and these others have in common is the attempt to recruit elements of the Black elite to an essentially counter-revolutionary enterprise. In this respect the 'new dispensation', the Slabbert-Welsh proposals, the Buthelezi Commission and similar schemes, represent a vital area of ideological convergence amongst disparate elements, linked to the monopoly capitalist class – either directly through economic interest, or intellectually by a commitment to the same objectives. The role that Gatsha and the Inkatha leadership have assumed in recent years is thus the practical political expression of a deeply rotted counter-revolutionary perspective and not merely the acting out of Gatsha's individual megalomania.

To be viable, the solutions proffered by the Buthelezi Commission would require a political vacuum in which the ANC is not an effective counter-pole to Inkatha – either having been weakened by repression or gone into decline as a result of its errors. Because as long as the possibility of defeating the regime is held out as a realistic objective to the Blacks, the temptation to seek a mealy-mouthed compromise is that much reduced. If we take the recommendations of the Buthelezi Commission as the goals towards which Gatsha is striving, our respective courses must inevitably collide. Gatsha has recently repeatedly assumed a posture of hostility towards the ANC and harps on the theme of reassuring the Whites of their future. This is the meaning of the minority veto. Neither is he ashamed of stating quite unequivocally that as far as he is concerned change is a hostage to White racist prejudices – this is the meaning of the finding that White fears of majority rule inhibit their support for reform. At the end of the day, what Gatsha proposes (if the recommendations reflect his political options) is a deal at the top, between an African leadership and the White monopolists, at the expense of the Black masses. Every constitutional model that abandons the unitary state, in preference for federal or consociational models has this as its principal objective.

Where then does this place our movement and its programme? What has become obvious is that we can no longer afford to mince words about the real meaning of the first clause of the Freedom Charter. Up to now we have couched our references to it in terms of universal suffrage – i.e. one person one vote. This is no longer sufficient since, as we can see, some elements in the enemy camp also accept this and we must differentiate ourselves from them. Universal suffrage must be linked to the demand for a unitary state. We would also submit that it is transparent political-double-talk to try to evade the implication that this will mean a state and a government dominated by the African people. At any rate, whether we admit it or not, the enemy and his allies understand it full well, so it only serves to confuse our own ranks. There cannot be anything wrong with such an arrangement (an African dominated state and government) in a country where the African people constitute 73% of the total population. Any suggestions that there should be parity between this 73% and the minorities (15%; 8.9%; 2.8% respectively) amounts to racial discrimination at the expense of Africans. This must be unequivocally stated and understood within our movement. At the same time, we must stress that the first clause is inextricably linked to the second clause which outlaws racial discrimination and guarantees the rights of minorities, not through inequitable and racist veto rights, but through the observance of democratic values.

Proposals for an Effective Counter

The ruling class and the regime have not been complacent about the crisis facing the system. They have already set in motion a number of political feelers whose ultimate purpose is as yet unclear. That such exercises coincided with the first major breach of the solidarity of the Frontline States is no accident when read in conjunction with Huntingdon's thesis (above).

One can never rule out the possibility that all these are part of an elaborate and well-planned psychological warfare stratagem, designed to identify possible weak points in our organisational solidarity. Yet the frequency with which they have descended upon us in the past eighteen months betrays the anxieties within the ruling class camp to find a solution. The veritable orchestrated campaign of editorials in the South African press since March 1984, soundings from the PFP, newspaper editors, the Harvey van der Merwe and the approaches by the monopoly capitalists themselves, all are indicative of actual shifts and the degree of uncertainty within the ruling class on how it should respond to the current situation.

The evident dead end of the Tri-racial parliament and the mass upsurge that has forced Botha to declare martial law have done nothing to allay the worst fears of those ruling class elements who are most apprehensive about the future. The response from the imperialist countries has done nothing to comfort the regime either.

The attempts to build constitutional models and toy with various schemes of elite accommodation are all designed to paint the liberation movement into a corner, salvage the essentials of the system of White domination and blunt the thrust of the revolution. The middle ground is here the area of contestation, with the ruling class (assisted by its satraps like Gatsha) trying to coopt the elements from amongst the oppressed as its allies. We must place ourselves in a position to pre-empt this strategy.

The offers that the ruling class has put on the table amount to a number of soft options for the Black elite. They are at the same time trying to paint us in colours that will appear threatening and dangerous to this self-same elite. We must at all costs work towards detaching this elite from the ruling class, not merely rendering it neutral but committing it to our objectives. We would suggest that the best means of doing this at this juncture would be the adoption of a Bill of Rights. The name we give it will not be that important but the constitutional rights and liberties it will embody could make a tremendous impact on the political scene at home and abroad. We do not suggest that such a Bill of Rights replace the Freedom Charter, quite the contrary. It should in fact be an extensive and comprehensive exposition of the rights and liberties South Africans would enjoy under an ANC government. Such a document could take many forms. We could model it on similar documents from other countries – the Declaration of the Rights of Man and Citizen comes to mind. Or we may come up with a totally new conception. Whatever form it takes it will explicitly declare apartheid, racism, fascism and Nazism illegal and punishable offences.

We shall also have to explicitly pronounce ourselves on the question of political pluralism (i.e. a multiplicity of political parties and political space for the loyal opposition). There is a sad misconception which has taken root amongst us, that radical social transformation is only possible under one party rule. This notion must be dispelled and laid to rest once and for all. It is neither intrinsic to revolutionary change that one party dominate the political process nor is it in fact the case in most socialist countries. In the countries where this is the case, particular historical circumstances created that situation and not the imperatives of revolution. Subject to the provisions of the maintenance of the crime of apartheid, there is no reason, in principle, why we should oppose a multi-party system. We would submit that as long as the ANC and its allies are capable of demonstrating through political argument, debate and open contestation that we have both the correct policies and the practical ability to address the burning social and political problems facing the people, we have nothing to fear from such a system.

The immediate political advantages of adopting such a Bill of Rights will be that it puts the ball in the courts of our opponents amongst the ruling class – on its right, centre and left. The Inkatha leadership and other pro-ruling class forces who oppose us will also be compelled to define their position in relation to it. If we adopt and publicise the document at the appropriate moment, it will become the focal point of political discourse inside the country. No one, even our worst enemies will be able to ignore it, and as such it will be an intervention that puts all other options in the shade. The question of timing will be all important (provided the idea is acceptable) so as to project the ANC even more firmly as the only viable alternative to continued racist domination. Such a document would have the effect of pre-empting the middle ground and can effectively counter the plans of the ruling class to recruit allies and helpers from amongst us.

FIVE

*Jordan describes himself as an 'unequivocally partisan' speaker among a panel of scholars – yet it is striking how well-researched and rigorous a paper he delivered, to the African Studies Association (USA) in Denver, Colorado, in October 1987. This paper was written in exile, and before the Internet existed to shrink distance; but its arguments are buttressed by telling details and quotations from a range of sources. He revisits the concept of counter-insurgency (see **Document 2**), arguing that the project still lay at the heart of P.W. Botha's strategies. But by contrast with 1983, the state was weaker: it had neither 'the capacity nor the political will to address the crisis it faces'. Forces opposing the state were remarkably resilient: a core group of organisations (including COSATU, the UDF affiliates, youth and student organisations) were all broadly 'Charterist' – an indication of the ANC's growing prestige and authority. In hindsight, Jordan's paper accurately depicted the balance of forces in 1987. The state could retain control through military power; but it had lost legitimacy and the room to manoeuvre. Time was on the side of the opposition.*

The Politics of the Current Conjuncture

Writing in 1983 I characterised the policies of the Botha regime as an 'Eleventh Hour counter-insurgency strategy'.[1] Some four years later is it improper to inquire whether this characterisation still holds true?

It can indeed be very cogently argued that during this period South Africa has experienced a major political upheaval whose internal and international impact has had a profound effect on the perceptions of all the actors. In such a situation can one continue to use terms we employed in 1983?

Yet I am still persuaded about the validity of my 1983 assessment. In this paper I shall attempt firstly to demonstrate that the counter-insurgency project still lies at the heart of Botha's policies. Secondly, that though the racist state has, through mass repression and the military occupation of the African townships, survived the wave of mass struggles of the recent past, it neither has the capacity nor the political will to address the crisis it faces. I shall, thirdly, be arguing that the initiative has decisively shifted from the racist state to the democratic oppositional forces ranged against it. Lastly, that among this wide array of political and social forces, in recent years, a core has crystalised, coalesced around the Freedom Charter as their common programmatic statement.

I am in the unfortunate position of being unequivocally partisan among a panel of scholars. While I make no apology for the views I hold I must, however, hasten to add that they should not be read as representative of the thinking of the ANC. I assume sole responsibility for the views expressed in this paper.

The dimensions of the dilemma confronting the apartheid state were perhaps most ably expressed in a report from the Human Sciences Research Council (HSRC), a government-related think tank based in Pretoria, during July 1985:

'Few social systems have a greater conflict potential than a group-differentiated configuration in which political dominance of a particular ethnic or cultural segment over a subordinate segment forms a dividing line that runs parallel with a socio-economic divide stratifying the two segments into a higher and lower class position respectively. And this is precisely what the matrix of intergroup relations in South Africa amounts to: Whites normally have a higher status along with more rights and privileges than other groups, particularly the Africans who are neglected to the lowest position in the hierarchy. The divisions between ethnic groups and classes converge in large measure.'

The HSRC concludes its report with recommendations based on a study of similar social configurations:

'Empirical evidence indicates that peaceful intergroup accommodation in deeply segmented societies is promoted to the extent that socio-economic strata cut across basic group cleavages such as culture, ethnicity, religion, language and race. Because this type of cross-cutting alliance promotes the development of common loyalties, multiple group attachments and common interests, it reduces the likelihood of certain cleavages becoming so politicised and mobilised that confrontation ensues between the groups concerned over wide front.'[2]

It might strike one as ironic that after almost forty years of National Party political dominance, the Botha regime has to be told that the institutional framework they have created is responsible for generating conflict. But, having arrived at this realisation the apartheid state has, since Botha took over leadership, sought to devise a strategy that would so restructure domination as to incorporate conservatives from the other racial groups in cross-cutting alliances strong enough to fend off those who seek fundamental change.

However, the very project of revising the terms of White domination has led to unanticipated consequences. The rigidities and certainties of old-style apartheid are not amenable to revision. The change from White exclusivity to the rhetoric of multi-ethnic consensus could not but result in a decline in ideological cohesion. The effort has yielded mixed results, none of which afford rightist backlash located amongst the lower middle classes, the lower reaches of the civil service and blue collar White workers. On the other hand it has brought into being institutions of doubtful legitimacy, manned by politicians who hold no mandate from their respective communities and are therefore keen to demonstrate their sincerity by continuously testing the limits of these institutions. The options he has chosen compel Botha to try to ride two horses, which threaten to fly off in divergent directions, repression and reform. A review of the politics of the ruling White bloc is the first section of this paper.

The Politics of the Counter-Revolution

Perhaps the most revealing event in White politics in recent months was the Whites only 'general elections' the regime chose to call two years ahead of schedule. Botha's reasoning for doing this was never a secret. It was openly stated that the National Party sought a mandate to continue along the path it had chosen and that Botha wanted to demonstrate the actual weakness of his parliamentary opponents. But the 'elections' permit us to examine the less visible dimensions of the ruling class a little more closely.

Since August 1984 the ruling circles of Pretoria looked on while their 'Total Strategy' was taken apart piece by piece until they were forced to face the reality that it had failed to stabilise the apartheid system. The internal aspect of 'total strategy' had been conceived as a mix of reformist and repressive measures designed to recruit supporters for the regime amongst Black petit bourgeoisie (by creating new opportunities in the economic sphere) while holding down radical opponents by raising the costs of consistent opposition. The revolt that erupted in the PWV region in August 1984 targeted precisely the co-optive structures the state sought to set in place and within a space of a year had either totally dismembered them or rendered them inoperative. The high visibility these struggles received through television coverage had the effect of mobilising international opinion against the regime at precisely a moment when it was anxious to demonstrate its reasonableness and reformist credentials. Faced with an unprecedented battle on two fronts, the Apartheid State perforce had to prevaricate. As the unrest spread geographically during 1985 it appeared that Pretoria was indeed persuaded to grasp the nettle of serious negotiations. The shallow hamming of 'Rubicon I 'was followed by Roelof 'Pik' Botha's grudging acceptance of the Commonwealth Eminent Persons Group (EPG) mission to South Africa.[3]

Acceptance of negotiations or their possibility in principle however had wider implications, which no one among the ruling clique was as yet ready to contemplate. The first of these was de facto recognition of the state's principle antagonists as legitimate interlocutors about the future of the country. Such recognition carried a derivative implication that the state was writing off its clients in the Tri-Cameral parliament and the bantustans.

Secondly, acceptance of the principle of negotiations implied also that at some point in the future the apartheid state would surrender power. Thus when finally forced to the brink, Pretoria had no other option than to scuttle the entire Commonwealth Mission in the dawn raids of May 19th 1986. May 19th signaled the regime's determination to hold onto power regardless of the external repercussions and the need to unleash terror against its internal opponents. It sounded the death knell of the reformist aspect of 'total strategy', effectively the abandonment of the strategy as a failure.

The terms of the 1983 constitution required Botha to call an election in 1989. He chose instead to settle accounts with his parliamentary opposition in 1987, while he was still visibly in command. At the same time he ignored those provisions of the constitution requiring simultaneous elections for the Coloured and Indian houses for fear of unleashing yet a second wave of boycotts similar to 1984.[4] Elections amongst the Whites alone would, he hoped, have the added bonus of shifting attention away from the democratic agitation on the streets to the White parliament as a site where the future of the country could be determined. He was assisted in this enterprise by the White Independents – Lategan, Malan and Worral – who for a time held the attention of international media as a possible middle road between the two principal antagonists.

In what must surely count as one of the greatest historic ironies, precisely in order to achieve his objective Botha was compelled to make the ANC and the democratic opposition the central issue of the elections. Illegalised for twenty-seven years and silenced by Botha's own proscriptive press regulations, the ANC featured in every rally and broadcast. Botha's intention was to play on the fears of the White electorate, but he could only do this by drawing their attention to political forces he sought to emasculate.[5]

The National Party campaigned on an explicitly counter-revolutionary platform, as did the far right parties. The liberal opposition and the Independents vainly tried to convince electors that theirs was a more viable strategy to defeat revolution but had nothing to upstage Botha's demonstrative 'kragdadigheid' in Botswana and Zambia. Despite rumblings about a boycott there was a high turnout in every province.

Though there are differing assessments of the results of the Whites only 'general election', all commentators agree that the National Party under Botha had pulled off a first - it had in fact transformed itself into a White national party, as against the Boer tribal party it had been since 1913. According to Willie Breytenbach of Stellenbosch University:

'No other White political party has achieved such a wide basis of cross-cutting support since 1910. In the past, election results showed clear language, ethnic and class patterns of support.'[6]

There was also a very evident rightward shift in White politics attested to by the losses sustained by the PFP in a number of urban constituencies and the decimation of the NRP in its former stronghold, Natal.[7]

Botha did indeed receive the mandate he had sought. The National

Party emerged with an overwhelming preponderance of seats. It owed at least a third of these to the electoral system, which favoured the incumbent party. Lest this recognition tempt one to hasty conclusions, it would be wise to remember that system of proportional representation would have favoured the far right opposition at the expense of the liberal opposition.[8]

The White electorate clearly voted for the continuation of the status quo created by the second state of emergency of June 1986. The reverses suffered by the parties that had been associated with the KwaNatal Indaba indicated that they were unwilling to accept even such peripheral tinkerings with the structures of racial domination.

The only persons who seemed to have expected such an outcome were the election strategists of the National Party itself. The dismay that greeted the narrow victory of Heunis over Worral testifies to the hopes many had invested in the 'new Nats'.

The 1987 elections recapitulated, with a few modifications, the alignments that had appeared during the 1983 referendum.[9]

THE PERMANENT STATE OF EMERGENCY

PW Botha acceded to the leadership of the National Party in the wake of the Information Department Slush Fund scandal (Muldergate). The manner in which the scandal was handled was indicative of irreconcilable conflicts at the highest echelons of Afrikaanerdom. Botha had the support of the top military commanders and was regarded as the candidate of Afrikaaner monopoly capital. He initiated an outreach campaign to non-Afrikaaner capital and won a measure of success through a series of government-big business conferences.

The confidence big business placed in Botha derived from a hard-nosed appreciation of its self-interest. Louis Luyt, Afrikaaner millionaire and erstwhile bag-man for the apartheid propaganda machine captured the spirit in which big business acted in 1985:

'Whether business likes it or not, it has benefitted from apartheid. It is only now that apartheid has turned against them that they are seeking its removal. For years big business did not want the situation changed.'[10]

If change had indeed become necessary, big business was determined to ensure that it occurred at a pace and in a fashion that did not unduly unsettle its equilibrium. Botha's approach of cautious restructuring while maintaining White security promised to achieve this.

The evident inability of the state to contain the upheavals of late 1984, 1985 and 1986 introduced an unaccustomed note of skepticism into the pronouncements of White capital at home and abroad. The first sign of unease was the Luangwa Valley safari undertaken by Gavin Relly and his colleagues in 1985. These second thoughts accumulated in the adoption of the Business Charter by the Federated Chamber of Industries, Assocom and the Afrikaans Handelsinstituut at the end of 1986. Business had repeatedly spoken in accents critical of the slow pace of reform but appeared unwilling to mark out a position separate from the state. After November 1986, sections of big business have sought to define an autonomous role, midway between the state and its opponents in the democratic opposition. Both the Independents and Van Zyl Slabbert's Institute for South Africa (IDASA) have benefitted from these anxieties. David Willers, London Director of the South African Foundation, who can be regarded as a representative voice of South African business circles recently explained that:

> '... if business is going to lay claim to any serious 'bridge-building role' it is obviously desirable that it retains its independent links with all the key actors, from the ANC to the National Party. The critical problem facing companies right now, whether foreign or local, is how to retain an independent stance and avoid becoming 'hijacked' both by the ANC/ UDF which seeks to co-opt business as an 'an objective ally', and the government which wishes to harness business talents in the total strategy effort.'[11]

Such considerations were proffered by ASSOCOM in explaining why it had changed its mind about demanding the release of political prisoners.

The leading business corporations and groups have at the same time demonstrated their preferences by enthusiastic support and participation in the KwaNatal Indaba. The Indaba, inspired by the recommendations of the Buthelezi Commission, proposes as a future constitutional

framework:
- the devolution of power to regional and municipal levels;
- a consociational process of negotiation among ethnic segments with the minorities enjoying a blocking veto;
- entrenchment of the rights of ethnic, cultural and linguistic groups;
- constitutional protection of the rights of property.

Gavin Relly, chairman of Anglo-American (AAC) and Jan van der Horst, chairman of the Old Mutual, have both given their personal endorsement to the Indaba.[12]

Big business's preference for a dispensation based on the Indaba is not difficult to explain. Having accepted that Black political empowerment is inevitable, White capital seeks to deflect the economic aspirations of the underprivileged through such devices as decentralization and to evade the economic consequences of such empowerment by entrenching property rights. In spite of its efforts to define an independent stance, big business has had to associate itself with the so-called 'moderate' centre as a possible third force.

Yet the most salient feature of the dilemma facing big business is its inability to create a convincing social support base for its programme. Apart from a handful of academics, the majority of Whites have demonstrated their preference for the security afforded by the apartheid state's Caspirs and Buffels. According to Willers,

> 'Raymond Ackerman, a top retailer, maintains that 98 percent of South Africa's chairmen support dismantling apartheid in its entirety - in other words, would support majority rule ...'[13]

But there is no agency capable of translating this potential support into reality outside the democratic opposition. When confronted with that choice the majority of businessmen prefer the devil of apartheid they know so well to the uncertainties of a democratic government.

The willingness of a significant section of White capital to collaborate with the racist state finds expression through the National Security Management System (NSMS). The system is headed by the State Security

Council, which is staffed by the chiefs of the security services plus the ministers of Defence and Foreign Affairs. The State Security Council has already set in place a sinister network of structures, parallel with the conventional civil administration, known as the Joint Management Committees, involving local politicians, business, the security services and Black collaborators. At present some five hundred of these are functioning. These are the most visible, yet ironically invisible, manifestations of the militarisation of the South African polity. The regime can no longer govern except by means of a more or less permanent State of Emergency.[14]

The restructuring of the institutions of racial domination has not resolved the crisis of apartheid. It becomes increasingly clear that the state has lost the initiative and been forced into a reactive posture – unable to determine the course of events. The National Statutory Council, originally conceived as the fourth chamber of the Tri-Cameral system, has been redefined at least twice even before it has been enacted as legislation. The executive state, in which the principle of accountability, either to the White parliament or the White electorate, has been eradicated appears to be the only option. The extent to which Botha will be able to carry out his slow strategic reforms while maintaining White power through repression depends on the politics of the revolution. It is to this that we shall now turn.

THE POLITICS OF THE REVOLUTION

In this section we shall be examining a wide spectrum of political and social forces who have in word, in deed identified themselves as advocates of a fundamental re-ordering of South African society.

The revival of organised mass opposition to the Apartheid State is the central feature of the recent period. Television and the press gave this a high international visibility, especially during 1985 and 1986 when huge funeral manifestations became almost a weekly feature of township life.[15] But equally important were the less visible debates and political struggles that engaged the democratic oppositional forces before, during and after this period of mass confrontations as they sought to define their strategy and political objectives. In this section I shall attempt to give an overview of both these aspects of the mass struggles of the recent period.

The PWV revolt of 1984 occurred in the context of the tri-cameral elections and the aftermath of the Nkomati Agreement. Both these had been held up as important achievements of the 'Total Strategy'. The one would draw significant allies to the regime's reform project, the other would create the space for reform to run its course by sidelining the ANC and everyone else who sought to change by revolutionary means.

The revolt broke out in Sebokeng, spread to the Witwatersrand, then to South Africa's industrial heartland, the Vaal triangle. It reached its first high point in November 1984 when a two-day strike on the 5th and 6th, involving 800 000 workers and 400 000 students, brought industry to a standstill. After an initial downturn during Christmas the revolt spread further afield, first to the Eastern Cape, then in quick succession overtook all the major urban areas outside Natal, so that by the end of 1985 unrest was endemic. During the first six months of 1986 the pace quickened. In addition to a number of industrial actions, three very successful stay-at-home strikes were waged. It was only after the military occupation of the African townships that the pace slackened and the situation became relatively stablised.

The effectiveness of the revolt and its rapid spread was assisted by the existence of a network of community, student and trade union bodies that had come into being during the preceding four years. The community organisations had been created to combat two components of the state's plans. In the Africa townships there were plans to impose the Black Local Authorities (BLAs) as one of the 'Koornhof Bills'; in the Coloured areas the Tri-cameral parliamentary elections were the issue. In addition, Black South Africa was experiencing severe economic difficulties, a number of which were directly attributable to the action of 'dummy' institutions.

During 1984, the PWV region, the epicentre of the revolt, was one of the hardest hit areas and its Black inhabitants were being burdened with additional costs for transport, fuel, water and rent. It was specifically the imposition of higher rents that precipitated the revolt. The region it next spread to, the Eastern Cape, was suffering an economic slump as a result of job losses and its townships were swollen by urban migration from the impoverished rural slums of the Ciskei.[16]

By giving voice to the anger of the township residents the community organisations grew and acquired credibility. During 1983 to 1984, a number of them affiliated to the United Democratic Front (UDF) which facilitated linkages between the local struggles and the wider national struggle for democracy.

Serious protests began in Port Elizabeth after the Port Elizabeth Black Civic Organisation (PEBCO) called for a stay-at-home strike for March 18th. On March 21st, the twenty-fifth anniversary of Sharpeville, a police riot squad fired on a peaceful funeral procession in Langa township outside Uitenhage, killing twenty people.

The Uitenhage massacre fanned the revolt. By the following week protest marches and vigils were taking place in Cape Town. When the victims of the massacre were buried, 80 000 mourners, including a number of prominent political figures, attended the funeral. Every township seethed with anger.

On May 1st, thirty trade unions called out their members to demand that May Day become a paid public holiday. By the beginning of May 1985, of the 104 BLAs that had been established throughout the country, only three were still functioning. The others had been rendered inoperative by mass resignations or by the flight of their members.[17]

In May 1985 a leaflet, titled 'ANC Call to the Nation – the Future is Within our Grasp.' made a dramatic appearance in all urban areas. The leaflet was the first massive intervention by the ANC underground during the entire period. It called upon the people to:

'... make the apartheid system more and more unworkable and the country less and less governable ... to ... replace the collapsing government stooge councils with people's committees in every block which could become embryos of people's power.'

The leaflet addressed a special call to the youth and students '... in every black community, school and university to find ways of organising themselves into small mobile units which will protect the people against anti-social elements and act in an organised way in both White and

Black areas against the enemy and its agents.'

In the months that followed the urban townships became the sites of intensive mass struggles – involving rent boycotts, stay-at-home strikes, mass consumer boycotts of downtown White commercial outlets, classroom boycotts by students. When the ANC met for its second national consultative conference at Kabwe, in mid June, many areas of the country were centres of general unrest.[18]

The murder of four prominent community leaders in Cradock during July escalated the level of the revolt. Matthew Goniwe, Fort Calata, Sicelo Mhalwuli and Sparrow Mkhonto were abducted by a murder squad acting on behalf of the state and brutally murdered. Their funeral on July 19th was a highly charged outpouring of mass grief and anger. Thousands from all over the country attended the funeral. For the first time in decades the red flag of the Communist Party was unfurled alongside the ANC banners. The murders and the mass response to them marked a qualitative change for both the people and the state.

Cradock, a small town in the Eastern Cape, had produced one the most active community organisations, CRADORA, headed by the late Goniwe. Pressure from the community had forced the members of the BLA to resign en masse and a number of their functions were taken over by the community organisation. Rather than waging a conventional rent strike, CRADORA had chosen to collect old rents and hold them in escrow, pending the outcome of negotiations with the municipal council.

The state and its agents had seriously miscalculated the mood of the country. Rather than cow Cradock's Black community, the quadruple murder spurred them to even bolder acts of defiance. On the weekend of the 19th July, in an admission of its powerlessness the regime declared a selective State of Emergency, affecting designated magisterial districts. With these emergency powers the regime could lay siege to a number of African townships in the Vaal triangle and the Eastern Cape.[19]

UNGOVERNABILITY AND THE EMERGENCE OF PEOPLE'S POWER

The upheavals that swept through South Africa in the wake of the PWV revolt of 1984 were probably the most sustained mass resistance movement the country has experienced since 1960. After the initial mass confrontations and public manifestations, the communities that became involved devised less visible but still highly effective means of resistance. The rent and consumer boycotts were the most hard-hitting of these and the relative ease with which effective protest was registered through boycotts popularised the method.

The chief organisers of the rent and consumer boycotts were the local UDF affiliates and trade unions. To co-ordinate action at the township level required the creation of base organisations to monitor participation and to ensure collective action. Such base organisations were usually small enough that a high degree of direct representation and accountability was possible. Beginning at the street, and even yard level, committees were set up. Each of these basic units (street or yard committees) elected representatives to area committees. Being made up of neighbours, these committees had the virtue of intimacy, making it difficult for spies and agents to penetrate them. This intimacy also made it easier for them to function without the formalities of usually associated with political organisation.

Originally, the committees were conceived as organs to conduct local struggles. As the state hit back in its attempts to cow the communities, they assumed responsibility for collective security -against anti-social elements and the state. Almost imperceptibility they became organs contesting the conventional organs of state at the local level. Through this process there came into being the rudimentary organs of popular power.[20]

The organs of popular power (OPPs) developed most effectively in the Eastern Cape, the PWV region and parts of the Western Cape. By addressing local grievances and relating them to the larger national political issues the OPPs were able to achieve a remarkable degree of unity and solidarity. Discussion and debate at the grassroots was their forte. By thus involving the 'ordinary' people, rather than the political activists, in the decisions about strikes, boycotts and the withholding of rent, the OPPs could attain an extraordinary commitment to the struggles waged from the communities.

In the majority of the townships of the PWV region the rent strikes launched in 1984/85 continue to the present. The consumer boycott of White commercial outlets was sustained for months at a time and the township traders, who usually stood aloof from political struggles, could readily see the advantage in supporting them.

Both the rent strike and the consumer boycott were apparently non-activists means of waging a struggle. Because of this it was relatively easier to convince the cautious and the less committed to participate in them. Their impact on the White business community and the state was far more profound than street battles and mass demonstrations. These tactics came into their own especially after the imposition of the selective State of Emergency in July 1985. Invariably the demand that the troops be removed from the townships was attached to a consumer boycott. By December 1985 the cumulative pressure of the consumer boycott compelled the White commercial sector in Port Elizabeth to pressurize the state into withdrawing its troops from the townships. Similar results were obtained in other towns such as Port Alfred and Cradock. The rewards of united action became readily visible when self-interest persuaded White traders to distance themselves from the state.

Parents and other adults were also attracted to the OPPs because they managed to impose a degree of control over the youthful 'comrades'. Discipline enforced by stewards and group leaders at public manifestations helped lower the tensions and reduced the risks of confrontations with the police. By diverting the energies of the youth to tasks of local mobilisation and more constructive political activities the OPPs won the respect of the older township dwellers.

Yet the Black urban communities had good cause to be disturbed by the situation as affecting particularly the youth during 1985. Since the first classroom boycotts of November 1984, schooling in the PWV had been disrupted. With the spread of student strikes during 1985 to other regions, practically all Black youth of school-going age had been absenting themselves from school. The banning of COSAS, the high school student's national organisation in August 1985, compounded the situation by destroying the only national institution capable of disciplining the students. By December 1985 the tensions occasioned by thousands of school-aged youth spending their days on the streets threatened to rupture the unity between parents and youth, trade unionists and students that had been so painstakingly built. To resolve the tensions a consultative meeting was convened by the Soweto Education Crisis Committee in January 1986. From this conference emerged a decision, jointly arrived at after lengthy consultation, that there would be a return to school. The Johannesburg meeting served as a launching pad for the nationwide conference, held in Durban over Easter, where a National Education Crisis Committee was formed to give organistional expression to the struggle over education.

The NECC drew support from teachers and students in the first instance but also deliberately drew in trade unionists, civic organisations, and other political bodies. The NECC adumbrated the notion of a 'People's Education', as an alternative emerging from the actual struggles waged over education and to be elaborated during the course of these struggles by the popular organisations.

In March 1986 when the regime lifted the State of Emergency it claimed that it had served its purpose. Both sides to the conflict knew that his was untrue. The urban Black communities had neither been cowed nor had the struggles that had been launched during 1985 subsided. Mass resistance affected areas far beyond the Vaal triangle and a vast array of grassroots organised formations had sprung up to co-ordinate and give leadership to the resistance. When PW Botha lamely pronounced that South Africa had outgrown apartheid during his 'Rubicon Two' speech, the state was once again vainly trying to catch up with the new realities.

THE TRADE UNION FRONT

The most vital element of this new reality is organised labour, which has in the past five years grown into the most effective sector of the democratic opposition.

The development of predominantly African democratic trade unions has been accelerated by the palpable improvements African workers have been able to attain through shopfloor struggles and strikes.

Consequently, for the first time this century the organised component of the Black working class numerically outstrips its White counterpart.[21] The development of these unions can be periodised into three phases. The first phase, commencing in 1973, which was characterised by the establishment of new unions and the appearance of general workers unions to bring organisation to the African workers. The second phase, linked to the findings of the Wiehahn Commission, saw the African workers seizing the space created by their earlier struggles and the gradual transformation of the general workers unions into industrial unions, and ends around 1984. The third and current phase is a period of consolidation and creation of unity whose finest fruit thus far is the creation of COSATU.

The re-emergence of industrial organisation amongst African workers after 1973 threw into sharp relief the issues of class and race, which every sector of the democratic movement had benignly neglected for almost three decades. With a few exceptions the dialectics of race and class in South Africa had not been seriously debated or discussed since the illegalisation of the Communist Party in 1950. The upshot had been that the liberal-academic critique of racial domination had been permitted to occupy this ideological space to the extent that it had taken root amongst sectors of the left. Precisely because of its intellectual inertia in this sphere, discourse on these issues has in large measure taken place outside the ranks of the Communist Party and in a number of instances to contest the Communist Party's stated positions.

While the relevance of these debates is not immediately apparent, they are important not only in shaping strategy but also have a bearing on the tactical options working class and national organisations have to make in the execution of their political tasks.

The debate has turned on three basic questions:

What is the relationship between the system of racial domination and the processes of capital accumulation? And arising directly from this:

Which social force is the agency for a radical transformation of South Africa? And lastly, the related question: What strategy and tactics are best suited to galvanise these social forces? A whole range of derivative and secondary questions are thrown up in the process of addressing these three major questions. These include the relationship between the trade unions, as the most basic form of working class organisation and the national movement; the relationship of the organised working class to other classes and strata amongst the oppressed, etc.

Many of these issues are in fact being resolved in the conduct of specific struggles even while some of the major strategic problems are still outstanding. For several years there were conflicting approaches on the question of direct involvement of the trade unions in political struggles outside the factory gates. A number of the leading figures in the former FOSATU were identified with this view prior to the November 1984 stay-at-home. It had then been argued that it was tactically unwise to jeopardise the space the trade unions had won by premature involvement. The primary task, they argued, was to build up organisational strength on the shopfloor so that the unions would be better able to withstand state repression. The countervailing argument was that political abstention would neither build the trade unions nor prepare the workers for future confrontation with the state. Only by active engagement in struggles would the workers acquire the experience to wage future struggles and build their unions as combative organs. The actual pace of struggle forced a resolution by imposing a choice that could not be evaded.

In the debate on strategy two poles of opinion have crystalised around what are called the 'workerist' and 'populist' positions.[22] Stated very briefly the two positions may be summed up as follows:

Workerist – racial domination is a function of the specific historical conditions of the development of capitalism in South Africa. Though the majority of the working class structure their identity around their status as members of an oppressed race and their economic position as an exploited class, economic exploitation is the determinant factor.

In the course of their struggles the working class have evolved a distinctive culture, of which the trade unions are one of many expressions, based on values such as solidarity, equality and collectivism. The working class should lead the struggle by entering any political struggle as an autonomous class force responsible only to itself.[23]

'Populist' – the populists would concur with the workerists on the relationship between racial oppression and capitalism. Where they would part company is on the weight they give political institutions in determining the form of the struggle. Thus they would argue that both race and class are determinant factors which have to be taken into account. Thus Black workers are not merely 'workers' but specifically Black workers in a racist society.

The existential situation of the Black working class indeed equips it to lead the struggle, but they can only give effective leadership by assuming responsibility for all those who are oppressed and are seen to be the greatest champions of liberation. The working class cannot hope to achieve pre-eminence except on the strength of recognition by all the other oppressed classes and strata. This requires it to interact at every level and in every conceivable struggle with the other social forces.[24]

The protagonists in this debate have yet to resolve their differences. But it would be misleading to suggest that a strategic line has not yet emerged within the trade union movement. At the recent second national conference of COSATU, the Freedom Charter was overwhelmingly adopted as 'a guiding document which reflects the views and aspirations of the majority of the oppressed and exploited in our struggle against national oppression and economic exploitation.'[25] During the course of the conference, Jay Naidoo, COSATU's General Secretary also outlined the movement's thinking on the question of alliances. He drew a distinction between 'strategic alliances' and 'tactical alliances', based on an assessment of programmatic and political affinity between the parties to the alliance. He envisaged the development of a closer relationship between COSATU, UDF and other mass organisations that would constitute such a 'strategic alliance'; while COSATU would always hold open its door to 'tactical allies' over specific issues with organisations such as AZAPO, the National Forum and the New Unity Movement.

The objective of 'one country, one federation' however, still remains elusive. When COSATU held is inaugural conference in 1985 a significant minority of democratic trade unions remained outside the federation. In 1987 these came together to found NACTU, a black consciousness oriented federation, comprising unions formerly affiliated to CUSA and AZACTU.[26]

The democratic trade unions have in many respects become the frontline trench of the democratic struggle. To equip itself to discharge these responsibilities COSATU's second national conference resolved to improve regional co-ordination and to wage its major campaigns in conjunction with its 'strategic allies'.

THE NATIONAL LIBERATION MOVEMENT

The single most important fact relating to the African National Congress (ANC) since its Second National Consultative Conference is its growing legitimacy, not only in South Africa, but most notably among the leading western nations.

The second consultative conference took place at Kabwe in Zambia at the height of the first wave of urban revolt, in June 1985. The conference itself and the events taking place inside South Africa raised the ANC's prestige immeasurably, so that within the space of two years, Pretoria's most intransigent defenders in the diplomatic arena had received the ANC President, OR Tambo.

The consultative conference had taken some two years to prepare, involving extensive pre-conference discussion within the movement's units in exile and insidfe South Africa.[27] Like the previous Morogoro conference it was necessitated by the unanticipated changes that had occurred in the country and in the region. Unlike Morogoro, the Kabwe conference had to address a crisis occasioned by the successes the movement had registered rather than reverses. It was called upon to address a number of issues: how valid was the ANC's strategy of People's War in the South Africa of the 1980's? How had the changes that had occurred since 1969 affected regional balance of forces? To what degree had the growth of a vibrant working class movement altered movement's perception of what was feasible? How was the movement to cope with Pretoria's determination to internationalise the conflict?

Most of the work at the conference was conducted in commissions, each of which had the opportunity to examine a series of background documents. The Commission on Strategy and Tactics and the Internal Commission grappled with the principle issues affecting the direction forward. Both largely endorsed the validity of the strategy of People's

War, though they were forced to make a number of key modifications to take account of the changed national and regional situation.[28] It was in the context of the work of these two Commissions that the conference adopted the highly controversial resolution on targets. The resolution said:

'G. Action Against the Enemy's Support Base.

We have always gone out of our way to avoid confrontation along racial lines and will continue to do so. But those among the white community who constitute the core of its social base for race domination are increasingly being mobilised in support of brutal repression. In particular the enemy has begun to transform almost every farm into a military outpost. Certainly in the countryside they are more and more blurring the distinction between what is civilian and what is military.

In many other ways, both in the urban complexes and in industry, it is also militarising its civilian support base.

Up to now our dedication to the avoidance of racial confrontation has often prevented us from dealing telling blows against the enemy and his installations for fear that white civilians would be caught in the crossfire or be killed or injured in the vicinity of an enemy installation.

We have even inhibited ourselves from inflicting direct blows against whites that are ostensibly civilians but are in fact part of the military, paramilitary and security machine.

The escalating brutality perpetrated daily against our people is now creating a new situation. We can no longer allow our armed activities to be determined solely by the risk of such civilian casualties.'

Sensation-seeking journalists and other detractors of the liberation struggle seized upon this resolution and construed it as a decision to attack 'soft targets'. Consequently the more significant matters were covered over. The thesis on the armed struggle drew attention to a number of features of the South African struggle, which would lead to divergences from the classical pattern.

'The classical approach,' the thesis said,' lays stress on the development of guerrilla warfare in the rural areas and designates a supportive role for urban warfare.

But the objective conditions of our situation reveal that:

- The rural areas are not as politically organised as the urban.
- Our organisational strength lies in the urban and surrounding areas.
- The bulk of our army comes from the urban areas.
- In the urban areas there already exist many organised units which have sprung up spontaneously from mass action and the resistance of our people to engage the enemy by violent means, using rudimentary weapons.
- The most advanced elements of our people, such as workers and the township youth, are in the urban areas.'[29]

Based on this assessment the thesis concluded that greater possibilities existed to root trained military personnel in the urban areas while conducting a campaign of harassment in rural areas with a view to establishing a combat presence which could begin to contest the enemy's over these areas.[30]

The ANC also spelt out in clearer terms its conception of People's War as primarily a political struggle, which must entail the 'active and conscious participation of the masses of the oppressed people themselves.' By this account, People's War was a comprehensive strategy which would unfold on four inter-related plains 'mass mobilization and struggle; the underground activity of the ANC and its allies; the armed struggle, spearheaded by Umkonto we Sizwe; and international solidarity to render the apartheid state weaker.'

Special emphasis was placed on the development of the democratic trade unions and the emergence of a combative organised working class. The conference endorsed the creation of one federation and pledged itself to work for the realisation of the project. It drew attention to the successful instances of united action between the trade unions and community organisations during November 1984 and later during the early months of 1985 as worthy of emulation. As at the Morogoro conference of 1969, the working class was designated the principal social agent of the revolution.

On the question of the regional balance of forces the conference acknowledged the assistance and support the movement received from the Frontline states but was forced to conclude that there was no prospect of securing a rear base for military operations anywhere in the region. To make up for this the ANC would have to harness the energies of 'the people in the political motion' by 'mobilising the masses into action wherever they are and in whatever formation they live.' The resolutions envisaged the creation of a network of alliances involving organisations of the working class, the women, youth, rural workers, the students and members of the religious fraternity united around common strategic objectives. The ANC would make an input into each of these through its underground activities but would preserve their autonomy and not compromise their legality.

After Kabwe the ANC had both a long term and an immediate programme of action. The key moments in each of these were mass mobilisation and activity. The skill with which the movement was able to implement these programmes contributed to its growing legitimacy among the various sectors of the democratic opposition. With increasing legitimacy amongst its friends came the added bonus of grudging recognition amongst its detractors and opponents.

THE PRESENT AND FUTURE

When the Apartheid State declared the second state of emergency on June 12th 1986 its authority had been irreparably eroded in many urban areas. To re-establish its power it acted with a finessed ruthlessness. Two days after its imposition, Adriaan Vlok, the Minister of Law and Order, stated explicitly that it was intolerable that a situation of dual power was developing in many townships and that it was his intention to uproot the OPPs. The police and the army set about the task by targeting street and area committees. The greatest number of those detained during the second emergency were members of OPPs.[31] In an insidious application of their counter-insurgency theory the regime's experts devised a plan to arm bands of thugs and vigilantes whom they unleashed against the most tenacious townships. By mid-1987 the townships of Uitenhage, which had been in the forefront of the struggles of 1985 and 1986, were under the effective control of armed vigilantes under the command of one Reverend Maqina. Crossroads 'squattercamp', outside Cape Town which had successfully resisted attempts to disperse its population by the state, was finally dispersed and the shacks razed by a gang of thugs named 'Witdoeke' (White Turbans) organised and armed by the police and army.[32] In the province of Natal armed vigilantes, inspired by Inkatha have kept up a spate of bloodletting that can only rebound to the state's advantage.[33]

By a combination of military occupation and vigilante terror the state was able to roll back the advances made by the mass movement in the previous years. Yet it can still not claim victory. After the initial shock of the regime's counter-offensive, the mass movement has adapted to conditions of effective illegality and is bitterly contesting every inch of the terrain. The rent strikes in the PWV region continue – no prospect of their termination in sight. During 1987 two very successful political strikes were organised to mark the Whites only elections and the anniversary of Soweto. The National Union of Miners was able to launch a strike that brought practically the entire mining industry to a halt. Important organisational gains were also made during this period. The South African Youth Congress (SAYCO) was launched at an underground conference; the UDF Women's league was successfully inaugurated.

Despite its 'Witdoeke' auxiliaries and kitskonstables (instant policemen) the regime has not been able to revive the BLAs or set in place credible organs of civil administration. For the present and the immediate future the regime will only be able to govern by employing martial law.

Yet the mass movement and the other sectors of the democratic opposition have sustained serious losses, both in personnel and in political gains. But it has displayed a remarkable resilience enabling it to fight back. Unlike the movement of the 1950s, it has become too well entrenched and strong for the state to crush either by conventional means or emergency powers. Within this movement there has now emerged a core group of organised formations – which includes COSATU, SAYCO, the UDF affiliates, the students organisations, NECC – which accepts the Freedom Charter as a common programmatic statement. All of these have a record of involvement in mass struggles and consequently command overwhelming popular support. This core has come to constitute one pole of the cleavage in South Africa.

At the other end of the political spectrum the Apartheid State is unable to extricate itself from deep crisis. These is a growing realisation among its strategists that even though for the present it still commands sufficient military power to fend off direct assault, time can only work to the advantage of its opponents.

The national liberation alliance led by the ANC enjoys a growing prestige and authority inside and outside South Africa. The most active elements of the mass movement accept its pre-eminence and identify with its objectives. The speed with which apartheid is consigned to South Africa's prehistory will in large measure depend upon the skill and tenacity with which the ANC pursues its goals.

Lusaka, October 1987

ENDNOTES

1 Z.P.J. Book Review: Black Middle Class – Eleventh Hour Counter-Insurgency or Acquiescence in Continued Domination. Sechaba. (Lusaka) May 1983. p.24.

2 Human Sciences Research Council. Investigation of Inter-Group Relations. (Pretoria) July 1985. p.151.

3 On May 19th 1986, a few hours before the EPG was due to meet Foreign Minister Roelof (Pik) Botha, the South African Defence Force launched co-ordinated attacks on ANC premises in Botswana and Zimbabwe. An air raid apparently targeted on the ANCs Information Department Complex in Makeni, a few miles outside Lusaka, overshot its target hitting instead a neighbouring UNHCR camp.

4 *The Sunday Times* (Johannesburg) 30th November 1986, suggested that P W Botha had struck a bargain with Coloured and Indian members of the Tri-cameral parliament, who feared a second humiliating election contest so soon after that of 1984, that we would leave them out of the elections in return for a promise that they would restrain criticism about the regimes inaction on Group Areas.

5 Heribert Adam in *Indicator – South Africa*, Vol. 4. No.4 1987, comments: One major winner of the election has been the ANC, which participated like a silenced phantom. Pretoria has elevated the ANC as the major threat to

white rule. It thereby makes the Congress the only alternative to the existing government and eliminates attempts to create a credible middle ground.

6   Willie Breytenbach: Election Signals – All Right, all white, alright? In *Indicator – South Africa* Vol. 14 No. 4 of 1987. p19.

7   Of the seven seats it held in Natal before the May elections, the NRP lost all but one. In the Cape it lost its only seat. In the Transvaal the PFP lost three of its nine seats; in the Cape it lost three of its eleven seats. In Natal the PFP did marginally better losing only one of its six seats.

8   Willie Breytenbach estimates that had a system of proportional representation been in force the liberal opposition would have fared even worse. The far right CP/HNP group would, however, have doubled its gains. Ibid.

9   During the 1983 White referendum 65,95% of the White electorate voted for the proposed new constitution. The majority of English-speaking voters deserted the liberal opposition to vote for the National Party. Similarly, during the May election some 40 to 50 % of the English-speaking voters defected to the National Party. Some 52% of the White electorate voted for the National Party in May 1987.

10 Quoted in Business and Reform in *The Financial Mail*, (Johannesburg) 6th September 1985.

11 David Willers, London Director of the South African Foundation told a Business International Conference in London during May 1987:
it is still the view of most businessmen that the ANC policies, the Freedom Charter notwithstanding, are inimical to business practice and that socialism and nationalisation on a large scale will be the consequences of its coming power.

12 Van der Horst told *Leadership – South Africa*:
I believe that if we can start talking and have a federal bias or direction to our talks we can work out a satisfactory solution. I recently saw Chief Buthelezi. We talked openly. To my mind our future lies in that direction, because we are dealing with a Christian, we are dealing with a man who has Western habits, and who believes in certain Western things such as private enterprise, the business of ownership, and so on. Chief Buthelezi is the leader f the most important tribe. In *Leadership – South Africa*, Vol. 5. No.6. of 1986. p.14

13 Willers, Ibid.

14 A Johannesburg City Councillor who recently made inquiries about the

JNCS was advised that the issues he was raising were classified information subject to the Protection of Information Act (sic).

Weekly Mail, (Johannesburg) October 30th to November 5th, 1987.

15 According to the South African Institute of Race Relations people lost their lives during the unrest of 1985 and 86.

Race Relations Survey. 1985 and 1986. (Johannesburg)

16 Race Relations Survey 1984 Johannesburg. Section on Employment. pp240 B298

17 *Rand Daily Mail*, (Johannesburg) 16th April 1985

18 African National Congress – Call to the Nation. (Lusaka) April 1985.

19 In addition to the townships in the Vaal triangle, East London, Port Elizabeth, Uitenhage, Cradock, Port Alfred and Bloemfontein had been drawn into the revolt.

20 Georgina Jaffe. Beyond the Cannon of Mamelodi. Work in Progress (Braamfontein) No. 41, 1986.

21 By July 1984 African workers constituted 43,4% of the unionised workers; Whites 33,9%; Coloureds and Indians 22,7%. At that time the Trade Union Council of South Africa (TUCSA) was the largest union federation, with 54 affiliated unions. The disintegration of TUCSA in 1985/6 leaves COSATU, with 33 affiliated unions, the largest federation.

22 The South African usage of the term workerist diverges from its original usage (ouvrieriste) in the context of debates within the French left during the 1970s. Populism as it is employed in these debates is also unrecognisable in terms of its original meanings.

23 Duncan Innes, Workers Politics and the Popular Movement in Work in Progress, (Braamfontein) No.41. 1986.

See also: Peter Hudson, The Freedom Charter and the Theory of National Democratic Revolution. In *Transformation* (Durban) No.4 1987.

24 Isizwe Collective, Errors of Workerism in South African Labour Bulletin. (Braamfontein) Vol. 12 No.3 of 1987.

Also: Isizwe Collective Workerism and the Way Forward: A Rejoinder in *South African Labour Bulletin*. Vol.12. No.5 1987.

25 Yunus Carrim. COSATU: Towards Disciplined Alliances, in Work in Progress, (Braamfontein) No.49 1987.

26 In September 1987 it was reported that NACTU had held a meeting with the

PAC in Dar-Es-Salaam, Tanzania, for an exchange of views on the situation in South Africa.

27 African National Congress Consultative Conference, June 1985. National Preparatory Committee Documents. (Lusaka) p.2.

28 African National Congress Consultative Conference, June 1985. Commission on Strategy and Tactics (Lusaka) p.15.

29 Ibid. p.19.

30 Ibid. p.19.

31 An estimated 30 000 persons were detained between 1985 and 1986. 25 000 under the state of emergency regulation; 3,989 under the Internal Security Act.

32 In June 1986 70 000 persons had been rendered homeless; 30 000 were moved to Khayelitsha, 20 Kilometers outside Cape Town.

33 Michael Sutcliffe. Summary Report of Political Unrest in KwaZulu-Natal, January 1986 to March 1987. (Durban) Reports that:

... bearing in mind that Inkatha is involved in far more identifiable unrest than any other group, one finds that most of the incidents attributed to Inkatha involve attacks on people. For example, comparing Inkathas actions to those of youths one finds that Inkatha initiated about seven times as many attacks on people than the youth. On the other hand, Inkatha was involved in about the same proportion of attacks on property than were the youth. (Emphasis added) p.13.

SIX

This paper was presented in Harare in September 1988, at a conference convened by the Southern African Development and Research Association (SADRA) and the Scandinavian Institute of African Studies (SIAS) on the theme of regional cooperation in southern Africa, from a post-apartheid perspective. Jordan provided a focused account of South Africa's mounting militarisation under P. W. Botha, and identified four phases of the 'war of destabilisation' waged by South Africa against neighbouring states during the 1980s. The paper concludes with an idealistic and somewhat rhetorical forecast that South Africa's post-apartheid regional policy would be based on 'mutual respect, mutual benefit and peace' (although he acknowledges that such programmatic statements, unless they are based in political praxis, may be 'little more than pious wishes').

Towards a New Regional Policy for South Africa: Study of the Internal Determinants of Pretoria's Regional Policy

O n 30th April, in London, it was announced that the first meeting between representatives of the People's Republic of Angola, Cuba and Pretoria would be taking place in that city in an attempt to bring to an end the undeclared war Pretoria has been waging against Angola. The first meeting duly took place on May 4th. US sources close to the talks expressed optimism about the good start that had been made. Subsequent meetings have taken place in Brazzaville, Cairo, New York and Geneva and visible progress has been registered in the resolution of the conflict in South-western Africa.

The thirteen-year-old war that Pretoria imposed on Angola has been as brutal as it has been costly. That real prospects now exist for it should be cause for satisfaction, amongst all those in southern Africa who have supported the Angolan cause. Precisely because we desire an end to racist aggression in the region and have campaigned internationally to attain it, it is incumbent upon those that grasp fully the meaning of the current negotiations, and the underlying causes of Pretoria's aggressive policies the better to ensure their total defeat.

There would indeed be no need for science and theory if there was an identity between appearances and reality. The ancestors of modern man, looking up at the skies, concluded from the evidence of their eyes that the sun revolved around the earth. It required science to uncover and elucidate the reality that the reverse is in fact the truth. So too in the affairs of human society and states what we most readily perceive may not necessarily be the reality.

In this paper, we shall attempt to delve a little deeper beneath the surface to uncover the determinants of Pretoria's regional policy and proceed from that to suggest the possible direction of a post-apartheid regional policy, whose purpose must include not merely a reversal of present-day policy but must also recast relations between South Africa and its neighbours on a more solid footing which shall enhance peace and mutual benefit.

The undeclared war that the Pretoria regime is waging against the states of our region has been widely reported and written about by a variety of authors. Most of this work has focused on the minutiae of specific actions and operations, often at the expense of an analysis of Pretoria's long term motives and the internal determinants of this aggressive policy. It is my contention that there are several structural determinants of the aggressive interventionist posture Pretoria has adopted towards the region. Secondly, that these are linked to and derive from the regime's efforts to recast the apartheid system in a 'reformist' mould that can either broaden its social support base or at least neutralise potential sources of opposition from amongst the oppressed. And, lastly, that Pretoria's efforts 'to shape by coercive methods' the regional context in which regional states act, cannot be regarded as incidental but is rather a dimension of the profound organic crisis afflicting the regime.

It has been said that what some regard as pessimism is in fact optimism without illusions. I remain an optimist and shall always be optimistic about the prospects of bringing peace to our region. Yet I am persuaded that our optimism must be tempered by an appreciation of the unpleasant realities that characterise the crisis of apartheid and the evident inability, until recent months, of the states of southern Africa to arrive at a coherent collective response to Pretoria's aggression.

TOTAL STRATEGY

The concept, 'total strategy' was formulated by P.W. Botha's policy makers in 1977 and given definitive shape in the White Paper on Defence which Botha, then B. J. Vorster's Minister of Defence, tabled in parliament during that year. This refurbished rendition of Pretoria' s security doctrine was further elaborated upon in the White Paper on Defence for 1982, which stipulated that 'total strategy' entailed action by the state, the private business sector, the universities and other institutions to repulse a 'total onslaught' by the forces of Marxism, orchestrated and guided from Moscow. Botha had the opportunity to give substance to his doctrine after the political demise of Vorster in the aftermath of the slush-fund scandal (Muldergate). That strategy assumed palpable form in several institutions and in the re-ordering of the alliances among the various fractions of the ruling bloc.

The architects of the 'total strategy' envisaged the creation of a national security management system (NSMS) to coordinate political, economic, socio-psychological, diplomatic and security measures to defend the substance of white power in South Africa. The first step in this direction was the inauguration of the State Security Council (SSC), as a super-cabinet, comprising the Prime Minister (now the executive President), the Ministers of Defence, Justice, Law and Order, Foreign Affairs, Finance and Constitutional Development. In addition, the heads of the National Intelligence Services, Military Intelligence, the Security Police and the Police force also joined it. For the first time, many senior civil servants were brought in to serve on a decision-making body.

The State Security Council (SSC) has its own Secretariat, headed by a senior military officer and staffed with commissioned officers of the South African Defence Force (SÅDF). It is at the pinnacle of a nation-wide Security Management System which has already marginalised the cabinet and repudiated the principle of accountability to white parliament. It is the most visible indicator of the militarisation of the South African polity.

Commencing with the Carlton Conference of November 1979, where 300 business executives met under state patronage, Botha has assiduously courted monopoly capital. Harry Oppenheimer, whose name is synonymous with big business, told the press afterwards that the meeting marks 'a new relationship between the state and private business in South Africa'. Botha, in turn, undertook to deregulate sectors of the economy, sell off to the private sector portions of the state sector and reduce state exchange controls, provided he could secure the cooperation of the private sector. The immediate upshot of this emergent new coalition was the Defence Advisory Council, composed of leading figures from the private sector. It included names such as Anglo-American's Gavin Relly; Barlow-Rand's Mike Rosholt; SANLAM's F. J. Du Plessis; Mutual's J. G. van der Horst; South African Breweries' Dick Goss and GENCOR's Tommy Muller.

Though militarisation became a dominant feature only during Botha's premiership (later, presidency), it had been a latent feature through-out the years of Vorster's leadership. Between 1966 and 1978, the South African military budget increased seven-fold. Between 1978 and 1983 the military budget doubled. During this same period, ARMSCOR, the para-statal charged with securing the production of arms and ammunition locally to evade the international arms embargo, grew into one among South Africa's largest corporations. Some 60 per cent of Armscor's production is outsourced to the private sector. Between 1978 and 1986 the number of private sector subcontractors undertaking work on its behalf grew from 800 in 1978 to 3,000 in 1986. One dimension of the 'new relationship' referred to by Oppenheimer, is the emergence of a military–industrial complex, involving South Africa's leading business corporations, whose executives have become active participants in the shaping of Defence policy.

The 1977 White Paper on Defence had identified the need to 'maintain a solid military balance relative to the neighbouring and other states of southern Africa' as the regime's priority. 'One means of achieving this', it argued, 'was the promotion of a Constellation of Southern African States (CONSAS), with South Africa as the pivotal member, to promote political and economic collaboration among the states of Southern Africa.' CONSAS was planned to include all the states of the region except for Mozambique and Angola. Its authors conceived of it as an economic association in which each individual member state would also be required to sign a 'non-aggression pact' with South Africa as a condition of membership. Such pacts, it was hoped, would lay the groundwork for possible defence pacts which, in the words of Roelof 'Pik' Botha, could bring about 'a common approach in the security field, economic field and the political field.'

At the 1979 Carlton Conference, it was again Harry Oppenheimer, speaking on behalf of his big business colleagues, who pledged their support for the project. 'CONSAS attracts us all' he said, 'and businessmen want to help.' His sentiment was echoed by the spokesman of the Associated Chambers of Commerce (ASSOCOM) who promised that its members would become 'ambassadors of prosperity' to the region.

The success of CONSAS relied on the regime's hopes for a Muzorewa victory in the Zimbabwean independence elections of 1980. The landslide victory won by the Patriotic Front alliance was a fatal reverse. The mortal blow was delivered by the coalescence of the region into the Southern African Development Coordination Conference (SADCC) with the primary purpose of de-linking their economies from South Africa's and reducing their dependence. Botha and the coalition of class forces he had brought together had been repulsed in their first sally against the region.

They felt the need to regroup end employ new tactics.

THE INTERNAL POLITICAL TENSIONS

During the decade of the 1960s the regime, under the leadership of Verwoerd and Vorster, had defeated the challenge from the democratic movement. Stability, imposed by repression, produced an environment of growing prosperity in the South African economy. Institutionalized White privilege had ensured that these benefits were distributed to all classes amongst the Whites. The chief beneficiaries however were big capital. It was during the halcyon days of the 1960s that the large Afrikaner controlled finance houses and monopolies came into their own, creating the opportunity to cement cross-cutting alliances amongst the monopolists that relegated the old Anglo/Afrikaner tensions to the past. Prosperity and the quiescence of the democratic movement enhanced the cohesion of the multi class bloc of Whites under the leadership of the National Party.

From the mid-1970s the crowing challenge from the black messes, led in the first instance by the working class, coinciding with the collapse of Portuguese colonialism heralded a new dangerous climate. The national uprising following Soweto in 1976, the re-appearance of the ANC's military activity, the growth of the democratic trade union movement coupled with more effective underground activity, placed new stresses on intra-ruling class cohesion. Within the ruling National Party, the leadership of Vorster was challenged by an emergent group associated with Afrikaner monopoly capital. 'Muldergate' – the slush fund scandal – proved an opportune pretext to strip Vorster of power. Outside the ruling party elite, this group was able to win the confidence of non-Afrikaner monopolists and rely on the support of the military. Botha, Vorster's Minister of Defence, was the candidate favoured to replace Vorster by this new coalition.

Botha had close ties with the top military commanders and was regarded as well suited for the role assigned to him – to check the challenge from below, while enticing the states of southern Africa into a de facto collaborative relationship with South Africa in return for economic benefits. To achieve the former, Botha hoped to employ a mix of cooptive and repressive tactics. To achieve the latter, he relied on aggressive diplomacy backed up by military power. But by the end of 1980, the initial phase of Botha's incumbency, he had not delivered on either aspect of his strategy. To increase its effectiveness a military-dominated administrative structure, parallel to and controlling the conventional structures of civil administration, has grown during the 1980s. These arrangements have the tacit backing of big business.

Before 1981, Pretoria's regional policy ran along two tracks – one persuasive; the other coercive. Economics was the key to the persuasive track, which Pretoria hoped would bind the regional states to the South African economy and act as an incentive to deepen that association. The coercive track sought to recreate the cordon santitaire formerly provided by the Portuguese colonies. This second track was given a higher profile during the 1980s after the creation of SADCC signalled the region's determination to disengage from the South African economy. SADCC was targetted on reversing the relationship with South Africa by addressing three immediate priorities transport and intra-regional communications; food security and industrial development and training. Mozambique and Tanzania with their long coast lines and rail links to the landlocked member states, were of key strategic importance for the realisation of the project. Mozambique's seaports offered realistic alternatives to the region's continued dependence on South African facilities. To the minds of the long-range strategists in Pretoria, unless these were rendered non-functional, there would be a decisive shift in the regional balance of power.

By an unhappy coincidence, Mozambique was also the most vulnerable of the SADCC states, barring the BLS countries. Under Portuguese rule southern and central Mozambique had been firmly integrated with the South African economy as sources of foreign migrant labour power. The peasant economies of southern Mozambique articulated with the South African mining industry to an extent that remittances from miners were an essential input for most peasant households. Central Mozambique too was linked to White-ruled Rhodesia as a source of seasonal labourers. Pretoria's war-planners perceived these historic links as a vital pressure point, which if consistently exploited, could unravel the fabric of SADCC.

THE WAR OF DESTABILISATION

The term 'destabilization' entered our political vocabularies through the US National Security Council, where Henry Kissinger had employed the term to characterize the comprehensive plans he had elaborated to subvert and overthrow the Allende Popular Unity Government in Chile.

The war of destabilisation Pretoria has waged against Southern Africa in the 1980s may be periodized into four phases. The commencement of the first phase was signalled by the Matola raid of January 29th, 1981. It was immediately after Matola that the racists launched 'Operation Protea', a major invasion of Angola, during which they established military occupation over vast portions of southern Angola. It was during this phase that Pretoria assigned a new role to the mercenary forces in its employ and deployed surrogate puppet armies in practically each state in the region. Two battalions, composed almost entirely of mercenaries, the 32nd and 201st, were assigned deep penetration duties inside Angola. The relations between Pretoria's Reconnaissance Commandoes and other mercenary forces also came to light during an abortive invasion of the Seychelles.

The election of Ronald Reagan as president of the US in 1980, proved to be a boon for Pretoria. The new administration confirmed its tilt in favour of Pretoria almost immediately after Reagan's inauguration, by introducing the element of 'linkage' as the only means of resolving the Namibian independence dispute. Linkage served Pretoria well by relegating to irrelevance South Africa's illegal occupation of Namibia, while placing the onus for the implementation of Resolution 435 on Angola and its allies. It also placed the Botha regime on a par with other African governments who were now compelled to regard it as a party with legitimate claims regarding its security. Other pronouncements made in the context of the 'constructive engagement' indicated that Washington would adopt a sympathetic approach to Pretoria's military adventurism in the region.

Destabilization entered its second phase in late 1982. The dominant feature of this phase was the intensification of military pressure against specifically targeted states, synchronised with intense psychological warfare and economic measures designed to produce disaffection and insecurity among the population. It was such tactics that extracted the secret 1982 Non-Aggression Pact from the Swazi government. At this time the strategists in Pretoria operated on the ' forward defence line concept', borrowed from Israel, whose intent was to ensure that the war with the liberation movement was fought outside the South African heartland by creating a cordon of instability among the neighbouring states which would compel them to drive the ANC out of the region. The 'forward defence line' had the bonus of wreaking mayhem in the targeted states. The destruction of infrastructure and causing of civilian casualties would serve as an object lesson to the countries not immediately affected about the costs entailed in antagonising Pretoria. If the southern African states could be forced to recognise Pretoria's military pre-eminence, the racist policy-makers hoped, these would each grudgingly face the necessity of dealing with apartheid South Africa.

Angola, Mozambique and Lesotho bore the brunt of this second phase which ended in early 1986. In January 1984, both Mozambique and Angola announced that they were entering negotiations with Pretoria. The outcome of both is a matter of historic record. In January 1986 Pretoria laid economic siege to Lesotho, only relenting after a military coup overthrew the Leabua Jonathan government.

After 1986 the regime expanded it activities to include the entire region. Botswana had suffered attack in June 1985; Zambia was subjected to aerial and ground attacks; in Zimbabwe, a campaign of bombings and small scale actions was mounted by gangs of well-armed spies and saboteurs, the Mozambican economy was subjected to every manner of disruption through acts of sabotage and economic reprisals. In Angola, the racists used their air umbrella to turn back FAPLA offensives aimed at Jamba. Through an informal alliance with the US, Pretoria and Washington jointly supplied and maintained the Savimbi's puppet army. This third phase of the war of destabilisation culminated in the massive invasion during the letter part of 1987.

It has been remarked that Pretoria's regional policy shall in the future be assessed in terms of the period before and after the battle for Cuito Cuenavale. In September 1987, the SADF launched a combined air and land operation, involving some 9,000 men, its Airforce, motorised units and long range artillery, against Angola. Their objectives were to seize two provinces in Angola in order establish Jonas Savimbi there as an alternative president. The racists' analysts had not reckoned on a tenacious resistance on the part of the Angolan forces. At Cuito Cuanavale, which it had employed as its staging post for its earlier drive to take Savimbi's headquarters at Jamba, the SADF offensive was stopped in its tracks. Improved Angolan air defence systems deprived Pretoria of the air superiority it had exploited in the past and its forces were compelled to dig in south of the town.

The SADF's long range artillery the G5 and G6 were employed to bombard the FAPLA but failed to dislodge the defenders. In mid-January 1988, the SADF launched a major offensive – using tanks supported by ground troops drawn from the so-called South West African Territorial Force and UNITA. This advance was beaten back.

Two further attempts to take Cuito Cuanavale failed during February. In March a major tank battle ensued as the SADF advanced within a kilometre of FAPLA's lines. The offensive was beaten back and the SADF tanks withdrew in panic, over-running several of their UNITA puppet troops in the process.

Pretoria's failure to take Cuito Cuanavale was compounded by a joint FAPLA-Cuban counter-offensive to the west, outflanking the SADF. It was in this context that Pretoria sought negotiations in April 1988. The threat of an effective Democratic Party Presidential candidate in the USA, who might sweep the Republicans out of the White House, lent urgency to need to find a settlement.

The battles in southern Angola revealed many of the fundamental weanesses in Pretoria's strategy. Apart from its corps of professionals, the SADF is forced to rely on youthful conscripts aged between 18 and 35. The Botha regime can ill-afford to lose too many of these in battle far from home. Thus, for example, in January 1986 the SADF's General staff calculated that Cuito Cuanavale could only be taken by a massive infantry assault. However, they estimated, this could well entail heavy casualties among the White South African troops. While the military risks made sense, the political risks outweighed them. Secondly, the SADF had always assumed its command of the air and was consequently ill-prepared for a reversal of roles. The air defence capacity of the SADF has never been developed thus laying it open to relatively risk-free air attacks from Angolan MIGs. In the last instance, it was the battlefield situation that persuaded Botha to talk. Pretoria entered the negotiations from a position of objective weakness and has not been able to dictate terms as they had done in 1984.

The Challenge from Within South Africa

After the signing of the Nkomati Accords Pretoria had boasted loudly that it had contained the threat of insurgency and would within a few months strangulate the ANC underground by cutting off its sources of supply from beyond South Africa's borders. Instead of the order and stability that the regime claimed it had delivered, in August 1984 a rent strike in Sebokeng escalated first into a regional uprising, and by the following year had engulfed all the major urban areas outside Natal.

It was in the context of this revolt that the latent lines of fracture began to reappear in the ranks of the regime's supporters, affecting even the ruling National Party. Tensions within the ruling bloc caused it to splinter in two directions. The dominant schism was to the right; the minority trend was to the left, led by reformists disillusioned with Botha and radical critics in search of a real alternative to apartheid.

Both the right and the left trends are minority tendencies within the white electorate. As the May 1987 elections demonstrated the National Party has been able to pull together a cross-cutting non-ethnic coalition, with some 40 per cent of the English-speaking voters supporting it.

However, the far-right has been the most significant factor eroding the cohesion of the regime's support base. It has detached significant numbers of the blue-collar White workers from the National Party and has made drastic inroads into its support base among medium size farmers in the Transvaal. In addition to the 29.5 per cent it polled in the May 1987 elections, it has scored highly visible by-election victories since then.

The 'leftward' drift among the regime's former supporters has been confined to the high-income bracket and professional strata. While many of these have parted company with Botha they have not discarded the ethos of white ethnocentricity and race privilege.

Ironically, the declining credibility of the regime amongst its former supporters is one of the factors reinforcing the trend towards militarization, as the Botha government seeks to recruit new allies and clients among the more conservative element in the Black communities, it has had to relinquish the rhetoric of racial exclusivity in preference for formulations about the 'defence of the free enterprise system'. In an attempt to lend substance to this new posture it has had to create some economic space for the Black middling strata at the expense of the white wage earners.

Judged against this backdrop the war of destabilisation and Pretoria's aggressive regional policy are necessary features of a highly militarised regime that seeks to impose solutions by force of arms. The rise of the military and the growth of the military-industrial complex are so intertwined with the crisis of apartheid colonialism that it is unlikely that one could eliminate the one without eliminating the other. The struggle for peace in the region has thus become inextricably related to the struggle for liberation in South Africa. A regional peace purchased at the price of compromising the South African and Namibian liberation struggles would be illusory.

Though it may be premature to speculate about the character of the regional policy of a post-apartheid South Africa, I submit that to the extent that negation implies assertion, we can, by careful extrapolation and projection into the future of those aspects of South Africa that are potentially beneficial to the region, deduce the rudiments of such a policy. Our ideas about a post-apartheid regional policy can be but a projection of the regional policies presently pursued by the anti-apartheid, liberatory forces of South Africa.

The Freedom Charter, adopted at the Kliptown Congress of the People, and subsequently embraced by both COSATU and the UDF in 1987, speaks in terms of 'peace and friendship' between a democratic South Africa and the rest of the continent. In its recently adopted Constitutional Guidelines for a Democratic South Africa' the ANC commits a future democratic government to a policy of non-alignment and close cooperation for mutual benefit with the states of the region.

Programmatic statements might be little more than pious wishes except if they are reflected in political praxis. Until it constitutes itself as a government, we can only judge the commitment of the South African liberation movement to these statements by its present-day practice. The ANC was a founder member of the Bandung conference of 1954. It attended the first Pan-African conference held on African soil, in Ghana, during 1958. It has been a member of the Afro-Asian Peoples' Solidarity Organisation for more than two decades and enjoys observer status in the Non-Aligned movement, the Organisation of African Unity and the United Nations. Within the region, it participates in the summits of the Frontline States and SÄDCC. While all these are extremely important fora from which to mobilise support for the liberation struggle, participation in them also commits the liberation movement to their goals. The adherence of non South African natives of the region to the ANC over many decades is a matter of historical record, as is the participation of South Africans in the movements of the regional states.

The bonds of solidarity among the peoples of the region, arising directly from the struggle for liberation, have laid the groundwork for a new regional order based on mutual respect, mutual benefit and peace. It is this potential that is consistently stifled by apartheid colonialism. Today, more than ever, in Southern Africa peace and freedom are indivisible.

SEVEN

*This paper, presented at a conference of ANC representatives and Soviet social scientists, held in Moscow in February 1989, revisits a topic explored previously by Jordan (**Documents 2** and **3**). It begins by noting than an earlier consensus – that an African middle class had no stake in the economy and would naturally make common cause with the masses – had 'all but broken down'. He argues that the liberation movement must 'contest every inch of the terrain' and 'detach the enemy's potential allies from his camp'. This is a less confident perspective than that articulated by Jordan a few years earlier (**Document 3**) – that the black bourgeoisie would be tugged by mass struggle into the ANC camp – and he now accepts that the possibility of the black bourgeoisie cleaving instead to white capital is a danger that 'should not be lightly dismissed'.*

The African Bourgeoisie –
A new look

INTRODUCTION

Since the publication of Nimrod Mkele's article, 'The Emergent African Middle Class' by Harry Oppenheimer's OPTIMA (Vol. 10, No. 4, 1960), it became generally accepted that despite the differentials in lifestyle, life chances and incomes separating the African petty bourgeoisie from the majority of the oppressed working people, the commonly shared burden of national oppression would ultimately make for a united front of all classes of Africans against white domination. As Mkele, quoting Monica Hunter, argued:

> 'While distinctions in wealth and education have become real among Africans and exert a powerful influence, 'There is no sharp cleavage between classes ... The cleavage between Bantu and European ... overshadows economic differences within the Bantu community itself.' Thus, Africans, suffering as they do from disabilities common to all classes, translate their struggle for status and personal recognition not into class terms which would cut across colour lines but into a struggle for the recognition of all Africans ... The African middle class has no stake in the country and sees its salvation in making common cause with the masses with whom it shares common disabilities.'

Until recently, few, if any, analysts within our movement took issue with this view. Indeed, it could be said that such a view is one of the cornerstones of ANC strategy, which emphasises the maximum unity of the various classes and strata in the black community against racist domination. ANC theorists have, moreover, argued that it is not merely sentiment that cements such alliance, but that it is grounded in material reality – a shared interest in the overthrow of the minority regime.

Thus Joe Slovo, in his 'South Africa – No Middle Road' (in Southern Africa: The New Politics of Revolution), states:

> 'In the case of the black middle strata, however, class mobility cannot proceed beyond a certain point; and again, this point is defined in race rather than in economic terms. Objectively speaking, therefore, the immediate fate of the black middle section is linked much more with that of the black workers and peasants than with their equivalents across the colour line.'

In similar vein, ZPJ, a reviewer in Sechaba, May 1983, dismisses the possibilities of 'elite accommodation' on the grounds that the disabilities of the African petty bourgeoisie will inevitably impel them to seek more radical solutions.

These approaches have come under the sceptical scrutiny of a handful of analysts, some from within the ranks of our movement and amongst our supporters, others from amongst critics and opponents of the ANC. Much of this scepticism has in part been occasioned by the role assigned to the African petty bourgeoisie in the South African ruling class's counter-revolutionary strategies and the designs of imperialism to subvert our revolution.

A number of these have remarked unfavourably on the growth of a highly visible, though as yet small, African petty bourgeoisie – comprising the urban commercial sector, the professionals, a sprinkling of African business executives in the employ of South African and Transnational corporations, government bureaucrats and officials. All these sectors of the petty bourgeoisie are organised into a number of formations – ranging from NAFCOC for the commercial sector, the

Black Management Forum for the executives to the various professional bodies for the professionals. Through organisation the African petty bourgeoisie controls its own independent assets, is able to galvanise a very articulate constituency and self-consciously tries to bring its ideological influence to bear on the rest of the African community. A myriad of other subterranean channels afford it access to all layers of the black community. Thus, despite its actual size, it wields influence far out of proportion to its numbers.

Some writers in our movement have, rightly, also expressed concern about the possibilities of an alliance between the commercial petty bourgeoisie and the state bureaucrats whom the regime has groomed in its Bantustan programmes. It is evident that this circle of paid functionaries are using the little power they have been delegated as one means of accumulation. 'Toussaint', writing in the African Communist (No. 64. 1st Quarter 1976), in a more pessimistic assessment of the petty bourgeoisie warns:

'But the growth of this black bourgeoise (sic) brings into being a group willing and indeed anxious to operate within the Bantustan establishment and from there – it is hoped – stake a claim to lead the nation ...'

Harold Wolpe has expressed himself in similar vein on many occasions as have other ANC social scientists.

Spokesmen and the ideologues of monopoly capital have also contributed to the debate on the African petty bourgeoisie. In addition to well-reasoned, but rather belated attempts at co-optation, they have come forward with innumerable hare-brained scenarios. Thus Leon Louw and Frances Kendall, propagandists for the Free Market Foundation – an outfit run by MC O'Dowd, one of the Directors of the Anglo-American Corporation – in a best-selling book they ambitiously named 'South Africa: The Solution' contend that:

'People are inclined to accept almost any political order as long as there is prosperity, growth and job opportunity. In Hong Kong, the Chinese do not have the vote, but they are too busy improving their standard of living in a booming economy to care too much about it. In many Swiss cantons, women received the vote only recently, but it was relatively unimportant to them because they were free and prosperous.'

At another point in 'The Solution' the two authors opine:

'If apartheid did no more than separate blacks and white, Soweto would be a flourishing city with a CBD, high-rise buildings, banks, department stores, supermarkets, prosperous business people and numerous entrepreneurs. But it is not. The reason for this is that blacks live in a socialist world – a world in which almost everything is owned and controlled by the state ... we have black socialism in South Africa.'

Louw and Kendall echo the words of Etheredge, former President of the Chamber of Mines, addressing NAFCOC's 17th Annual Conference:

'... the blacks were entangled in a web of laws which restricted their mobility, which was the very heart of the free market system, and controlled them in so many ways that it was totally wrong to suggest that they lived in a capitalistic state, when they in fact lived under socialism.'

The monopoly capitalists and their house-trained intellectuals have their own ideas about the role that the African petty bourgeoisie should play in South Africa. Since 1976, through such agencies as the Urban Foundation, they have assiduously cultivated it as an alternative to the revolutionary liberation movement. One of the means so employed is to label apartheid as 'socialist'.

The consensus that previously existed in our analysis of the African petty bourgeoisie has all but broken down. The emergence of differing assessment is indicative of a need to re-examine a few assumptions.

Lenin remarks somewhere that advocacy of a people's revolution should never inhibit us from recognising the real and potential class contradictions that exist amongst people.

Nicos Poulantzas, in his 'Classes in Contemporary Capitalism' more explicitly says:

'... every class alliance of the popular masses (the 'people') involves a series of real contradictions which have to be seriously taken into consideration and resolved correctly ...'

It is generally accepted that the ANC is a multi-class coalition made up of a range of class forces. The Mass Democratic Movement (MDM), composed of a series of constituency organisations, is even more diverse in the class allegiances of its adherents. However, it is generally accepted that the working class is the leading force amongst this alliance of classes. Though it is rarely stated, there is an underlying assumption implicit in positing a leading or hegemonic class. This is that the various classes and strata that make up the coalition are motivated by differing, and perhaps even contradictory, class aims and therefore differ in their commitment to radical change. This being the case one class within the coalition will emerge hegemonic.

This brief study seeks to do two things. Firstly to subject to critical scrutiny one specific stratum within the African community, the petty bourgeoisie in its various fractions. Secondly to assess the efficacy of our movement's efforts to 'resolve correctly' the contradictions between the differing class aims of this stratum and the leading class in our revolution.

For purposes of this study I shall focus on the most articulate and best organised fractions of the African petty bourgeoisie, in the hope that a survey of their activities and ideologies will offer us some clues to their class objectives.

Defining our Terms

Before we proceed it is necessary that we first define exactly whom we are referring to. The classical definition of the petty bourgeoisie bases itself on the place this stratum occupies within the relations of production. The petty bourgeoisie is distinguished by:

• Small scale productive or commercial property; and/or
• Control over marketable professional skills;
• Typically the same agent/person is both the owner of his/her means of production and the direct producer;
• If and where he/she employs hired labour the scale is typically small,

seasonal or intermittent, being more an extension of, rather than a substitute for, their own labour.

As with all definitions this is a very broad generalisation which does not necessarily capture the character of any particular historical petty bourgeoisie. In each particular country or region the petty bourgeoisie will have its own specificity, shaped by history. Thus is can be said that in general the European petty bourgeoisie belongs to the simple commodity mode of production, which was historically the form of transition from feudalism to capitalism. Yet, despite this, it is equally true that this stratum has displayed a remarkable resilience and a capacity to survive into the era of monopoly capitalism and even beyond, outstanding examples of such adaptation being the artisan bakers one finds in France, the Federal Republic of Germany, Austria and some of the East European Socialist countries.

In general, we may also characterise the petty bourgeoisie as a transitional stratum, that recruits its ranks from the two major classes in capitalist social formations. The upwardly mobile proletarian is first transformed into a petty bourgeoisie before he can hope to enter the ranks of the bourgeoisie. The bankrupted capitalist descends first into the ranks of the petty bourgeoisie.

In capitalist social formations, the petty-bourgeois property owner is overwhelmed by a sense of contingency, whose source is the cyclical fluctuations of the capitalist economy. The precariousness of his existence marks the political attitudes of the petty bourgeoisie, hence he prefers stability to the uncertainties of change.

The petty commodity producer, artisan, trader and professional, works in isolation from others of his stratum, whom he perceives as competitors in the market place. His life is determined by individual exertion and initiative. Hence he tends to be individualistic. Fear of change and individualism dispose the petty bourgeois towards political conservatism.

In the classical literature of Marxism the petty bourgeoisie is typically referred to as a vacillating stratum. More often than not this stratum will be pulled in different directions in the face of a political crisis.

One section will side with the forces of change, while another will side with those for the status quo, and yet a third will attempt a precarious balancing act between the two extremes. This indecisiveness, like the political conservatism of the petty bourgeoisie, has its basis in material reality.

Being an intermediate stratum, which draws from both the proletariat and the bourgeoisie, the petty bourgeoisie has interests in common with both major classes. As direct producers the petty bourgeoisie has points in common with the proletariat, but as property-owners they also share common interests with the bourgeoisie. Beyond this are the links, sometimes as recent as one generation, to one or other of the major classes carried by recent arrivals to the petty bourgeoisie. Thus moods, ideas, movements and trends within the major classes inevitably produce resonances within the petty bourgeoisie. This is the material basis of their oscillation between left and right.

With the development of capitalism the variety and the range of marketable professional skills that the petty bourgeoisie may command has been vastly expanded. Besides the traditional professions, the ever-growing needs for renovation that keep the processes of capital accumulation in motion have generated new spheres of specialisation and highly-skilled labour both in the productive and the non-productive sectors of capitalist social formations. These have called into being what may loosely be referred to the a 'new petty bourgeoisie', whose distinguishing hallmarks are possession and control over marketable skills and training

THE SPECIFIC CHARACTERISTICS OF THE AFRICAN PETTY BOURGEOISIE

When examining the African petty bourgeoisie in our country, the general definition can guide us, but we must be keep in sight the peculiarities that mark out this petty bourgeoisie from others. The features we can most readily isolate are:

- Unlike the classical European petty bourgeoisie, the African petty bourgeoisie came into existence as a result of capitalist development during the epoch of imperialism.

- This stratum is specifically composed of upwardly mobile individuals, drawn from the traditional or modern peasantry, or from the proletariat. None of its recruits derive from declassed bourgeoisie.

Historically, the African petty bourgeoisie came into existence as the step-child of British colonial policy in South Africa. In both the Cape and Natal imperialist policy-makers had encouraged the growth of a stratum of African petty commodity producers on the land, both as a means of transforming the traditional African peasantry into consumers of British goods and as a means of undermining the authority of the traditional rulers who led the military opposition to colonialism.

The only area of capitalist economy in which Africans were allowed to gain an insecure foothold for accumulation during the late 19th century was commercial agriculture. Beginning in 1880 this economic niche was savagely attacked by the colonial state in its drive to create a mass labour force to feed the insatiable appetite of the mines. The crowning event in this process was the Native Land Act (1913).

The Natives' Land Act of 1913 achieved two purposes. It places a racially-determined ceiling on the capacity of the modern African peasantry's ability to accumulate capital and develop by restricting access to land to the 'Native reserves', comprising less than 13% of the land area of South Africa. Secondly, it restructured South African agriculture by abolition of tenant farming and compelling the African tenant farmers to become tenant labourers. At the stroke of the legislator's pen the pre-capitalist relations on the land were transformed into capitalist relations.

Extruded from the land the African petty bourgeoisie survived by entering the professions. It was from this stratum of professionally trained Africans that both the commercial petty bourgeoisie and the other fractions of the petty bourgeoisie emerged in the post-war years as stable urban African communities grew up.

In order to prosper that African petty bourgeoisie was forced to explore and discover those areas of commerce into which white commercial capital was either unable or unwilling to go. Its existential situation was typically a rearguard action to fend off encroachments on its living space by either white capital or the state. Ironically, it was racist legislation that for a long time afforded it some protection by giving it an unchallenged foothold in segregated African townships.

The other fractions of the petty bourgeoisie that we will refer to have slightly different origins.

By 1905 the colonial state sharply changed direction in its attitude towards the African petty bourgeoisie. The African petty commodity producer on the land was regarded as a potentially dangerous competitor by the white commercial farmers; the policy-makers had lost interest in his utility as a stalking horse in opposition to chiefly authority; the African professional stratum came to be regarded as the principal organisers of a modern political opposition and the mine-owners saw new possibilities of harnessing s superficially 'traditional' hierarchy as a vital constituent of its system to draft African labour to the mines. After the 1905 Native Affairs Commission, the state elaborated a patron-client relationship between itself and appointed pseudo-traditional chiefs, to whom it delegated certain powers of labour impressment and land distribution in the 'Native reserves'.

The thrust of state policy was finally rationalised in terms of the 1927 Natives' Administration Act, which designated the Governor-General as the 'Supreme Chief' over all 'natives in the Union', with absolute power to appoint and depose any of his subordinate chiefs – i.e. the so-called traditional hierarchy. The minority state thus dispensed with the services of the professional petty bourgeoisie but in turn created a bureaucratic stratum, partially drawn from the remnants of the pre-colonial African aristocracy but in every respect resembling the petty bourgeoisie. As state policy evolved into its present form, this bureaucratic stratum was given greater latitude and additional powers. By design and explicit intent these powers will never be permitted to develop to a point that will enable the bureaucratic petty bourgeoisie to sever the umbilical cord of dependency on the racist state. This stratum is a creature of Pretoria, dependent upon manning the structures of apartheid for its livelihood and very existence.[1]

The new petty bourgeoisie comprises all those persons who, in both the industrial productive and the tertiary sector of the economy, exercise supervisory and managerial functions over those engaged in the productive process. In terms of the racist practices of South African finance, industrial and commercial capital over the decades, this is a relatively new fraction of the petty bourgeoisie whose origins do not date further back than the mid-1970s. Ironically this petty bourgeoisie fraction owes its new-found life chances to mass struggles in which its members and other fractions of the petty bourgeoisie played a minimal role.

Stimulated by the struggles waged inside South Africa, anti-apartheid forces in the US and Western Europe increased pressures on companies investing in South Africa. One outcome was the Sullivan Code, adopted by the US Transnational Corporations and the EEC Code of Conduct for Western European countries. Both codes were devised to deflect the disinvestment lobby by promising promotion of blacks into executive and managerial posts. South African corporations soon followed suit with similar programmes, explicitly pursued with a view of creating a section of blacks 'who have a stake in the system.'

The first posts opened up to these black managers were invariably in the field of personnel management. With time more found their way into other positions but in the main the recently arrived black executive is still trapped in marginal roles and rarely has authority over whites. Despite their extremely small numbers, this fraction has already organised itself into a Black Management Forum and publishes a journal, significantly called The Black Leader. Occupationally the back manager or executive is set on a collision course with an overwhelmingly black labour force. It seems difficult to define a route whereby the conflictual relationship that necessarily exists between management and employees can be resolved. We shall return to this point later when we discuss ideology.

THE DISABILITIES OF THE AFRICAN PETTY BOURGEOISIE

When the African commercial petty bourgeoisie launched its first national organisation in 1964 a veritable minefield of regulations and discriminatory laws inhibited its ability to develop. The main reasons in force laid down:

- No African may occupy more than one business building.
- No African businessman could erect his own business premises. He

was constrained to occupy buildings erected and controlled by the local authorities.

- No African was permitted freehold rights in an urban area.
- No African was permitted to form a partnership, a limited liability company or run a wholesale business in the urban areas.
- African traders were permitted to sell only a limited number of commodities, designated 'daily essentials'.
- Trade permits for Africans expired annually and were renewed by the Bantu Administrations Board if the applicant for such renewal was deemed 'fit and proper' by the BAB officials.

The state made no effort to conceal its motives which were to drive African businessmen out of the urban areas and force them to relocate in the 'Native reserves'. Despite petitions and a deputation of 44 members of the National African Chamber of Commerce (NACOC) executive, the state would not relent. However, between 1964 and 1968 the Minister of Bantu Affairs and Development (BAD) received deputations of NACOC. At their meeting in 1968 the minister made it clear that he was no longer prepared to receive a 'national' deputation as this ran counter to regime policy which recognised nine separate ethnic 'nations'. So unless NACOC fragmented itself into separate Zulu, Sotho, Pedi, Tswana and Xhosa chambers of commerce, he could no longer enter into discussions with them.

In its dealings with the Minister of BAD, NACOC was speaking from a position of extreme weakness. Yet its response to this challenge was most revealing. In an attempt to accommodate the minister while retaining its own self-perception, in 1969, NACOC transformed itself into the National African Federated Chamber of Commerce, broken up into fifteen regional chambers of commerce, none of which conformed to the ethnic boundaries the minister was insisting on. We may draw two conclusions from this episode:

- The leadership of the commercial bourgeoisie is committed to a non-ethnic organisational structure both as a matter of principle and as a source of tactical strength in dealings with other classes and the state.
- The commercial petty bourgeoisie defines its interest in pan-South

African terms, transcending ethnic affiliation and deriving from a common class situation in the context of an economically united South Africa.

The Minister of BAD was unwilling to accept this apparent compromise and cancelled all future meeting with NAFCOC.

Since 1976, when for the first time after eight years, the Minister of BAD agreed to see a NAFCOC delegation on 20th August, the state has gradually lifted the restrictions it had formerly placed on the African commercial petty bourgeoisie. In 1977 after various white business interests, including the Federated Chamber of Industries (FCI), Afrikaanse Handels Instituut (AHI) and the Association of Chambers of Commerce (ASSOCOM) took up the cause of NAFCOC, the state made a number of concessions. Africans were permitted to operate more than one business; all trades and professions were opened to African traders; and licensing laws were brought into line with those for whites. In the following two years, the 99-year leasehold for urban Africans was introduced and African traders were permitted to expand into the service sector. At the Carlton Conference in 1979, PW Botha announced a new development strategy which would include the promotion and development of service industries in African urban areas. Anton Rupert, Managing Director of the Rembrandt Group, piloted the establishment of a small business development corporation, as a joint state-private sector venture to 'encourage small business entrepreneurship amongst small population groups'. In 1985 the state 'accepted the principle of ownership rights for blacks in the urban areas outside the national states' (i.e. Native reserves).

The relaxation of the constraints imposed on African business led to a growth spurt. NAFCOC now has over ten thousand paid-up members, spread over ninety-seven chambers of commerce. The NAFCOC leadership has exploited this new situation with a tactical acumen that invites admiration. The Soweto Uprising of June 1976 forced open the Minister of BAD's door. Though the African commercial petty bourgeoisie played little or no role in that and subsequent uprisings, it has undoubtedly been the chief beneficiary of the mass struggles of the last twelve years. It has been courted by every quarter of the ruling class (with the exception of the neo-fascist far right) who see in it an objective ally against the propertyless classes. In these circumstances NAFCOC has sought to maximise its position by driving a hard bargain in dealings with the more powerful fractions of white capital.

Though the business climate for the African commercial petty bourgeoisie has changed dramatically since the early 1970s, there is still a ceiling beyond which the African business community cannot rise. This ceiling is defined both by their economic weakness and in terms of race. Compared with the well-capitalised white monopolies, the projects NAFCOC has succeeded in mounting are shoestring operations. Even as they rush to take advantage of the new opportunities that have opened up to them the African traders find they have to seek loans and assistance from white monopoly capital. While Dr Samuel Motsuenyane might sit on the board of the Anglo-American Corporation, any white derelict who might panhandle him for a hand-out has more rights than him.

Within the context of apartheid and the stifling hold white monopoly capital has on the economy, the aspirations of the African commercial bourgeoisie are unlikely to be realised.

The Ideology of the Petty Bourgeoisie

NACOC came into existence during the period of induced political quiescence, following the Rivonia convictions. Weak ad indecisive, it was deferential and abject in its dealings with the regime and seemed ready to seek any shoddy compromise even at the expense of the perceived class interest of its constituency. Unable to take a firm stand, the commercial petty bourgeoisie toyed with the option of making the Bantustan scheme workable in the hope of raising loans through the Bantu Investment Corporations.

The upshot was however that the BIC granted loans to whites on better terms than for Africans.[2] NAFCOC appeals for redress against such patently inequitable treatment were to no avail.

Having been failed by the Bantustans the leadership of NAFCOC attempted to jump onto the Black Consciousness bandwagon by promoting 'economic nationalism' through a 'Buy Home Week' in the townships. This was, however, doomed to failure as township shops were constrained to selling a limited range of goods and moreover charged higher prices. It would appear that NAFCOC finally opted to challenge the state policy in 1973 when Motsuenyane in his Presidential Address repudiated the notion of ethnic and racial separation.

Despite indecision and political flabbiness, NAFCOC remained committed to a pan-South African identity as a class and strove to preserve this in the face of pressure from the state. The commercial petty bourgeoisie began to discover its gumption only when the mass movement, under the leadership of the black working class, displayed signs of revival. It cannot be accidental that Motsuenyane repudiated separate development in the midst of the Durban strikes. In the wake of the post-Soweto mass struggles NAFCOC became more assertive of its sectional petty-bourgeoisie interests, and was no doubt assisted in recouping the reverses the petty bourgeoisie had endured in the sixties and the insecurity these struggles instilled in the white monopolists.

NAFCOC as the principal mouthpiece of the African commercial petty bourgeoisie espouses a classical bourgeois ideology of the free market, free enterprise and minimal state interference. There is, however, an awareness within its ranks that, unaided by state intervention to at least equalise the odds, it cannot hope to compete with white monopoly capital. Nonetheless its President, Motsuenyane, has lent his name to the propaganda of the Free Market Foundation, by penning an introduction to the Louw and Kendall book. While its interests dictate that it oppose apartheid without reservation, its membership pragmatically recognise that township boundaries for the present protect their captive market against more powerful fractions of white commerce. The material conditions of his life still compel the petty bourgeois to vacillate as he tries to negotiate the treacherous reefs of contingency.

Unlike his counterpart in the commercial sector the African business executive is not self-employed. He is invariably one among a large number of employees possessing certain skills. He is essentially a team player whose chances of success depend as much on his native ability as on how well he integrates himself in the team. Ideologically he is shaped by these considerations. Since it is the large business concerns that have opened their executive suites to blacks, the new African petty bourgeois usually works for a monopoly which no longer fears innovation and experimentation. So, unlike his small trader counterpart, he must be bold and initiating if he is to get on in his career. As he owes his very position to the erosion of racial barriers he is implacably opposed to any system that does not recognise his individual merit, thus he does not equivocate on the issue of apartheid. He is, however, aware of the symbiotic relationship that has long existed between racial oppression and capitalism but tends to regard this unholy alliance between the system he regards as basically sound (capitalism) and a savage survival from South Africa's prehistory.[3]

Being a relatively recent arrival on the political landscape this new petty bourgeoisie is as yet ideologically unformed. But its livelihood is tied to monopoly capital's project to deracialise capitalism. It remains to be seen to what extent this fact will determine its ideological orientation. Suffice it to say at this point the organ of the Black Management Forum echoes many of the ideas and opinions of the leading monopolists on issues affecting the economy.

It is anticipated that the numbers of this new petty bourgeoisie will grow in the immediate future in response to the demands anticipated by economic planners. JL Sadie of Stellenbosch University complains that the ratio of managers to labour force in South Africa is one to every 52 workers. He found this unacceptable. To correct this deficiency other experts suggest the training of 74 000 African managers between 1985 and 2000. Recent figures stand at 2 794. The rate at which the number of managers has increased may be judged by comparing the figures for the period 1960 to 1980 against those of today. Human and Hofmeyr say that 300 Africans were appointed to managerial posts between 1960 and 1980 (i.e. at a rate of 15 per cent a year). This suggests that the remaining 2 494 achieved their promotions in the last five to seven years.[4] At the same time Arthur D Little and Co., an independent US Research Agency, found that between 1984 and 1985, foreign firms had all registered a drop in the numbers of Africans promoted to managerial posts.[5]

How We View the African Petty Bourgeoisie

In the recent period analysts and writers within the broad democratic movement and others outside it have commented extensively on the role, actual or potential, of the African petty bourgeoisie. Their comments have ranged from the dismissive 'left' positions adopted by Sarakinsky, to the pessimistic view adopted by Toussaint, Wolpe, O'Meara; or the downright cynical Heribert Adam and Connor Cruise O'Brien. Mike Sarakinsky, for example, writing in Africa Perspective (New Series. Vol. 1. No. 3 and 4 1987) discerns:

'There are two strands to NAFCOC's political discourse. Firstly a reformist appeal to white capital and the state in terms of free enterprise morality, which at the same time emphasises the benefits, political and economic to be derived from the emergence of a 'black middle and entrepreneurial class'. Secondly, an appeal is made to racial identity in an attempt to represent the interests of African entrepreneurs as the interests of all Africans.'

He concludes:

'They (NAFCOC) have been pragmatically conciliatory towards the state, and their relationship with white capital has been contradictory.'

Sarakinsky has of course discovered nothing startlingly new. The behaviour he describes could have been anticipated given the real relations of power between the forces involved.

Toussaint, Wolpe and O'Meara also evince an abiding lack of faith in the African petty bourgeoisie. A typical assessment is that of Wolpe, penned in 1976:

'... the direction of the political line of African petty businessmen seems to have been far removed from any kind of direct challenge to the structure of racial domination. The main thrust of their politics has been, on the one hand, to demand the removal of restrictions imposed upon their trading and business rights within the townships.'

Further on he links the three major fractions of the petty bourgeoisie in the following terms:

'It is, however, the petit-bourgeoisie – both the traditional and, given the administrative/bureaucratic structure, important sections of the new petit-bourgeoisie which is linked to the former – in the Bantustans – which is of prime importance.'

Then he draws the conclusion:

'… that in the present conjuncture, at least in the Bantustans where its political position is of much greater importance than in the white urban areas, the African petit-bourgeoisie stands, not merely outside the mainstream of the liberation movement but as a force for reaction.'

The congruence between this and the views of 'Toussaint' quoted in the introduction are self-evident.

The most alarming view however is a cynical instrumentalist one pronounced y two foreign academics who have taken a keen interest in South Africa, Adam and O'Brien. Both regard apartheid – old style or reformed – as a lost cause. In their calculations they assign the African petty bourgeoisie the task of political reconstruction but specifically as the 'pacifier' of the black have-nots and at their expense. Thus O'Brien:

'But the new black South Africa, unlike the other African countries, will have a large black middle class … In these conditions the new black government would need such allies as it could find. And it would be likely to find allies among the whites. A multi-racial coalition … could be expected to emerge: a coalition of all those with something to lose, whatever the colour of their skin.'

In a similar vein, Adam and Moodley project:

'… a historic compromise among big capital, small traders and bureaucrats would not founder on class antagonisms. To be sure the aspiring black 'bourgeoisie' would not be enticed to capitalism without capital, but, like Afrikaners before them, they could realistically hope to acquire their share of capital through control of the state.'

The scenario painted by Adam and O'Brien represents the fondest dreams of the monopoly capitalists and imperial policy makers. As such it need not detain us except to note these objectives and the need to contest them.

Of greater significance for our purposes are the views expressed within our own movement and the mass democratic movement at home. As noted earlier, Sarakinsky has uncovered nothing new. That the African commercial petty bourgeoisie, on assessing its strength and capacity in opposition to that wielded by the state, pragmatically seeks to avoid confrontation in which it will inevitably be bested can only be seen as realism. Its dependence on white capital, both for financial support and as a lobby to win more living space is a matter of record. It is rather the significance Sarakinsky, and in their own way Toussaint, Wolpe and others, attach to these well-known facts that should be a matter of concern.

Since 1976 white monopoly capital and the 'reformist' element in the state have made no secret of their own agenda for the African petty bourgeoisie. Through the Urban Foundation. Leading corporate figures and their organised bodies have told us they intend cultivating these strata as a buffer against pressures from the black working class and rural poor. Undoubtedly the economic weakness and dependency of the African petty bourgeoisie makes them all the more vulnerable to co-optation. Recognition of these realities should, however, not tempt us into accepting that such co-optation has already been realised.

Sarakinsky, Toussaint, Wolpe and O'Meara seem to believe that it is impossible to contest the plans of the ruling class. In spite of their best intentions they forsake the battlefield before issue has been joined, thus handing victory to the principal enemy without a fight.

The tasks of the national democratic movement is to contest every inch of the terrain, and where possible, detach the enemy's potential allies from his camp. It is my considered view that the Freedom Charter, as the movement's programmatic statement, is singularly equipped to achieve this.

As has so often been stated, the Freedom Charter is not a socialist programme. What has unfortunately not been as forcefully underscored is that it is neither a conventional bourgeois democratic programme. In its economic clauses – dealing with monopoly capital and the land – the Freedom Charter envisages the seizure of economic assets presently owned or controlled by white monopoly capital and large landowners. The immediate impact of the operationalisation of these clauses would be to break the stranglehold monopoly capital currently has on the economy, thus creating the space for the small entrepreneur, trader and businessman to realise his ambitions for growth. In point of fact it will remove numerous constraints presently inhibiting the flowering of the African petty bourgeoisie.

At the same time the transference of ownership of the commanding heights of the modern economy to the democratic state will also lay the basis for further revolutionary advance by the working class and its allies. What I am suggesting, therefore, is that for the petty bourgeoisie the Freedom Charter is a maximum programme – which opens up the way for the realisation of their class ambitions. For the proletariat, on the other hand, it represents a minimum programme which creates the preconditions for a second phase of the revolution. Thus are the 'real contradictions', referred to by Poulantzas, programmatically resolved. There is, however, an obvious tension here because the various classes coalesced around this common programme have to coexist through a dialectic of unity and struggle – i.e. a struggle amongst themselves for hegemony over the coalition. These tensions need not be explosive if creatively handled by the national democratic movement.

Yet the dangers we are constantly warned against should not be lightly dismissed. It is vital that the movement demonstrate to the petty bourgeoisie, in all its fractions, that it is only under a democratic government that it can register real advances. The ANC's own experience with NAFCOC, Inyandsa, elements of the Transkei bureaucracy and CONTRALESA is indicative of the potential amongst these strata. Stripped to its essentials what the movement has to get across is that only by dismantling the white monopoly over productive property, the professions, commerce, the higher reaches of the civil service and skills can these strata hope to secure their property and their skills. Moreover, it should be stressed that the democratic state will require the skills and services of competent managers, administrators and technical personnel since the existing white bureaucrats and managerial cadre would be a potential fifth column.

Released from the oppression of monopoly capital the African petty bourgeoisie will have the opportunity to give its undoubted talent and initiative full scope to flourish. In the sphere of small scale enterprises, especially in the service sector, its role would be indispensable in assuming responsibility for the sort of venture that even the most radical democratic state would find an encumbrance.

ENDNOTES

1   The growth of the bureaucratic petty bourgeoisie since the implementation of the Bantustan programme can be gauged by the following figures:
In the Transkei in 1963 there were 2 476 civil service posts. 76% of these were occupied by Africans. In 1973 in the Transkei there were 4 383 civil service posts. 92.4% of these were filled by Africans.
Source: Muriel Horrel. The African Homelands of South Africa (Johannesburg) 1973.

2   The Rand Daily Mail, 7th September 1974 reported that during its existence the BIC (1959 to 1974) provided loans to the value of R77 million, divided as follows:
African-owned businesses: R14 million
White-owned businesses: R43 million
BIC-owned enterprises: R20 million

3   See *The Black Leader*, August 1987, 'Business and Apartheid – An Unholy Alliance.'

4   See: 'Black Advancement: Strategies for Survival' an address by Mr Gaby T. Magomola. Black Management Forum Seminar. 23rd July 1987.
Also: 'Business should be a Microcosm of a New South Africa.' Address to Total (SA) Ltd Board of Directors by Don D. Mkhwanazi.
Race Relations Survey, 1985 SAIRR (Johannesburg) 1986, p.10.

5   Ninth Report on the Sullivan Principles. Arthur D. Little and Co. (Boston Mass.) 1985.

EIGHT

In this letter, written in 1989, one meets Jordan bristling with polemical flair. The letter, which the African Communist refused to publish, was in response to an article on Trotsky and Trotskyism by 'Dialego', the pseudonym of British political scientist John Hoffman. Jordan – writing under his nom de guerre – challenges Dialego's negative assessment of Trotsky's role, and does so by quoting copiously from Trotsky, Lenin and others. Dialego (Jordan notes) 'does not think it worthwhile to let us in on Trotsky's thinking', but relies instead on his own, partisan construction of Trotsky's views. Jordan really has two targets in his sights: Dialego – 'a political Peter, plugging the leaks in the ideological dykes occasioned by glasnost with the puny fingers of his dogmatism' – and those who 'had become accustomed to the rigid, intellectually stultifying practices of Stalinism'. Jordan would certainly have regarded as Stalinist some elements of the South African Communist Party – and in retrospect it is unsurprising that the journal declined to publish the letter.

Letter to the Editor

African Communist (unpublished)

Dear Comrade Editor,

My letter concerns the article on Trotskyism ad the life and times of Leon Trotsky, contributed by Comrade Dialego. (African Communist No. 115, Fourth Quarter 1988.)

There are numerous questions one could ask about the life of any revolutionary activist. These could include:

- What contribution did he/she make to the shaping of the movement's ideas, strategy and tactics?
- What active contribution did he/she make to the practical work of the revolutionary struggle?
- What role did he/she make to the process of reconstruction after the successful seizure of power?

Some of the possible answers to all these questions, respecting Trotsky, are those proffered by Comrade Dialego in his article, summed up in his basic conclusion that for the greater part of his political career. Trotsky 'hindered rather than helped the struggle of socialism'.

In 1966, Eric Hobsbawn, probably the doyen among historians writing in the Marxist tradition in English-speaking countries, wrote that it would be difficult if not impossible for Marxist historians to do a proper assessment of Leon Trotsky's role in the Russian Revolution as long as a great deal of mythology attached to his name.[1]

Almost daily new facts (or perhaps old facts previously concealed) uncovered in the Soviet archives, are being published shedding new light on the roles of Trotsky, Zinoviev, Bukharin, Kamenev, Rykov, and other leading Soviet Communists of the October days and the 1920s who perished during the nightmare of Stalinism. One would have thought that a degree of circumspection was advisable – at least waiting until all the facts are in – before rushing to judgement and committing one's self on paper.

Comrade Dialego's purposes are evidently not to set the historical record straight. I am compelled to conclude that he has added nothing to our knowledge of Trotsky or Trotskyism. I find this unfortunate because Comrade Dialego could have performed a real service had he at least tried to demythologise Trotsky.

My answers to the questions I pose at the beginning of this letter will differ fundamentally from those of Comrade Dialego. I claim no special expertise on the subject but will bring out what was deliberately left unsaid by Comrade Dialego.

Dialego builds much of his case against Trotsky on the latter's 'non-Bolshevism' prior to April 1917. This is of course old hat and an incontrovertible historical fact which is not contested even by the most ardent of Trotsky's supporters and defenders. The spirit in which Comrade Dialego approached his subject is set within the very first few paragraphs of his article. Where we encounter the startling allegation that Trotskyism is a form of Utopian socialism. This too is most unfortunate and suggests a lack of theoretical rigour and a desire to pronounce anathemas rather than clarify issues.

Comrade Dialego's negative assessment of Trotsky tempts him to make extravagant claims such as that Trotsky made no constructive contribution to the tasks facing Soviet society after 1917. He displays a rash zeal to gloss over facts which appear inconvenient to the case he wishes to make, which reinforces the impression I've formed of one with a political axe to grind. Comrade Dialego's Manichean scheme cannot account for Trotsky's conduct during 1917, the War of Intervention, NEP the Debate on Industrialization, etc.

1905

It is my view that one can begin to untangle this conundrum by re-examining 1905. It is the manner in which the various classes and their political representatives responded to the revolutionary crisis of 1905 that determined how all revolutionaries regarded them.

It is my impression that Comrade Dialego has either misunderstood the issues that divided the Russian Social Democrats after 1903 or that he so oversimplifies matters as to suggest a clear demarcation between angels and devils but which does not do justice to the complexity of the issues. The catch-all 'Menshevik' deserves to be treated with some caution by the historian. Careless use of this term can, in my view, obscure the highly variegated spectrum of political opinion. There are obvious and glaring differences among Plakhanov, Martynov, Martov, Dan and Trotsky, though all four were adherents of the Menshevik faction of the RSDLP. 1905, more than any other event, brought these to the fore.

From the Bolshevik perspective the issue in 1905 was which class *would* and *could* and *therefore should* lead the bourgeois-democratic revolution. It was in addressing this issue that Lenin wrote 'Two Tactics of Social Democracy in the Democratic Revolution' (henceforth 'Two Tactics'). There was no difference of opinion as to the social character of the revolution among the various social democratic factions. All were agreed that it was bourgeois democratic in character. Where they parted company was on the issue of class hegemony over the revolution.

The classic Menshevik position, against which Lenin polemicized, called on the proletariat to exercise restraint so as not to frighten the bourgeoisie into the arms of reaction by active intervention in the revolution. To the Menshevik leadership it appeared logical that since the revolution was bourgeois-democratic in character, the bourgeoisie should lead it and by so doing fulfil its historic task of building capitalist democracy. The role of the proletariat in the context of such a revolution was to stand back and not get in the way.

Lenin dismissed this line of reasoning, warning that the bourgeoisie was a treacherous and politically flabby class that lacked the political courage and social vision even to perform its historic mission. The role of leadership therefore devolved on the proletariat.

'Marxism teaches the proletarian not to keep aloof from the bourgeois revolution, to be indifferent to it, not to allow the leadership of the revolution to be assumed by the bourgeoisie but, on the contrary, to take a most energetic part in it, to fight most resolutely for consistent proletarian democracy, for carrying the revolution to its conclusion.'[2]

He derisively mocked the Menshevik concern not to alienate the bourgeoisie: '... the bourgeoisie is inconsistent, self-seeking and cowardly in its support of the revolution. The bourgeoisie, in the mass, will inevitably turn towards counter-revolution, towards the autocracy, against the revolution and against the people ... There remains 'the people', that is the proletariat and the peasantry: the proletariat alone can be relied on to march to the end, for it is going far beyond the democratic revolution. That is why the proletariat fights in the front ranks for a republic and contemptuously rejects silly and unworthy advice to take care not to frighten away the bourgeoisie.'[3]

Trotsky, unlike the Menshevik leadership, had a similar assessment of the bourgeoisie and the role of the proletariat:

'To imagine a revolutionary democratic government without representatives of the proletariat is to see the absurdity of the situation. The refusal of the social democrats to participate in a revolutionary government would make such a government quite impossible and would thus be equivalent to a betrayal of the revolution. But, the participation of the proletariat in a government is also objectively most probably, and permissible in principle, only as a dominant and leading participant. One may, of course, describe such a government as the dictatorship of the proletariat, peasantry and intelligentsia ... but the question nevertheless remains: who is to wield the hegemony in the government itself, and through it in the country.'[4]

There is a common thread linking both Lenin and Trotsky's views with the standpoint of Marx in his Address to the Central Committee of the Communist League in 1850:

'While the democratic petty bourgeoisie want to bring the revolution to an end as quickly as possible, achieving at the most the aims already mentioned, it is our interest and our task to make the revolution permanent until all the more or less propertied classes have been driven from their ruling positions, until the proletariat has conquered state power and until the associations of proletarians has progressed sufficiently far – not only in one country but in all leading countries of the world – that competition between the proletarians of these countries ceases and at least the decisive forces of production are concentrated in the hands of the workers.'[5]

It is in this connection that the interpretations of 'permanent revolution' associated with Lenin and Trotsky respectively can usefully be discussed. Comrade Dialego does not think it worthwhile to let us in on Trotsky's thinking. We have to rely on his construction of Trotsky's views.

The parting of the ways between the two appears to be the role of the peasantry. In 'Two Tactics' Lenin contends:

'The peasantry includes a great number of semi-proletarians as well as petty bourgeois elements. This causes it also to be unstable and compels the proletariat to unite in a strictly class party. But the instability of the peasantry differs radically from the instability of the bourgeoisie, for at the present time the peasantry is interested not so much in the absolute preservation of private property as in the confiscation of the landed estates, one of the principal forms of private property. While this does not make the peasantry become socialist or cease to be petty bourgeois, it is capable of becoming a whole hearted, and most radical adherent of the democratic revolution.'[6]

Trotsky, on the other hand, was dismissive of the peasantry, stressing instead its instability, its petty bourgeois character and backwardness:

'... the policy of the peasantry, in view of their social diversity, their intermediate position and their primitiveness; the policy of urban petty bourgeoisie, once again owing to its lack of character, its intermediate position and its complete lack of political tradition – the policy of all these ... social groups is utterly indefinite, unformed, full of possibilities and therefore full of surprises.'[7]

The logic of Trotsky's distrust of the peasantry was rejection of the worker-peasant alliance and therefore exclusive reliance on the proletariat, not merely as the leading class in the revolution, but shaping it independently of class forces and potential allies. This accounts in many cases for the charge levelled against him that he wished to skip stages. He concludes his argument:

> 'Political supremacy of the proletariat is incompatible with its economic slavery, whatever may be the banner under which the proletariat will find itself in possession of power, it will be compelled to enter the road of Socialism.'[8]

But those who are quick to judge Trotsky as the skipper of stages would do well to contemplate the words of Lenin written in September 1950:

> 'From the democratic revolution we shall at once, and precisely in accordance with the measure of our strength, the strength of the class conscious and organised proletariat, begin to pass to the socialist revolution. We stand for uninterrupted revolution. We shall not stop half-way.'[9]

Anticipating a speedy transition from the bourgeois-democratic to the socialist revolution does not necessarily imply skipping of stages, unless one regards these stages as discrete historical epochs, separated by years. Textual comparison suggests that at this time the issues that separated Lenin and Trotsky were those of strategy – who could be mobilised for the revolution – and not as some allege the stages the revolution would entail.

THE PARTY AND THE WORKING CLASS

The character and tasks of the revolutionary party were the source of the original schism among Russian Marxists in 1903. Comrade Dialego unfortunately vulgarises the viewpoint of Lenin's opponents to the point of caricature and appears unwilling to explore the possibility that they may have raised some valid points or have foreseen some of the problems that could arise. I feel it is worthwhile to re-examine the objections of at least two of the leading revolutionaries of the time.

The split in the RSDLP occasioned discussion and debate throughout the ranks of the Second International. Russian Marxists were of course the principal protagonists but other leading theoreticians of the movement also were drawn in. Among these can be counted Karl Kautsky, Karl Liebknecht, Rosa Luxemburg. The main criticism raised by many of these, all of whom opposed Leni's prescription, was that it smacked of Blanquism (associated with the 19th century revolutionary socialist, August Blanqui). Blanqui had advocated a conspiratorial revolutionary party, composed of professional revolutionaries, which would act as the custodian of the revolutionary vocation of the working class. At the propitious moment for insurrection, this party would galvanise the working class for seizure of power and institute a revolutionary dictatorship of the proletariat. Lenin, basing himself largely on the theoretical writings of Kautsky, held that capitalist productive relations masked the exploitative character of the employer-employee relationship. As a result, the proletariat tended to perceive only its immediate interest as sellers of labour power on the market. Acting on this perception it struggled to improve its relative position vis a vis the capitalist classes. It required science to bridge the distance between what was immediately perceptible and the reality – that the relationship is essentially exploitative irrespective of the remuneration the proletariat receives. Science or revolutionary theory therefore had to [be] brought to the proletarian movement from outside it, by the bourgeois intellectual who had forsaken his own class for the proletariat. Theory not only clarified the exploitative character of class relations but also provided the means of synchronising the struggle for reform with the revolutionary project. According to Lenin, the instrument for this was the revolutionary party, which itself had to be a highly disciplined organisational formation made up of professional revolutionaries.

Rosa Luxemburg took issue with these ideas, arguing:

'The fact is that the Social Democracy is not *joined* to the organisation of the proletariat. It is itself the proletariat. And because of this, Social Democratic centralism is essentially different from Blanquist centralism. It can only be the concentrated will of the individuals and groups representative of the most class conscious, militant advanced sections of the working class. It is, so to speak, the 'self-centralism' of the advanced sectors of the proletariat. It is the rule of the majority within its own party.'[10]

She rejected also Lenin's view of the relationship between class consciousness and the revolutionary party. While accepting that revolutionary theory would come from outside the day to day struggles of the class, she held that it was the actual struggle that was educative in class politics:

'The proletarian army is recruited and becomes aware of its objectives in the course of the struggle itself. The activity of the party organisation the growth of the proletarian's awareness of the objectives of the struggle and the struggle itself, are not different things, separated chronologically and mechanically. They are only different aspects of the same process.'[11]

She insists also that centralism and the discipline demanded by Lenin are no guarantee against deviations. Indeed, according to Luxemburg, it might pose the graver danger.

'It is by extreme centralism that a young, uneducated proletarian movement can be most completely handed over to the intellectual leader staffing a Central Committee.'

In a last cautionary note she says:

'The working class demands the right to make its mistakes and learn in the dialectic of history. Let us speak plainly. Historically, the errors committed by a truly revolutionary movement are infinitely more fruitful than the infallibility of the cleverest Central Committee.'[12]

It was Trotsky, perhaps, who carried the 'Blanquist' charge the farthest:

'In contrast to the 'economists' the 'politicians' (meaning the Leninists) take as their point of departure the *objective* class interests of the proletariat, established by the method of Marxism. But with the same fear that the 'economists' have they turn away from the 'distance' which lies between the objective and the subjective interests of the class whom they 'represent' ... Thus if the 'economists' do not lead the proletariat because they are dragged *behind it, i, the 'politicians' do not lead the proletariat because they themselves carry out its obligations.'*[13]

Hindsight makes Trotsky's warning about future dangers quite ironic:

'In the internal politics of the party these methods leads, *as we shall yet see*, to this: the party organisation is substituted for the party, the Central Committee is substituted for the party organisation, *and finally a 'dictator' is substituted for the Central Committee ...'* (emphasis added)[14]

It may be argued that neither Trotsky nor Luxemburg presented viable alternatives. Moreover in the case of Trotsky, he implicitly came to accept Leninist party principles in practice by joining the Bolshevik party. I would however suggest that it is reckless to dismiss these criticisms out of hand in the light of the tragic events we have become all too familiar with in the experience of socialist construction. Comrade Dialego, by implication, seems to suggest that all the revolutionaries who opposed Lenin were by virtue of their opposition, less committed to the revolution. As for his charge that Trotsky regarded political consciousness as 'a metaphysical property, which is always there', is yet another example of Comrade Dialego's zeal getting the better of his judgement.

TROTSKY AS A REVOLUTIONARY LEADER

How then does the Leon Trotsky who differs so fundamentally with Lenin find himself at Lenin's side in 1917? Comrade Dialego here again descends to irresponsible puerilities rather than engaging in serious analysis by suggesting that Trotsky dissembled his conversion to Bolshevism (p. 72).

Lenin in fact provides part of the answer. Criticising Trotsky's theory of 'Permanent Revolution' he wrote:

'Trotsky borrows from the Bolsheviks their call for decisive revolutionary struggle and the conquest of power by the proletariat, and from the Mensheviks, their repudiation of the role of the peasantry.'[15]

This assessment is repeated by A.S. Lunarcharsky in his semi-official collection of biographies, 'Revolutionary Silhouettes', published in the Soviet Union in 1922. In his essay on Trotsky, Lunarcharsky says:

'Of all the Mensheviks, Trotsky was then the closest to us (Bolsheviks) ...'[16]

And later:

'The fact that he was quite incapable of fitting into the ranks of the Mensheviks made them react to him as though he were a kind of social-democratic anarchist and his behaviour annoyed them greatly. *There was no question at that time of his total identification with the Bolsheviks.*'[17]

Lunarcharsky sums up his appraisal of Trotsky with the words:

'Trotsky's political career has been somewhat tortuous: he was neither a Menshevik nor a Bolshevik but sought the middle way before merging his brook in the Bolshevik river, and yet in fact *Trotsky has always been guided by the precise rules of revolutionary Marxism.*'[18]

This [is] a Trotsky very different from the portrait we have from the pen of Comrade Dialego!

At the outbreak of the First World War, though Trotsky did not join the Bolsheviks he was closely identified with the left wing of the Second International. Like Lenin Liebknecht, Luxemburg and others he was a defeatist and an advocate of transforming the imperialist into civil war. He was among those who tried to rally the left at Zimmerwald in 1915. His opposition to the war was such that he was driven from one

European capital after the other and was forced to find refuge in the then neutral USA.

The acid test however was October 1917 itself! During 1917 Trotsky, together with a large number of leading and rank and file socialists, who were committed to revolution adhered to the Party they all had come to realise was really serious about it, the Bolshevik Party. Trotsky's role in the events of that year is legendary and does not require repetition. Suffice it to remind readers that John Reed was so impressed that he dubbed Trotsky 'the greatest Jew since Christ'. While one may reject Reed's over-enthusiastic description, it is clearly indicative of how the chronicler of the October revolution had come to regard Trotsky.

This 'eleventh hour Bolshevism' was the outcome of Trotsky's belated recognition of his underestimation of the peasantry in 1906. The indefatigable energy with which he performed his tasks in the Petrograd Society, the Revolutionary Military Committee of the Party and, after 1918, in organising the Red Army as Commissar of War during the War of Intervention, is attested to by numerous historians. Hardly the actions of one who 'hindered the struggle for socialism' or was equivocal in his commitment to the socialist revolution! Judging from the accounts of contemporaries (including Lunarcharsky) there were times during this period when Trotsky was considered second only to Lenin in the leadership of the Soviet State. It is obviously untrue that he made no positive contribution towards the construction of socialism. Between 1917 and 1926 Trotsky held three senior ministerial posts in the revolutionary government, served on the Political Bureau of the Central Committee of the Bolshevik Party and on the leading organs of the Communist International.

Perhaps the best authority to turn to in assessing Trotsky during these days is Lenin himself. In his last letters Lenin assessed the leading figures in the Central Committee of the Bolshevik Party. One of these letters was republished in 'Umsebenzi' during 1988.

In the first and second portions of this letter Lenin is concerned with the possibility of a split in the party. He presciently warns of the tensions between Stalin and Trotsky.

'… I think relations between them make up the greater part of the danger of a split …'

He warns also against the powers Stalin had amassed in his office as General-Secretary. He is fulsome in his praise of Trotsky '… distinguished not only by outstanding ability. He is perhaps the most capable man in the present CC …' but equally does not play down his faults – 'excessive self assurance' and: 'pre-occupation with the purely administrative side of work.' He nonetheless describes these two – Trotsky and Stalin – as '… the two outstanding leaders of the present CC'. He recalls also the weakness displayed by Zinoviev and Kamenev during the October Revolution and in this context recalls also Trotsky's late adherence to Bolshevism. He obviously did not want any of these to be forgotten but warns against their being held against the individuals.

The third portion of the letter is the most revealing. Here Lenin specifically castigates Stalin as '… too rude …' and suggests that the CC find ways of removing him from his post. Significantly, Lenin says:

'This circumstance may appear to be a negligible detail. But I think that from the standpoint of safeguards against split and from the standpoint of what I wrote above about the relationship between Stalin and Trotsky it is not a detail, or it is a detail which can assume decisive importance.'[19]

It is evident from this letter that whatever else Lenin may have thought of the leadership of the party, he had come to the conclusion that Stalin constituted a danger to the stability of the party and its leadership and wanted him removed.

Lenin's negative view of Stalin was reinforced by a personal affront to Krupskaya. He concludes a letter to Stalin, dated 5th March 1923 with the words:

'I ask you, therefore, to think it over whether you are prepared to withdraw what you have said and to make apologies, or whether you prefer that relations between us should be broken off.'[20]

In contrast to this fraught relationship with the General-Secretary, from these letters, it appears Lenin had come to rely heavily on Trotsky to convey his thinking on important matters to the CC. On December 12th 1922, for example, he wrote to Trotsky:

> '... it is my request that at the forthcoming plenum you should undertake the defence of our common standpoint on the unquestionable need to maintain and consolidate the foreign trade monopoly.'

Later during the same month:

> 'I consider that we have quite reached agreement. I ask you to declare our solidarity at the plenum. I hope that our decision will be passed ...'

He also advised Stalin of the requests to Trotsky:

> 'I have also come to an arrangement with Trotsky to stand up for my views.'

On March 5th 1923, in yet another letter to Trotsky:

> 'It is my earnest request that you should undertake the defence of the Georgian case in the Party CC.'

It is apparent that while distancing himself from Stalin, Lenin was tilting in the direction of the other 'outstanding leader in the present CC'. Would a political leader of Lenin's calibre have placed so much confidence in a person approximating the image of Trotsky Comrade Dialego painted? I acknowledge it's possible, but find it somehow doubtful.

There is no doubt that even during the period before Lenin's death there were differences between Trotsky and Lenin in the councils of the CPSU. But to give the impression, as does Comrade Dialego, that Trotsky alone was periodically at loggerheads with Lenin is misleading if not mischievous. One may agree or disagree with Trotsky's views in these disputes, but what is incontrovertible is that in terms of the

CPSU's statutes and the traditions of the Bolshevik party, he had the untrammelled right to hold these views and to express them within the Party's structures and in its press. It is also clear that according to the Leninist norms, as practised under Lenin, no one, least of all a member of the Central Committee, was required to renounce sincerely held views merely because they were at variance with those of the majority. One may infer this from the manner in which Lenin treated Zinoviev and Kamenev after the October incident. Both were given posts in the revolutionary government and retained their party membership in spite of their actions. Bukharin and the 'Left Communists' of 1918 opposed Brest-Litovsk to the bitter end. They retained both the Party and government posts. Kollontai and the members of the 'Workers' Opposition' of 1922 were similarly treated. There is evidence too that during Lenin's leadership like-minded individuals were permitted to group together as a platform and to engage in political struggle within the party to advance their viewpoint. This was permissible so long as it did not jeopardise or undermine the capacity of the party to act in unity on matters that had been decided. There is no record of an 'opposition' being hounded out of the party by Lenin – let alone judicially murdered or assassinated!

Unless Comrade Dialego is of the view that sincerely held opinions should be suppressed or self-censored because they are minority views, I cannot see why he holds it against Trotsky (and any of the other oppositionists) that he would not relent in his opposition to policies he thought ill-advised.

Comrade Dialego had an opportunity to add to our understanding of an important historical figure. Instead he has chosen to perpetuate the demonization of Leon Trotsky. He had in fact merely rehashed the old calumnies from the 1930s, slightly refurbished to take account of the new political climate – hence his rather mealy-mouthed admission that most people no longer believe that Trotsky was a fascist agent.

After reading Comrade Dialego's article I formed the impression of him as a political Peter, plugging the leaks in the ideological dykes occasioned by glasnost, with the puny fingers of his dogmatism. Glasnost is gradually beginning to restore the norms of democratic discussion and debate that had been at the heart of the Bolshevik Party's practice before being so brutally supressed by Stalin and his henchmen. That some, who had become accustomed to the rigid, intellectually stultifying practices of Stalinism feel discomfort is perhaps unavoidable. But I would suggest that the experience of socialist revolution and construction will prove worthless to humanity unless socialists have the moral courage to face up squarely to the errors, mishaps and crimes that have been committed during their course. This does not, and never has, implied rejection of socialism or the need to struggle for it. Trotsky, Bukharin, Zinoviev, Rykov, Kamenev and all the other Soviet Communists who fought and struggled for the establishment of the first workers' state but opposed Stalin and his policies with the sincere conviction that they were wrong, have for too long been victims of slander and the most criminal libels. Comrade Dialego dishonours the cause of socialism by continuing this shameful practice. I would make so bold as to say it is the attitudes reflected in his article that have for the past forty years 'hindered rather than helped the struggle for socialism.'

I do not call into question Comrade Dialego's right to hold a negative view of Trotsky, Bukharin, or for that matter, Gorbachev or any other Soviet leader. I would however suggest that it is irrational to cling to a point of view where there is overwhelming evidence that it is not well-grounded in facts.

In the Year of Mass Action for Peoples Power,
Mahlubi Nkomonde.
Lusaka, Zambia. March 1989.

ENDNOTES

1 Hobsbawn. E.J. 'Revolutionaries'. London. 1973. pp. 190–120.
2 Lenin, V.I. 'Two Tactics of Social Democracy in the Democratic Revolution.' In Selected Works. Vol. 1. Moscow. 1954.
3 Lenin, V.I. 'Two Tactics'.
4 Trotsky, L.D. 'Results on Prospects' (published in Daniels, R.V. (ed) 'A Documentary History of Communism'. London. 1987. p. 30–32.)
5 Marx, Karl. 'Address to the Central Committee of the Communist League. March 1850.' In Marx. 'The Revolutions of 1848.' London 1973. pp. 321.
6 Lenin. V.I. 'Two Tactics'.

7   Trotsky, L.D. 'Results and Prospects.'

8   Trotsky, L.D. 'Results and Prospects.'

9   Lenin, V.I. Collected Works. Volume 9. Moscow. 1964. pp. 236–7.

10 Luxemburg, Rosa. 'Organisational Problems of Russian Social Democracy'.
    In Luxemburg, Rosa. 'The Russian Revolution and Leninism or Marxism'.
    Ann Arbor. 1962. pp. 81–108.

11 Luxemburg, Rosa. 'Organisational Problems'.

12 Luxemburg, Rosa. 'Organisational Problems'.

13 Trotsky, L.D. 'Our Political Tasks'. In Daniels R.V. (ed) Op. Cit. pp. 20–22.

14 Trotsky, L.D. 'Our Political Tasks'.

15 Lenin, V.I. Collected Works,. Volume 21. Moscow 1964. p. 419.

16 Lunarcharsky, A.V. 'Revolutionary Silhouettes'. London 1967. pp. 59–73.

17 Lunarcharsky, A.V. 'Revolutionary Silhouettes'.

18 Lunarcharsky, A.V. 'Revolutionary Silhouettes'.

19 Lenin, V.I. Collected Works. Volume 36. Moscow. 1966. pp. 595–597.

20 Lenin, V.I. Collected Works. Volume 44.

NINE

Probably the best known, and most cited, of all Jordan's writings. It appeared first in Lusaka in February 1990 (with the subtitle 'A Critical Review of Joe Slovo's 'Has Socialism Failed?''); it was published in a slightly amended form in Transformation six months later, and subsequently reprinted in several other outlets. It was (writes Alan Wieder, Slovo's biographer) 'by far the most thoughtful critique' of Slovo's essay. Jordan welcomed Slovo's candour and courage in criticising socialist countries and communist parties, but argued that Slovo had only begun rather than concluded a journey. Jordan 'expanded Joe's thesis historically, politically, and sociologically', Wieder notes, deepening an understanding of the failures of state socialism. Jordan is also far more critical of the SACP than Slovo could be, accusing it of having a political culture that nurtured 'a spirit of intolerance, petty intellectual thuggery and political dissembling'.

The Crisis of Conscience in the SACP

In *Transformation*, 11 (1990), pp. 75–89.

'Has Socialism Failed?' is the intriguing title Comrade Joe Slovo has given to a discussion pamphlet published under the imprint of 'Umsebenzi', the quarterly newsletter of the SACP. The reader is advised at the outset that these are Slovo's individual views, and not those of the SACP. While this is helpful, it introduces a note of uncertainty regarding the pamphlet's authority.

The pamphlet itself is divided into six parts, the first five being an examination of the experience of the 'socialist countries', and the last, a look at the SACP itself.

Most refreshing is the candour and honesty with which many of the problems of 'existing socialism' are examined. Indeed, a few years ago no one in the SACP would have dared to cast such a critical light on the socialist countries. 'Anti-Soviet,' 'anti-Communist,' or 'anti- Party' were the dismissive epithets reserved for those who did. We can but hope that the publication of this pamphlet spells the end of such practices.

It is clear too that much of the heart-searching that persuaded Slovo to put pen to paper was occasioned by the harrowing events of the past twelve months, which culminated in the Roumanian masses, in scenes reminiscent of the storming of the Winter Palace in October 1917, storming the headquarters of the Communist Party of Roumania. It beggars the term 'ironic' that scenarios many of us had imagined would be played out at the end of bourgeois rule in historical fact rang down the curtain on a 'Communist' dictatorship!

We may expect that, just as in 1956 and 1968, there will flow from many pens the essays of disillusionment and despair written by ex-Communists who have recently discovered the 'sterling' qualities of late capitalism.

Comrade Joe Slovo remains a Communist, convinced that the future of humankind lies in the socialist development of society and the social ownership of property. He therefore feels compelled to explain what could have gone so terribly wrong as to bring about the events we witnessed on December 22nd and 23rd 1989.

MISSING QUESTIONS AND ANSWERS

I read and re-read Comrade Slovo's pamphlet in the hope of finding such an explanation. It proved well-nigh impossible to discover a coherent account of what had gone wrong. Reducing the arguments advanced in his pamphlet to their barest minimum we are left with a handful of causes, which however beg, rather than answer, a number of questions.

Slovo points to the economic backwardness of a war-weary Russia, forced to build socialism in one country because the European revolutions it had hoped for failed to materialise. He also attributes a degree of blame to the necessities imposed upon the Bolsheviks by the intervention of the capitalist powers in 1918. He discerns too a rather mechanical dismissal of the virtues of bourgeois democracy by Lenin in his 'The State and the Revolution.' He detects also some responsibility attaching to the non-existence of 'democratic traditions' in Tsarist Russia. Lastly, he faults all the ruling Communist Parties for institutionalising their role as 'vanguard' through law rather than on the basis of popular endorsement by the working class and the majority of society.

The combination of these factors, acting upon each other and inter-penetrating, by Slovo's account, led to the one party dictatorship over the proletariat and society. To sum up, he offers one major objective factor (economic backwardness in the context of war-weariness coupled with political isolation) plus four subjective factors.

WHAT OF DEMOCRATIC TRADITIONS?

Slovo argues that the lack of a democratic tradition in Tsarist Russia contributed to the absence of democracy after the revolution. This implies that in other countries of Europe bourgeois democracy had been achieved and provided traditions that foster democracy.

It is one of the perennial weaknesses of South African Communist theorists that they appear to have accepted as gospel the much touted lie that capitalist societies are either basically democratic, or require democratic institutions, or thrive best within a democratic political order. The experience of both the 19th and, more so, that of the 20th century, demonstrate that this is untrue.

This was equally so in the case of the leading capitalist powers on the eve of the First World War!

In 1914 the state of the art with regard to democratic institutions among the capitalist powers was as follows:

Britain was a constitutional monarchy in which universal male suffrage was a mere 39 years old. The supremacy of Parliament had only recently been established in 1911, at the instance of the Asquith government that passed legislation ending the Royal prerogative to veto Acts of Parliament.

Female suffrage was still some years away.

France was the classic bourgeois democracy in which the universal male suffrage was well-established since the Second Empire (1851). French women still battled for the vote.

Germany and Austria: the monarchs of the two German states were indeed Emperors. Both possessed inordinate powers (which a British monarch last enjoyed in 1688!) vis-à-vis their parliaments. Yet a balance of power, arrived at through compromise, gave parliament power over fiscal policy. The franchise was restricted to men only.

Japan was still a classic oriental despotism, though much reformed by the ruling Meiji dynasty. The Japanese Diet, very much like the Tsarist Duma,possessed little real power in relation to the crown.

The United States was the closest thing to a white-male-capitalist republic,in which people of colour were regularly lynched for daring to express the wish to vote.

Most other capitalist nations were either constitutional monarchies (like Sweden, Netherlands, Belgium, Italy), clerical authoritarian states (as in the case of Portugal, Spain, Greece and Turkey) or dominions (as were Canada, Australia, New Zealand, South Africa.)

On the face of it, Tsarist Russia was not as exceptional as Slovo would have us believe. In 1914, democratic traditions were extremely thin on the ground, existing more in the rhetoric of politicians' war speeches than in substance.

To give Slovo the benefit of the doubt, he is perhaps referring to the institutions of 'liberal constitutionalism.' In this case he might be able to make out a strong case for France, Britain and some of the smaller constitutional monarchies of Europe. However, I would urge him against too hasty a judgment even in that respect.

However, a different kind of democratic tradition existed in all the countries referred to. This democratic tradition was part of a counter-hegemonic popular politics that had evolved among the middle classes, the urban working people and (especially in France and the United States) among small farmers, in the wake of the French Revolution. The ruling classes were compelled to respond to this, especially in their efforts to win support for the First World War – an act of cynical manipulation – but one which nonetheless institutionalised democratic practices.

Tsarist Russia was no exception to this pattern. Since the Decembrist Rising of 1825, radical intellectuals had disseminated the ideas of the French Revolution and subsequent revolutionary thought among the popular classes. The vibrancy of these popular traditions is evidenced in both the practice of the Soviets (i. e. the workers and peasants councils of 1905 and 1917) in the militias and neighbourhood committees that arose during the course of the 1917 revolution.

In this respect, I would say, Slovo has confused the democratic traditions among the people with the dominant ideology in the leading capitalist states. What needs to be explained is how and why the healthy democratic currents in the radical Russian political culture were subverted and finally extinguished.

Slovo acknowledges that there were terrible abuses of political, civil and human rights in all the countries of the socialist bloc. He admits also that during the days of the Communist International (Comintern) – and perhaps even after – the interests of other Parties and peoples were often subordinated to the perceived interests of the Soviet Union. He does not dispute the mounting evidence of corruption and moral degeneration among the CP leaders in many of these countries – leading to the scandalous charges of graft, money-laundering and skimming off the top!

He has identified the symptoms of the illness but not its basic causes. He has, perhaps, also provided us with evidence that in a particular economic and social climate the viruses that give rise to the illness may thrive and prove lethal, but we remain with the illness itself undiagnosed.

Marxism prides itself in its ability to uncover the reality that lies hidden behind appearances. Marxists therefore cannot be content with expressions of shock, horror and condemnation. It is our task to explain what has led to the atrocities we condemn! This is the missing element in Slovo's otherwise very useful pamphlet.

A FORGOTTEN TRADITION

Among the Marxist-Leninists parties that once constituted the world Communist movement, attempts to come to grips with the problems of socialist construction are extremely rare and have for decades been muted if not actively suppressed. This is as true of the South African CP (perhaps more so) as it is of the Communist Parties that have achieved power and the others.

The exceptions to this pattern were the Chinese Communist Party (CCP), in the immediate aftermath of the uprisings in Poland and Hungary during 1956; and the Italian Communist Party (CPI), which began to define a new identity for itself, after the death of Palmiro Togliatti in 1964.

Previous to this, the only other attempts were undertaken in the ranks of the Communist Party of the Soviet Union (CPSU) itself, by the two oppositions associated with Trotsky-Zinoviev and Bukharin respectively. This tradition has been almost totally suppressed in the Communist movement, and despite the political rehabilitation of Bukharin and the judicial rehabilitation of Trotsky, Zinoviev and the other Left oppositionists, is still largely forgotten.

Latterday Marxist oppositionists have been branded as 'counter-revolutionaries', 'spies' and 'provocateurs' by the Communist Parties, in much the same way as their predecessors (Trotsky, Zinoviev, Bukharin, etc) were so labeled in the frame-up trials of the 1930s. Their works have consequently been ignored by Communists, only to be taken up by the real counter-revolutionaries, spies and provocateurs, as sticks with which to beat the left in general.

It is striking that the Soviet press, which has in recent years elevated Bukharin to the status of a Bolshevik martyr, prints little of his analysis of Soviet society during the 1930s! The concept 'the Dictatorship of the proletariat,' which owes more to French revolutionary practice than to Marx and Engels, may indeed have to bear some blame for the horrors perpetrated in its name. It was precisely this that the CCP attempted to examine in 1957 in a short pamphlet titled 'On theHistorical Experience of the Dictatorship of the Proletariat.' It is an index of the extremely unhealthy climate that prevailed in the Communist movement at the time (which was exacerbated during the Sino-Soviet dispute) that this remarkable piece of writing is virtually unknown except among specialists.

In analyzing the previous forty years (1917 to 1957) the Chinese Communists drew analogies between the socialist revolution and the bourgeois-democratic revolution. They correctly assert that for the first 100 years of its existence bourgeois democracy was in fact precisely that – democracy for the bourgeoisie – as only property-owners had a franchise. In addition, at that very moment (1957) the leading bourgeois democracy still excluded African-Americans from the franchise on racist grounds. The pamphlet went on to argue, that while the proletarian dictatorship was imperfect and deformed in many ways, most of these distortions were attributable to the security considerations imposed by capitalist encirclement and active hostility. Its basic character, however, was sound because of its commitment to the creation of a classless society. In what was then an amazing departure from conventional orthodoxies, the CCP argued that 'the dictatorship of the proletariat' had already given rise to a variety of institutional forms. Among these it enumerated the

Yugoslav system of workers' councils, the Chinese 'Peoples' Democratic Dictatorship', etc. This was among the first official CP documents to suggest that the Soviet model was not universally applicable!

The Italian Communists in many respects followed a line of argument similar to the Chinese until the mid-1980s, when Enrico Berlinguer castigated the Soviet model as a failure which should be abandoned. During the 1970s a whole range of other parties also took the plunge, but most of their writing was unoriginal, repeating the formulations of others.

The class character of the Soviet model (which was emulated in most socialist countries) has been precisely the central focus among those Marxists who take their inspiration from the Bolshevik oppositionists and other East European critics of Stalinism. In their polemics against Stalin and Stalinism both Trotsky and Bukharin make reference to the class character of Soviet society at the time. The same is true of the Yugoslav oppositionist, Milovan Djilas in his 'The New Class'; Karol Modzelewski and Jacek Kuron, two Polish left oppositionists from the 1960s also point out the class roots of the degeneration of the Socialist countries, as does Rudolph Bahro, the most recent left critic of Stalinism from inside a ruling Communist Party , in his 'The Alternative in Eastern Europe.'

While Slovo recognises that the socialist countries degenerated into police states, with their administrative and repressive organs possessed of inordinate powers, he never seems to broach the rather obvious question: What gave rise to the need for such practices? Was it not to contain and suppress a fundamentally explosive contradiction in these societies that the ruling partiesconstructed such formidable armouries of police powers?

ARE CASTE AND CLASS USEFUL CONCEPTS?

The most famous critic of Stalinism was doubtlessly Leon Trotsky. Setting aside for a moment our opinion of him and his political career, we can nonetheless agree that, employing the method of historical materialism, he provided one of the most original critiques of the Soviet system. It was Trotsky's contention that the backwardness of Russia, the depredations of the War of Intervention, followed by the famine, and the failure of the European revolution conspired to so isolate the young Soviet republic that it was compelled to fall back on its own meagre resources in order to survive. The price exacted was that a bureaucratic caste, drawn from the working class leadership itself, reinforced by the NEP-men and other non-working class strata, was permitted to usurp power from the proletariat, because the proletariat required their expertise and skill to maintain the state. This caste, having developed from within the working class and ensconced in its party, employed the language of socialism and was compelled to defend the gains of the October Revolution (on which its very existence depended) was nonetheless a parasitic layer battening on the surplus produced by the working class. According to this account, a relationship that was historically unprecedented thus developed – it was not exploitative in the true sense, since the bureaucracy did not own the means of production; yet it was exploitative in the sense that the bureaucracy was above the class of direct producers and consumed the surplus they produced. According to Trotsky, the dictatorship of Stalin was the political expression of this fraught internal contradiction.

While Bukharin would have parted company with Trotsky as regards his conclusions, he nonetheless sought to employ the same method, historical materialism, to explain the problems of Soviet society. Bukharin stressed the social character of the alliance between the proletariat and the peasantry, which undergirded Soviet power. According to him, the problems arose as a result of the abandonment of the NEP in favour of the five year plans. All these, Bukharin charged, were premised on the accumulation of capital at the expense of the peasantry and were bound to rupture the alliance. Having ruptured the worker-peasant alliance, the Soviet state lost the support of the vast majority of the population (the peasants) and was consequently tempted to act no differently than the Tsarist state before it – in a dictatorial manner. Bukharin and Trotsky concurred that Stalin had become the leader of this omnipotent state and epitomised its cruelty and callousness.

Most subsequent oppositional writings, with the exception of the Chinese and Italians, derive from these two main sources or at any rate regard these as their baseline. Milovan Djilas, for example, contended that the process of socialist construction had brought into being a 'new class,' unknown to the Marxist classics and to the experience of bourgeois sociology. This new class's power derived from its control (rather than ownership) of the means of production and its capacity to command the labour power of others, in much the same way as the high priests of Sumeria had commanded the labour of their fellows. The locus of this 'new class,' Djilas contended, was the leadership of the Communist Party.

The two Poles, Modzelewski and Kuron, recapitulate the essence of Trotsky's argument except that they insist on greater freedom for small property-owners and private enterprise in the tradition of Bukharin. They agree that this deep-seated cleavage is potentially explosive and could lead to loss of power by the bureaucracy/ new class/ Stalinist state. As a result, the state acts in a paranoid fashion, fearful of any criticism or dissenting voices, irrespective of the intent of the critics. The one party state, based on the false claim that only one party can correctly interpret the interests of the proletariat, enhanced the authoritarianism of the system by pre-emptively silencing oppositional voices.

Rudolph Bahro, a former member of the Socialist Unity Party (SED) of the GDR, who had held a number of responsible posts under both Walter Ulbricht and Erich Honecker, while acknowledging an intellectual debt to Trotsky, holds that Stalinism was inevitable in the context of a backward Russia that still awaited the capitalist development of the productive forces. 'Despotic industrialization' was the necessary outcome of the drive to transform an agrarian into an urban industrial society. Stalinism, by his account, had outlived its historically necessary role once such an industrial base had been established. However, because the bureaucracy that had been created to manage this earlier phase of economic development had acquired a vested interest in power, it resisted change to the point of violence, as in Czechoslovakia in 1968.

This bureaucracy, Bahro argued, behaved like a class in that it is able to reproduce itself, through easier access to better education; favoured treatment for its members and their families; special status in all spheres of public life.

These explanations apart, it is true that Stalin's policies were actually supported by the overwhelming majority of Soviet Communists during the 1920s and '30s. Both the Trotskyists and the Bukharinists were outvoted in the Party congresses. It was precisely because he had such support that Stalin found it possible to perpetrate the abuses of the late 1930s and 1940s.

The only anti-Stalinist who acknowledges and has sought to explain the pro-Stalin consensus in the CPSU is Isaac Deutscher, who asserts that by a skilful combination of Marxist rhetoric and an appeal to atavistic Russian nationalism, Stalin was able to weld together an alliance among the party apparatus and the basically conservative bureaucracy at the expense of the CPSU's revolutionary democratic traditions.

Whether one agrees with it or not, this oppositional intellectual tradition must be taken into account by a Marxist who wishes to understand the 'socialist countries'.

The Implications of Class

The question we have to pose is: could a new class of bureaucrats, responsible for the smooth functioning of the state, who have however, acquired an identity and interests apart from the rest of society, possibly have come into existence?

Historical materialism teaches that the basis of class lies in the social productive relations, and not in the real or apparent relative affluence of individuals. To answer this question leads us straight back to the classical Marxian conception of the dictatorship of the proletariat, which Frederick Engels said he discerned in the institutions of the Paris Commune of 1871.

Apart from democratising the state, the Paris Commune attempted to create a legislature and administration that would remain close to the working people. This was institutionalised in the rule that no law-maker or civil servant shall earn a salary higher than that of a skilled workman:

This was intended, in the first instance, to discourage those who saw government service as a means of self-enrichment; and to contain the tendency for legislators to become alienated from their constituencies. A second provision, linked to the first, subjected all legislators to immediate recall by the electors, thus imposing on them greater accountability to the voters.

One would be hard put to find a single socialist country that has adopted these very sound principles as the basis of government. If the evidence of the recent events is to be believed, it seems clear that they were honoured in blatant breach. The elite's hunting lodges, the exclusive suburbs and ornate palaces of the 'proletarian dictators' indicate gross violations of the principles handed down from the Paris Commune. If one were to judge by the evidence of this alone one could indeed be persuaded that we had witnessed the emergence of a new class.

What then are and were the social productive relations in the existing socialisms?

It is clear that a number of modes of production existed side by side in the socialist countries and that among them one could point to a variety of social productive relations. While this is true, we can also refer to a dominant mode, based on state-owned property. The Stalin model, whose roots lie in the specifics of Soviet history, shall for purposes of this paper serve as the universal model.

The Stalin model had its origins in the defeat of the left and right oppositions to Stalin during the 1920s and '30s. It involved a dramatic reversal of all the policies pursued during the NEP and the near total etatization of the economy. The task of the state, as understood by the pro-Stalin majority in the CPSU, was to set in motion the processes of primitive socialist accumulation. The techniques employed to achieve this were not altogether different from those pioneered during the early phases of capitalism. Coercion and extra-legal methods became the order of the day.

These in turn created their own dynamic. The egalitarian ethos, which had been the hallmark of the Communists during the period of War Communism, was replaced by a strongly anti-egalitarian ethic, decreed from the topmost leadership of the CPSU. The rationale for these steps was elementary – there was no other way of enforcing work discipline other than the methods that had served capital so well?

Christian Rakovsky, a Bulgarian by birth but a Bolshevik by persuasion, explained the transformation that occurred in the following terms: 'When a class seizes power, a certain part of this class is transformed into agents of the power itself. In this way the bureaucracy arises.'

Rakovsky continues:

'... that part of those functions which formerly the whole party or the whole class itself carried out has now shifted to the power, i.e., to a certain number of people from this party, from this class.'

The impact of the war and the famine had in fact drastically transformed the Bolshevik Party since October 1917. At the end of the Civil War it had become a party of committeemen, professional revolutionaries, administrators and state functionaries rather than a party of working class militants rooted in their factories and in their neighbourhoods. It was less and less the working class, but the committeemen, the cadres and functionaries who served in these capacities, who framed policy. The extent to which this was true is evident from the census of party membership published by the Central Control Commission of the CPSU in 1927:

- Workers engaged in industry and transport   430, 000
- Agricultural workers   15, 700
- Peasants   151, 500
- Government officials of peasant origins   151, 500
- Other government officials   462, 000

The disproportionate representation of state officials (one and a half times the number of shop-floor workers) was perhaps unavoidable in light of the demands of the moment, but it has to be admitted that it changed very fundamentally the character of the CPSU. It was these realities that persuaded Rakovsky that:

'Neither the working class nor the party is physically or morally what it was ten years ago. I think I do not exaggerate when I say that the party member of 1917 would hardly recognise himself in the person of the party member of 1928...'

Such were the imperatives imposed by the rhythms of primitive socialist accumulation!

However, once we posit the category 'class' we are by implication also positing its corollary, 'conflict.' I am still not persuaded that a social class of owners and controllers of the decisive sectors of the means of production existed in the Soviet Union and other socialist countries. which leads in the direction of an examination of the nature and character of this conflict.

Primitive Socialist Accumulation.

As early as 1921, the 'Workers Opposition,' a faction within the CPSU led by Alexandra Kollontai, complained bitterly about the introduction of one person management in all the factories.

The relegation of the Committees for Workers' Control at factory and plant level, though important for efficiency, stripped the working class of a most fundamental conquest of the October revolution – the power to determine the character and rhythms of the labour process. The Soviets (the democratically created councils of workers, soldiers and peasants) too saw their powers diminished by appointments made by the apparatus. The Bolsheviks harvested the bitter fruits of these developments when the sailors of the Kronstadt garrison, known from the days of October and throughout the War of Intervention for their heroism and revolutionary zeal, mutinied in March 1921, denouncing the Soviet government as a new tyranny.

> '... The most hateful and criminal thing which the Communists have created is moral servitude: they laid their hands even on the inner life of the toilers and compelled them to think only in the Communist way' declared the Temporary Revolutionary Committee of Kronstadt.
>
> 'With the aid of militarized trade unions they have bound the workers to their benches, and have made labour not into a joy but into a new slavery.'

In both his seminal works, 'From NEP to Socialism' and 'The New Economics,' written during the 1920s, the left oppositionist, Eugene Preobrazhenskymakes clear that in the absence of massive capital inflows from advanced countries, the Soviet Union would have no option but to construct its industrial base at the expense of the peasantry. It was his contention also that the proletariat, at the lathe and the bench, would have to submit itself to the most rigorous work discipline in order to construct an industrial society at breakneck speed.

By 1934, Lazar Kaganovich, one of Stalin's leading henchmen, could remark that 'the earth should tremble when the director is entering the factory.' This new style 'socialist' director was a petty tyrant on his own patch. All other structures in the factory – such as the trade union – existed not to obstruct or contain his power, but rather to assist it in realizing its objectives.

The demands of constructing an industrial society in conditions of economic backwardness in a huge territory, surrounded by extremely hostile enemies, placed enormous strains on the political institutions of the young Soviet republic. The Bolsheviks had never been a mass party, even of the working class, before or after the October Revolution. The party had indeed won the confidence and support of millions of workers and soldiers. The land reforms, taken over holus-bolus from the programme of the Social Revolutionaries (SRs), had also earned them support among the peasants. The nationalities programme gained them the confidence of the Asiatic peoples formerly oppressed by Tsarism, enabling the Bolsheviks to hold the line against the White Guards and their foreign allies for three solid years of war.

It was only at the end of that war that one can properly say the Bolsheviks began to govern.

Though they had fought to defend the conquests of the revolution – especially land – the peasants in fact had not become solid supporters of the Bolshevik party. The illegalisation of the SRs and the other right-wing socialist parties during the war did not assist matters either. The dispersal of the urban proletariat, as factories ground to a halt and mass starvation threatened the cities, meant that the Bolsheviks also lost their sheet anchor in the working class. Kronstadt was an indication that even among its most stalwart supporters the Communist government's base was no longer secure.

Taking fright at these developments, the Tenth Party Congress of the CPSU, in March 1921, instituted the most fateful reforms of the party statutes, outlawing factions. The sixth Thesis of the resolution on Party

Unity explicitly prescribed expulsion for anyone who did not observe this new rule. More fateful were the 'Resolutions on the Syndicalist and Anarchist Deviation in Our Party', adopted by the same congress. It was these resolutions that, for the first time in the history of the Communist movement, designated a 'deviation' as treason to the working class. The relevant section, which deserves to be quoted in full, stated:

> 'Hence, the views of the 'workers opposition' and of like-minded elements are not only wrong in theory, but in practice are an expression of petty bourgeois anarchist wavering, in practice weaken the consistency of the leading line of the Communist Party, and in practice help the class enemies of the proletarian revolution.'

The result of these reforms was the reversal of long-standing Bolshevik practice, which had permitted like-minded members of the party to combine and present a common platform to the party for debate and resolution. Such a debate, on 'The Trade Union Question,' had just been concluded a few weeks before the Tenth Party congress. During the course of the debate, 'Pravda', the CPSU's official organ, had published a series of articles representing differing viewpoints from among the CPSU leadership. At least three public debates had been held in Moscow and Leningrad, at which the various viewpoints were aired before an audience of party militants and the public.

Many who voted for the resolutions of the Tenth Party congress and subsequently became oppositionists had those fateful words flung into their faces with a vengeance by the torturers and bully boys of the NKVD (Soviet Intelligence and Security, renamed the KGB in subsequent years)! But while wiser counsels prevailed in the Politburo of the CPSU no party member needed to fear for his/her safety. The Congress resolved '... to wage an unswerving and systematic ideological struggle against these ideas;... 'At that point, 1921, the struggle was aimed at the incorrect ideas – the sin, so to speak, but not the sinner. However, the malignancy had been planted in the body of the party and all it required was a new environment, provided by the death of Lenin, for it to become dangerous. Just as Zinoviev and Trotsky supported the outlawing of the ideas of the 'Workers Opposition' in 1921, so too in 1927 Bukharin supported the outlawing of those of the 'Left Opposition.' In 1933, others supported the outlawing of the views of the 'Right Opposition'. Each of these successive layers prepared the ground for their own demise by compromising the intellectual climate in the party and subverting its traditions of debate and ideological contestation. Thus, once the CPSU succumbed to the imperatives of primitive socialist accumulation there was no mechanism available to break out of the logic of this grim cycle. Once caught on this demonic treadmill, the party membership either kept going or went under.

The regime this system imposed in the factories, plants and fields was as authoritarian as it was rigid. The concept 'alienation,' employed by the young Marx to describe the plight of the worker in capitalist industry, has been borrowed in this instance by Slovo, to explain the profound scepticism (if not cynicism) of the Soviet workers about their employers 'the socialist' state.

In the capitalist countries the attitude of the workers is determined by their age-old recognition that no matter how much their immediate conditions might improve, the relationship with their employers remains exploitative.

There appears to have been a similar feeling in the Soviet Union, fuelled no doubt also by the regime of lies and falsehood that the logic of monolithism persuaded the CPSU leadership to embrace. If deviation equals the ideology of the class enemy, was it not logical to conclude that the bearer of that ideology was also the class enemy?

Thus did the wheel come full circle – since the Party felt it could no longer rely on the working class, it fell back on its own resources and instituted a system of control essentially no different from that of the capitalists. But, having chosen that option, it left itself no means to reconquer working class confidence and, though ruling in that class's name, both it and the working class knew that this was a lie, eroding further the working class's confidence in the Party.

In a heart-rending reflection on his past, Rudolph Bahro said inter alia: 'You'll find it difficult to imagine how proud we were then, I and countless other young comrades, to wear this party badge with the intertwined hands set against the red flag in the background.

And now I ask myself and I ask all those young comrades from those thirty years: How has it come about that today we are ashamed to pin on this badge? The essence of the matter is that we learned quite gradually to be ashamed of the party to which we belong, this party which enjoys the notorious distrust of the people, which holds people in political tutelage day in and day out, and which still feels obliged to lie about the most ridiculous trivialities.'

Rulers bereft of the confidence of the ruled lack legitimacy. In that respect the Communist Parties, not socialism, have indeed failed!

INEVITABILITY, NECESSITY AND ACCIDENT

The question does arise: was it inevitable, given the complex of circumstances and the historical legacy of Tsarist Russia, that the first socialist state should evolve in this direction? Related to this question is a second, did Stalinism and its horrors flow logically from Leninism and Marxist theory?

Throughout this paper I have sought to demonstrate that the Soviet leadership faced a range of alternatives at all the crucial turning points of early its history. Inevitability is, therefore, not part of the question. I am persuaded that a number of circumstances – among which we cannot exclude personality – conspired to influence their choices in particular directions. Having chosen those specific options, the Soviet leadership by that action, renounced others.

Rather than inevitability, what we are dealing with is necessity. This implies an element of choice, but not unlimited choice, for the alternatives themselves were structured by previous choices and inherited circumstances. To speak with the Karl Marx of 'The Eighteenth Brumaire of Louis Bonaparte':

'Men make their own history, but they do not make it as they please; they do not make it under circumstances chosen by themselves, but under circumstances directly encountered, given and transmitted from the past.'

Necessity, Marx tells us, plays itself out in the shape of accidents. In this regard one may say that it was an accident that Lenin died at a moment when his leadership qualities might have prevented the tensions he detected within the CPSU from spilling over into splits. Equally, it may be counted as an accident that the man who became General Secretary of the CPSU was a ruthless, de-frocked, Georgian priest. Yet another accident was the murder of Kirov immediately after the 1935 'Congress of Victors.' But it was all these accidents that conspired with given circumstances and those created by the CPSU's own choices, to place inordinate powers in the hands of Stalin and his henchmen. It is this uncanny synchronization of chance and causality that constitutes necessity.

Restoring Confidence in Socialism and the Communist Movement.

If Comrade Slovo's pamphlet (and remember, it does not necessarily reflect the SACP's views!) is to serve any useful purpose it must at the very least assist Communists in coming to terms with the history of their movement. This requires that they begin to settle accounts with the oppositionists, left and right, who stood up, very courageously, against the degradation of the ideals of communism.

South African Communists would do well to turn to the works of the anti-Stalinist Marxists and Communists to rediscover the true meaning of this vision which has, over centuries, persuaded thousands of militants to lay down their lives; which has inspired thousands with the courage to storm the citadels of power even when the odds appeared insuperable; which moved great artists to create magnificent works. The South African Communist Party owes it to itself and to the cause it espouses that it boldly grasp this nettle! One cannot lightly accept at face value Comrade Joe Slovos's protestations about the SACP's non-Stalinist credentials. Firstly, there is too much evidence to the contrary. Any regular reader of the SACP's publications can point to a consistent pattern of praise and support for every violation of freedom perpetrated by the Soviet leadership, both before and after the death of Stalin*. It is all too easy in the context of Soviet criticisms of this past for Comrade Slovo to now boldly come forward. Secondly, the political culture nurtured by the SACP's leadership over the years has produced a spirit of intolerance, intellectual pettiness and political dissembling[1] among its membership which regularly emerges in the pages of the Party's journals. If we are to be persuaded that the Party has indeed embraced the spirit of honesty and openness, expected of Marxists, it has an obligation to demonstrate this by a number of visible measures.

As a token of the SACP's commitment to a new path and political practice, Comrade Slovo's pamphlet could serve as the opening sally in a dialogue among South African socialists – including every persuasion - to re-examine the meaning of socialism and the implications of its distortion in the socialist countries. I submit that it is only by an unsparing interrogation of this past that we can hope to salvage something from the tragedy of existing socialism.

---

1 By way of explanation of this past it has been suggested that these were necessities imposed by diplomatic considerations. I insist that after the dissolution of the Comintern there was no requirement that any CP blindly support the crimes of Stalin or his successors. Silence was an option that would have given no offence but at least would not have compromised the SACP's moral integrity.

TEN

This is another thoughtful piece, based on an impressive array of sources. It was delivered to a conference in Zimbabwe in 1990. The first half provides a condensed history of the foreign policy of the Soviet Union and its application to South Africa of Lenin's 'Theses on the national and colonial question'. The second half analyses, and illuminates, the New Thinking on foreign policy under the Gorbachev leadership. Its cardinal aim was to create a new framework for international relations, and this hastened Soviet enthusiasm for settling regional disputes (such as the war in Angola). Jordan distinguishes between 'globalists', 'regionalists' and 'internationalists' within perestroika's New Thinking and considers the implications of these for a negotiated settlement in South Africa.

The Southern African Policy
of the Soviet Union

with s pecific reference to South Africa

1. For purposes of scientific analysis the term 'superpowers' is not very helpful, as it does not assist our understanding of the fundamental issues separating these powers nor does it offer any insight into the specifics of their internal structure, which determines their respective roles as actors on the world stage. Despite these strictures, for purposes of these notes, I shall conform to the terms our conference organisers have chosen.

2. Soviet Foreign Policy: The foreign policy of the USSR is in large measure determined by the circumstances under which the Soviet Union, as a nation state came into existence during the 1920s. The First World War (1914–18) had a devastating impact on the moribund Russian Empire resulting in revolution.

   That the revolution broke out in Europe's least developed country demonstrated that the working classes of the most advanced capitalist countries had rejected revolutionary politics. As early as 1858 Friedrich Engels had drawn attention to the 'embourgeoisement' of the proletariat, especially that of Britain. He had suggested that as long as the proletariat is not ready to make revolution in its own behalf, the majority of the class would regard the existing bourgeois order as the only possible one. Within it they would constitute themselves as the 'tail of the capitalist class, its extreme left wing.'[1] This planted the seed of the notion that only enduring economic tension would sustain the class consciousness of the proletariat as the negation of capital. Periods of relative stability, it was argued, would result in the working classes falling under the ideological influence of the bourgeoisie. 'Embourgeoisment' entailed the working class leadership, pursuing its immediate economic interests, shelving the decisive historical interests of the class, to pursue palpable immediate and intermediate gains.

It was his grasp of such realities that underpinned Lenin's scathing critique of the 'economists' and the right-wing of Social Democracy. If societal relations are class relations, Lenin argued, they determine the discrepancy between appearance and reality – i.e. between phenomena and their essence. Therefore, what the proletariat can be – the negation of the capitalist system – will not necessarily find reflection in the everyday activity of the class or in its actual consciousness.[2] The stabilization of capitalism, as a consequence of imperialism, persuaded numerous European socialists not only of the utility of the export of capital but also of the possibility of relying on the political weight of the working class vote to improve the class situation of the proletariat by incremental reforms. This was the position advanced by the right wing of international Social Democracy at both the Stuttgart and the Amsterdam Congresses of the Second International.

In opposition to this view, Lenin, Luxemburg, Liebknecht and other partisans of the left, held that stabilization was a temporary phenomenon which was bound to erupt in wars amongst the imperialist powers or in sharpening economic crisis within the respective capitalist countries. The task of revolutionaries, they argued, was not to attempt to improve the capitalist framework but rather to work to synchronise proletarian political consciousness with its historical mission. As Rosa Luxemburg emphasised in her famous pamphlet, 'The Mass Strike, The Political Party and the Trade Unions': 'And what it is, that should it dare to appear.'[3] Luxemburg's formulation, once again captures the classic construction of dialectical reasoning, appearance contradicts essence. In this case, the reformist appearance contradicts the revolutionary essence.

The events of August 1914 were the realisation of the worst fears of the revolutionaries. The working classes of Europe, ideologically dominated by their rulers and ill-served by their leaders, flocked to the banners of their respective bourgeois governments, each chanting 'Defence of the fatherland'. The revolution in Russia in historical fact turned out to be an exception, rather than the first spark of a continental conflagration. In spite of numerous valiant attempts in Berlin, Budapest, Munich and Hamburg, the revolution in the rest of Europe failed to take hold and the USSR came into being in 1924 as a lonely beach-head surrounded by hostile and powerful enemies.

3. The realities of the Tsarist Empire had compelled the Bolshevik Party to come to terms with the numerous pre-capitalist socio-economic formations that constituted the hinterland of the Empire and the greater part of the earth's surface. Lenin, building on Marx's own rather suggestive remarks in his correspondence with the Russian populists,[4] had theorised the bourgeois-democratic dictatorship of the proletariat and the peasantry to take account of this.

    Before Lenin, Karl Kautsky, writing in 1902, had expressed the opinion that '... the revolutionary centre was shifting from the west to the east... the new century opens with events that induce us to think we are approaching a farther shifting of the revolutionary centre, namely to Russia. 'Lenin, in two articles on China written in 1909, had tentatively drawn similar conclusions.

    These ideas were only fully theorised in Lenin's conclusion that the chain of imperialism must be broken at its weakest link. This 'weakest link' could, as has been noted, change its locus from one period to the next. However, the success scored in Tsarist Russia tended to shift the emphasis to the predominantly agrarian hinterland of capitalism where the weaknesses of imperialism offered greater chances of success.

    The strength of reformism in the European working class movement resulted in the failure of what may be termed the first round of proletarian revolutions. When they initiated the founding of the Communist International (Comintern) in 1919 the Bolshevik leaders still anticipated a European revolution. Hence they regarded Moscow as the temporary headquarters of the world revolution. Its rightful place was Berlin, where it was hoped a successful revolution would soon enable the Comintern to move. Lenin and his colleagues, however, recognised that certain short-term expedients would be necessary to tide them over the transitional period. Before her death Rosa Luxemburg had directed some of her most critical barbs at them for this, while nonetheless recognising that these had been imposed on the Bolsheviks by the failure of the world proletariat to come to the rescue of backward Soviet Russia.

> 'Everything that happens in Russia is comprehensible and represents an inevitable chain of causes and effects, the starting point and end term of which are: the failure of the German proletariat and the occupation of Russia by German imperialism' Luxemburg wrote in 'The Russian Revolution.'
>
> 'It would be demanding something superhuman from Lenin and his comrades if we should expect of them that under such circumstances they should conjure forth the finest democracy, the most exemplary dictatorship of the proletariat and a flourishing socialist economy. By their determined revolutionary stand, their exemplary strength in action, and their unbreakable loyalty to international socialism, they have contributed whatever could possibly be contributed under such devilishly hard conditions.'

Yet she added the warning,

> 'The danger begins only when they make a virtue of necessity and want to freeze into a complete theoretical system all the tactics forced upon them by these fatal circumstances, and want to recommend them to the international proletariat as a model of socialist tactics.'

The failure of the European revolution transformed the anticipated transition into a rigid status quo. Temporary expedients too had to be re-adapted and became long term policies.

The territorialisation of revolution and reformism – the one with its centre in the Soviet Union, the other in the advanced capitalist countries – compounded the division between these two trends in socialism. Underlying the evolution of Soviet foreign policy is the reluctant acceptance that revolution in the west has been effectively contained. The Seventh Congress of the Comintern (1935) signalled the acknowledgment that revolution was improbable by committing the Communist Parties in Europe and the Americas to a minimum programme of defence of the bourgeois democratic state. Consequently the international Communist movement, boxed in by these developments, was compelled to turn to the anti-colonial movement in its attempts to re-awaken the revolutionary potential of the working class in the advanced capitalist countries.

Socialist, or more correctly, Communist-led revolutions in fact were waged, not by the proletariat, but by peasants in the main. If the impact of the stabilization of capitalism in the late 19th century had led Lenin to argue that revolutionary theory must come to the proletariat from outside that class, the history of revolution in the 20th century tempted Mao Zedong to suggest that even revolutionary praxis will have to come from outside the proletariat. With the emergence of this second discrepancy – that between theory and praxis – matters reached an impasse. The geo-political division of the world between mutually hostile armed camps appeared to freeze the history of the 20th century into these contending blocs. Every struggle waged in the twentieth century was played out against its backdrop.

4. Intrinsic to the foreign policy of the USSR is an internal tension occasioned by its empirical existence as a nation state, which came into being and has survived despite the worst intentions of its imperialist counterparts, on the one hand, and its initial self- perception as the first bridgehead of the international proletarian revolution, on the other. The unmistakable threat of the enemy at the gate, moreover an enemy who has more than once actually breached the defences, has loomed large in the consciousness of all Soviet policy formulators. They have invariably been torn between two options – either to

purchase time at the expense of the state's revolutionary vocation, or to go over to the offensive by opening up a front in the enemy's rear by assisting the revolutionary process. Though these are often perceived as alternatives, reality has usually dictated that the USSR attempt a reconciliation of the two. Raison d'état and the demands of the world revolution have invariably collided in the evolution of Soviet Foreign Policy giving rise to charges of 'selling out,' 'capitulationism,' etc from allies and former supporters.

Our task as historians, however, is neither to pronounce anathemas nor to fabricate elaborate alibis. It is rather to attempt to understand the forces that have moulded this policy and, on the basis of that comprehension, to predict its probable future directions.

A number of writers have suggested that the only area in which there has been a consistent continuity between Bolshevik theory and Soviet foreign policy practice is on the issue of national liberation and the anti-colonial struggle. Helmut Gruber, for example, insists that though the spirit of Bolshevik nationalities policy was frequently violated, necessity compelled the Soviet government to de-colonise 'Great Russia' in order to win the support of the former subject peoples and thus maintain the traditional frontiers against the foreign interventionists.[5] Pragmatic appreciation of the value of allies in the colonial world, in the absence of reliable ones in the advanced capitalist countries, may be said to be a cardinal feature of Soviet foreign policy since the 1920s.

5. While Lenin and the Russian Marxists evolved a strategy for harnessing the national struggles of oppressed peoples to the cause of proletarian revolution, the Austro-Marxist Rudolph Hilferding, was developing his own theory regarding the evolution of the capitalist system. Hilferding held that under the leadership of finance capital, entire national economies would be mobilised for expansion, which would, through the collusion of large scale monopolies tend towards international economic as well as political integration, under the control of the most powerful capitalist interests. According to Hilferding, a supra-national cartel, capable of manipulating the contradictions of the capitalist system by maintaining uniformly

high wage levels within its own area of dominion at the expense of intensified exploitation of the markets and populations that fell outside it, would emerge. For its realisation, he contended, liberalism would be replaced by an aggressive, militarist nationalism and authoritarianism.

The views expressed by Hilferding were echoed by Karl Kautsky, long regarded as the doyen of Marxism, in his theory of 'Ultra-Imperialism'. It was Kautsky's contention that the imperialist countries were evolving towards a mutually acceptable modus vivendi that would entail the peaceful resolution of their differences and enhanced levels of cooperation among themselves at the expense of the colonised peoples. According to Kautsky, this arrangement would result in all the imperialist states voluntarily submitting to the leadership of one of their number.

The political settlement after the conclusion of the Second World War, accompanied by the Cold War, produced an international situation that bears a striking resemblance to the predictions of Hilferding and Kautsky. During the last forty-five years the imperialist powers appear to have composed their differences and by mutual consent have intensified the economic exploitation of the third world to sustain relative prosperity in their own countries.

The apparent resolution of inter-imperialist rivalries has placed an inordinate burden on post-revolutionary societies. They have been forced to face the combined might of the entire imperialist world – in the shape of trade embargoes, the arms race, systematic covert campaigns of subversion and overt attempts at counter-revolutionary invasions. As Ralph Miliband and Marcel Liebman have noted these policies are inspired by the hope that: 'The Soviet Union must be 'deterred'; but it is from extending help to revolutionary movements that it must be 'deterred', rather than from launching a military attack on the West, an eventuality in which no serious politician truly believes.'[6]

6. South Africa and the Soviet Union: Soviet interpretations of the South African problem and apartheid derive from the Comintern and subsequent scholarly work on South Africa undertaken in that

country. The manner in which the Comintern construed the political economy of South Africa has its roots in the second congress of the Comintern (1920) when under Lenin's guidance, the world body adopted his 'Theses on the National and Colonial Question.' Lenin based his theses on two considerations:

- that support of the bourgeois democratic movements in the colonies would expedite the disintegration of imperialism and thus bring nearer the day of the socialist revolution;
- that the revolution in the advanced capitalist countries and the struggle of the colonial peoples were mutually reinforcing because a socialist Europe would have no interest in subjugating other peoples.

In Lenin's view, this made possible an alliance between these two struggles. During the debates in Commission, serious differences of opinion had emerged between Lenin and an Indian Communist, M. N. Roy. Roy drew a sharp distinction between what he regarded as two autonomous streams in the colonial liberation movements. The one, he said, was a bourgeois-led movement for independence which sought to impose the hegemony of the indigenous propertied classes over the liberation movement. The other was the as yet inchoate movement of the peasants and nascent working class, striving for liberation from all exploitation. Roy argued that the task of the Communists in the colonies was to foster the independence of this second movement from the first.

Though the report of the Commission sought to reconcile these divergent viewpoints, the tension remained to haunt the Comintern's strategy in one anti-colonialist struggle after the other. Beginning with the Chiang Kai-shek's notorious massacre of the Communists in 1927, the spectacle of bourgeois nationalists slaughtering Communists with arms provided by the Soviet Union has been repeated with terrifying regularity.

South Africa was unique among sub-saharan African countries because of its large, naturalised White population, spread across all classes, who had come to regard South Africa as their home. The classic colonial power relations in the South African instance were structured by this reality. Mining had set in motion an industrial revolution and given birth to a rapidly developing industrial proletariat. During the 1920s, South Africa was the only African country that had an organised Communist presence, even though it was located within the White labour movement.

7. In an essay written in May 1933, the words of Dr W. E. B. Du Bois resonate with the South African experience:

> 'The second influence on white labour – both in America and Europe – has been the fact that the extension of the world market by imperial expanding industry has established a world-wide proletariat of coloured workers, toiling under the worst conditions of 19th century capitalism, herded as slaves and serfs and furnishing, by the lowest paid wage in modern history, a mass of raw material for industry. With this largesse the capitalists have consolidated their economic power, nullified universal suffrage and bribed the white workers by high wages, visions of wealth and the opportunity to drive 'niggers'. Soldiers and sailors from the white workers are used to keep the 'darkies' in their places, and white foremen and engineers have been established as irresponsible satraps in China and India, Africa and the West Indies backed by the organised and centralised ownership of machines, raw materials, finished commodities and land monopoly over the whole world.'[7]

The Sixth congress of the Comintern adopted what has come to be regarded as the definitive Communist statement on the South African problem, 'The Black Republic Thesis'. It characterised South Africa as a British dominion of the colonial type, politically and economically dominated by a white settler bourgeoisie. It defined the principal feature of the South African regime as the dispossession of the indigenous people of their land. The two dominant political economic trends, it said, were the merging of white settler capital with British finance and industrial capital, which would lead to a growing affinity between Brit and Boer; the development of secondary industry, iron and steel production and the commercialisation of agriculture. All these, the thesis said, would result in the rapid proletarianisation of the Black majority.

These developments were of immediate relevance to the main tasks of the Communist Party, centred on three inter-related areas:

- The national character of the Communist Party;
- The relationship between the Communist Party and the national movement;
- Trade union and agitational work.

The institutions of national oppression in South Africa, the thesis held, rested on the expropriation of the African people of the land and its wealth. To be meaningful, national liberation must necessarily entail the restoration of the land to the indigenous people. The chief agency for such a national revolution, it said, would be the African peasantry in alliance with and under the leadership of the working class.

It posed the principal strategic task for the Communist Party as the need to forge an alliance with the African National Congress. Such an alliance, it anticipated, would involve the quantitative and qualitative growth of the ANC.

It order to be effective, the ANC would have to mobilise the peasants and the workers. But the influx of such an organised peasant and working class presence would in its turn transform the ANC, radicalise it and weaken the grip of the conservative petty bourgeois element then in its leadership.

To achieve all this, the Comintern document argued, the Communists would have to constitute themselves as the core of a radical bloc within the ANC, while maintaining their independence as the party of the working class. '... the basic question in the agrarian situation in South Africa is the land hunger of the blacks and that their interest is of prior importance in the solution of the national question.'[8]

The Black Republic itself was conceived of as the apex of revolutionary struggle waged by the African peasantry. Among the first items on its agenda would be addressing the resolution of the land question.

The Comintern thus set out a strategic approach to the South African problem that underscored the colonial character of the system of White domination based on five inter-related features.

- The system was based on the colonial conquest of the indigenous people, who were explicitly ruled as a conquered and colonised people who could claim no rights other than those the dominant white minority conceded.
- The dominant White minority enjoyed an undisguised monopoly over political, economic and social power legitimated in terms of race. All Blacks, irrespective of class status, were statutorily excluded from the exercise of political power, they were non-citizens.
- The seizure of the land and its wealth through conquest has resulted in an extremely inequitable economic situation in which the decisive centres of productive property – in land, mining, industry and commerce – were the exclusive monopoly of the White minority.
- It was a system of labour coercion in which a multiplicity of extra-economic devices were deployed with the specific purpose of compelling the indigenous people to make themselves readily available as a source of cheap labour power.
- The system required a highly repressive state, directed against the conquered people whom it regarded as a rightless mass to be held down by force of arms.

Since the colonial state (the White minority state) and the conquered people shared the same land mass, there was logically no way in which the two could co-exist. One would have to give way to the other. A Communist Party of South Africa pamphlet published in 1934, characterized the Independent Black Republic as:

'... first and foremost means the anti-imperialist revolution, i. e. the driving out of the imperialists and the national liberation of the country.... But the revolution against the imperialists, the anti-imperialist revolution ... will not be a socialist, but a bourgeois-democratic revolution, as it is usually called. Not the immediate building of socialism but the liberation of the country from the imperialist yoke – this is the essence and the task of the anti-imperialist revolution.'⁹

As an essentially national democratic revolution, the Black Republic would not address issues of class conflict – latent or actual – among the oppressed. It would, however, entail the seizure of economic assets, such as the land and its wealth, from the incumbent (white) ruling class. Thus, though it would have a very distinctly national character – a revolution by the oppressed Black majority – the Black republic would also have its distinct social character -a revolution of those deprived of property and power by the incumbent rulers. 'The bourgeois democratic revolution' projected here would be more far-reaching than a conventional one. The 1928 Black Republic Thesis of the Comintern, with slight modifications at various points in time, has formed the basis of both Soviet understanding of the South Africa struggle and the strategic thinking of South African Communists until recently.

8. Perestroika and the New Thinking on South Africa: Perestroika was the option chosen by the leadership of the Communist Party of the Soviet Union, identified with the ascendancy of Mikhail Gorbachev to the post of General-Secretary.

Gorbachev and his supporters chose Perstroika in order to break the Soviet system out of a profound socio-economic crisis, occasioned not so much by stagnation, but by the phenomenal development of the USSR over the previous thirty years (1955 to 1985). As Moshe Lewin has stated it:

'Since the 1950s the country has continued to become increasingly urbanised, educated, professionally differentiated, and politically, ideologically and culturally diversified. The political facade of monolithic uniformity can no longer be taken seriously by anyone. Complex urban networks shape individuals, filter official views, and create an infinite welter of spontaneities.'¹⁰

During the Brezhnev years the Soviet Union achieved military parity with the USA and its influence in the world, especially among the developing countries, grew. These developments reached their peak during the mid-1970s. With specific reference to Southern Africa, it was the impact of Soviet policy in this region that brought an end to Portuguese colonialism and Ian Smith's UDI.[11]

Despite such advances the Soviet Union still remained a minor player in the world economy. Though it was undoubtedly an industrial society, like the countries of the third world, the Soviet Union earned its foreign exchange reserves by the export of minerals, oil, natural gas and other raw materials.

This paradox was expressive of the internal crisis that became increasingly evident during the 1980s, a decade of stagnation. The recognition that thoroughgoing change was necessary in order to stimulate the creative energies of the population came to the CPSU leadership rather late.. 'Democratization was to be the instrument of reform.'[12]

The New Thinking, associated with the reformist policies of the Gorbachev leadership, has been applied in the main to the area of foreign policy. They executed a dramatic change of direction from the Brezhnev leadership who had contested the USA's strategic-military ascendancy and sometimes registered a few successes. The Breznhev leadership corps's tack was to employ Soviet military parity to extract certain recognitions from the USA during the 1970s. Firstly, the Soviet Union's status as a world power, with an equal claim to a recognised role on global issues. Second, and derivative from the first, was the need to reduce the risks involved in this Soviet-US rivalry by reaching ad hoc agreements and the policy of detente.

The New Thinking relinquished the use of the Soviet Union's immense military power as a lever in dealings with the USA. In its place the new approach posited the inter-dependency of the international community, which required enhanced levels of cooperation among nations, despite their differences. From this first premise it derived three related principles:

- The survival of the human species transcended all considerations of class, nationality, region or state. Therefore it was the responsibility of the powers to do everything possible to eliminate the threat of nuclear war.

- Given the mutual dependence of the planet, no single nation, no matter what its size or military capability, could any longer seek to impose its own decisions on the rest of the world. Due consideration had to be given to the larger global picture, even at the expense of self-interest. In other words, real security would not be achieved by pursuing it at the expense of the other side's interests.
- Given the immense capacity of the industrial powers, Soviet and Western, a reduction of international tensions in earnest would release resources that were currently being wasted on arms and defence systems, for the general upliftment of the common people in every part of the world.

The cardinal aim of this new thinking was the creation of a new framework for international relations.[13] The United Nations, as the one world forum where every nation is represented, assumed a new significance in this context because of its potential in multilateral negotiations.[14] It is in the context of these principles that the settlement of regional disputes by political means assumes significance as one more measure to ensure the reduction of tensions.

Speaking at the 27th Congress of the CPSU, Mikhail Gorbachev had identified four components as essential to the creation of a new system of international security.

These were:

- respect for the right of all peoples to choose the political and economic system under which they wished to live;
- just political settlement of international and regional conflicts;
- confidence building between and among nations and the creation of effective guarantees against foreign invasion; and
- effective means to combat international terrorism and ensuring the security of land, air and sea travel and communications.

These concepts were directly applied to Southern Africa on two separate occasions after the 27th Congress. The first was in a joint

Soviet-Angolan Statement in May 1986; the second was during President Chissano's state visit to the Soviet Union in August 1987, when explicit reference was made to South Africa.

9. In examining the 'new thinking' in its application to South Africa one has to be careful to separate out official Soviet views from the views expressed by various scholars, commentators and journalists. Recent visitors to the Soviet Union have noted that there is a wide spectrum of opinions, ranging from those close to the ideas of the ruling National Party to the opposite extreme, exponents of the view of the national liberation movement.[15] Partly because we have become accustomed to a conformist repetition of the official view by scholars and journalists, many have been tempted to read new directions and approaches into the pronouncements of persons who do not necessarily have that authority. It is proper, however, also to remind ourselves that the differing opinions one hears expressed from various quarters within the policy formulating institutions of the Soviet Union today probably reflect processes previously hidden from public view. The major difference is that they now take place more publicly and no longer behind closed doors.

One can therefore legitimately speculate that though the varying opinions of academics and commentators do not bear the authority of official policy, they nonetheless echo bodies of opinion within the foreign policy formulating community in the Soviet Union. They shall be treated in that light in this paper.

For purposes of simplification I divide the Soviet foreign policy formulating community into three groups, whom I characterise as:

- Globalists – those who emphasise securing a modus vivendi with the US as the key to a lasting peace and new international system of security;
- Regionalists – those who insist that each regional conflict has its own specificity and as such should be treated case by case taking account of these specifics. International peace, by this account, can be attained by the piecemeal resolution of each individual case of conflict;
- Internationalists – those who are persuaded that there are

overarching international considerations that shape local and regional conflicts and that such conflicts cannot be addressed except in that context. Reduced to their essentials, these over-arching considerations are the divergent political economies of the capitalist West and the socialist countries.

In the case of South Africa, as in others, these discrete categories lend themselves to much smearing at the edges. There is therefore no pure and simple internationalist, just as there is no pure and simple globalist. All three these broad groups subscribe to the new thinking, though offering divergent counsels on how its objectives are to be attained.

10. The Globalists: The proponents of this view are in the main academics associated with American Studies in the Soviet Academy of Sciences. Among their number may be counted Yakovlev, Arbatov, Vasilikov and Utkin. All four are linked to Institute on the USA and Canada of the Soviet Academy of Sciences.

Broadly speaking the globalists regard both the USA and the Soviet Union as global powers whose actions and options impact on the rest of humanity. As such they would say, a special responsibility devolves on these two to so conduct themselves that the pursuance of their self-interest does not inadvertently result in an exacerbation of tensions whose consequences extend far beyond these respective countries. With specific reference to South Africa, they would argue that both the USSR and the USA have an interest in the resolution of the problem, but neither one has a vital interest in the region.

This was the view stated by Dr Vitaley Vasilikov at conference in Vienna in May 1989. In a paper, titled 'Possible Soviet-American Cooperative Efforts in Southern Africa,' Vasilikov argued:

'It follows that the USA is sincerely interested in changing the apartheid regime, and proceeds from the assumption that apartheid politically discredits the capitalist system in the eyes of the whole world, has become an obstacle to South African economic progress, hence of the Transnational corporations' profits, radicalises the regional situation and is fraught with social outburst which may result in the protracted wrecking of the RSA's economy, and in this way, deny the West reliable access to the region's raw materials, complicate relations with its allies, provoke public indignation throughout the world, contribute to the sharpening of ethnic relations and human rights problems in the Western countries and so on. A considerable role for the USA (is) also (its) concern that the USSR can use the crises situation for gaining unilateral benefits.'

He continues:

'The USSR indeed remains committed to the support of the people's struggle for independence and sovereignty but this interest may not always be so diametrically opposite to the respective interests of the West, as it has been considered for a long time.... The new political thinking, while not ignoring differences, sometimes serious ones, which may occur among national states in the international arena, as distinct from ideological differences, suggests some more enlightened vision of the Third World. It's high time to admit, for instance, that nationalism may well be the principal ideology in the majority of developing countries, thus making a contest for gaining Eastern or Western ideological 'allies' counter-productive and unworthy. It is also true, that the development of capitalist relations may often be more historically justified and thus progressive in these countries, than artificial and premature imposing of pseudo-socialist models, which only discredit real socialism. That way of thinking, instead of striving against capitalism, (places before us) the task of encouraging its development in more civilized, democratic and moral forms (and opposing) the reactionary ones, such as apartheid, for example.'

By this account, since the USSR and the West, for differing reasons, both recognise the need to get rid of apartheid, cooperation between them on this score should be possible. What is perhaps more interesting are the conclusions Vasilkov derives from his analysis.

'... the main national interest of the USSR now seems to be a regime of 'non-apartheid' (sic!) in the RSA, i. e. a democratic, non-racial and steady (stable?) government, with which the Soviet Union will be able to establish mutually advantageous diplomatic and economic relations without harming the rest of its foreign policy interests. This embraces a sensible view on the white community's legal interests, real power and contribution to South African development.'

Then comes a statement laden with implications:

'That is why, the single active element in the Soviet approach toward South Africa until recently – support of the ANC – means unilateral and narrow Soviet dependence on this organisation's policy, to the same , if not to the larger extent as the United States policy means dependence on Pretoria's position. More than that, the ANC's monopoly on Soviet support can lead the ANC to an orientation of complete and uncompromised victory, that can give rise to dogmatism and scare away both the whites and the blacks.'[16]

We can glean a number of notions from these two passages.
• Vaslikov envisages a post-apartheid state that takes account of the 'interests' of the Whites.
• That he wishes the Soviet Union to move away from exclusive support to the ANC-led liberation alliance.
• Such a move away from the ANC will compel it to be less 'uncompromising' and orient it away from pursuit of 'complete victory'. This then will be the basis, as Vasilikov sees it, on which the 'USSR and the USA may be expected to find a common ground...'

Though they do not exclude unilateral actions, the Globalists underscore the need for multilateral action. According to them, the over-riding need to avoid global conflict, detonated by a regional war, makes multi-lateralism necessary.

One of their number, V. Kazakov, writing in 'International Affairs' saw the problem in these terms:

'Regional conflicts have become most dangerous today, especially because they occur amidst the global arms race and the general growth of international tensions. The inter-relationship is obvious here, all the more so since the art of warfare has been developed to the point where, as was predicted by Lenin, 'not only would a war between advanced countries be an enormous crime, but would inevitably undermine the very foundations of human society.'[17]

The implications of the globalist view are that not only should the two great powers act with restraint, but that the principal players (the ANC and the White Racist regime) too should find ways of accommodating their opponents, and in the instance that they cannot do this on their own account, the Soviet Union and USA should find ways of assisting them in that direction. The Soviet Union could, they contend, by the judicious application of its moral authority in such circles, nudge the ANC towards moderating its demands, they would argue.

11. The Regionalists: This is a body of thought which comprises a number of academics, journalists and foreign ministry specialists. The most prolific among them is perhaps Boris Asoyan, Deputy Chief of the African Department in the Soviet Ministry of Foreign Affairs.

Asoyan first took issue with the conventional Soviet approach to Africa in a series of articles, the most significant of which was titled 'Africa Is Not So Far Away: How We Looked at That Continent Yesterday and What We See There Today.

'The main thrust of Asoyan's argument was that Soviet journalists based their work on Africa on threadbare dogmas derived from a faulty understanding of the continent, its peoples and its problems. Proceeding from dogma, rather than facts about the continent, these journalists did their reading public a grave disservice.

'A serious and, more importantly, a sober attitude toward socio-economic and political processes in developing countries has been replaced by a bureaucratic approach that concealed the truth, shamelessly glossed over unpleasant realities, passed off wishes for reality, and bent the facts to fit theories and models as short as the Procrustean bed.'

In a passionate appeal for honesty and truthfulness he concluded:

'The Africans themselves speak of these mistakes and miscalculations honestly and frankly. We, for some reason, find it awkward – might they take offense? They will not take offense. On the contrary, they will be grateful, if the criticism is accurate and the reasons are correctly indicated. They may be offended by sugary pictures having nothing in common with reality and by formless images created with the help of inner or external censors.'[18]

The thrust of the regionalists' position is that conflicts in the Third World have their roots in very specific regional conditions that cannot be derived from a single source. They de-emphasise the role of external forces, focusing rather on internal factors. Asoyan, in particicular, has stressed that Soviet analyses in the past under-estimated the complexity of Third World countries and the relative autonomy from international currents, of political processes in these countries.

While he continuously stresses the specificities of each region, Asoyan too seems unmindful of these when he gets down to cases. In an article of his carried in Pravda on 20th August 1989, Asoyan, borne on the wings of his own enthusiasm speaks of:

'The reforms (Botha's) have, for the last 11 years fundamentally changed the political situation in the country.'

Later he detects important shifts in the Black population which he claims have led to the 'emergence of a relatively numerically strong middle class which is interested in stability (and) peaceful means of resolving the existing conflict. The colour of one's skin is losing significance as a determinant of economic life.'[19]

None of these bald assertions is substantiated with a single fact! The specifics of the place and situation of the Black middle class Asoyan has so belatedly discovered would have revealed that skin colour has everything to do with economic life. Despite its growing numbers, this stratum of Blacks contributes less than 1% to South Africa's GDP! They do not manage, let alone own, a single company listed on the Johannesburg Stock Exchange! They are still systematically excluded from meaningful participation in South Africa's managerial staffs! But perhaps the demands of space precluded such critical examination of the facts.

More startling however are his claims for the bona fides of the South African regime.

'Of principal importance in this regard was the unexpected (for many) decision by Pretoria to sit at the negotiating table with Angola and Cuba. The very fact that efforts are being continued to untangle other sources of tension in Southern Africa bears testimony to Pretoria's realisation of the futility of forceful military methods in (dealing with) controversial situations (and to) the emergence of a real possibility of peace in this part of the globe.'[20]

Here the man who insists on facts ignores his own very sound advice and substitutes his wishes for reality. He ignores or down-plays the loss of air-superiority, the over-extension of the SADF's lines, the heavy losses in personnel, the projected human cost (in White personnel) of a concerted infantry assault – in short, he discounts all the factors that weighed so heavily in the Pretoria regime's reluctant acceptance of the need to negotiate. It appears he thinks that goodwill and common-sense alone determined their decision.

A more balanced regionalist approach is that of V. I. Tikhomirov, attached to the Institute for African Studies of the Soviet Academy of Sciences. In a short article, titled 'South Africa: Is A Political Settlement Possible?' Tikhomirov begins with an analysis of the particular features that have made the South African problem so intractable.

'Racial and national discrimination is only an outward manifestation of the entire complex of South African problems. The crux of the matter lies in the social and economic structures which are the pillars of apartheid. Historically, the social and class division of South African society coincided with its racial and national division. As a result, the anti-apartheid struggle aims at putting an end to discrimination and racism and, simultaneously, at substantially changing the social and economic order. The overwhelming majority of South African political leaders, including representatives of the ruling quarters, are aware of the fact that the former objective cannot be attained without the latter and that even the formal achievement of the former goal will raise basic questions about fulfilling the latter task.'[21]

Despite these problems, Tikhomirov detects the possibilities of a political settlement because of the overwhelming support for change from among the Black majority and a growing number of Whites. In the context of this development, he predicts, an opportunity for Soviet-US cooperation to speed the process of change by taking a number of limited steps can arise. These could include:

'... a joint Soviet-US declaration outlining the basic principles and objectives of the two powers in southern Africa...'[22]

At the end of the day both globalists and regionalists concur that agreements between the Soviet Union and the USA are crucial to solving the problems of the region and only such cooperation offers any prospect of success. This has inevitably led many observers and people in South Africa to speculate about the dangers of a Soviet-US con-dominion over South Africa.

12. The Internationalists: The Internationalists among the Soviet foreign policy community, though equally committed to the new thinking, tend to view international relations from the perspective of partisans of an economic system that stands in fundamental contradiction to the world capitalist system. They are very cognisant of the intrinsic instability of Third World countries in general, occasioned by their

poverty and the impact of imperialism. This being the case, they have sought to define a role for the Soviet Union, which while not seeking to take advantage of such instability, accepts it as a reality which will neither be wished away nor suppressed by arms or diplomacy.

Concerning the relative autonomy of processes in the Third World, the internationalists are closer to the regionalists but, with greater consistency, insist that solutions should derive not from the possible role of the great powers, but rather from the actual balance of socio-political forces on the ground in each specific case. As distinct from the regionalists, they do however see imperialism as a major factor in instigating and compounding conflicts whose primary sources are regional or local. The role of the US and Pretoria in the Angolan conflict being a case in point.

13. The conflicting and divergent counsels emerging from the foreign policy community in the Soviet Union are rooted in the paradox of a nation state which is ideologically committed to the transformation of the existing international economic order but is nonetheless compelled to conform to the norms of international relations. This is a tension I refer to earlier in these notes.

As a nation state, the Soviet Union has certain interests which are accepted and can be recognised even by its worst enemies. On the other hand, as a proletarian state committed to Marxism-Leninism, it can be no respecter of an international status quo built on the exploitation of the majority of humankind by a handful of powerful western nations. In a context when, for their own reasons, leading statesmen and politicians from these very western nations have recognised that the inequities of the existing international economic order pose a danger not merely to the peoples of the Third World but to the human race itself, apparent acceptance of the status quo by the Soviet Union would be untenable.

Viewed exclusively from a pragmatic assessment of its own nation state interests, there is an obvious advantage to the Soviet Union in assisting aspirant nations and oppressed peoples to achieve their national freedom and independence. In the first instance, the struggles for independence waged during this century have been directed at imperialist countries – the principal antagonists of the Soviet Union. Consequently, in the assessment of even the most short-sighted policy-maker, the Soviet Union stood to gain to the extent that it won one more region away from the sphere of domination of its adversaries.

Secondly, the Soviet Union developed isolated from the outside world during its first thirty years. It only stood to gain by the break-up of the old colonial empires and the emergence of independent states. But the advances made by Third World countries have at the same time been a mixed blessing for the Soviet Union. In many parts of the ex-colonial world the Soviet Union is perceived as an important counter-weight to the dominance of the Western powers, especially the US, and its assistance is inevitably sought in all instances of confrontation with the West. It is a matter of record that the Cuban revolutionary government could not have survived except for the assistance of the Soviet Union and other socialist countries. Soviet assistance to the Vietnamese war effort during the US aerial war and in the period of reconstruction afterwards is also well-known; as is the debt this region owes to Soviet military equipment for its defence against South African aggression.

Third World governments and countries have ironically become an additional burden on the stretched resources of the Soviet Union, contributing to, rather than alleviating its economic problems. Because the Soviet Union's principal exports are, like those of Third World countries, raw materials, minerals and oil, opportunities for trade between the Soviets and new allies in the Third World are extremely limited. The Soviet Union has to compete for western markets with its friends in the Third World, since neither of the parties to this relationship can export to the other. Global political considerations, rather than economics, tend to determine the trade and terms of trade between the Soviet Union and Third World countries. Though this might be more equitable by ethical standards, by world market standards, this can often prove uneconomic.

The aggressive, interventionist posture assumed by US imperialism with the arrival of three successive Republican administrations in

Washington made matters worse by imposing additional costs on the Soviet economy through the wasteful arms race.

This paradox is compounded by the virtual extinction of the revolutionary politics among the working class in the advanced countries which is attributable, in part, to the unattractiveness of 'existing socialism' as it was constructed in the Soviet Union, China and other countries. The 'new thinking' evolved as one more attempt to thaw the frozen history of the 20th century.

Southern Africa in general, and South Africa in particular, is but one arena of this global terrain. If today it appears that a negotiated settlement is likely, this owes more to the struggles waged by the South African people than to the strategies devised by policy makers in either Moscow or in Washington. Doubtless the de-demonisation of the Soviet Union has assisted the process as has the strength of the anti-apartheid lobby in the US and other western countries. To that extent we may say 'new thinking' has been one, among many factors, that have contributed to the breakthrough everyone hopes for.

ENDNOTES

1   Friederich Engels; The Origin of the Family, Private Property and the State in Selected Works (Moscow) 1986. p. 579.

2   V. I. Lenin. Collected Works. Volume 5. (Moscow) 1961. p. 383. Lenin inter alia quotes Kautsky to the effect that:

> But socialism and the class struggle arise side by side and not one out of the other, each arises under different conditions. Modern socialist consciousness can arise only on the basis of profound scientific knowledge. Indeed, modern economic science is as much a condition for socialist production as, say, modern technology, and the proletariat can create neither the one nor the other, ...

> The vehicle of science is not the proletariat, but the bourgeois intelligentsia, it was in the minds of individual members of this stratum that modern socialism originated, ...

3   Rosa Luxemburg, The Mass Strike, the Political Party and the Trade Unions. in Rosa Luxemburg Speaks. (New York)1986. p. 218.

4   Cf. [Ed. E. J. Hobsbawm] Karl Marx, Pre-Capitalist Economic Formations.

Letter to Vera Zasulich. (London) 1978. p. 142–145.

5   Helmut Gruber, International Communism in the Era of Lenin. New York. 1967.

6   Ralph Miliband and Marcel Liebman. Reflections on Anti-Communism in Socialist Register. 1984. (London) 1984.

7   W. E. B. Du Bois. Marxism and the Negro Problem. in [Ed. Julius Lester.] The Seventh Son(New York) 1971. p. 294.

8   Resolution on the The South African Question adopted by the Executive Committee of the Communist International following the Sixth Comintern Congress. in South African Communists Speak – 1915–1980. (London) 1981.

9   Communist Party of South Africa. What is the Native Republic? (Johannesburg) 1934 Mimeograph.

10 Moshe Lewin. The Gorbachev Phenomenon. (London.) 1988. p. 147.

11 Boris Kagalitsky. Perstroika: The Dialectic of Change. in New Left Review. No. 169. May–June 1988.

12 Ibid.

13 M. Gorbachev. Political Report of the CPSU Central Committee to the 27th Party Congress. (Moscow) 1986. p. 94.

14 A Utkin. Broadening Multilateral Approach: Prospects for Soviet Policy Flexibility. (Moscow) 1989. Mimeograph.

15 Steven Friedman and Monty Narsoo. A New Mood in Moscow: Soviet Attitudes To South Africa. (Johannesburg) 1989.

16 Vitaley Vasilikov. Soviet-American Cooperative Efforts in Southern Africa. (Moscow) 1989. Mimeograph.

17 In International Affairs, No. 2. 1987. p. 46.

18 Boris Asoyan. Africa is Not So Far Away in Literaturnaya Gazeta. 7, October 1987. (translation by Lucky Mabasa)

19 Boris Asoyan. The South African Experience. in Pravda, 20, August 1989. (Translation by Lucky Mabasa)

20 Ibid.

21 V. I. Tikhimirov. South Africa: Is a Political Settlement Possible? in SAPEM, May 1989.

22 Ibid.

ELEVEN

*This article was originally published in Southern African Report, a Canadian solidarity journal edited by John Saul. It is a kind of companion piece to Jordan's critique of Slovo's 'Has Socialism Failed?' pamphlet (**Document 9**). It summarises and assesses South African defences and criticisms of Slovo, written from a variety of political standpoints which Jordan characterises as Defenders of Orthodoxy, Left Oppositionist Critique, and Independent and New Left. He also discusses (and contests) Slovo's response to his critics – which turned out to concentrate almost exclusively on Jordan. The article warns that in almost every newly independent African state 'the class of people who acquired control of government used it as their chief means of accumulating wealth and becoming capitalists': an outcome discussed by Jordan years later (**Document 29**).*

A Survey of the South African
Debate on the Decline of Socialism
in Eastern Europe

Socialism, as it was understood by Marx and Engels, would be the first phase in the process of creating a society that would have no need for repression and oppression because it had overcome economic scarcity. Marx and Engels envisaged a society in which the social productive forces had developed to a point that they would be capable of producing such a surplus of goods and services that the majority of people would no longer have to spend the greater part of their lives in work. The planned allocation of resources and human labour, in such a future society, would also ensure that no one would have to degrade themselves by working for another human being in order to survive. Instead of work being something we all try to avoid, it would gradually be transformed into one of a wide range of creative activities people engage in to make their lives meaningful.

For centuries the wisest human minds and the most far-sighted of our thinkers had thought about and tried to work out plans for a human society not dominated by exploiters, be they slave-owners or captains of industry: A society in which human beings could enjoy the fullness of life without the need to make others their servants, or to be servants of others. Marx and Engels predicted that the development of the productive forces under industrial capitalism would for the first time in human history build the material basis for such a fundamental transformation of society.

Marxists have always stood opposed to the proposition that it is the destiny of most human beings to live an unfulfilled life. For example, Marx in his essay, 'The Future Results of British Rule in India' wrote:

> 'When a great social revolution shall have mastered the results of the bourgeois epoch, the market of the world and the modern powers of production, and subjected them to the common control of the most advanced peoples, then only will human progress cease to resemble that hideous pagan god, who would not drink the nectar except from the skulls of the slain.'

Marx's statement implies that human progress has until our day relied on the grossest forms of oppression and misery. But it also says that such economic exploitation, oppression and repression, though regrettable, are unavoidable features of human history as long as the combined output of human labour, science, the machines and technology people have created, is not large enough to provide sufficient food, shelter, recreation, education and necessary luxuries for everyone. Socialists call this condition 'economic scarcity.' Economic exploitation, oppression and repression, to the Marxists, therefore, pose not an unchanging human problem, but are historical problems which could disappear when our productive forces have developed to an extent that nobody goes without what they need for a fully human life.

The realization of that vision today seems even more remote after the collapse of 'existing socialism' in Eastern Europe and the Soviet Union. Its deep crisis in China, Cuba and the post capitalist states in Asia means there is an increasing likelihood that it might completely disappear. There are many enemies of socialism who hope it will destroy itself because of its internal contradictions. One cannot however rule out the possibility of imperialist intervention, tempted by the crisis of socialism, especially in the case of Cuba, to bring down socialist governments.

Unusually, it was from a non-governing Communist Party in the third world that the most searching critical appraisal of this crisis has emerged. The work in question has excited a great deal of comment precisely because it was produced by the General Secretary of the South African Communist Party, Joe Slovo.

Joe Slovo's intervention is important in other ways as well. The SACP is among the oldest Communist Parties, founded in 1921, four years after the October Revolution. The SACP is a highly respected ally in the national liberation alliance, in marked contrast to the discrediting of both socialism and Communist Parties in the Soviet Union and Eastern Europe. As one reporter remarked, as fast as red flags come down in Eastern Europe, an equal number are raised in South Africa. At the very moment of the decline and collapse of its sister parties in Europe the SACP appears to be on the verge of success. The White liberal press might make nasty jokes about it as the 'last Marxist-Leninist Party.' But, unlike the trend in most other capitalist countries, in South Africa the Communist Party is not irrelevant, it is in fact a political force that cannot be ignored. In this article I shall be addressing the responses to Joe Slovo's pamphlet, 'Has Socialism Failed?,' especially among writers in this region and the debate his intervention has initiated about both the crisis of socialism and the nature of socialism itself.

Slovo called for 'an unsparing critique' of existing socialism so that socialists could 'draw the necessary lessons.' Frankly, though his pamphlet was a refreshing breeze, Slovo did not live up to his words in his analysis of the Soviet experience. This does not merely reflect subjective weaknesses but suggests an unfortunate underestimation of the severe damage Stalinism has inflicted on both the ideals of socialism and the societies on which it was imposed. This shortcoming is the result of too long an association with the least attractive traditions in Marxism which discouraged a critical look at 'existing socialism,' above all, as it was practiced in the Soviet Union.

Responses to Slovo's invitation varied in both their general thrust and in quality. A number of Marxists not associated with the SACP, who are active in the democratic and the labour movement came forward to engage him specifically on the distortions of socialism in Eastern Europe and the Soviet Union. A considerable number of writers in the Trotskyist tradition saw this as a long awaited opportunity to reopen the old debates, not only about the nature of socialism but also the line of march of the liberation movement. One or two writers, among them supporters of the SACP, came to the defence of the time-worn empty phrases of orthodoxy, while a few others seized the occasion to vent their anger on the SACP and all its doings.

Slovo himself was afforded the opportunity to respond to these critics on the occasion of the Monthly Review anniversary in November 1990. He has also developed and elaborated on his views in a number of interviews carried in left-wing magazines such as 'New Era,' 'The South African Labour Bulletin' and 'Work in Progress.'

The hardest hitting among Slovo's critics was Professor Archie M. Mafeje, an Oxbridge trained South African social scientist, who has become a regular contributor to 'Southern Africa Political and Economic Monthly' (SAPEM), a regional journal published in Harare.

Mafeje unfortunately did not engage with Slovo, choosing instead to scold the SACP and its ally, the ANC, about the policies they are pursuing to bring down apartheid. Although Professor Mafeje could have made a number of valid points, these got lost because of the Africanist stance he adopted. This was unfortunate because South African Marxism has an extremely under-developed theoretical tradition to which Mafeje might have made a more substantial contribution if he had contained his bad temper. In this instance his eagerness to settle accounts with ideological opponents got the better of him. He was even tempted into making factually incorrect assertions, that are easily be disproved, that the SACP is a White party.

Few other writers followed Mafeje down this ill-chosen path, the overwhelming majority chose to conduct their arguments with restraint.

DEFENDERS OF ORTHODOXY

Given the traditions of the SACP, Slovo's essay must have arrived as a major shock to a number of the old-guard Communists and former party members. Slovo was ready to drop a number of ideas and criticise many practices that had been considered beyond reproach in the Communist Party. His pamphlet, however, was published as a 'discussion document,' explicitly not as a document representing the SACP's collective views.

This perhaps reflects the reluctance of the majority of the leadership to come to grips with the true character of the crisis and the implications it has for the cause of socialism in South Africa and the world.

In the past South African Communists had usually explained away the glaring shortcomings of Soviet socialism by appealing to the fact that the Soviet Union was the first ever socialist society. No road-maps, so we were told, had been provided to assist the young socialist republic to find its way on the unknown terrain it had ventured into.

This is the main line of argument in an apologetic article written by Harry Gwala, a veteran SACP leader from the Natal Midlands, published in the 'African Communist' (No. 123. Last Quarter, 1990.)

Relying on the standard arguments, Gwala urges Slovo to 'Look at History in the Round,' suggesting that he has focused too narrowly on one aspect of a complex process. Gwala argues that Slovo is being wiser after the event and moreover is overlooking the economic and political circumstances under which socialism had to be built in the Soviet Union. Economic backwardness was bound to lead to a backward form of socialism, Gwala asserts.

A similar line of reasoning is followed by Mike Neocosmos, who ironically joined the debate with a view to defend Slovo against two of his critics. The Communist Parties, Neocosmos claims, cannot be held accountable for 'the muck of ages' which resulted in the bureaucratic degeneration of socialist countries and their institutions. Neocosmos gives us a clue to his political preferences by permitting himself a rather vicious swipe at the Workers' Organisation for Socialist Action (WOSA), a Trotskyist group. The most hardline defence of orthodoxy came from a very unlikely source, David Kitson, a former member of the SACP underground during the 1960's who served a 20 year sentence for his role in the activities of Umkhonto weSizwe. Writing in the Johannesburg based monthly, 'Work in Progress,' (No 73, April 1991) Kitson asks: 'Is the SACP Really Communist?'

Kitson's answer is implicit in the question. To prove his assertion, Kitson subjects Slovo's pamphlet to a comparison with certain writings of Lenin. Kitson says that by abandoning the concept 'the dictatorship of the proletariat' Slovo has joined the revisionists and class traitors who have given up the fight for socialism. He rests a large part of his argument on Slovo's use of Rosa Luxemburg's critique of the Bolshevik Party, which Rosa Luxemburg wrote shortly after the October Revolution, 'The Russian Revolution.' In that book, while recognising the achievement of the Russian working class movement, Rosa Luxemburg, referring to the banning of free political debate during the Civil War, criticises the Bolsheviks for arguing that such an unpleasant necessity is a good thing. This, Kitson charges, demonstrates that like Rosa Luxemburg, Slovo (and by implication the SACP) has abandoned a class approach to the question of freedom.

The defence of orthodoxy amounted a plea for understanding of the vast discrepancies between the original vision and the reality of existing socialism. Gwala reminded us of the continued presence of an armed enemy at the gates of all socialist countries. In 1918 there came first of the nine capitalist powers that invaded to assist the old ruling classes of Russia. Then in 1941 the Nazi hordes invaded the USSR. After that war and until quite recently, the socialist countries were ringed with aggressive alliances – NATO, SEATO, CENTO and the other arms of US world hegemony. The socialist countries, Gwala argues, lived under an unrelenting state of siege and therefore never experienced stability. It escapes these apologists that this permanent state of emergency might have been relieved had the Communist Parties taken the working class into their confidence and not tried to force them to support socialism. That would have proved its most effective line of defence. That the methods they prescribe have in fact failed has taught the orthodox nothing. At best they will concede that the CPs administered too much of it, but they insist the medicine they were applying is good.

THE LEFT OPPOSITIONIST CRITIQUE

Trotskyism, as in most countries, is a minority trend among democratic activists on the left. Crises in the Soviet bloc have inevitably made many who resisted it in the past, rethink what the Trotskyists have said in their criticisms of Soviet political practice. For instance, after the uprisings in Poland and Hungary in 1956, Trotskyism attracted a number of left students. Those who escaped imprisonment during the repression that followed the Rivonia Trial in 1964, gradually drifted out of active politics. The crude repression of left and right wing critics in the Soviet Union at the height of the Brezhnev era drove most of the rising left intellectuals who came into the movement during those years away from socialism.

South African Trostkyists had been forced into an uncomfortable silence during the 1980s as the SACP's influence and visibility grew within the mass democratic movement. Slovo's intervention helped to make it legitimate to criticise the Soviet Union in the eyes of many activists and the Trotskyists were not slow to seize the opportunity.

Since the mid 1980's the Workers Organisation for Socialist Action (WOSA), led by Neville Alexander, has provided a political home for those Trotskyists operating outside the Charterist camp, while the so-called 'Marxist Workers' Tendency' has been the rallying point for those within it. Writing in the non-sectarian 'South African Labour Bulletin' (SALB Vol. 15. No 3.) WOSA linked the degeneration of socialism in the Soviet Union, to Stalin's policy of building 'Socialism in One Country.' This, WOSA argued, was the result of a counter-revolution in the Soviet CP and marked a crucial retreat from Leninist principles and practice, which led to a lack of commitment to proletarian internationalism, on the part of the Soviet leadership, if not outright appeasement of international imperialism for the sake of peace.

After the defeat of the Left Opposition (in 1927), so WOSA argues, the Soviet Union became a country which was not prepared to upset the international order and became more concerned to secure its own international boundaries and was therefore prepared to buy peace with imperialism by discouraging revolutions in other countries. WOSA relates this to the SACP's own strategic line, the theory of Colonial of a Special Type (CST), adopted by the SACP after the Sixth Congress of the Comintern in 1928. This, they argue, is the South African face of Stalinist appeasement of the bourgeoisie as it committed the SACP to the pursuing of bourgeois-democratic goals, – such as the franchise, redistribution of the land, the right to trade anywhere, etc – rather than posing a socialist alternative to apartheid capitalism. Only by abandoning this theory will the SACP demonstrate its turning away from Stalinism, they say.

A more thoughtful critique from the Trotskyist perspective came from the pens of Themba and Mathole, two writers who pose the question: 'Has Socialism as Yet Come into Being?,' published in SAPEM alongside Archie Mafeje.

In sixteen tightly argued theses Themba and Mathole subject the practice of both the SACP and the Soviet Union to a searching critique. They generously acknowledge that the SACP's newssheet, 'Umsebenzi' has begun to break out of the Stalinist mould but nonetheless point up the SACPs decades-long record of abject apologism for the CPSU and former Soviet bloc countries.

> 'The Party and its press,' they jeer, 'imposed silence on those who wished to voice their reservations about all these.'

The main points of their argument are that it was incorrect to refer to the eastern European countries, China, North Korea, Cuba and the Soviet Union as socialist because socialism had not been realised by any of these countries. Socialism, Themba and Mathole assert,

> '... would be a society of free producers, working under a rationally planned economy and no longer made up of buyers and sellers trading products through the market, but a community of people who turn out goods for society at large and receive them for personal consumption from society's common pool, This vision posited a society so wealthy, so educated, so cultured that there would be no need or necessity for instruments of direct or indirect coercion. Socialism, ... would thus be a post industrial society.'

Communist-led revolutions, however, came first in under-developed and semi-colonial countries and led to the creation of 'post-capitalist' societies in places that lacked the industrial infra-structure capitalist development would have created. The task of primitive accumulation – that is, assembling the material and human resources for industrial development – consequently had to be undertaken by these post-capitalist societies, resulting in the betrayal of the working class and other working people whose struggles had brought about change.

In an innovative departure from the orthodox Trotskyist approach, they cite three contradictions within the post-capitalist societies, using Russia, China and Cuba as their examples. The first is the requirement, imposed by economic backwardness, that the working class party and state supervise the extraction of surplus value from the workers. The second, deriving from the first, is the role the workers' state assumed as the central player in the economy. The third, they say, derives from the character of the working class itself, which is a constantly changing class made up of persons from a number of different backgrounds. The consciousness of the working class, as a result, is always altering, and this fact makes it necessary that a vanguard party assume the role of custodian of its revolutionary role.

Like many others, Themba and Mathole, charge that Slovo's account of the roots of Stalinism is inadequate, personalized and not consistent with historical materialism. At the end of their article they pose a challenging question: Is the Soviet Union (and by implication, similar social formations) deserving of the international solidarity of the working class?

They answer their question in the affirmative, invoking Trotsky's defence of the Soviet Union on the eve of World War II. Trotsky had argued that despite Stalinism, it was the duty of the international proletariat to defend the Soviet Union because, deformed though it was, it was the only existing alternative to the barbarism of imperialism.

Unlike WOSA, Themba and Mathole do not draw negative conclusions about the SACP's programme on the basis of their critique of the CPSU. By concentrating on the silences and the weaknesses they detect in Slovo's pamphlet they do, indirectly, pose serious questions about the real possibilities of the socialist revolution in South Africa. They make out a strong case to demonstrate that in the absence of an industrial base plus the experience of the economic and political struggles of a modern proletariat, it is well-nigh impossible to construct socialism. It is a pity they did not follow this up by looking at the implications this has for the prospects of socialism in South Africa itself.

WOSA, on the other hand, appears to treat the notion of Socialism in One Country as an original sin, which led to a fall from grace in every other respect. CST, and many other 'sins' are thus attributable to it. But this is rather hard to understand because WOSA itself presently advances the immediate strategic objective of a democratic revolution with a socialist transformation growing out of it. Leon Trotsky, from whom WOSA presumably derive their inspiration, in his letter to South Africa written in the 1930s, warmly commended the 1928 Black Republic, the basis of CST, to his followers in South Africa. One is left wondering what immediate strategic tasks WOSA wishes to pose for the South African left.

Themba and Mathole, on the other hand, leave the distinct impression that they support the idea that Stalinism was inevitable, when one takes account of all the circumstances surrounding the Russian Revolution. Citing the fictitious character, Boxer, created by George Orwell in his satire *Animal Farm*, they claim:

'... the working class is betrayed, and has to be betrayed in this process, because in order to create a better tomorrow, it must be deprived today...'

If there is indeed this element of inevitability, does this not imply that socialism was indeed a failure?

The challenges Themba and Mathole address to Slovo at the end of their article will be with us for a long time. These are the dilemmas every left movement has had to grapple with in assessing not only the Soviet bloc, but also the newly independent ex-colonial states and revolutionary movements that are still engaged in the struggle for power. They correctly warn against the trend to treat all dictatorial regimes as if they are one and the same and the adoption of 'a plague upon both your houses' as impractical options in a world where imperialism seeks to establish global dominance. Though there are no easy choices, choices have to be made.

THE INDEPENDENT AND NEW LEFT

I was among the few members of the ANC who took up Slovo's challenge to debate the issues raised by his pamphlet, in an article titled 'Crisis of Conscience in the SACP,' published first in 'Transformation' and SAPEM and later republished in both Work in Progress and the SALB.

My line of argument was that though Slovo's pamphlet signalled the emergence of a refreshing critical spirit in the ranks of the SACP, he offered an incomplete explanation of the root causes of Stalinism. I reminded readers of a long tradition within Marxism that was critical of Stalinism, dating back to the writings of Soviet leaders such as Trotsky, Rakovsky and Zinoviev during the 1920s, down to those of Rudolf Bahro, from the former GDR, in our day. These writers had sought to explain the phenomenon in terms of the material conditions in Soviet Russia after the Civil War, especially the need to industrialize and, given the insufficient numbers of personnel possessing managerial skills, the growth of a class of bureaucrats who took charge of the state and the economy. I stressed the dispersal of the working class in the chaos occasioned by the Civil War and the political crisis the Bolsheviks faced in the cities in the early 1920s when some of most revolutionary workers and sailors refused to recognise the party's leadership.

I said the Bolsheviks faced dilemma. They took decisions which they hoped would be short-term expedients, but because the international situation did not change were forced to adapt these to long-term policies. I suggested that this was perhaps one of the elements that made them lose sight of their original goal. An extreme pragmatism, that took little account of principles, was one of the hallmarks of Stalinism. I specifically challenged the argument put forward by the liberals that Stalinism was the logical outcome of Marxism-Leninism and invited the South African Communists to have a second look at the work of anti-Stalinist Marxist writers.

Karl Holdt, one of the editors of the SALB, approached the problem from a different direction, the thrust of his argument being that Lenin and the Bolsheviks had a rather weak conception of civil society and consequently tended to regard the party as the principal active element of society. In Holdt's view, this encouraged the trend to vest too much authority in the party.

Ironically, when Slovo was afforded the opportunity to respond to his critics he appeared to ignore all the others to concentrate only on mine.

Even here, however, he excluded the greater part of my arguments from consideration choosing the unfortunate course of challenging me that a critique of Stalinism from a Trotskyist perspective is less than useless since Trotsky himself was not committed to democracy. This gave the impression that my point of departure was Trotskyist. While Trotsky was one of the many Communist opponents of Stalinism I cited, there were others, such as Bukharin, Djilas, Kuron and Bahro, to name a few.

The weakness of Slovo's reply is that it raises even more questions than his original pamphlet. He seems to base a large part of his argument on a quick reading of Isaac Deutscher's 'The Prophet Armed' and a less than certain grasp of the issues involved in the Trade Union Debate which took place in the Soviet Union between 1920 and 1921.

Slovo suggests that the seeds of Stalinism were in fact sown by the future oppositionists themselves – and he specifically names Trotsky, Bukharin, Kamenev and Radek as among those responsible for sowing them long before Stalin was in the saddle. The barbs he directs against the opponents of Stalin amount to petty debating points when one considers that the terror of the mid-1930s would probably have descended on the Soviet Union at least a decade earlier had these Bolshevik leaders not been there to frustrate Stalin's plans. I find it strange that Slovo cannot give them credit for trying to defend what was best in Lenin's party.

None of Slovo's critics, let alone I, suggested that Stalinism appeared like mushrooms after the rains during the 1930s. But the question must be posed: by seeking to spread the blame, is Slovo not indirectly letting Stalin, its chief architect, off the hook?

Whatever faults in Bolshevik theory and practice assisted Stalin's rise to a leading position in the Party, there was a point at which a crucial transformation – a qualitative change occurred – separating Stalinism from all that preceded it. That critical point entailed, among other horrors, the slaughter of precisely the oppositionists Slovo suggests should now share the blame with their murderer!

None of Slovo's critics played down the responsibility that the old Bolsheviks bore for that outcome. On the contrary, I stressed the grave error they all committed by supporting the outlawing of the ideas of the Workers' Opposition in 1921. Unless Slovo wishes to suggest that

Stalinism was latent in Bolshevism, his arguments on this score are extremely shaky.

Slovo evades the most important points of my argument, which he dismisses as 'class reductionism.' In opposition he argues that since economic rewards under socialism are still determined by the contribution the individual makes rather than need, those who contribute more will receive more and that is bound to lead to some being more privileged than others. This is uncontested by myself or others. More to the point, however, a distinction must be drawn between a system that recognises the unavoidable and unpleasant necessity of such differences in incomes and power and one that glorifies it, as Stalinism did.

Slovo does not even mention the empowerment of factory directors (beneath whose feet Kaganovich expected the earth to tremble) and their superiors (before whom the planets presumably trembled), at the expense of the working class, with a glibness that I find alarming. It is evident that these state and government officials were not merely persons who received larger pay packets because of the value of their contribution. They had in fact been transformed into petty tyrants with immense powers over the working class.

According to Bahro, members of this stratum could pass these privileges on to their children from generation to generation, just as rich people pass on their property to their children under capitalism. The wide gulf between them and the working class can be measured by their showy, privileged life style – the hunting lodges, exclusive suburbs, holiday homes, special shops, limousines. But more importantly, I pointed up the position they occupied, as early as the 1920s, within the CPSU itself, as indicated by the census of party membership for 1927!

The way in which this caste functioned, the manner in which its members related to each other and the rest of society are not the small matters Slovo seeks to reduce them to. They lie at the root of the mass dissatisfaction with socialism that finally persuaded millions of east German workers that it was preferable to be governed by Kohl, the Conservative Prime Minister of West Germany, rather than by the Communists, Erich Honnecker or Egon Krenz.

In the Soviet Union itself the 'unthinkable ' has happened. Socialism, in whatever shape or form, is totally discredited and pro-capitalist, nationalist and Russian chauvinist elements have acquired the upper hand. The democratic version of socialism, let alone the views of the Bolshevik opposition to Stalinism, has been completely marginalised and receives very little hearing. For the time being, it can be said that socialism has been defeated in the former socialist countries of Europe.

By the early 1990s Perestroika had failed and existed only in name. The social and political forces whom Gorbachev had welded into a winning coalition in the CPSU had all but abandoned it or were exhausted. The liberal intelligentsia, oddly dubbed the 'left' by the western media, had become explicitly pro-capitalist and their leader, Boris Yelstin, had taken up the banner of Russian nationalism.

Part of the explanation for this reverse is that in Eastern Europe, with the exceptions of Yugoslavia and Albania where it had won widespread popular support through the anti-Nazi war of liberation, 'communism' was regarded as an imposition by a much hated foreign country. It had never been a popular cause. Ordinary people's view that communism came from outside was reinforced especially by the events of 1956 in Poland and Hungary and yet again in 1968 with the suppression of the Prague Spring. Communists could thus be portrayed as collaborators who persecuted their countrymen to please a foreign government. The right-wing, including rabid anti-Semites and racists, and anti-Communist liberals were cast in the role of patriots. Continued reference to these pro-marketeers and laissez faire capitalists as the 'left' also helped to obscure the fact that in western countries the views they hold are associated with politicians on the far right – Margaret Thatcher and Ronald Reagan.

Even the harshest critics of Stalinism had not expected such an outcome in the Soviet Union. But the true extent of the degeneration of 'communism' became evident when a tiny group of narrow-minded government officials, this time identified as 'Communist hardliners' by the western media, attempted a coup to get rid of Gorbachev in August 1991. Not only did the CPSU prove powerless against these would-be-coup-makers, no one in the entire country came out onto the streets in opposition to the junta to defend socialism, let alone the CPSU. It was the explicitly pro-capitalist Yelstin and his supporters who organised demonstrations and were able to mount any mass resistance to the coup. The public's participation in these events was uneven and it would appear most Soviet citizens were too confused to react, except passively. After the coup was crushed and Gorbachev returned to Moscow, his first action was to resign as General Secretary of the CPSU then to shut down the CPSU's entire central apparatus. On November 7th, the anniversary of the October Revolution, Yelstin banned the CPSU in the Russian Federation!

These events that changed the shape of the world, have their roots embedded deep is the history of the Soviet Union and the countries of eastern Europe after World War Two. Socialists are called upon to study and analyse this Stalinist past without fear or favour. This is a task we must approach with the utmost seriousness and we cannot shrink from what such study discloses because it might ruffle feathers in certain high places. Slovo's reluctance to rise to the demands of the occasion was not of service to the South African Communist movement.

SPIN-OFF AND DERIVATIVE CRITIQUES

The majority of liberal and right wing social scientists did not bother to address the issues raised by Slovo. The media and spokespersons of big business crowed with satisfaction because they thought these events demonstrated the bankruptcy of socialism. The pro-capitalist politicians waxed eloquent about the virtues of the free market. Among the liberal scholars, Heribert Adam, a visiting professor from the University of British Columbia, Canada, entered the debate.

Heribert Adam is a German sociologist. He has written extensively on South Africa since the early 1970s and though he is an outspoken opponent of racism, has also been a severe critic of the national liberation movement and seems more comfortable in the company of the liberal opposition.

Adam appears to be opposed to socialism as such rather than being a critical partisan. He criticises Slovo from the point of view of one who is fundamentally opposed to what Slovo stands for. Though many of his points are well taken – for example, the sense of betrayal felt by the common people of eastern Europe – he is off the mark on other counts.

Adam charges that Slovo's argument boils down to that there was essentially nothing wrong with the socialist system except for the persons placed in charge of it, i.e. Joseph Stalin and the men who followed him. As Adam would have it, pilot error and not the design of the craft was responsible for the disaster.

From this point Adam goes on to criticise the SACP and the ANC's policies for South Africa's future. He even seems reluctant to defend the principle of state intervention in the economy, which has been extensively applied in even the most devoutly 'free enterprise' systems, lest someone accuse him of secret Bolshevik sympathies. He does however agree that affirmative action, to redress the racial imbalances produced by decades of White privilege, is necessary. But in the next breath he reduces the true significance of affirmative action by suggesting that it is a clever way to secure the plums of public office for a Black petit bourgeoisie. That affirmative action, which has only been tentatively applied in the US, could be extended to make more meaningful inroads into areas of White privilege and thus benefit not only the Black poor but all disadvantaged people, does not occur to him. Adam also suggests that the leadership of the national liberation movement must inevitably sell-out its poor constituency in order to reach agreement with the White ruling class. Indeed, if he sees any use in the SACP, it is that it could more easily persuade the young militants, the working class and the poor to accept such a 'sell out' because they have faith in the SACP.

Quite a startling lesson to draw from the experience of Stalinism!

Stalinism and the unfortunate tradition among many Communists, including the SACP, to extol it as 'existing socialism' have, certainly, made socialism an easy target for attack by liberals, social democrats and, nowadays, even by the right. Nothing Adam says distinguishes him from this chorus of complacent fat cats who seem to feel the demise of the Soviet Union vindicates their own short-sighted contempt for the most elementary principles of social justice.

Adam, unfortunately, added nothing to our understanding of either the phenomenon of Stalinism or the movement that had spawned and embraced it. He does not offer serious criticism, on which one could build and improve the national liberation movement, but chooses instead to find fault. As a result his criticisms contributed nothing to the search for solutions which could assist socialists in South Africa in creatively recasting communism in a democratic mould.

IN LIEU OF A CONCLUSION

Slovo's pamphlet, with all its weaknesses and faults, was able initiate a much-needed dialogue among South African socialists. Few others enjoy the moral and political authority to have done this. No one suggests that the debate about the character of socialism and the impact Stalinism has had on it has now been exhausted. But the seriousness with which the subject was approached is indicative of the profound questions which the experience of 1989, 1990 and 1991 have raised in the minds of those activists who see socialism as the future of our country.

Despite the differences in emphasis and the awkward defense of orthodoxy, all the participants showed a concern to learn from the errors of the past and to get to the root of the problems of socialism in the Soviet Union and eastern Europe. They appear to agree that a socialism that is not democratic ceases to be socialism. They differ among themselves on the exact character of the democratic institutions that should be the basis of a socialist society. While none of the contributors dismiss parliamentary democracy, few of the contributors regard it as the ultimate solution to the problem. They agree that there must be a role for an autonomous civil society and democratic accountability to the working class, written into the law, in a socialist society.

With the exception of the left oppositional critics, the other authors tend to downplay the dangers of the emergence of a 'new class' or bureaucratic caste and the new contradictions this generates in a society that is attempting to build an egalitarian socio-economic order. This is rather ironic because in almost every newly independent African state the class of people who acquired control of government used it as their chief means of accumulating wealth and becoming capitalists. This bureaucratic bourgeoisie has become the bane of African countries, and many liberation alliances (including those that say they are socialist) have produced one. In South Africa, where the majority of the working class were deliberately under-educated, kept unskilled and denied basic knowledge about the world because of racial oppression, extreme concentrations of power, knowledge and skill in the hands of an elite are very likely. When we add to this that the best educated, most articulate and skilled, even in the liberation alliance, are likely to be Whites rather than Blacks, the gap between those who lead and those who are led is likely to be even wider.

South Africa moved to become an industrial capitalist country one hundred years ago. But by world standards it still needs to develop much, much more than it has up to now. Primitive accumulation will remain among the many tasks a democratic or socialist regime in South Africa will have to undertake. The existence of a White South Africa, that looks and lives like an advanced capitalist country, cheek by jowl with a Black South Africa, that lives and looks like any third world country, will act as a spur to solve these problems by the fastest possible route. Under such circumstances, leaders will be tempted to cut corners and to silence critical voices that insist on counting the costs. These dangers should not be played down. An historical materialist analysis of the sources and class forces responsible for Stalinism could assist us to avoid them.

Is There a Way Forward?

The decline and the fall of 'existing socialism' has been a severe setback for the forces of socialism internationally. The worst defeat suffered by socialism this century was the crushing of the working class movement in Germany and Austria by the Nazi juggernaut. The disintegration of socialism in eastern Europe and the Soviet Union are probably the second only to that. Yet it would be foolish to abandon hope in the promise held out to humanity by the socialism of Marx and Engels. Even in the leading capitalist countries, such as the USA, Japan and Germany, late monopoly capitalism has proved incapable of solving even the basics of human existence – such as decent housing, health-care, schooling and work – for all citizens. Few Black working people in South Africa have any illusions about the benefits of capitalism. The idea that it shall dominate the entire world can only fill one with dread.

Socialism must be saved from what the CPSU and its sister parties throughout the world reduced it to. There seems little likelihood that such a revival could come from the small and discredited Communist parties of Europe and north America. As the one country in which the working class still has faith and hope in the party, the SACP could take the lead in restoring the original vision to socialism. But in order to do this the SACP will have to look back over its own political record and that of the Soviet party from which it took its inspiration.

I would therefore repeat my challenge to the SACP to begin a thorough re-examination of the meaning of socialism that draws in all South African socialists. Such an exercise will assist the SACP to discard those aspects of Stalinism it still carries and put new zest into its intellectual life. Those socialists who saw and spoke up about the shocking shortcomings of 'existing socialism' never lost hope that socialism can be achieved, despite the stinging criticisms we made of the Soviet Union, China or the eastern European countries. The collapse of Stalinism offers all socialists, including those who blindly followed Stalin and his successors, to make a new beginning. Hopefully this time no one will demand that they show 'solidarity' with the 'vanguard of vanguards.'

TWELVE

This delightful piece is in part an obituary of bassist Johnny Dyani, and in part an aficionado account of jazz in South Africa in the 1950s and 1960s. It recounts how 'a tiny fraternity of black musicians' in Cape Town, Port Elizabeth, East London, Queenstown and Johannesburg found an affinity with the pioneers of modern jazz like Charlie Parker, Dizzy Gillespie and Thelonious Monk: the South African jazz artists were 'young, daring and talented'. The article lovingly recounts the history and heroes of this musical development, including those like Dyani who wound up in exile with the legendary Blue Notes. (The text first appeared in Rixaka: Cultural Journal of the African National Congress, *in 1987; was reworked when it appeared in* Two Tone, *in 1992; and is slightly edited in this version.)*

Freedom on the Bass-line

Johnny Mbizo Dyani, one of the most accomplished bassists to have come out of South Africa, died on October 26th, 1986, after having collapsed after a concert at the Berlin Festival ten days earlier.

His first instrument was the piano, but he was later attracted to the bass which, to him, had the deep notes resonant of the folk choirs back home.

His path to music began like that of many others, in the bustling townships of South Africa's urban areas. But he was fortunate in one singular respect: an early exposure to some of the leading musicians of the black community.

From an early age Dyani rubbed shoulders with seasoned professionals. His home, in East London, had for years been a regular stopover for musicians on the road. Much of their skill was passed on to the impressionable youth.

He displayed a precocious interest in the double bass, first picking up tips from itinerant musicians, then beginning to play with his peer group.

The formative influence at this point is his life was Tete Mbambisa, an exceptional pianist, composer and arranger. It was as part of a group of singers and dancers, led by Mbambisa, that Johnny made his stage debut. Throughout his musical career singing remained one of his great passions.

Touring the coastal cities along the garden route, the quintet made a big hit with their spirited and highly original renditions of such standards as A String of Pearls, My Sugar (Is so Refined), This Can't Be Love and others.

It is a lasting testament to both his talent and perseverance that from these small beginnings, in non-amplified, dingy, draughty dancehalls, he grew into a much sought-after international talent.

During the 1950s, the decade during which Dyani entered his teens, the most influential band in East London was led by Eric Nomvete. Playing a very eclectic repertoire that included jazz standards from the swing era, waltzes, the tango, mbaqanga, bebop and a host of other dancehall favourites, this band, together with others, directly impacted the moulding of his tastes and the breadth of his musical vision.

But the decisive influence of Johnny's musical career came from outside his immediate environment.

In Cape Town, Port Elizabeth, Johannesburg, Queenstown and East London, a tiny fraternity of black musicians found an affinity with the pioneers of [the] modern jazz movement in the United States – Charlie Parker, Dizzy Gillespie and Thelonious Monk.

They were avid collectors of records and sheet music, and incorporated the influences of the bebop style in their own music. Many of the names that have since become legendary in South African music were members of this group. One thinks of names such as Kippie Moeketsi, Mackay Davashe, Sol Klaaste, Christopher Columbus Ngcukana, Cups'n'Saucers Nkanuka, Gideon Nxumalo.

And, amongst the younger generation of musicians, Abdullah Ibrahim (then Dollar Brand), Dudu Pukwana, Chris McGregor, Hugh Masekela, Jonas Gwangwa and Johnny Gertze.

The modern jazz movement struck roots in the major metropolitan areas, especially the port cities of the Cape, through which the musical journals and records from abroad were imported.

It was a movement of the young, daring and talented.

From the beginning modern jazz was a minority taste, patronised by black workers and intellectuals in the urban areas, a growing number of the 'off-beat' white students and artists, and the occasional music business impresario. Its breeding grounds were centres such as Dorkay

House in Johannesburg, run by the Union Artists, the Ambassador's Jazz Club in Cape Town, the Blue Note café in Durban, and university campuses.

During this period the very notion of an African making a career in music was legally impossible. That a musician should hope to prosper by playing modern jazz was even more farfetched. But despite this, the pioneers of the movement were prepared to brave the worst adversities.

Perhaps it was their youth; that most did not have the additional responsibility of raising a family enabled them to steer the perilous course between the shoals of racist laws and discriminatory practice. Life itself was a tightrope act, governed by numerous dodges to circumvent the pass laws, the Urban Areas Act, and the Group Areas Act. All this made it hard to form stable bands or groups. Record dates were even harder to come by.

At the time, the major outlet for black talent was the African Jazz and Variety show, owned and managed by the musical huckster, Alf Herbert.

Most of the adherents of the modern jazz movement had passed through the mill of African Jazz and Variety, where they had learned the bitter lessons of cultural exploitation and artistic prostitution that Herbert was notorious for. Their determination to preserve their cultural and musical integrity was in great measure a direct consequence of this experience.

One of the country's first stable modern jazz groups, the Jazz Epistles, was made up of Kippie Moeketsi (alto sax), Hugh Masekela (trumpet), Jonas Gwangwa (trombone), Abdullah Ibrahim (piano), Johnny Gertze (bass), and Makaya Ntshoko (drums). At the time Ibrahim also led his own Cape Town – based trio, comprising Gertze and Ntshoko, which regularly featured at the Ambassador's Jazz Club in Cape Town.

It was into this milieu that a bright student of the SA College of Music entered. His name, Chris McGregor, the Transkei-born scion of white missionaries. McGregor was strongly influenced by the intellectual currents affecting Europe and the United States in the period immediately after the Korean War.

He had become a well known figure in Cape Town artistic circles as an exponent of existentialism and as a modern jazz pianist. Using both the campus of the University of Cape Town and the fledgling jazz clubs around Cape Town as his base, he had integrated himself with a group of black musicians from the townships of Cape Town.

Among this number was Cups Nkanuka, the tenor saxophonist from Langa, with whom he often shared the stage, 'Mra' Ngcukana, Danayi Dlova, an alto sax man, the bassist Martin Mgijima. In 1961 McGregor developed a lasting and extremely fruitful relationship with Dudu Pukwana, an alto sax player from Port Elizabeth.

1960, the Sharpeville Massacre, the banning of the African National Congress and the declaration of the State of Emergency, inaugurated the campaign of massive repression that characterised the next two decades. The regime definitively cut off all avenues of peaceful struggle, forcing the national liberation movement to reassess its entire strategy.

An aspect of the new strategy was a concerted campaign to isolate the apartheid regime in the world community. This necessitated the creation of the ANC's international mission to coordinate and plan this campaign.

The decade of the sixties was to be the turning point in Dyani's life. The nodal movements were the jazz festivals at Moroka Stadium in 1962 and at Orlando Stadium in 1963. At the '62 Moroka festival, McGregor fielded a septet drawn from Cape Town musicians; Pukwana came with a quintet The Jazz Giants, including tenorman Nick Moyake and pianist Tete Mbambisa.

A group from East London, led by Eric Nomvete, included trumpeter Mongezi Feza. All these were promising musicians, destined to win recognition not only in Johannesburg but also internationally.

In 1963 they were all brought together in one group, The Blue Notes, led by Chris McGregor.

By 1963 each of the members of the band had evolved tremendously. Leader McGregor had continuously interacted and sought opportunities to perform with all the key musicians of the modern jazz movement since the late 1950s. His academic training had contributed to his skill as an arranger and transcriber.

Playing with the like of 'Mra', Kippie, Nkanuka, Dudu, Gertze, Winston Mankunku Ngozi, and Mackay Davashe had helped McGregor to grow from an emulator of Bud Powell into a definitively South African pianist, partaking in and contributing to the cosmopolitan melting pot of its evolving culture. His fellow musicians in The Blue Notes: Pukwana, Moyake, Feza, Dyani and drummer Louis Moholo each had matured within their original settings and in the band.

The Blue Notes were preparing to go overseas. The trip materialised in 1964.

Their popularity and prestige brought them to the notice of the European jazz critics. Consequently, the band was invited to play at France's Antibes Festival during the summer of 1964. Assisted by a grant raised among the Rand mining magnates, the band left for Europe in mid-1964,

Antibes was to be a gateway to a new world for all of them.

After the initial impact at the festival, The Blue Notes had to weather the storms and chilly winds of the 'free market place', dominated by the entrepreneurs of the music business, whose chief concern is business and not the promotion of talent.

The first three years after Antibes were the hardest. Flushed with a perhaps naïve enthusiasm for the relative freedom of Europe, the musicians fell victim to one flim-flam artist after another.

To all intents and purposes The Blue Notes ceased to exist in 1965. Moyake opted to return to South Africa. Dyani and Moholo joined up with the US saxophonist Steve Lacey and became stranded in Buenos Aires. Dudu, Mongezi and Chris made their way to London where they tried to make ends meet with intermittent club dates.

Somehow the dispersed members of The Blue Notes managed to retain their old loyalty to the conception of the original group. Huddling together for warmth in London, the core group assisted the two prodigals from Argentina back to London.

By the time Dyani and Moholo came back to Europe in 1967, the modern jazz school had undergone its most far-reaching metamorphosis since Parker and Gillespie at Minton's in the late 1940s.

The names associated with these changes are Texas altoist Ornette Coleman, tenorman John Coltrane, a former Dizzy Gillespie band member, later with the Miles Davis Quintet, Eric Dolphy, a former Mingus sideman, Albert Ayler, a tenor player from New Jersey, and

Archie Shepp, a tenor saxophonist from Philadelphia.

The accent among these innovators was on freedom. Freedom, they said, could be attained by breaking out the conventions of bebop and seeking out new modes of expression by total improvisation.

They forcefully reasserted the African musical idiom, borrowed freely from Indian, South American and modern European traditions. For good measure they threw in elements from the Shamanism of Asia and North America for further experimentation.

It was called the New Wave or Avant Garde.

Individually and collectively the members of The Blue Notes had kept abreast of these developments. The core group in London was already making a mark on the Avant Garde scene where they had a regular weekend gig at Ronnie Scott's Old Place in Soho.

On their first weekend in London, Dyani and Moholo demanded to be allowed onto the bandstand after the first set. In sensational second and third sets, the reunited Blue Notes set the club on fire. There was an evident empathy amongst the musicians despite the years of separation.

Critical acclaim was not long in coming, followed by a recording date early in 1968, the outcome of which was an album, Very Urgent. Featuring compositions by Pukwana and McGregor, the album was expressive of the mastery of the musical idiom of Avant Garde by the leading South African musicians in Europe. It remains a collector's item.

During the succeeding years, the different directions sought by the individual members of the reunited Blue Notes contributed to the dissolution of the group. By 1970 Johnny was freelancing with various British, Continental and American groups in addition to leading small groups of his own in and around London. The extreme fluidity of the Avant Garde assisted in his development.

Stable groups were the exception rather than the rule as musicians from the US, South America, Europe and Africa sought each other out for the chance to perform together and thus share experience and ideas in the act of creation. For a little while Paris became the centre for American Avant Garde musicians, who coalesced around the BYG label.

The strength of the Avant Garde was that it arrived at a moment when developments in the electronics industry made recording facilities more readily available to small scale operators. This effectively broke the monopoly over reproduction formerly held by the record companies. The musicians, too, were more concerned to effect direct communication with their audiences rather than transmittal through radio and the record industry.

Small clubs proliferated. Concerts, festivals and loft gigs, closely associated with the changes in lifestyle, had also undermined the star system so assiduously cultivated by the promoters and music hustlers of the 1950s.

Dyani made his own distinctive contribution to the contemporary cultural climate of a healthy cosmopolitanism, reflective of the recognition of the universality of aesthetic values and the need for humanity to share its common cultural heritage.

His first album featured Feza plus a Turkish drummer, Okay Temiz. This was to be characteristic of all his subsequent albums. Caribbean, American, Danish, South African, North African ad Swedish musicians all, at one time or another, were drawn into his various small bands, the most recent of which was called Witchdoctor's Son.

Among his musical co-workers can be numbered some of the most outstanding exponents of the Avant Garde school. These include Don Cherry, John Tchicai, Allen Shorter, Oliver Johnson, plus his old colleagues from South Africa, Dudu, Louis and Chris.

The memorial album, dedicated to Mongezi Feza, Blue Notes for Mongezi, and a subsequent album, Blue Notes in Concert, are glowing examples of their mature interpretation of the Avant Garde idiom.

Dyani gave his work an explicitly political tone in recent years, with albums such as African Bass, Born Under the Heat, and Mbizo.

He was also an invaluable partner in a most fruitful collaborative relationship with Abdullah Ibrahim, the products of which were Good News from Africa and Echoes from Africa.

[In] 1972 Dyani once again moved from London, settling first in Denmark, then in Sweden. It was from here that he led his most stable group, Witchdoctor's Son, a band with a heavy mbaqanga sound which became a regular feature at jazz festivals through western Europe.

Throughout his musical career, Johnny has actively associated himself with the liberation struggle. During Festac '77 in Lagos, Nigeria, he was part of a small ANC delegation. At the Gaborone 'Culture and Resistance' Festival, he proved an articulate spokesperson on behalf of the musicians in a number of panels. In Scandinavia, he was an active member of the ANC regional structures, often contributing his services to raise funds for the movement.

In Dyani's death, we have come to the end of a brilliant chapter in South African cultural history. It marks the final disappearance of The Blue Notes. One member of the famous band survives, Louis Moholo. Nick Moyake died in Port Elizabeth in 1965, Mongezi Feza died in London in 1975, Dudu Pukwana died in London in 1990, and Chris McGregor in France the same year.

Dyani's passing leaves a gap among committed South African musicians that will be hard to fill. During his all too brief life, he had left an indelible imprint on black South African music and the international jazz scene. Through his music Johnny managed to reach out to millions – touching each of their hearts with that subtle and sensitive blending of hopes, sorrows, desires and struggles of the South African people.

In his music one could hear the rhythms of protest, so eloquently expressed in the work songs of unskilled labourers; one could feel the moving pathos of the songs of widows of the reserves; one could be swept up in the spirit of defiance and revolt conveyed in the surging freedom songs.

But, above all, his music resounded with a joy in life, which is at the core of our musical traditions.

Johnny, like most of our musicians, was sprung from the loins of the black working class. He was, in the best meaning of the term, a man of the people. From an early age he was possessed of a quiet dignity and self-assuredness, endowed with a vast capacity for hard work and sustained effort. These were the qualities he brought to his first love – music – which was his chosen career.

Johnny was never a pompous or conceited person.

Amongst his friends and colleagues he was known for his wit – a digging, ribbing sense of humour so common in the Eastern Cape.

Unlike many of his peers, he was perhaps fortunate in having had the opportunity to go abroad. In the world beyond South Africa's borders, despite the many hardships he suffered, he was at least free from the ubiquitous racial barriers, restrictions and constraints that have smothered so many other talents amongst our people.

As we cast our eyes back over the life and times of this outstanding young musician, we can feel proud of a record of no mean achievement. Yet this same record serves to remind us also of the thousands of others who never even received the opportunity to develop their potential, because of the system of national oppression that holds our country in thrall.

Johnny Mbizo Dyani was not the type of artist who subscribes to the notion that 'the double bass is mightier than the sword'. He knew from his experience as a man, and through his sensitivity as an artist, that the freedom he sought could not be achieved solely in the key of 'B flat' or 'C major'.

He clearly understood that freedom, for the artist and in the arts, is inextricably bound up with freedom in society. It was this recognition which determined the path to which he hewed, as a politically committed artist.

THIRTEEN

A response to a letter by Stephen Mulholland, managing editor of Times Media Limited, which combines humour and a stringent critique of Mulholland's claims.

Letter to the Editor

Sunday Times, 3 February 1992

Sir.

I was persuaded that either the English language has become a little opaque or my ability to express myself clearly in it has become impaired after reading Mr Stephen Mulholland's letter in the Sunday Times, 2nd February 1992.

I find it odd that Mr Mullholland seems think that racial laws came onto South African statute books with the National Party's victory in 1948. Surely he is aware that many of these preceded the 1948 elections by at least 38 years, beginning with the exclusion of people of colour from a full franchise in terms of the 1909 Act of Union. Others, carried over into the Union, came into effect in the British colonies and the Boer republics during the 19th century. I was under the impression that such facts were imparted as part of the high school history syllabus.

The laws I was specifically referring to are the 1913 Natives Land Act; the 1923 Urban Areas Act; the 1927 Native Laws and Administration Act; the 1936 Natives Land and Trust Act and the 1946 Asiatic Land Tenure Act.

Though the National Party opposed none of these laws, it was not directly responsible for any, except for the 1927 Native Laws and Administration Act. After 1948 the National Party built on and elaborated the edifice of racial laws it found in existence, tightening up their provisions and introducing a consistency born of its own fanaticism.

Responsibility for the destruction of the property-owning classes among the African people and other black groups must therefore be shared among both the National Party and the former South African Party/United Party axis.

All serious historians recognise the role played by both the mining houses and White agricultural interests in pressing for the 1913 Land Act: The mining houses motivated by a desire to secure their labour supply; the White farmers to eliminate a troublesome potential competitor. Attempts to saddle the National Party, and by implication its constituency, alone with these pernicious policies will just no longer wash!

The point I wished to make is that having deliberately engineered this set of circumstances through its exclusive hold on political power, the advantaged racial community today insists that property rights are sacred and should not be tampered with.

There is an old Yiddish saying: 'Please do not piss on my back and tell me its rain! 'I fear Mr Mullholland seems intent on doing exactly that to your readers. Successive White governments, before and after 1910, have ridden roughshod over the property rights of every black group in this country! The principle, if that is what it can be called, we are being asked to accept is that the property rights of Whites are sacred and should not be tampered with!

My recounting of the tale about the ANC branch in Drakenstein was to illustrate the effect that the power wielded by the property-owning classes, (who now are, thanks to the laws tabulated above, almost exclusively White) over the propertyless. Yes, the AWB; CP; Boerestaat Party and even the Ku Klux Klan may all demand access to meeting halls on farms. The crucial difference however is that these right wing parties do not need to seek access to such halls, because their members, unlike the workers at the Drakenstein estate, own farms! Their ability to exercise their right of freedom of expression consequently is not affected by their economic circumstances. Mr Mulholland's inference that I demand access to such facilities for the ANC while denying them to the AWB is not based on anything I have said or written. In fact, he has erected a straw man.

As Mr Mulhholand probably well knows, in many rural areas of the Cape; the Free State and Transvaal, the only public building is a school room. More often than not these are part of a farm-school – i.e. they are located on the private property of some landowner. If access to these is withheld workers on these farms effectively have no place to meet. To invoke the abstract possibility of holding a meeting some place else – in a town-hall which is miles away and to all purposes inaccessible – is reminiscent of the sort of cynicism that made Marie Antoinette remark 'If they can't have bread, why don't they eat cake?'

A wee bit of sensitivity to the real, as against the imagined, circumstances in which millions of his fellow citizens live would greatly assist Mr Mulholland in appreciating the clear and present dangers to democracy represented by the existent distribution of economic power in our country.

Everyone accepts that South Africa is moving towards elections. Does Mr Mulholland think these can and will be free and fair under circumstances in which some parties will be excluded from access to voters (who, owing to no fault of their own, live on their employers' property) at the whim of a landowner? Will such elections be free and fair if potential voters can effectively be denied the ability to hold meetings, discuss the issues of the day, meet with candidates and question them on their political platforms at the whim of some landowner?

A morality that sanctifies the rights of property and elevates the claims of the property-owner above everything else loses sight of too many considerations for one to embrace without reservations. Surely the demands of justice and equity must sometimes over-ride the rights of property! Mark you this not some radical new principle. It was applied by a Republican President of the USA in 1863 to effect the emancipation of theslaves!

I cannot imagine what motive persuaded Mr Mulholland to refer to the 'Marxist-Leninist roots of the ANC' if it was not to mislead his readers. 'Roots', as employed in this sense usually implies origins or inspiration.

Unless Mr Mulholland is absolutely ignorant of the history of the ANC and the intellectual traditions from which it drew inspiration he cannot contend that they are Marxist, let alone Leninist. To assist him in filling this yawning gap in his knowledge I refer him to the four volume work, 'From Protest to Challenge', compiled. by a group of US Academics, which is available from a number of Johannesburg bookshops. Perhaps to his amazement, he will discover that the political tradition with which the ANC identifies begins with the Magna Carta and includes the American Declaration of Independence and Bill of Rights; the French Declaration of the Rights of Man and Citizen; Woodrow Wilson's Fourteen Points; the Atlantic Charter and the UN Declaration of Human Rights. At least three of those documents precede the birth of Karl Marx. Four precede the Russian Revolution!

We would appeal to the public to judge the ANC on its political record and not the ill-informed assertions of Managing Editor of the TML.

Sincerely,

Z. Pallo Jordan.

FOURTEEN

This document echoes heated debates within the ANC and the SACP in 1992 and 1993. Jordan takes a tough and (in the judgement of some) extreme position in response to the document 'Strategic Perspective' written by Slovo. He castigates 'Strategic Perspective' as a fundamental departure from long-term ANC objectives; he contests the assertion that there was an objective basis for cooperation with F.W. de Klerk's government; and he insists that negotiations have been improperly elevated to the status of strategy. At the time, and afterwards, Jordan insisted that he was not hostile to negotiations per se. He told an interviewer eighteen years later that his debate with Slovo had been misunderstood: 'It was not whether to negotiate or not – it wasn't that. The issue was how far are you prepared to go.' (The footnotes that appear here were added by Padraig O'Malley when he reproduced the article on-line.)

Strategic debate in the ANC.
A response to Joe Slovo.

The African Communist, no. 131, 4th quarter 1992

Since the adoption of the document 'ANC Strategy and Tactics' by the Morogoro Conference of 1969 the ANC has held the view that the contradiction between the colonised Black majority and the White oppressor state is the most visible and dominant within South Africa. It has further argued that this contradiction cannot be solved by the colonial state 'reforming it-self out of existence', and consequently, only struggle to overthrow the system of colonial domination could lead to the resolution of this contradiction. Moreover, it has been the ANC view that since the colonial state and the colonised people cannot be spatially separated, there is no possibility of the two co-existing. In the South African context, this necessarily means that the struggle must result in the destruction of the colonial state. This thesis, generally described as the theory of Colonialism of a Special Type (CST), has been the core the ANC-led alliance's strategic approach to the liberation struggle.

There is now a perceptible shift in thinking on these basic strategic questions amongst some of us. This is, in fact, not a thought-out process, let alone the outcome of agreement within the leading bodies of the movement. It is better described as a change of gear among some of the leadership. They have canvassed their view of the current situation, without benefit of any discussion in the fora of the movement, in public sources. While their right to do this is not in question, the wisdom of such an undertaking at a time when unity is essential for contesting power with the De Klerk regime can be questioned.

This gear change became evident during an NWC Meeting during the last week of October, when we were called upon to discuss a document titled 'Strategic Perspective'.[1]

Though the document in question, 'Strategic Perspective', in its rhetoric, does not depart from the strategic objectives of the movement, once read it becomes clear that the logic of the paper is a fundamental departure from those objectives. Because there is no explicit statement denoting such a departure, it shall be my task in this paper to demonstrate the departure by dissecting the internal logic of the 'Strategic Perspective' document.

The Stated Premise of the Paper

The central flaw in the paper is to be found in its fifth section. Here the authors suggest that there is an objective basis for a large degree of cooperation between the De Klerk regime and the ANC-led alliance. According to the authors the basis of such cooperation is the mutual need for each other 'to move the peace process forward'. They then proceed to assert that a relationship of cooperation and competition has in fact been imposed on the ANC alliance and De Klerk government by circumstances beyond the control of each – by 'the balance of forces'. I shall return later to this conception of the balance of forces as a preordained reality that seems impervious to human will.

At this point the authors perform what can only be described as a political sleight of hand. At 5.4. they invoke the movement's acceptance of the need for an Interim Government of National Unity (IG) to give credence to a point they want to make in 5.5.[2] suggesting that the IG is premised on the assessment of the 'objective character' of the 'balance of forces' they have previously presented.

Firstly, the notion of an IG was never premised on a balance of forces that made it a political necessity. The IG derives from our Harare Declaration. It was refined and subsequently elaborated as an Interim Government of National Unity, without any reference to a so-called balance of forces. It was, from the beginning, regarded as one of the steps to facilitate the transfer of power, which took account of the reality that some form of continuity was inevitable. As originally conceived, it was to govern by decree – in much the same manner as provisional governments in Mozambique, Angola and Zimbabwe had done. To now invoke it by way of substantiation of an insubstantial line of argument is to mislead.

I strongly contest the assertion of an objective basis for cooperation between the regime and the ANC alliance.

There have indeed been situations where such an objective basis for cooperation does exist between a national liberation movement and an incumbent government. Mozambique and Angola were such instances. Those were situations arising from an anti-colonial liberation war at the end of which the colonial power had made the political decision to give up control of the colony. (It does not affect the argument whether this was voluntary or imposed.) Both the national liberation movement and the incumbent government, in such instances wish that the process of disengagement proceeds as swiftly and as unimpeded as possible. It is that common interest, for differing motives, that is the objective basis for their cooperation.

In the South African instance this is not the case. No amount of clever word-spinning about disaggregating the immediate from the ultimate objectives can conceal the fundamental reality that the dominant aspect of our relationship with the De Klerk regime is that of opposition. To reduce this to 'contradictory elements of cooperation ...and competition...' as if we are discussing a difficult marriage, is not only misleading, but dangerous.

As I see it, the reality is that the regime's objective – however defined – is to retain the essentials of White power – i.e. the accumulated, palpable privileges that the Whites, as a dominant racial group, enjoy in terms ownership and control of the decisive sectors of productive property; domination of the civil service; control over the decisive organs of the state. While quite prepared to make room for Blacks to enter the political domain, the regime is determined to so condition what power the majority acquire that it will frustrate any attempts to tamper with these essentials of White power.

The ANC alliance, on the other hand, has the national liberation of the most oppressed and exploited as its central objective. The realisation of that project necessarily includes the dismemberment of the racist state as one of the priority items on its agenda. In other words, to directly tamper precisely with one of the core institutions sustaining White power. To characterise this fundamental contradiction, this collision of basic interest, as 'competition' is to make nonsense of the English language.

Objectively, the relationship between the ANC alliance and the regime is conflictual. This is also not because we desire it, let alone because I say so. The conflictual nature of the relationship is structured by the diametrically opposed interests the two represent. In the case of Angola or Mozambique such diametrical opposition did not dictate no basis for cooperation. In the South African instance it does dictate it because the colonial power shares the same geographical space with us.

The Elevation of Negotiations

Negotiations cannot and will never be a strategy in any political conflict, whether the conflict be between states, classes, nations or oppressor and oppressed. Negotiation is an aspect of a strategy.

A tactic, as conventionally understood, is a conjunctural instrument of policy, employed to achieve an objective that is relevant within a set time-frame. For example, the tactic of boycott of a particular institution (like the Tri-Cameral parliament) is determined by the specific set of circumstances in which the movement and the country find themselves, and not by a pre-existing and eternal principle. In a particular context it may be employed, at another moment, depending on circumstance the movement may choose not to employ it.

The attempt to elevate negotiations to the level of strategy is fundamentally flawed and betrays a misunderstanding of negotiations.

To illuminate the point let us look at negotiations in the context of an industrial dispute. Proceeding from the premise that the relationship between employers and workers is fundamentally antagonistic, there are parallels between that situation and the national liberation struggle. The class struggle proceeds both openly and covertly, and it is irrelevant to the argument whether or not there is a conscious striving towards revolution. In general terms, the working class (in all its fractions) strives to improve its bargaining position in the market-place. The strategy it employs to attain this is to achieve as much control as is possible over the commodity the working class has on offer, its collective labour power.

This strategy itself can, however be broken down into a number of aspects. Regulation of the pace of work and production is one aspect; enforcement of certain codes with respect to the conditions under which the workers labour is another; ensuring that experience and length of service are remunerated is another. Broadly stated, the working class strives to achieve as much control as is attainable over the conditions of its reproduction.

Matters sometimes reach a flashpoint – say a strike. Both sides to the conflict however recognise that, unless they have decided to go for the final showdown, they must compose their differences. Negotiation then is the manner in which these differences are composed, and each side chooses to enter into negotiations at a moment which it feels will give it greatest advantage.

In the course of the negotiations, one or other side may choose to break them off, as a means of enhancing its bargaining position. That – the breaking off, or resumption of negotiations – is a tactic; the negotiations themselves are not. The negotiations feature as an aspect of the strategy being pursued by the working class (or a section thereof) in a particular dispute with the employers. They can never be a strategy, any more than strike action can be a strategy, or working to rule can be a strategy, or factory occupations can be a strategy.

Though there are similarities, the national liberation struggle diverges from the above in that it is explicitly about the striving for power. Moreover, since a transfer of power to the oppressed cannot co-exist with the retention of power by the oppressor, it is a final showdown. Historically the ANC's strategy was to harness every conceivable instrument of struggle into a multi-pronged offensive which would draw the broadest front of opposition to the apartheid regime into active struggle. In these terms the ANC always posed its objective as the seizure of power, not in the poetic sense of the Storming of the Bastille, but in the sense of taking power against the will of the oppressor. At no time, since 1969, did the ANC ever elevate any one of the prongs above the others, though it was understood that there would be moments when one or other prong might acquire a higher profile than the others. (For example, during the 1984–86 mass uprisings, when mass struggle acquired a profile over and above the others.) It was understood that the thrust of ANC strategy was to knit these prongs together, through mutual reinforcement, so as to merge them into one huge current, culminating in the overthrow of the racist regime. Each of the prongs would make a contribution, though at a specific crisis point one of them would prove decisive.

Even while we pursued the four pillars of our strategy, the ANC never excluded negotiations as an aspect of its strategy. The movement had repeatedly argued that at some point negotiations must inevitably arise, even if merely to receive the surrender of the enemy. When they seriously came onto the agenda – beginning with the soundings from prison and the various contracts with the regime – the ANC said negotiations are a terrain of struggle, no different from the others. Implicit in this was the understanding that negotiations are neither a tactic nor a strategy but an aspect of strategy. As such, its relative weight is far lower than that of the four major prongs of strategy. They feature as a subsidiary means for the realisation of the objectives pursued through strategy. Hence, the ANC never saw any contradiction between negotiations and waging the armed struggle. Which is what 'Strategic Perspective' implies! Equally, we saw no contradiction between continuing either underground work or mass political mobilisation and negotiations.

However, there is a crucial difference between the analogous industrial dispute and the national liberation struggle. Industrial disputes – including any negotiations they entail – are waged in a manner that will enable both sides to co-exist, as antagonists to be sure, but to co-exist nonetheless. In the case of the national liberation struggle, one or other party to the dispute must go under. Negotiations, in such a situation, are not aimed at composing differences, but are aimed at the liquidation of one of the antagonists as a factor in politics. This crucial distinction, in turn, should determine the alliance's entire approach to negotiations.

The manner in which the document poses the issue at section 2, 'Negotiations the preferred option of the liberation movement' is indicative of the utter confusion of the authors. Here they confuse non-violent struggle with negotiations. The ANC alliance resorted to arms when all avenues of non-violent struggle vanished, not when the possibility for negotiations vanished.

The unstated premise (that non-violent struggle and negotiations are synonymous) not only raises negotiations to the strategy, but by so doing suggests that everything else, all other prongs and aspects of strategy, must merge into this dominant thrust, negotiations, to which they are all subordinated.

This has far-reaching consequences for the ANC's entire approach to the liberation struggle which requires examination in depth.

What we are encountering is in fact a fundamental revision of the ANC's conception of struggle as consisting of mutually supportive prongs and replacing that with a conception of a hierarchy (like a series of terraces), one of which will provide the breakthrough to success. Thus, the other prongs support this one, which, because of its primacy over the rest, must be preserved at all costs.

The danger concealed beneath the fine words of the authors of 'Strategic Perspective' is that by elevating one aspect of strategy above the others, the ANC would in fact be stripped of crucial instruments of policy. The logic of a hierarchy is that certain aspects of strategy necessarily recede in importance. These may, therefore, either be dropped or relegated to a lesser role maintained merely as a hedge against contingencies. That aspect which has acquired (or rather has been attributed) primacy, on the other hand, in turn requires the greatest investment in time, effort, talent and perhaps even finance.

The unwarranted elevation of negotiations to the ANC's primary strategy has the unfortunate outcome of re-orienting the movement away from confrontation with the enemy to a search for common ground. 'Strategic Perspective' exudes a desperation to discover such common ground at all costs. Rather than discovering ways of enhancing the growing confidence of the mass of the oppressed as the agency of their own liberation, it advises the ANC to discover new ways of facilitating communication between its leadership and the regime. Amazingly, this is seen as a 'breakthrough'. 'Breakthrough' into what? One may well ask!

The harm this can inflict on the movement is already evidenced by the confused signals which have emanated from the NEC - its oscillation between militancy and complacency.

Trapping Our Victories in the Jaws of Defeat

It would seem we all agree that it was the combined impact of the many prongs of ANC strategy that compelled the enemy to seek negotiations. Quite correctly, we claim that as a victory! We proceeded from there and said the challenge facing the ANC was to skilfully employ negotiations to expedite the transfer of power from the enemy. This has been a process characterised by an ebb and flow, forwards and backwards. (The suspension of negotiations in 1991, followed by a successful CODESA 1 in December 1991; the deadlock at CODESA 2; the suspension of talks after Boipatong; etc). We have, however, been able to marshall both internal pressure, through mass mobilisation, which has in turn generated international pressures, plus the pressure arising from this indecisive inter-regnum (e.g. a continuing investors' strike) to force the regime to yield. Thus we characterised our unprecedented mass action as a victory. Its immediate outcome was the Record of Understanding, which objectively regarded was the ANC compelling the De Klerk regime to accept our terms. Once again we said this was a victory. Its immediate fruits were the release of some of the remaining and most prominent political prisoners. We correctly claimed that too as a victory.

Important to recognise in the context of these most recent victories is that De Klerk could quite easily have denied us these by taking formative action himself. He has consequently been seen by his constituents and his allies as submitting to the ANC alliance's agenda.

There is consensus in the NWC that the ANC alliance can win at the negotiating table only that which it has secured through struggle. In other words, the struggle, which continues with negotiations as one of its aspects, is the factor in determining the balance of forces - leave aside whether these are tactical or strategic shifts.

It is this movement that stands at the head of a series of victories, which every NWC member claims to recognise, which is now being advised to act in the following manner:

- The regime has put forward a Constitutional Plan that seeks to make power-sharing mandatory and coalition governments, in which it has a decisive voice, constitutionally compulsory. The 'Strategic Perspective' document advises that we comply, not in terms of a constitution but by accommodating the regime for a while – three years, five years, ten years?
- The regime wishes to retain its security services, shield them against possible prosecution now or in the future, integrate the members of MK (and possibly APLA) as subordinates and as secondary factors in the security services. The 'Strategic Perspective' advises us to comply.
- The regime wants to retain the essentials of the colonial administration it has run since 1910, to provide sheltered employment for incompetent and badly trained Afrikaners and other Whites from the lower middle strata, continue with feather-bedding and grossly inflated, wasteful bureaucracies (in triplicate to boot!), permit them to waste, squander and embezzle taxpayers' monies. Such strategically placed persons would also have the capacity to thwart every democratic reform the democratic state wishes to implement. The 'Strategic Perspective' advises us to comply.
- The regime would like the boundaries, powers and the configuration of future regions to be determined outside the Constituent Assembly. Its purpose is to try to ensure that it can gerrymander boundaries that will advantage it and its allies. The 'Strategic Perspective' says we should accommodate them.

There appears to be a deep-seated pessimism that runs through the entire document. True, as the document says, we have not defeated the regime. But neither has the regime defeated us! The thrust of the document suggests that we are suing for the best terms we can get from a victorious enemy.

To be generous, the authors appear charmingly ignorant of the history of the 20th century. These measures, which would amount to capitulation to some of the core objectives pursued by the regime at this time, we are advised to adopt as a hedge against the destabilisation of democracy by the SADF, SAP and the racist civil service. That there are people who fondly imagine that the appetites of repressive armies and police forces can be stilled by appeasement is alarming. If, as the authors seem to fear, the officer corps and ranks of the SADF and SAP are likely to be opponents of a democratic order, I would have thought that underlined the need to have them vacate these strategically important posts as soon as possible. The gravest danger to a transition and the democratic order is precisely such potential fifth columnists. Had the government of the Spanish Republic been firmer in its attitude to Franco to begin with, there is the great likelihood that he could never have been emboldened to make his coup! The history of this century is literally strewn with similar examples – every repressive military formation that has been coddled by the democratic forces has not had its teeth drawn, instead it has taken courage from such leniency.

Conceptual confusion runs through this section of the document as well. I find it alarming that the authors seem to think that the motivating factor in the action of potentially subversive civil servants is their individual pensions, job security and perks. A first year sociology student knows that the actions of a corporate body do not reflect the individual wills of its members; that the actions of a class or a dominant racial, or ethnic group are not the arithmetical aggregate of the wills of its members. That being the case, it is foolhardy to imagine that a democratic state will contain subversion by the racist civil service by giving guarantees about pensions, job security and perks. If they act they will act as a corporate body, on behalf of their perceived interest as a group and appeals to individual benefits accruing from loyalty will be seen for what they are – attempts at bribery to desert their side.

The authors also seem to have no appreciation of the feather-bedding and wastefulness of the incumbent regime. The dictates of austerity alone – leave aside politics – would compel a democratic state to take a very sharp axe to the bloated bureaucracy which the regime created to make comfortable jobs for Afrikaner sons and daughters. A single example: The creation of one education system, something a democratic regime will ignore at its peril, alone would immediately render three parallel bureaucracies redundant! The entire machinery of 'Native administration'; 'Coloured administration'; 'Indian administration', etc. will also disappear.

Setting the politics aside, how can the ANC alliance give assurances about the continuity of the existing civil service?

Once we factor in considerations of competence, honesty, public service ethos, and loyalty to the democratic political order the case becomes hopeless. The imperatives of good government - which our posters boldly proclaim our people should vote for - would dictate that we take another very sharp axe to the racist civil service!

THE ISSUE OF VIOLENCE

I have often questioned the realistic prospect of the regime embarking on serious negotiations, in the full realisation that their inevitable result must be the loss of power. I have consequently insisted that the alliance must take seriously De Klerk's words that he seeks to reach an accommodation about sharing power, and not to surrender power.

In other words, the regime would like to arrive at a formula that would make possible the co-existence of CST and democracy. I am, consistent with ANC strategic thinking up till now, convinced that such co-existence is impossible. That democracy requires the uprooting of CST.

De Klerk's strategy – a mix of reformism, coupled with the systematic destabilisation of the ANC alliance – has as its immediate objective rendering the ANC too weak to resist such a compromise. There is ample evidence that the SADF, the overt and covert security services, assisted by a range of irregulars and freelance auxiliaries, have been assigned the task of continuing the counter-insurgency war. Contrary to what some, including the authors of 'Strategic Perspective' appear to think, there is no contradiction between reformism and the 'informal repression' that the De Klerk regime is employing. We are not by this suggesting that each and every cabinet member knows the operational details of the strategy, but it is clear that its broad parameters are the outcome of collective decision. De Klerk's demonstrated unwillingness to do anything to stop the violence can have no other explanation.

The authors, inexplicably, treat the SADF and SAP as if these are autonomous players and not parts of the state machinery De Klerk uses against us. I cannot decide whether this is yet another instance of conceptual confusion or a deeper malaise. I do not suggest that specific agencies of the state lack the capacity to act independently and in defiance of their political masters.

But at this point in time, there is nothing to suggest either that the SADF or SAP is acting in this fashion, or that they entertain the ambition to act in such a manner.

The De Klerk regime obviously has not come to terms with the inevitable outcome of serious negotiations. It has not arrived at the seminal political decision that it must give up power. The violence betrays that; its negotiations position betrays that; its clinging to its alliance with the IFP betrays that.

Happy Trails to You, or Riding Into the Sunset Together?

It has been suggested by one of the sources of inspiration of 'Strategic Perspective' that the sort of compromises the movement should make are such as will not undermine its strategic objectives or subvert the achievement of national liberation.

I have already indicated, and it would seem many agree, that the ANC alliance and the regime both decided to explore the path of negotiations, but with diametrically opposed immediate and long-term objectives. It is my contention also that this opposition is rooted in the fundamental contradiction of our society.

The national liberation project includes not only the creation of a democratic state, but crucially, the dismemberment of the racist state. The central components of this state are its coercive arms – the army, police, law courts, the prisons; and its persuasive arm – the civil administration, civil service, the state ideological apparatus (like SABC, schools, etc.). It is precisely these organs of White minority state power that we are now being told should not be tampered with, so as to enable the liberation movement and the regime to ride blissfully into the sunset together.

(Images of Roy Rogers fill our tearful eyes!)

Such an option, I submit, will permanently block the path to any meaningful change in this country. We would, by choosing such a course, do two things. We would keep in place a civil service that has no interest in serving the mass of the oppressed who are the ANC's constituency; a civil service that will do everything to undermine the democratic government. At the same time we would be keeping under arms the agency that can ensure that the democratic forces dare not touch that civil service when its disloyalty is uncovered. A national liberation movement that did that would not be riding into the sunset, it would be building its own funeral pyre! Not only does that option lead to a dead-end, it is suicidal!

Negotiations are a key aspect of ANC strategy at this time. Within their context we have employed various tactics, both to keep the process on course and to pressure the regime.

No one in the ANC wants to see them fail.

While we will not get at the table what we have not won on other fronts, we should be equally careful not give away what we have won on these fronts at the negotiating table. I fear 'Strategic Perspective' is a prescription to do that. This attempt to revise the ANC's strategic perspective and these latter notions form a composite whole, linked by a radically misguided conception of what is possible in the present. It must resolve itself in a perspective that projects or accommodates the piecemeal eradication of the substantive elements of CST – a reformist perspective!

Unfortunately, it does not work. Look at the history of social democracy! .

ENDNOTES

1   Jordan is referring here, and throughout, to the first document with this title drafted by the ANC Negotiations Commission, dated October 1992 [ed].

2   5.4 and 5.5 refer to paragraphs in the ANC Negotiations Commission paper. These paragraphs no longer appear in the ANC NEC paper [ed].

FIFTEEN

*This was written as a discussion paper in preparation for the ANC's 50th National Conference, held in Mafikeng in December 1997. Although it ranges quite widely over South African history and politics, the paper is underpinned by a somewhat rueful recognition of 'compromises, some concessions and postponements' in the negotiated agreement. The paper concludes with a measured warning of the potential in South Africa for ethnic mobilisation and entrepreneurship – 'the gravest single threat of destabilisation and subversion in our new democracy'. In a passage that prefigures **Document 44**, Jordan contemplates the disestablishment of so-called 'traditional' leaders, retaining their ceremonial titles and roles, but not entitlement to state powers by virtue of these titles.*

The National Question in
Post-1994 South Africa

'The danger begins only when they make a virtue of necessity and want to freeze into a complete theoretical system all the tactics forced upon them by these fatal circumstances ...'

Rosa Luxemburg wrote that about the Bolsheviks in 1918. Could that admonition not also be directed at the South African national liberation movement (NLM) and the ANC?

Comrade President Mandela has often remarked that we should not behave as if we are dealing with an enemy whom we defeated on the battlefield. Implicit in this warning is that the enemy is still strong and might well have un-exhausted reserves of power and energy that he could marshal against us.

What remains unsaid, but should be read between the lines, is that the elections of April 1994 entailed a degree of compromise, some concessions and postponements, many of which took account of the enemy's real strength and untapped power. Others were made to draw to our side of the conflict vacillating class elements and strata who might otherwise have reinforced the ranks of an as a yet undefeated enemy. Yet others were made to widen the fissures and cracks within the enemy's own ranks and to buy time that would enable us to consolidate the gains made. There were also compromises forced upon us because we could ill-afford to jeopardise the larger prize – majority rule – in pursuance of a few uncertainties.

It is in this context that I want to locate the national question in the post April 1994 period, focusing specifically on the issues of uprooting the institutions of Colonialism of a Special Type (CST), on Ethnicity and Culture and Affirmative Action.

SOME COMPARATIVE COMMENTS

1997 marks the 50th anniversary of Indian Independence, it will also be the 48th Anniversary of China's Liberation on 1 October. These two anniversaries and the movements associated with them probably were the central influences on the post-World War II process of decolonisation.

In many respects the two movements are contemporary and their victories are just two years apart. Yet they are referred to very differently by both protagonists and antagonists. We speak of the 'Struggle for Indian Independence', but we speak of the 'Chinese Revolution'. Is there any significance in how we refer to these two movements? Does our mode of expression point up a fundamental difference between the two?

The attainment of Indian Independence was of great political, social, psychological and symbolic importance to all the peoples in the colonies. India was the world's largest colony. It was probably the richest British colony – fondly referred to as the 'Jewel in the Crown' in the literature of imperial nostalgia. The independence of India in 1947 was the first decisive triumph of the liberation movements in the colonies and semi-colonies. Independent India was also the very first country to place the issue of racial oppression in South Africa on the agenda of the newly founded United Nations Organisation. As such, Indian independence had a very direct bearing on the struggle of our own people. For the other colonies it represented the implicit guarantee of colonial freedom. It gave a very positive impetus to the irresistible drive towards colonial freedom that unfolded during the 1950s and 1960s.

Yet, the emancipation of India came in a form that was far less than the movement for independence had striven for. The country was partitioned along religious lines. The creation of Pakistan was a totally arbitrary act of colonial despotism, because there was no precedent of such an entity

– a Muslim confessional state – in pre-colonial India. That act built into India's hard won independence a virtually permanent source of tension. A cancer, so to speak, that has bled since 1947.

The liberation of China came about by a very different route. An armed struggle, characterised by two revolutionary Civil Wars, briefly interrupted by a War of Resistance to Japanese imperialism, culminated in the routing of the Goumindang's armies and the armed seizure of power by the Communist Party of China at the head of a successful peasant's revolt.

Yet the 'un-finished character' of Indian independence, is echoed also in the liberation of China. With the support and assistance of the US, Taiwan seceded under Guomindang rule; the British were allowed to remain in Hong Kong until July 1997; and the Portuguese in Macao.

Despite their unfinished character, both these movements were nonetheless victories. And the significance of their achievements is not diminished by the concessions that had to be accepted or that were foisted upon them.

Virtually all the liberation movements that attained victory after 1947, including our own, have been forced to make compromises at the point of victory. National liberation has rarely come in the form that the movement sought. Consequently, the terrain on which the triumphant movement has to manoeuvre after victory is not necessarily all of its own choosing or making.

Anniversaries are important as marking a climax, the crucial nodal point in time – the people finally assuming power. But, while we might focus on a single day, or a single event, or happenings – revolutions are not a moment, they are processes. Processes in which there are nodal moments – like 27 April 1994 – but they are a continuum.

Our own national democratic revolution is no different. April 27, 1994 will remain a very significant day in South African history, but in reality it merely marks a high point in a continuing process. In that ongoing process there will be moments of rapid advance, but there will also be the need, sometimes, to retreat. Retreating does not mean conceding defeat, it is most often a tactical manoeuvre undertaken to put off till a more opportune time, action one would have preferred to take in the present.

What I am suggesting therefore is that national liberation movements have, in many cases, been compelled to postpone aspects of their programme and policy in the light of an intractable tactical conjuncture. The retreat, in other words, is undertaken in order to prepare for a more coherent and better planned advance.

It is important that we boldly acknowledge and accept that the movement has had to seek compromises and make concessions to the old order so that we could attain the important beach-head of majority rule in 1994. A victory that was further consolidated with the signing into law of the constitution in December 1996.

How Did We Understand Apartheid?

Since 1969 Morogoro Conference the ANC has held the view that the contradiction between the colonised Black majority (Africans, Coloureds and Indians) and the White oppressor state is the most visible and dominant contradiction within apartheid ruled South Africa. It has further argued that this contradiction could not be solved by the colonial state 'reforming itself out of existence', and consequently, only struggle to overthrow the system of colonial domination would lead to the resolution of this contradiction. Moreover, it was our view that since the colonial state and the colonised people could not be spatially separated, there was no possibility of the two co-existing - as is the case in classic colonialism where the colonial power packs off its staff and goes home, leaving the former colony to fend for itself. In the South African context, this necessarily meant that the struggle would have to result in the destruction of the apartheid state.

The ANC always regarded apartheid as much more than mere racial discrimination, though, of course, racial discrimination was central to its practice. We regarded apartheid as a multi-faceted and comprehensive system of institutionalised racial oppression with the following characteristics:

- It was a system of White minority rule in which the Black majority were statutorily (i.e. by law) excluded from the political process. Political power, except for some marginal delegated powers, was explicitly the monopoly of the White minority. The indigenous people were ruled as a conquered and colonised people.

- It was based on the conquest and dispossession of the indigenous people of their land and its wealth. This dispossession was itself institutionalised in formal legislation. The watershed law was the 1913 Natives Land Act in terms of which 13 per cent of the land area of the country was set aside as 'Native Reserves' and Africans were excluded from land ownership, save by special licence, in the remaining 87% of the country. Consequently, access to the decisive sectors of productive land was racially determined to the advantage of the Whites. The dominant White minority enjoyed an undisguised monopoly over economic power – the land, mines, industry and commerce – which was racially apportioned to its advantage. As a result the propertied classes were virtually exclusively White, while Blacks, on the whole, owned little or no property.
- It was a system of labour coercion in which a multiplicity of extra-economic devices had been deployed with the specific purpose of compelling the indigenous people to make themselves readily available as a source of cheap labour power.
- In order to function, the system had required a highly repressive state machinery, which was directed against the conquered people whom the apartheid rulers regarded as a right-less mass to be held down by force of arms.

All of this was rationalised on the basis of the racial superiority of the Whites.

Apartheid was, however, also a racial hierarchy, graded on the basis of skin colour, resulting in a high degree of differentiation among the oppressed in terms of job opportunities, access to certain types of training, the exercise of property rights, etc. At the core of the system of national oppression was the conquest and domination of the African majority who were the most exploited and oppressed.

National oppression thus found expression in the palpable form of a number of economic, social and developmental indicators - such as poverty and underdevelopment, the low levels of literacy and numeracy among the oppressed communities, their low access to clean water, the non-availability of electricity where they lived, their low food consumption, their invariably low incomes, the poor state of their health, the low levels of skills, the generally unsafe environment in which these communities lived, etc. Thus, the uprooting of national oppression required, amongst other things, the correction of precisely these conditions. In the view of our movement the content of freedom and democracy would be the radical transformation of South African society so as to create an expanding floor of economic and social rights for the oppressed majority. The changes that we felt would bring about this transformation were set out in our programme, the Freedom Charter. Though it is not a programme for socialism, the Freedom Charter envisaged the seizure of economic assets in the land, the mines and monopoly industry as essential to the transformation of South Africa.

How Do We Understand April 1994?

It would not be unreasonable to characterise 27 April 1994 as the commencement of a new phase of South Africa's national democratic revolution. The democratic elections ushered in political democracy, enabling the people of this country for the first time to put in office a government of their choice. But the political democracy that came into being was one based on a host of preceding institutional arrangements.

Firstly, it was parliamentary democracy, on the British model, which prescribes that the executive be constituted by the party that held the majority of seats in parliament. Secondly, there were the terms agreed at Kempton Park, that parties that polled more than five percent of the total poll could enter into a coalition of national unity.

However, political democracy also placed in the hands of the democratic government, led by the ANC, levers of power which could be used to address the most immediate and pressing social and economic needs of the oppressed communities. The RDP was an attempt to reconcile our vision of transformation with what was immediately attainable in practice. The RDP has been further refined through the government's GEAR strategy, which is aimed at operationalising the RDP in the context of the global environment within which South Africa has to live.

But parliamentary democracy means that the ANC has now entered the era of electoral politics. Winning a working majority in the legislative chamber at local, provincial and national levels determines whether or not we will be given the mandate to govern. Electoral politics requires that we package our policies and tasks in a platform that can muster the votes needed to win at the polls.

Without the mandate of the electorate, the movement will not have the authority to put in place the programmes that can bring nearer the attainment of our strategic goals.

Our message of a 'Better Life for All' in 1994, was a bid to encapsulate the long term and immediate objectives of the movement in a catchy and memorable phrase. True to itself and its traditions, the ANC also addressed itself to the entire nation, rather than a section thereof. In spite of this, the election results demonstrated that we garnered support mainly from the African people, sections of the Coloured and Indian middle classes and a tiny fraction of Whites. In KwaZulu-Natal a sizeable portion of the African rural population supported the IFP, as did sections of the White and Indian professional classes. The overwhelming majority of Coloured and Indian working classes voted for the National Party (NP). Whites went overwhelmingly for the NP; a sizeable fraction of the Afrikaners voted Freedom Front (FF), while the remainder, a tiny fraction totalling 2% of the electorate, voted Democratic Party (DP).

The policy positions the ANC put forward could not be faulted by any of its opponents. Some even sought to mimic them! But the election results indicated that in many instances it was identification with particular parties and fear of others, rather than political platforms per se that persuaded voters how to cast their votes. Race, ethnicity, gender and class were very evidently salient factors in voter choice.

THE NATIONAL QUESTION IN CONTEXT

As conventionally understood in South Africa, as elsewhere, the National Question concerns the oppression of one or a number of other people/s by a dominant external or colonial power. Consequently, the right to self-determination or to national freedom/independence does not apply to the dominant group, but is applied exclusively to the oppressed or dominated group. [Thus it would have been absurd for Britain to have characterised the decolonisation of India as an act of British self-determination.] International law, as it evolved after World War II, including a number UN Security Council resolutions on South Africa, further underwrote this interpretation of the right to self-determination. International law, convention and established tradition does not recognise any right to self-determination by an oppressor group or nation. This is a right that can be claimed exclusively by the oppressed!

What then is the relevance of this to South Africa today?

Among the tactical options the ANC was compelled to consider was that of accommodating the demand for a Volks chamber on the part of the White ultra-Right. I submit that it would be utterly wrong to interpret this as some form of recognition of the right to self-determination on the part of the Afrikaners.

Firstly this would violate every precept of international law as it has evolved since 1945, and would also run counter to the ANC's own conception of self-determination.

How then do we view our acceptance of the notion of a Volks chamber?

The example of the Volks chamber serves to highlight a concession that is most glaringly inconsistent with both the democratic foundations of the South African constitution and the tradition to which the ANC has always adhered. There are a number of others, perhaps less jarring, which had to be made at the time as a means of smoothing the transition. It is, however, of paramount importance that we assess whether these were temporary expedients which should not be allowed to congeal into a status quo or were regarded as options that could become permanent. I would like to discuss some of these concessions, as well as their tactical significance in relation to how we view ethnicity, the issue of culture, affirmative action and the emergence of a black capitalist class.

It has become impolitic in South Africa to speak of tribalism. Firstly, because this is an expression that has been used by racists and other enemies of the African people as a means of stigmatising Africans as peculiarly prone to 'tribalism'. Secondly, many have argued that what are usually referred as 'tribes' in the African context, in Europe would be called nations, or at least nationalities. 'Tribe' by this account is yet one more example of derogatory language applicable exclusively to Africans as a way of belittling us. Thirdly, the term 'tribalism' is itself highly politically charged and consequently adds more heat than light to an argument. We have developed a preference for 'ethnicity' as a consequence.

The South Africa that was finally brought under White control and domination at the end of the Anglo-Boer War had formerly been divided amongst at least nine different African political communities. In the south east there had been the kingdoms of the Xhosa, sub-divided into a number of principalities (or paramountcies as the colonialists preferred to call them); in the north east the Zulu Kingdom; the Tsonga kingdom; and the Venda Kingdom. On the highveld were the baPedi kingdom, the Tswana and southern Sotho Kingdoms. In addition to these there were the independent Coloured principalities of the Gri(qua) and Nama(qua), under the leadership of Kapteins (Chiefs) At the Berlin conference of 1884 the colonial powers of Europe had shared Africa out amongst themselves. In many instances the newly established colonial borders divided these kingdoms, as was the case with the Swazi kingdom, whose people lived on either side of the borders, the southern Sotho, the Tsonga and many of the Tswana.

Conquest, accompanied by the growth of agrarian capitalism and later mining, had set in train a number of socio-economic processes that continue to unfold till this very day. The colonial authorities regarded all Africans, irrespective of their affiliation or origin, as a conquered and subject people. A handful could, by the grace of the colonial regime, buy their way out of their helot status by acquiring property of a certain value, or by practising a profession or by engaging in a trade that earned a certain income. These were the 'exempted Natives', who in the Cape and Natal were allowed to vote and were not required to carry passes. Large numbers of Africans, formerly outside the modern economy, were drawn into it first on the mines, then in the developing urban areas.

Most importantly, conquest had drawn African, Coloured, White and the most recent immigrant population, the Indians, into a common society in which the capitalist economy, dominated by the Randlords of

British descent was pre-eminent. The Africans' shared status as colonised people conspired with the economic evolution of the country to create the material conditions for the birth to a national consciousness. This emergent national consciousness was articulated first by the African intelligentsia – clergymen, professionals – in the first decade of the 20th century.

Before and immediately after the Anglo-Boer war, the Colonial authorities in London, had mitigated the worst excesses of the settler White minority in South Africa. Indeed Britain had entered the war proclaiming the amelioration of the condition of Africans in the two Boer Republics as one of its war aims. As a result of this, Black intellectuals and political leaders had come to regard the British government, and those South African Whites who identified with the imperial power, as protectors, patrons or as allies. Britain promptly betrayed these undertakings once the Boers had been defeated and instead sought an accommodation with her former enemies to 'keep the darkies in their place.' The 1905 Native Affairs Commission sealed the British imperial state's betrayal of the hopes of all Blacks by confirming their colonial status in no uncertain terms. National consciousness emerged as a response to conquest and the shedding of past illusions about the imperial state.

The main agencies for the socialisation of Africans into modern life were the mines and factories, churches, schools, formal and informal organisations, and as literacy grew, the press and other media. All of the latter were controlled by the Black intelligentsia. Acculturation thus unfolded largely as a process guided by them and on their terms. This accounts for the extraordinary ideological hegemony of this stratum over modern African communities despite its puny numbers. The values and mores of this intelligentsia were quintessentially the product of transition from pre-colonial to colonial society. In the urban areas new opportunities arose for mixing with Africans and other Blacks from diverse social, ethnic, linguistic, cultural and religious backgrounds. In the towns education, training, skill, wealth and other achievements were the measure of status rather than lineage and descent. New points of contact based on economic, social and political activity in this new environment assisted in forging new identities. The jettisoning of some inherited values, the retention of others and the embracing of new ones, made for a more variegated cultural surroundings which offered more opportunities for the energetic, the creative and talented.

At the same time the homogenising effect of urbanisation on the whole society expanded the area of shared values among Africans, Coloureds, Indians and Whites as members of a common society. The Black – African, Coloured and Indian – leadership that grew within these circumstances accepted the modern world because they recognised its liberatory potential in opening up new vistas for themselves and their people. They were modernists.

Thus by the time the Act of Union was passed in 1909, Africans drawn from varying ethnic stocks belonged to the same church, worked at the same jobs, played the same games, read the same newspapers, belonged to the same sports clubs and shared the same political ideals. Thus a person could be of Zulu birth, be a member of the Congregational Church, work as a clerk on the mines, be a star soccer player, a reader of The Star, and a member of the Native Voters Association, like his neighbour who was Venda, Xhosa, Tswana, Sotho, etc. Such urban Africans shared many of these affiliations with Whites, Coloureds and Indians.

The modernist African intelligentsia consequently evolved an inclusive vision of South Africa, embodied in Rev. Z. R Mahabane's invocation of: 'The common fatherhood of God, and the brotherhood of man'. From its inception African nationalism in South Africa eschewed ethnicity, racism and tribal particularism in favour of a non-racial national agenda expressed in the preamble of the Freedom Charter as 'South Africa belongs to all who live in it....'

This process of homogenisation grew apace with time, picking up speed particularly during and after World War II when millions of Africans from the rural areas were called forth to man industry. As the members of this urbanising African community restructured and reconstituted their identities to take account of the new roles that living and working in a modern economy imposes on them, so too have the significance of particular language communities and ethnic backgrounds assumed diminished importance in the manner in which they conduct their lives.

The concept of a common society was also embraced by the left-wing of the then pre-dominantly White labour movement, organised as the South African Communist Party, in 1924. A handful of White liberals within the dominant capitalist classes began to see it as the inevitable result of the changes wrought by World War II. White liberalism made its last ambivalent attempt to force this recognition on the rest of White South Africa through the 1946 Fagan Commission on Native Laws. Otherwise the majority of White South Africans rejected the notion of a single society, and insisted on excluding Blacks from common citizenship.

Colonialism of a Special Type (CST) carried within it two contradictory tendencies – the one, segregationist; the other, its counter-vailing trend, an integrating impulse. Capitalist development in a colonial setting co-opted the numerous existing instruments of coercion, including racism, and created others of its own for purposes of capital accumulation. Victorian racist ideology, merged with that of the ex-Boer Republics, was the chief instrument of the emergent capitalist classes. The empirical facts of institutionalised racial discrimination, arranged in the hierarchical manner already referred to, have acted upon the consciousness of South Africans to the same or a greater degree than the objective socio-economic forces. The society at large, including the economic institutions themselves, have been the objects of forces and political currents generated within the dominant racist order.

The Segregationist Forces

The principal countervailing tendencies to integration were the economic interests of the dominant White capitalist classes – in mining and agriculture – and the sectional interests of the Afrikaner petty bourgeoisie.

Like any other dominant class, the White oligarchy in mining and commercial agriculture sought to limit access to their economic and social status. Law, inherited custom and the mores of British colonialism in Africa were used to deny Africans access to various forms of productive property. This was first applied in the mines, but was incrementally extended to commercial agriculture, then to various trades and professions, then to a number of commercial activities, culminating in 'Stallardism', that excluded Africans from the urban areas except when 'ministering to the needs of the Whites'. By the 1920s all Whites, including the recently landed immigrant and even the beggar, were defined as members of an exclusive community, collectively endowed with certain rights and prerogatives solely on account of their race.

Racial domination – in its various guises of 'white supremacy with justice' a la Smuts' United Party, or the 'apartheid' of the National Party – was also the means of domination employed in the pursuance of particular class interests. By legislative fiat and administrative measures, the White autocracy steadily destroyed the property-owning classes among Blacks. Beginning with the Natives Land Act of 1913, these measures were followed up by the Natives Land and Trust Act of 1935, the Asiatic Land Tenure Act of 1946, The Group Areas Act of 1951, the Bantu Authorities Act of the same year and a host of others that bankrupted the Black property-owning classes by restricting their rights to own property and engage in commerce. Policies such as the 'civilized (read White) labour policy instituted by the Nat-Labour Pact government after 1924, then further elaborated in the Job Reservation Act of 1954 also made certain forms of skilled work the exclusive preserve of Whites. State policy thus created a racial hierarchy graded by skin colour, with Whites at the top and Africans at the bottom.

An intricate dialectic of race and class was thus devised, resulting in a class stratification coinciding in large measure with a racial hierarchy, so that in general terms the overwhelming majority of Blacks were property-less working people, while the propertied classes were virtually lily White. The ANC's policy thrust of tilting in favour of the working class and its mass organisations is grounded in this reality. Historical experience is also the basis of the alliance with the Communist Party and COSATU.

These racial exclusions were institutionalised in the 1909 Act of Union, then by extension differentially applied to the other Blacks. Indians, as a numerically weak minority of recent immigrants, were the easiest victims. Coloureds, the majority of whom were the descendants of property-less servants and former bonded persons, were to witness steady encroachments on their rights well into the 1970s.

The second powerful reinforcement of racism came from the sectional interests of the Afrikaner petty bourgeoisie and intelligentsia.

British victory in the Anglo-Boer War destroyed Afrikaner independence and threatened to plunge the Afrikaner people into a cosmopolitan, industrialising society dominated by British monopoly capital. The impoverished Afrikaner ex-farmer of the early 1900s, like his African and Coloured counterparts, entered the job market as the least skilled and least acculturated to urban life. All three these groups of former peasants now had to re-invent and restructure their identities as new persons living in a common society. From the perspective of the Afrikaner petty bourgeois intelligentsia – whose domain was the Dutch reformed churches and its educational institutions – this process held out the prospect of the urbanising Afrikaner community drifting away from the church, the 'volk' and other institutions dominated by themselves.

Consequently, the bearers of Afrikaner nationalist ideology were the small property owners and related strata amongst the Afrikaners, whose livelihood depended on the preservation and elevation of that community's distinct language, the preservation of its churches and exclusive schools, as well as other institutions. They manipulated the totems and symbols of the Afrikaner's recent past - defeat in war, the destruction of their republics, suffering at the hands of the British occupation forces, etc. – to cocoon their community against the influences of the cosmopolitan environment. An ethnic nationalism, which alleviated the pain of the Afrikaner working people's alienation, but could not redress their political and economic subordination was the result. Afrikaner ethnic nationalism defined an ethnic 'home' for a people who had been rudely torn from their pre-industrial life by war and bankruptcy and placed them under the ideological domination of the Afrikaner propertied classes who thenceforth employed ethnic mobilisation as the means to carve out a niche for themselves in South Africa's developing capitalist economy.

The Afrikaner nationalists found ready helpers among the right wing of the White labour movement, led by the South African Labour Party. An electoral pact between the two in 1924, defeated Smuts' South African Party and began an inexorable reinforcement of racism through law.

The White labourites hoped to promote the claims of White workers to certain rights by an appeal to their status as Whites in a colonial society. White labourism's alliance with the racists was sealed at the expense of the Black people in general, but the Black working class in particular. As the majority of White workers embraced racism, so too did they drift away from the Labour Party which virtually disappeared from White South African politics by the outbreak of World War II. This led to the coalescence of a racial bloc – Whites as a dominant racial group – led by the capitalist classes, who projected the particular interests of the White propertied classes as the general interest of all Whites.

The third, but no less important countervailing trend was White racist state policy. Once institutionalised, racial domination and its twin, racism infected every pore of society. The compound labour system, originally designed to give mining employers greater control over their work force, was extended to virtually every section of African workers. After the Report of the Stallard Commission in 1923, Africans were arbitrarily defined as aliens in all the urban areas of the country. They were residentially segregated to improve control over their movements and residential segregation quickly became the norm in urban areas outside a few areas of the Cape, Natal and some freehold locations in Johannesburg.

THE EVOLUTION OF SO-CALLED 'AFRICAN CUSTOMARY LAW'

But the chief institutional plank of segregatory politics came as a response to an emergent, inclusive African nationalism as expressed in the phenomenal growth of the ICU during the 1920s. The formulation of 'Native policy' in the Nat-Labour Pact government of 1924 was in the hands of so-called 'experts' from Natal, schooled in the Shepstonian policies of divide and rule.

Dismayed at the ability of the urban Blacks (mainly African and Coloured) to master the organisational skills appropriate to their environment, these experts hit on the notion: 'Bantu communalism rather than Bantu Communism' as a riposte. This was translated into the Native Laws Amendment Act of 1927 – the earliest attempt to create a comprehensive legal framework for racial oppression – which statutorily changed all African monarchs into servants of the state and elevated the Governor-General to the status of 'Supreme Chief of all Natives' (in much the same fashion as the king of Britain was Emperor of India.) All Africans, irrespective of their preference, would henceforth be assigned to a 'tribe' and placed under the authority of chief or headman to whom they would be obliged to pay allegiance. The chiefs and headmen were given extra-ordinary powers of coercion over their 'subjects'. They were granted power to administer the distribution of land, 'tribal' justice, and the system of labour recruitment and control. Thus a parallel legal and administrative regime, applying exclusively to Africans, was established. Its impact was, and continues to be, particularly severe on African women whose rights are radically curtailed in terms of what purports to be 'African customary law'. A key component of the 'triple oppression of African women' were the institutions of so-called 'customary law', which reduced them to the status of legal minors, constricting even further the very limited rights African women could claim under apartheid.

These measures were touted as the promotion of 'traditional' forms of African government and the recognition of 'traditional' African leaders, whom the racist state saw and treated as a counterweight to the modern political leadership offered by the intelligentsia and the urban labour movement.

There was, however, little or nothing that was traditional about these 'traditional authorities' created and installed by the White minority government. No nineteenth century African king or prince would have recognised himself in the tinpot autocrats invented by the 1927 Act.

The institutional incorporation of 'traditional' leaders was a thorough corruption of pre-colonial legal traditions and merely an extension of racial domination by proxy. As a system of indirect rule favoured by colonial powers everywhere, its purpose was creating a caste of relatively privileged Africans who would thus acquire a direct material interest in the preservation of the institutions of racial domination at the expense of their own people. The fact that some of these co-optees could trace descent from the pre-colonial heads of kingdoms and other notables was purely incidental. The White minority state repeatedly demonstrated its low regard for such niceties by the arbitrary deposition of legitimate chiefs and the elevation of lesser figures in a lineage purely on the basis of their attitude towards the racist state.

Because their livelihoods depended on it, these 'traditional' authorities acquired an interest in fostering an ethnic consciousness by wielding the totems, symbols and other paraphernalia of a particular 'culture' or practises that differentiated their subjects from those of other chiefs. Language and 'customs' proved useful foils in such an exercise. The power of 'traditional' authority was augmented with the active connivance of the mining industry who agreed to recognise 'tribal' affiliation in the housing of their labourers in the compounds. This device was eagerly seized upon by other employers of migrant workers who readily recognised it as a cheap means of extending further control over their workforce.

Thus was 'bantu communalism' harnessed to combat, not only communism, but more importantly, an inclusive, progressive African nationalism. The revival of African ethnicity thus had little to do with nostalgia for past greatness on the part of the Africans. It was even less the articulation of a 'psychological urge' (as the theorists of ethnicity claim) to cohere as members of a unique ethnic community. It clearly was a deliberate act of state policy to subvert the struggle for equality and freedom on the part of the African people.

After 1927 the African chiefs and other notables, who had been accorded a special status as an 'upper House' in the ANC, with some outstanding exceptions, withdrew from the national liberation movement. By 1936 the House of Chiefs had fallen to disuse. It was finally abolished under A.B. Xuma's Presidency in 1943.

Verwoerd and the Rise of the Ethnic Entrepreneur

The NP's victory at the polls in 1948 marked the political defeat of those amongst the Whites who had accepted a common society. The White electorate effectively turned its back on liberalism in '48 offering it only the extra-parliamentary route to attain its goals. African Nationalists, Communists, liberals and other democrats collectively would thenceforth have to devise new strategies to realize a common society.

Though the White minority regime had assigned 'bantu communalism' a distinct role in the strategy of domination, it vacillated in its use of the chiefs as an instrument of power. It was only under the post-1948 NP regime that Verwoerd set out quite deliberately and more consistently to sponsor the 'traditional leaders' as the state's front forces of repression in the rural areas set aside for African occupation and as a rival centre of political authority to the national liberation movement.

Verwoerd's method differed from that of previous White pro-consuls over the 'bantus' in that he invested both money and personnel in raising the stature of the 'traditional' authorities to transform them into the central players in a chain of political patronage, presided over by Pretoria. The 'traditional authorities' would be the vital transmission point for such patronage. By this device Verwoerd hoped to endow the 'traditional leaders' with a greater degree of authority by disbursing tangible material rewards to them, which they in turn could dispense to helpers, supporters and collaborators.

Verwoerd theorised his strategy in terms of apartheid ideology, arguing that South Africa was not a common society. An historical accident, the NP ideologue contended, had resulted in the artificial forcing together of members of a number of discrete nations. Thirteen of these were the 'bantu nations', the others were the Afrikaners, the Brits, the Coloureds and Namas, and the Asians. By his account, each of these 'nations' was striving for independence, which apartheid was designed to facilitate, by creating the space for each to 'develop along its own lines.'

The first step the regime took in this direction was the Bantu Authorities Act of 1951, which further inflated the powers of 'traditional leaders', but simultaneously increased the apartheid state's control over them as well. All through the 1950s into the early 1960s, peasants' resistance to the impositions of the racist regime, converged with the resistance of specific chiefs and lineages to the corruption of African tradition as they understood it. The upshot was the peasant uprisings in Witzieshoek (Qwaqwa), Sekhukhune (Lebowa), Rustenburg and Zeerust. The exception to this pattern was the revolt of the Transkei peasants in 1960 to 1961, which was directed against both the newly installed 'Bantu authorities' and their paymasters in Pretoria. That revolt was inevitably led by commoners who identified with the modern liberation movement and whose assemblies adopted the Freedom Charter as their programme.

In the wake of African independence and the rural uprisings of the 1950s and early 60s, the apartheid regime took its strategy still further. Still under the guidance of Verwoerd, by then elevated to the post of Prime Minister in recognition of his services, the 'Bantu Self-government Act' was passed in 1961, ostensibly as the first step to granting independence to the developing 'bantu nations'. The 13 percent of the land area of South Africa set aside as 'Native Reserves' in 1913 was now redefined as 'Bantu homelands' where, Verwoerd proclaimed, all African political aspirations would have to be realised. By definition all African claims in the rest of the country were thus illegitimate and intrinsically seditious.

The act was however an extremely cynical political sleight of hand designed to delegate further repressive powers of control to the 'traditional leaders' and to enmesh them even more thoroughly in the enforcement of apartheid. To make the package more attractive to those who would go along with it, the means of political patronage were greatly augmented as were the arbitrary powers 'traditional authorities' were granted over their subjects. Verwoerd's pro-consuls assiduously revived long forgotten chieftaincies and scoured even urban townships to uncover individuals with some tenuous link to an obscure lineage in order to give substance to this new policy thrust. Once found, such non-entities were encouraged to stake their claims and were duly crowned as 'headmen', 'chiefs', or 'paramount chiefs' by the 'supreme chief of the Natives'. The 'traditional leaders' were encouraged to become ethnic entrepreneurs, who could acquire the status of 'royalty' and enrich themselves provided they were prepared to do the bidding of the apartheid regime. To lend some dignity to this deceitful exercise, the regime also assisted its appointees to constitute what were purported to be modern political parties, but were in fact machines for the dispensing of patronage. The Chief of the Buthelezi clan in KwaZulu proved to be the most adept at using the instruments of the 'homeland' system in constructing a political machine and an effective system of patronage.

At the same time the draconian powers that the 1927 Act had vested in the 'supreme chief of the Natives' were wielded with a new vigour to depose those who proved unwilling to cooperate; to exile and deport those who were defiant; as well as to elevate the most willing collaborators. Thus, for example, Chief Kaiser Matanzima, from a relatively junior lineage among the Tembu, was raised to the same status as his cousin, King Sabata Dalindyebo. And at the other extreme, Chief Moroamocha of the baPedi, who refused till his dying day to cooperate with the apartheid state, was deposed and condemned to internal exile!

Ethnicity, specifically that associated with the 'homelands' and 'bantustan' politics, quite clearly has nothing to do with 'blood', 'the ancestors, 'the soil' and other attributes which ethnicists invariably invoke. It does however have everything to do with White racist policies to thwart the aspirations of our people for freedom, democracy and equality.

THE NATIONAL QUESTION IN POST-APARTHEID SOUTH AFRICA

The sub-heading elicits the question: Is there a national question in post Apartheid South Africa? The easy answer is: not in the form in which it is conventionally understood! Racism is no longer institutionalised; all South Africans now have the franchise; racial restrictions on property rights and on access to the professions, trades, forms of work have been abolished; the instruments of labour coercion have been done away with; and a democratic constitution has put an end to legal repression.

Yet no one can pretend that South Africans share a common patriotism and a common vision of the future of their society. Ours is still a highly racialised society and, since the 1970s, racism has been amplified with a sharpening of ethnic attitudes.

Both racism – attitudinal as well as institutional – and ethnicity are functions of the development of South African capitalism in a colonial milieu. Ethnicity, we have demonstrated, was artificially fostered by the Afrikaner nationalist intellectuals and the White minority state. In the one instance as an instrument of ideological domination over the Afrikaner working people; and in the other, to create an opposing centre of authority to the political leadership coming from the modernist intelligentsia and the labour movement.

Though rooted in these material realities, both forms of ethnicity have produced resonances within the society, and often for very similar reasons.

Less stable and consequently more erratic, is the ethnic consciousness presently found among the Coloured and Indian communities. As Black national minorities both these communities suffered under the apartheid regime, though the extent was marginally better than that endured by Africans. What is peculiar about both is that neither is an assertive identity of 'selfhood'. In the case of both communities there is a dependent identification with their former White masters who are now regarded, at best, as 'the devil we know', and at worst, as a bulwark against a perceived 'black peril' – the African majority – which supposedly will take away their jobs, housing and welfare opportunities.

The driving force behind this ethnic' consciousness is competition with fellow Blacks over scarce resources. The perception of Africans as a clear and present threat is reinforced by a powerful mood of contingency – a fear of change – which would much prefer the known world to remain as it is, rather than risk the uncertainties of change. To the sections of these communities who embraced this outlook, the NP represented the continuity they craved. The electoral behaviour of Coloured and Indian working people is unlikely to change until visible delivery on the part of the democratic government demonstrates that there could be sufficient resources for all the disadvantaged.

Affirmative Action, Corrective Action and the Freedom Charter

This paper proceeds from the premise that the ANC had to make a number of distasteful concessions to the old order in order to secure the beach-head of majority rule in 1994. These were made with the implicit understanding that the main thrust of movement policy would be to consolidate that beach-head and employ it to lay the foundations of a truly democratic society.

We have further argued that the economic unification of the country spawned a number of centripetal forces which have conspired to create a common South African society. However, the productive relations structured and determined by CST, reproduced a racial hierarchy which was institutionalised and has engendered equally centrifugal forces reinforced by the racial and ethnic divisions sponsored by the apartheid state.

Our third premise is that the national liberation movement, with the ANC at its head, has been the most consistent advocate of an inclusive South African nationhood rooted in the universalist, liberatory outlook of modernity and the realities and imperatives of South Africans of all races sharing a common territory. Arising from these, I would contend that issues of democracy, non-racialism and national liberation, on the one hand, and those of racial oppression and ethnicity, on the other hand, come together in acute fashion. And that the attitude one adopts to these two sets of issues defines distinct commitments.

The ANC has always held that democracy, national liberation and non-racialism are inseparable. But, we have equally forcefully said that for democracy to advance national liberation it must entail the empowerment of the oppressed and most exploited – the Africans, Coloureds and Indians. The institutional form this democracy assumes therefore is of crucial importance to us. The Freedom Charter remains the seminal statement of our movement's vision. Empowerment as laid down in it envisages the radical restructuring of key aspects of the economy so as to destroy the material basis of the White racist power structure.

It is this context that I want to pose the issues of Affirmative Action and Corrective Action.

No serious person, even from among our opponents, could pretend that South Africa today is not a country of far greater opportunity than it was ten years ago. The opening up of new opportunities for many who never had a chance to pursue their own ambitions, aims and individual aspirations before has created an environment conducive to the emergence of a class of Black capitalists, a stratum of very senior Black managers and business executives, a stratum of senior Black civil servants and bureaucrats, a stratum of Black professionals, as well as a Black lower middle class. And, Sandile Dikeni's tastes notwithstanding, there is nothing wrong with this.

After all the struggle for democracy was also a struggle to create opportunities for men and women of colour to rise as high as their talents can take them. Obviously the ANC cannot bar Blacks from becoming and being capitalists, any more than it could debar them from becoming lawyers, doctors, accountants, engineers, skilled workers, etc. The high visibility of these strata should not deceive us. In absolute terms they number far, far fewer than their equivalents among Whites.

The vast majority of Blacks, however, remain workers and other working people.

The movement adopted as policy the conscious and deliberate de-racialisation of South Africa by undertaking a host of measures, among which are affirmative action, to ensure that the results of decades of systematic discrimination and denial of job opportunities are reversed. In other words, the purpose of affirmative action is to create circumstances in which affirmative action will no longer be necessary.

The practical implementation of these policies, outside the public sector, has however been problematic. In both the Western Cape and KZN, the impression has quite deliberately been fostered that affirmative action entails the laying off of Coloured and Indian workers or denying opportunity to Coloured and Indian workers to create opportunities for Africans. The mischievous intent of these practices is obvious and it has already produced handsome returns for the NP and DP in both constituencies.

Racial and ethnic flashpoints over what are seen as diminishing job opportunities are thus being created to compound the existing tensions encouraged by the racial hierarchy in jobs and skills of the past.

The questions we have to pose are, do we see it as one of our tasks, among others, to legislate and lay down strict guidelines for the implementation of this aspect of policy? Should such guidelines apply to all categories of jobs or only to certain ones? Would the most effective means of implementation require the setting of targets by government and the private sector? To what extent should government hold the public sector corporations to account for their implementation of affirmative action?

Beyond the sphere of employment, systematic exclusion from opportunity and property rights has also left a legacy of unrepresentativity in every sector of the economy. Captains of industry in South Africa are invariably White males. The same category of persons dominate the boardrooms of every major corporation in mining, industry, banking and commerce. Commercial farming is virtually by definition the preserve of Whites.

In the de-racialisation of society, is the fostering and encouragement of these emergent Black middle classes one of the ANC tasks? And, if we say it is not, what will be the consequences of that choice? [because like it or not, these classes and strata are emerging and will evolve.] If the ANC does not relate to them other political forces will. Who will those forces be? With what consequences? What will/should the content of our engagement with these emergent middle classes be?

The ANC itself is a multi-class movement, yet it would be correct to say that historically ours is a movement that has received far greater support from certain classes than from others. Since the 1940s, it is specifically the African working class of town and country who have been the movement's main base of support. Historically the movement has employed the classic weapon of working class struggle – the general strike – as its principal method of peaceful struggle. Because of the relative weight of the working class and other working people among the oppressed the ANC has also tilted unambiguously in favour of their cause and aspirations.

But we insist that the multi-class bloc constituted under the leadership of the ANC is essential for the transformation process. I would suggest that this implies that the ANC's engagement with the emergent Black bourgeoisie should involve the elaboration of certain standards of conduct and a business ethic that will speed the realization of the postponed goals' of the national liberation movement. In the immediate timeframe this must include job creation, the fostering of skills development, the empowerment of women, the strengthening of the popular organs of civil society, and active involvement in the fight to end poverty.

The ANC must also encourage this Black bourgeoisie to cultivate within their own enterprises and in those where they hold executive positions, the creative management of the conflict potential in industrial relations. In other words, the ANC must influence the Black bourgeoisie to assume certain RDP related responsibilities and to give the lead to the business community with respect to responsible corporate behaviour.

Since 1994 the multi-class character ANC itself has of course changed.

Whereas in the past there were no captains of industry in the leading organs of the ANC; today an NEC member heads one of the largest conglomerates trading on the Johannesburg Stock Exchange. This corporation, moreover, employs thousands of other ANC members as well as ANC supporters! Prior to 1994 Transnet, one of the biggest state-owned corporations which employs thousands of ANC supporters and members organised in the South African Railways and Harbours Workers' Union (SARHWU), was headed by one Johan Maree. Today its MD is a member of the NEC.

We will neither handle the tensions this new situation can give rise to by denial nor by a blind insistence that there is no conflict potential between the director of a corporation and the workers employed by it.

THE STRUGGLE WITHIN THE STRUGGLE

Proceeding from what we have said before, it is clear that the movement's own non-racialism and non-ethnic ethos is not merely a matter of high moral principle. The endurance and sustenance of these norms which many today take for granted, has not been unproblematic. The ever present racism in South African society and the ethnic and tribal segmentation encouraged by the White minority state were powerful currents against which our movement has had to contend.

The movement itself has consequently been the site of intense politico-ideological struggles around the issues of ethnicity, race, class and gender. During the 1930s, for example, a conservative section of the ANC's founding fathers led a campaign to expel Communists from the movement and to move it closer to the liberal fraction of the White establishment. At around the same time Dr John L. Dube, led the bulk of the ANC branches in Natal out of the mother body to set up his own regional organisation in opposition to the ANC.

It was only in 1948 that Chief Luthuli and others were able to win back the ground lost to Dube branch by branch, until they could compel re-affiliation of the province.

At the height of the struggles of the 1950s a group of dissidents, led by Potlako Leballo, tried to manipulate the justifiable anger of Africans against their oppressors on an 'Africanist' platform, a large component of which was also opposition to Communism. The majority of ANC members resisted these siren songs despite the evident emotional appeal of the 'Africanist' slogans. The dissidents walked out of the ANC to constitute themselves as the Pan Africanist Congress (PAC) in 1959. [And, it is important to underline that the 'Africanists' were NOT expelled from the ANC! They left it voluntarily, as they had joined it, voluntarily!]

There have been repeated attempts through the years by others to whip up residual ethnic loyalties and sectional inclinations as a means of mobilising support around platforms of dubious credibility. To the credit of the ANC's membership, none of these attempts have been successful.

Which raises the question: Is the ANC leaving those of our people who identify ethnically to the political wolves of ethnic entrepreneurship by continuing to discourage ethnicity and favouring an inclusive nationalism?

Perhaps that question is best answered by posing others.

What honour would accrue to the ANC if it were to compete with the PAC on the issue of 'Africanism'?

Or better yet, can the ANC ever hope to outdo the IFP in the promotion of a Zulu ethnicity and chauvinism?

And, if it did try to compete on such terrain, what price would the movement have to pay in order to do so?

And, what price will it have to pay for having done so?

A third question: Would the ANC profit by trying to pander to the baser instincts of the Coloured and Indian working people?

It's proper that we remind ourselves of our strategic goal - creating a democratic, non-racial, non-sexist society. The radical transformation of the quality of life of the Black majority is central to these objectives. Putting an end to poverty, hunger, insecurity, and economic exploitation should therefore be at the top of the ANC's agenda.

To the ANC, democracy, non-racialism and non-sexism do not mean that every five years Tony Leon and his African domestic worker can stand in the same queue in Houghton to vote. They mean creating the conditions in which that domestic worker's daughter, has a fair chance of competing equally with Tony Leon's son,

- for a place at the best schools in South Africa,
- for a chance to play the same sports, on sporting facilities of the same quality,
- to have access to the best cultural amenities,
- to compete with him for a place at Wits,
- to become a lawyer (or doctor, etc) if she so wishes,
- and to move in next door to Leon (or even Harry Oppenheimer for that matter), if that is what she wants.

The ANC's vision of empowerment of the mass of our people requires a highly critical attitude towards ethnicity and sectional claims. This does not imply insensitivity to the sense of grievance felt by many African communities and language groups about the relegation and corruption of their languages and cultural practices. I would however argue that the redress of these does not require recognition of special ethnic claims or the politicisation of the issue of language. More specifically, with regard to the claims of the pro-apartheid Afrikaners and Afrikaans speakers, the democratic traditions offering constitutional and other special protection to ethnic and linguistic minorities were designed to secure the rights of oppressed groups whose rights would otherwise be threatened by dominant oppressor groups. Latter-day attempts to appeal to the authority of that tradition as a means of sheltering the privileges of racist and oppressive minorities do violence to that tradition and are patently fraudulent.

TOWARDS SOLUTIONS

Solving the national question requires that in the first instance we pose the correct questions and not buy into the mythology and metaphysics of ideologists. As in all instances, the national question in South Africa is undergirded by the material realities the development of capitalism in a colonial setting and the institutions created to sustain those productive relations.

To return to Rosa Luxemburg, we cannot hope to address these problems by uncritically embracing some of the temporary expedients the movement had to adopt in the context of a negotiated settlement.

With the exception of the most backward and fanatical racists, the Afrikaner petty bourgeois intellectuals have forsaken ethno-nationalism, hoping to constitute a multi-racial coalition of conservative forces to oppose the national liberation movement in the hustings. They can be expected to continue engaging in a modified form of ethnic mobilisation around the issue of the Afrikaans language for the resonances it can produce among sections of the Coloured population, but most realize that such a policy thrust will prove unattractive to the majority of voters.

Ethnic mobilisation and entrepreneurship, in its various guises – including that of federalism – however still poses a serious problem and represents the gravest single threat of destabilization and subversion in our new democracy. The tap root of ethnicity and political adventures based on it, are apartheid and the artificial revival of so-called 'traditional' institutions undertaken first in the 1920s then pursued with fanatical zeal by Verwoerd and his acolytes after 1948. The so-called 'traditional' leaders' all have, to one degree or another, acquired an interest in these institutions. In addition to power and prestige, these institutions have become a lucrative source of income and patronage. Their propensity to reproduce new generations of ethnic entrepreneurs cannot be under-estimated.

A possible solution could be the dis-establishment of so-called 'traditional' leaders, which would include their being allowed to retain their ceremonial titles and roles, but they should enjoy no state powers by virtue of these titles. The stipends they presently enjoy from government could also be phased out over time. Such a step would necessarily also require the reduction of the house of traditional leaders to a purely ceremonial one and its eventual elimination as an institution of state. Recognition of a 'traditional' leader should become a voluntary matter, with persons voluntarily agreeing to pay allegiance, tribute or any other dues that the office 'traditionally' entitled its holder to claim. 'Traditional' leaders should be relieved of various powers - such distribution of land – that they still retain, despite the democratic constitution. Their judicial powers should also be subjected to rigorous review to ensure that all South Africans, especially Africans, are completely equal before the law. The time frames for such reforms can be negotiated, but the need for change has to be accepted in principle.

The democratic breakthrough of 1994 has created conditions which enable the ANC and its allies to steadily eradicate the material base of racism in our society. Measures that address the capacity of ethnicists to reproduce ethnicity will greatly assist in undermining its appeal among certain sections of the population. It can be expected that the NP will try to employ a modified form of the 'black peril' to mobilise electoral support amongst a segment of the Coloured, Indian and White population, but that too will loose its appeal as the democratic government's reforms make it plain that there is sufficient wealth to address the quality of life problems of all working people.

If we accept that the racialisation of South African politics was rooted in specific historical and material conditions, there is no reason why radical transformation of those conditions cannot result in an end to racism and provide a solution to the national question. This will probably require the ANC to pursue de-racialisation with the same determination and tenacity as the racists pursued racism and division. This must be done as a matter of conscious policy. We should give no quarter to any form of racial discrimination in schooling, employment, housing and recreation; and must positively reinforce all efforts at de-racialisation. This will not prevent a person who places some value in being identified as Venda/Sotho/Tswana/Zulu/Xhosa, etc. from doing so, but it will not require another, who sets no store by that, being compelled to do so. It does however require us to reject the insistence of ethnicists and racists that ethnic origin or race defines an individual's identity or should take precedence over everything else in defining it.

Acknowledging the un-finished character of our national democratic revolution is not to detract from the significance of the gains our movement has made. It should rather spur us to press even harder for the commencement of the next phase of an unfolding democratic revolution. Now more than ever the slogan of the day should be 'A luta continua' – the struggle continues!

SIXTEEN

A short article which links in interesting ways to earlier pieces on the black bourgeoisie and to Jordan's views on the negotiated settlement: 'The historical upshot turned out more complex than any of the theorists and strategists had anticipated,' he notes drily.

The Changing Character of the National Democratic Alliance

Mail & Guardian, 24–29 April 1998

The Black (African, Indian and Coloured) political movements that pioneered the democratic struggle were initially led by an educated elite who had embraced democracy and modernism as universal visions. 'Modernism' has been used in two senses, one technological, the other socio-political. Its technological dimension assumed humanity would incrementally attain mastery over nature by the application of science and technology. This is a view rooted in the belief that, provided it is not circumscribed by either secular or clerical authority, human endeavour has unlimited possibilities. Modernism is also rationalist, asserting that reasoned debate, inquiry and investigation are the only reliable basis of human knowledge.

Modernity in South Africa had two loci. One of the urban areas, where modern technology was visibly opening new frontiers and drawing millions of Blacks into a vast economic system that spans the world. The other was the schoolroom, where the elite itself had acquired the knowledge and skills, as well as the self-confidence to challenge the White rulers on their own terms.

The Black elites advocated a society in which the ability and worth of a person would be judged on the basis of their performance rather than ascribed from some alleged racial characteristics. Such a society, they believed, would encourage progress by rewarding talent, Black or White.

The political leadership of the Black working class has also been unabashedly modernist. The working class, like the productive forces it mans, is the object of a continuing process of renewal, improvement and refinement. The demands and rhythms of the economy require that the working class constantly change and adapt itself to technological progress. Thus while not denying the brutalising impact of industrialization on pre-capitalist African societies, the working class leadership has preferred to focus on its transformative and progressive aspects.

The rationalist bias of modernism includes the interrogation of traditional belief systems, customs and accepted mores. Such questioning undermines the existing order by subjecting authority to the scrutiny of reason. The modern political ideals of popular sovereignty, government by the consent of the governed, and equality before the law collided directly with the institutions of White overlordship, kingship and chieftaincy. The modernists, the corollary of the notion that some people are born to rule, is that others are born to be ruled, which flies in the face of the principle of equality. Modernism implicitly challenged the legitimacy of both the White state, with its racist doctrine, and the traditional African aristocracy.

Progress, thus is itself contradictory. It disrupted the lives of entire communities; continuous change produced profound uncertainties. Many individuals, however, prefer the predictability of the known present or the past to the maelstrom of change. Thus, though conservatism sits uneasily with the existential situation of the urban working class, large sections of it have recourse to tradition, its language and its symbols for warmth and comfort.

Since the publication of Nimrod Mkele's article, 'The Emergent African Middle Class' in *Optima* (Vol 10, No.4. 1960), it has generally been accepted that despite differences in lifestyle, life chances and incomes, the African petty bourgeoisie and the majority of African working people would ultimately make common cause because of the shared burden of national oppression. By extension, the same was assumed to apply among Coloureds and Indians as well. These assumptions were the cornerstones of liberation movement strategy. This perspective excluded the possibility of an elite accommodation because, it was argued, the disabilities of the Black elite obliged it to seek more radical solutions.

The historical upshot turned out more complex than any of the theorists and strategists had anticipated.

Rather than through the seizure of power, change came to South Africa as negotiated settlement with a host of explicit and implicit compromises. The radical courses that both Black elites and working people would otherwise have followed have been deferred. The struggle has resulted in an unfinished revolution based on a settlement that privileges the rights of property at the expense of its obligations. This could produce tensions in the multi-class national democratic alliance forged during the struggle for liberation. Elite accommodation is now being pursued in earnest. But there is nothing inevitable about the success of such a project.

My difficulty with Heribert Adam is that he appears not to have proceeded beyond the first year in his study of Marxism. Had he done, he would be conversant with the Hegelian concept: 'the cunning of reason', with which Marx's writings on India, China and the American Civil War are suffused. It suggests that even malevolent intent, employing vile methods, can nonetheless have desirable consequences. He would also be familiar with the clear distinction Marxists draw between a bourgeoisie, like the French, who attained ascendancy by revolutionary means; and others, like the Germans, who rode to it in the slipstream of the reforming Prussian state. All bourgeoisies, of course, wish to maximise their profits, but that does not mean they are identical.

I agree with Cronin that class and race have begun to diverge and that we should be alive to the real, though latent, contradictions that could now affect a hitherto unified bloc of national democratic forces, but there continues to be an objective basis for unity among this broad alliance.

With the state's capacity to intervene so severely constrained, are there no possibilities for Black owned companies, pursuing rich dividends to be sure, to contribute to economic development, working in creative alliances and joint ventures with union investment houses, CBOs and state corporations? New forms of public ownership that do not necessarily entail state ownership could also be explored.

Greater enthusiasm is needed in seconding government-led initiatives. Black-owned corporations could drive these by giving a lead. The working poor and the Black bourgeoisie have a shared interest in the implementation of those aspects of the democratic programme that have for the moment been deferred.

Should these not be the Sunrise Clauses for 1999?

Z. Pallo Jordan.

Cape Town.

SEVENTEEN

This is a partisan but entertaining analysis of election slogans and images used by the New National Party, the Democratic Party, the Inkatha Freedom Party, and other smaller parties in the 1999 general election.

Values and Virtues of
Lamppost Literature

Business Day, 19 May 1999

S top an ANC Two-Thirds majority, screamed and the blue, white and
yellow poster from the lamppost. Tony Leon Needs You, proclaimed
another in the same hues. Thus began the Democratic Party's (DPs) drive
to encourage its supporters register as voters.

Not to be outdone the New National Party (NNP) summoned its
forces with stirring call to Register Against crime. Running true to form,
the NNP peddled its stock in trade, encouraging fear and insecurity in
the electorate.

Supporters who might have been confused by the name change were
reassured by the constancy in party colours: orange, white and blue, the
colours of the apartheid republic's flag and the insignia, NP, sans the N.

Many supporters of both parties remained unconvinced about doing
the right thing. Their uncertainty was reinforced by the court action of
the authors of these slogans.

Evidently unsure that their negative messages would have the desired
effect, both the DP ad the NPP sought relief form the court to compel
the Independent Electoral Commission (IEC) to allow unregistered
voters to vote. A ruling in their favour would have rendered their posters
superfluous.

Once registration had passed the election campaign began in earnest.

From its initial Kitchener image, the DP moved to that of Churchill, decking lampposts with Tony Leon's picture alongside the slogan The Guts to Fight Back.

This belligerent tone was sustained in a second and third poster in what appears to be an unfolding campaign to convince us that the DP are not wimps. Repeating the same Fight Back in poster number two and ending with a third – You have the Power. Fight Back.

Less imaginatively, the NPP sought to ride on Leon's cattails with Mugabe has Two Thirds. And, depending on where you live, the NNP exhorted you to Hang Rapists and killers to show No Mercy for Criminals.

Interestingly in the Western Cape, a proactive plagued by the very 'rapists and killers' whom the NNP assures us it will hang, its blood-thirsty battle cry has been played down in favour of a variety of messages targeting different constituencies

In Cape Town's city centre, the leafy suburbs along the Table Mountain green belt and in historically coloured areas of the Cape Flats, the NNP's message Keep the ANC out the Western Cape, alternates with Keep the Western Cape NP – without qualifying 'new. In Khayelitsha and Gugulethu the posters read: For the Future of your Children, Keep the Western Cape NP. Old habits die hard as these separate but equal posters testify. The NNP campaign is unfocused. Its strategists seem to believe in a blunderbuss approach. Fire away in the hope that at least some of the pellets will inflict some damage.

It has peppered the streets with a variety of negative messages ranging from the wild assertions that axes have gone up under the democratic government to No jobs for Matriculants. Make SA Governable, declared the IFP's family group of three elephants, mimicking a slogan coined by the African National Congress underground during the second half of the 1980s.

As if to give the lie to the party's commitment to good governance, on Tuesday last week one of its leading legislators lead the police to an arms cache he and others had secreted in bunkers close to Ulundi.

The Freedom Front offers Die Span Met 'n Plan never quite defining what the plan is.

More modestly the Pan Africanist Congress of Azania has produced busy little posters with print that is illegible except to the most laid back pedestrians who can take time out to read them. But then, clarity was never this party's strongest point.

The even tinier African Christian Democratic Party seems confused about the real purpose of elections, salvation or constituting a government.

From the election posters, of the main opposition parties, a new voter, unfamiliar with SA politics, would find it impossible to get a firm grip on the issues.

None of them advocates a single solution to SA's problems- except the NNP, which seems to think that blood sacrificed by the state will create jobs, build schools and uplift the poor.

A more disturbing spectacle is the DP's campaign. Vote Your Hopes, Not Your Fears, the DP said during the whites-only referendum in 1992. This time it is telling voters to damn hope and voter their fears. Its logo also conveys an uncomfortable message – a small yellow (the colour of cowardice) circle, in the embrace of blue (the colour of conservatism) wings, enfolded within a larger white (the complexion of the party) circle.

The ANC'S understated, nonhysterical campaign that has dwelt on the real political issues presents a sharp contrast to the belligerent tone of the DP and NNP's hangmen.

It's Your Future, Protect it, Register to Vote, ANC posters read. Suiting words with deeds, when the IEC had difficulties in manning registration stations, ANC members volunteered to assist, much to the chagrin of a churlish opposition which preferred to sit on its hands.

Except for one mischievous stunt by its Western Cape region, who thought they could unpack the subtext of the DP's Fight Back slogan, the ANC has abstained from negative campaigning. A Better Life for All in a country with endemic unemployment, hunger, and a spiraling crime seems to make more sense than promising a good fight or rapists the rope.

Mbeki for President is a slogan for which the opposition has no riposte. None of them can field a credible presidential candidate. The ANC has approached SA's second democratic election with a dignity worthy of its age. Its campaign evinces the quiet confidence of a party that knows what it is doing and where it is going.

At every point it has homed in on the burning issues that affect the quality of ordinary people's lives. Its eyes squarely fixed on the prize of a convincing majority, it is aiming for a clear mandate to translate its manifesto into a vigorous programme of reform.

Perhaps that is the distinction between the politics of hope and the politics of despair.

EIGHTEEN

Another riposte – this time to Andrew Kenny, who had accused the ANC of re-racialising politics, but with the Democratic Party also at the receiving end of Jordan's sardonic humour. Their 'muscular liberalism', he sniffs, 'is merely flabby conservatism'.C

A Witches' Brew with the Tongue of Newt

Business Day 19 August 1999

Muscular liberalism is merely flabby conservatism. After his election as US president in 1948, the Democratic administration of Harry Truman passed the Civil Rights Act. The law targeted government institutions in the first instance, among them the US defence force.

One of the instruments employed to ensure that action suited the fine words in the law was the careful monitoring of the numbers of African-Americans enrolled in the US military academies; the employment of policies of corporations that received defence contracts; the number of companies owned and run by racial minorities that received such contracts and so on.

These practices were later extended to other sectors of the federal government and are still in force. The US defence force is probably the most integrated institution in the US today, with women and members of minority groups well represented at every level.

A corporation that is putting a new product on the market will usually undertake extensive market research to test the waters and once the product has been launched its performance in the marketplace will be closely monitored.

Within a few months the corporation will have a fairly clear idea whether or not its previous research was accurate and whether or not it has invested wisely in its new product line.

Monitoring and regular review of performance indicators are tried and tested methods employed in every facet of human endeavour to assess success or failure.

During the course of the last half century virtually every government has also used them as a tool to weigh the efficacy of policy. Why should their application with respect to the achievement of racial equality in a deeply divided society striving to overcome the legacy of racism cause such a furore.

Andrew Kenny claims that government policy is re-racialising SA politics. Indeed, the Democratic Party (DP) made this charge one of its key election themes, especially when addressing Indian and coloured voters.

'Your colour still matters,' Tony Leon declaimed. 'What about merit?' the DP challenged.

Abstractly considered, these might be telling points. But they betray a profound insensitivity to the realities of SA life and the experience of the black majority.

It is interesting to note that the opponents of Truman's policies also screamed 'racism in reverse'!

They were, of course, unabashed white supremacists, racists and conservatives, anxious to keep things as they were.

Kenny, like many latter-day SA liberals, subscribes to the hoary old dogma that any form of intervention has a distorting effect on the market. The underlying assumption is that the market, left to its own devices, will invariably optimise performance and consequently contribute immeasurably to the public good.

While the market can very easily assess the value of a host of commodities, it finds it difficult to, or understates, the value of intangibles that we cannot buy and sell. Clean, fresh air, the pristine beauty of a landscape, the diversity of natural life – all these have suffered immeasurably as the dogmatists of the free market have translated their ideas into social policy.

There are many other things the marketplace prices wrongly – education, public infrastructure, public health, research and the quality of good governance. It is self-evident to most sensible people that the market, left to its own devices, does not necessarily deliver.

Hence state intervention – to regulate the market, to correct imbalances it might produce and to achieve those desirable public aims it cannot weigh – is widely accepted by social democrats, liberals and socialists as vitally necessary in virtually all democracies.

The greater majority of SA's people have stated their preferences through the ballot box. While the view of the majority by no means closes discussion on any social issue, it does reflect what they expect of government.

That the African National Congress, which was elected to address these expectations, finds it difficult to lend a polite ear to the free market blather from the mouths and pens of the well heeled and well fed is hardly surprising.

Kenny confuses the intent of policy with its instruments. I assume he accepts the de-racialisation of our society as an objective government should pursue.

The setting of targets (or quotas, the term preferred by our SA liberals) by which we can measure the success of policy surely must be one of the tools government employs. To put it bluntly, unless we can count heads – the heads of the blacks, women, the disabled and others who have been discriminated against in the past – there is no way to assess the extent to which we are reversing the consequences of apartheid policy.

Yes, to that extent, all these things still matter and will matter until policy has rendered them irrelevant. Does it surprise Kenny that those most likely to benefit from such procedures read opposition to them as an attempt to retain the status quo?

The party that claims to be the flagship of liberalism in SA today appears to have sold out virtually every liberal principle and seems driven by an obsessive antagonism to the ANC. What has been termed a muscular liberalism by its proponents is a profoundly uncharitable conservatism, rooted not in sound liberal principles but in latter-day conservatism associated with Ronald Reagan in the US and the Monday Club in the UK.

Ironically it is the supporters of this brand of liberalism who have most consistently cast a damning spotlight on its essentials.

Stephen Mulholland, for example, boasts that the DP is in the good company of the US Supreme Court in opposing affirmative action. Little does Mulholland realise that the current US Supreme Court bench is probably the most conservative since the mid 1930s.

Every virtue of liberalism has been incorporated in our democratic constitution. This, incidentally, includes the obligation to redress the legacy of apartheid. One such device, but by no means the only one, is affirmative action.

This is in the best tradition of western liberalism and was originally crafted by the Johnson administration in the US during the 1960s. the US politician who distinguished himself by nay-saying affirmative action was Spiro Agnew. It should be a cause of embarrassment that he is one of the DP's kindred spirits.

I shall return to the unpleasant Nigel Bruce affair because I was integrally involved. That Kenny cannot name a single African editor who has used the offensive terms he quotes tells its own story.

Whatever Bruce's intentions were, I was among the first people to draw his attention to the offensive nature of his remarks.

It might be easy for Kenny, who has probably never been at the receiving end of vile and degrading racist jibes, to prattle lightly about such matters. But those who are demeaned and humiliated by them find them deeply offensive.

I would have thought any decent human being would retract and apologise when it was pointed out that he had inadvertently caused offence.

On three separate occasions before this year's elections, when offered the opportunity to do so, Nigel Bruce refused. Does that not suggest that the offence was indeed intended?

What SA is facing is a rearguard action by the unreconstructed who are employing every device to hold back change and not a new McCarthyism. It is a witches brew that stands before us with the tongue of Newt floating among its ingredients. Is it not time that genuine liberals called a halt to this weird sister's dance?

NINETEEN

A comment on the centenary of the South African (or Anglo-Boer) War that is written across the grain of most accounts of the anniversary. Jordan insists on the culpability of British colonial policy ('legalised brigandage' as James Connolly dubbed it); he also remarks on the historical amnesia attached to the centenary – the crushing of the Venda, the deaths of African prisoners of war in British and Boer hands. (The quotation in the penultimate paragraph is by Rosa Luxemburg.)

Observing the Anglo-Boer War

Business Day, 1 November 1999

We observe anniversaries to recall specific events, and through ritual attempt to imprint them on the collective memory of present and future generations. It was therefore to be expected that the centenary of the outbreak of the Anglo-Boer War would be marked by a number of ceremonies. Key nodal dates in that conflict will be likewise noted.

Those who observed from afar and did not see or experience the carnage, the brutalities and human misery the war entailed, romantically referred to it as 'the last gentleman's war'. Afrikaans writers, until recently, called it 'the second war of liberation' (Die Tweede Vryheidsoorlog). It has now been rechristened the Anglo-Boer South African War.

At the end of the week the war broke out, the Irish socialist, James Connolly, penned a damning indictment of British colonial policy, denouncing it as legalised brigandage. Connolly was of course writing from an Irish perspective. With Ireland's own experience of some 200 years of British domination he readily identified with another people who had fallen victim to Britain's taste for empire.

Connolly's words echoed around the world. In South Africa John Tengo Jabavu, the doyen of African journalism and the founder-editor of 'Imvo Zabantsundu', despite decades of loyalism to the Empire, editorialised so vigorously against the war that his newspaper was banned. Anti-British sentiment also found resonances in the Swazi royal family which sent a delegation to Paul Kruger with an offer of military assistance.

In Europe itself, with the exception of Turkey, virtually every government stood opposed to Britain. A consensus arose among otherwise mutually competitive powers, who became odd bedfellows in their shared antagonism towards British aggression. Within each of these nations too, public opinion was overwhelmingly critical of Britain for provoking a war with what Connolly described as a 'simply peasant nation'. On this issue Tsar Nicholas II, and his arch enemies – the populists, the social democrats and anarchists – found themselves on the same side. In Germany, the Kaiser was able to exploit vocal anti-British sentiment to his advantage and piloted a naval construction programme through the Reichstag virtually unopposed. In France too, the socialists and radicals sat comfortably in the company of their political opponents on the right.

Britain was at the pinnacle of her career as an imperial power in 1899. Unencumbered by alliances in Europe, other than her long-standing commitment to the preservation of the Ottoman Empire as a bulwark against Russia, she conducted her diplomacy and fought the war in 'splendid isolation', supported by troops from her far flung empire.

The British generals and colonial officials had anticipated a short, inexpensive war. The upshot was a war that lasted four years and cost the British exchequer in excess of 200 million pounds. It proved the costliest war Britain had fought in the colonies that century.

James Connolly can be forgiven for viewing the South African events through green-tinted lenses. Unlike the European powers, who contented themselves with bombastic diplomatic notes, a number of Irishmen suited their sentiments with deeds by volunteering and fighting in the Boer trenches against the perceived common enemy. Tsar Nicholas raised an ambulance brigade to help the Boers by kept his troops at home while a number of Russian volunteers made their way to South Africa.

What is remarkable about this centenary, presumably observed to ensure that we do not forget, is the historical amnesia that accompanies it.

In 1898, Petrus Joubert had led the armies of Kruger's Zuid Afrikaanse Republiek into the Zoutpansberg to crush the last independent African kingdom in South Africa. In a brutally fought campaign, Joubert blasted last-ditch resisters out of their caves and forced Makgatho and Mphephu to surrender. Like the communities conquered before them, the Venda had to submit to Kruger's taxes and to forced labour. Had James Connolly known, he would have recognised the methods of Ireland's British tormentors in the practices of the 'simple peasant nation' to whose defence he had sprung. He would have been even more deeply shocked had he heard of the Boer's policy on captured African combatants and helpers fighting on the British side. Is it not a little curious that while much has been written and said about the Africans who suffered and died in the concentration camps, there is a deafening silence about African prisoners of war held by the Boers?

Within a year of the outbreak of war in South Africa, European imperialism dropped its mask when a Chinese peasants' secret society, the Yo Hetuan or the Boxers, rose up against foreign encroachments on China's sovereignty. A German general, Waldersee, led an expeditionary force drawn from the European powers, the Untied States and Japan, that marched on Beijing and suppressed them. It was, parenthetically, in that context that the Kaiser coined the phrase 'yellow peril'. On that occasion, the sensibilities that had inspired so much sympathy for the Boer cause were conspicuously absent.

With a hundred years of hindsight, a British royal may today dismiss the war as 'pointless'. But in 1899 it seemed to make perfect sense to spend 220 million pounds, to send 29 000 men to their deaths, to destroy the farms and homesteads of Afrikaaners [sic], and to starve 272 000 women, children and men to death in concentration camps, if the prize was Southern Africa's mineral wealth and securing the sea routes to Britain's richest colony, India.

Controversial and conflicting interpretations of the war, by whichever name it's called, very likely will continue well into the next century. But I have still to be convinced that the conclusions of one commentator, written thirteen years later, were misguided. She wrote of the parties to the conflict:

'Both competitors had precisely the same aim: to subject, expel and destroy the coloured peoples, to appropriate their land and press them into service by the abolition of their social organisation. Only their methods of exploitation were fundamentally different. While the Boers stood for out-dated slavery on a petty scale on which their patriarchal peasant economy was founded, the British bourgeoisie represented modern large scale capitalist exploitation of the land and the natives.'

The outcomes of the war – the Peace at Vereeniging, the 1905 Native Laws Commission, the Act of Union, and the 1913 Land Act – all seem to bear out that interpretation.

TWENTY

Jordan marks the ten-year anniversary of De Klerk's famous speech historically, reviewing events and developments during the 1980s that led the State President to that point. February 2 earned De Klerk his place in history, Jordan concludes, although the National Party 'proved unequal to the stature he had attained'.

How the Rubicon Finally Came to be Crossed

Business Day, 2 February 2000.

The liquidation of the system of apartheid by the speediest possible route was the centerpiece of the African National Congress's (ANC's) political agenda during the 1980s. Mapping out the transition from apartheid to a democracy preoccupied the movement's key strategist for the entire decade. The 1980s saw the most determined attempts by the National Party (NP) government to suppress the democratic movement. There were two states of emergency. Cross-border raids into Mozambique, Lesotho, Botswana, Swaziland, Zimbabwe and Zambia became a regular feature.

Its strategy also entailed the extensive use of armed surrogates to complement its security services.

The Witdoeke changed THE Crossroads squatter camp from a centre of resistance to a stronghold of reaction. Armed gangs of vigilantes, with the help of security forces, wreaked terror on ANC-supporting townships. A low-intensity war, funded and fanned by the most elements in the security forces simmered in KwaZulu-Natal.

But the mass struggles waged during the mid-1980s had effectively legalized the ANC, though it remained an illegal organisation in law. Even the SA Communist Party's (SACP's) banner had been defiantly unfurled during a funeral in Cradock.

The issue of political power became central to all political campaigns. The ANC openly declared its immediate strategic task as gearing all its forces – legal and illegal, armed and unarmed – for a strategic advance for the seizure of power. Operation Vulindlela under the personal supervision of Oliver Tambo and Joe Slovo, was set in motion in 1985. At its congress, held in Havana during 1989, the SACP adopted a strategy of armed insurrection.

Yet there was a discernible narrowing of the gulf between the apartheid regime and its opponents in the broad democratic movement on a range of issues.

In 1985 a subcommittee of the ANC national executive committee (NEC) was set up to explore the issue of negotiations. A statement on talks, adopted by the NEC in October 1987, fleshed out the ANC's conception of these more fully. In 1989 the NEC adopted the Harare declaration. The option of a negotiated settlement was under serious consideration by both camps by the end of the decade.

The first tentative signals that the NP was in earnest came during the second half of 1989, after FW de Klerk received the solid endorsement of the white electorate during a 'whites-only' election, when all the Rivonia trialists bar Nelson Mandela were unconditionally released from prison.

The announcement on February 2 1990 was therefore not a surprise. The ANC leadership expected something dramatic on that day. What some of us found rather disappointing was De Klerk's evident reluctance to grasp the nettle of responding to the Harare declaration. It was, however, clear that he faced objective pressures to which he had to respond.

Equally clearly, the NP Government had not yet attained coherence about its strategic direction.

But De Klerk had moved quickly to place his cabinet at the center of all decision-making processes. He restructured the central bodies of power, relegating the state security council to a secondary status, infuriating sections of the military-security establishment.

He was also compelled to keep a tight rein on the NP's parliamentary majority. But he did not seem to realise that the results of his actions would no longer be within his effective control.

He had taken an irrevocable step. Political terrain we would all be compelled to operate on was radically different.

The ANC leadership had been primed for this well in advance. No sooner had the announcement been made than the movement went into high gear, pulling out all the stops and catching the NP government off guard.

But the ANC had ignored two salient facts in its assessments.

In weighing the opinions and the views of the Afrikaner business circles, academics, writers, journalists with whom it had interacted, it took little account of the agenda of these interlocutors. The movement made no attempt to weigh their views against independently acquired political intelligence.

The ANC thus based many of its approaches on the views of the interested parties, which it had accepted at face value.

There was consequently little critical appreciation of the inversion of the fear factor. The NP had for decades frightened white voters with the prospect of an 'ANC Communist' government.

After February 2 the NP employed the prospect of dire consequences – more sanctions increased international isolation, economic decline – for the same purpose. It made absolutely no mention of democracy or of its desirability. It presented the prospect of talks in a political vacuum, as a virtue in itself.

In contrast to the black majority, which saw De Klerk's actions as the beginning of something, most whites viewed them as the end of something.

The movement was compelled to undertake painful introspection. Was it being adequately served by its intelligence and information-gathering agencies? The ANC's inability to get a handle on the third force violence that escalated after Mandela's release was the price exacted for this weakness.

Secondly would the ANC be adequate to taking on the NP in an election campaign, and should it not immediately create the structures and skills base appropriate to that task? Within months of its legalization, the ANC was up and running, with efficient political, operations. They proved themselves in the landslide victory of 1994. The ANC's negotiating team outperformed anything the NP could field.

February 2 earned De Klerk his place in history… The political party he led, however, proved unequal to the stature he had attained.

TWENTY-ONE

This lecture was delivered at the University of the Witwatersrand on the anniversary of Ruth First's murder, 28 August 2000. At its heart is an account of African nationalism in South Africa and its engagement with modernity. Jordan depicts the black intelligentsia as having had to confront an agonising dilemma: 'either to confidently confront the uncertainties of progress and the future, or cling to the dubious comfort of a disintegrating past'. He argues that the black working class has historically been a protagonist of modernity and of a multilingual, multifaith and multiracial society. The lecture concludes by calling on the left to make a strategic intervention so as to shift debate to the issue of redistribution, and to elaborate a realistic development model as an alternative to GEAR.

Ruth First Memorial Lecture

Delivered by Z. Pallo Jordan at University of the
Witwatersrand, 28 August 2000

The Ruth First Memorial lecture does not mark a happy occasion. In fact it marks a murder. The death of the comrade whom we are honouring this evening was the result of a vile deed. An act of violence that is but a link in a long chain of repression that commences with the illegalisation of the Communist Party of South Africa (CPSA) in 1950, the illegalisation of the ANC and the PAC in 1960 and the so-called Political Interference Act of 1968. The torture and murder of political prisoners in detention, leading inexorably to the formal repression through state-employed murder squads and 'unofficial' death squads, were all expressions of the same brutal response. There was a diabolic consistency to the logic of Verwoerd and his successors. As demonstrated by these and their subsequent actions, they hoped to banish from the South African political landscape the real alternative to apartheid by statutorily defining any efforts to recast South Africa along non-racial lines as seditious.

Verwoerd's successors made a further attempt to crush that alternative by statute and imprisonment in October 1977 when they banned the 17 organisations, and 'The World,' shortly after murdering Steve Biko.

These acts of repression testify to the desperation of the apartheid regime, which, thirty two years after banning the CPSA, found it necessary to take the killing fields from the streets of Soweto and other townships into the capitals of the region.

The full weight of the blow struck against us when the apartheid regime ordered the assassination of Ruth First is felt at moments like the present. Her incisive, analytical mind would have greatly enriched the national debate both inside and outside the liberation movement and helped to define the way forward. Comrade Ruth First was outstanding because she had taken to heart Marx's eleventh Theses of Feuerbach:

> 'Philosophers have only described the world in different ways, the point however is to change it!'

She was a militant South African democrat and a Communist who became one of the foremost campaigners for the independence of Namibia, both here at home, and during her years in exile. As an internationalist, she was also deeply involved in the liberation struggles of other African countries, especially the former Portuguese colonies, Mozambique, Angola and Guinea-Bissau. It was these qualities that made the comrade whose murder we are marking today so formidable an opponent of the apartheid regime.

Ruth First was among that generation of liberation movement militants who occupied the frontline trenches in the fight for freedom after the Second World War. She was one of a talented corps of men and women, nationalists and Marxists, who initiated virtually all the major decisions that shaped the destiny of the liberation movement, and consequently our country. Their political baptism was the 1946 African Mineworkers strike. They were prominent in the Passive Resistance Campaign of 1946-47. It was they who led the Defiance Campaign of 1952. It was they who led the campaign for the Congress of the people in 1955. It was they again who took the decision to launch the armed struggle in 1961.

Her primary sphere of activity was journalism. She served as the Johannesburg editor of 'The Clarion,' 'Advance.' 'New Age' and the 'Spark,' weekly newspapers that were successively banned by the apartheid regime. She also served as editor of 'Fighting Talk,' the monthly magazine founded by the Springbok Legion, a non-racial ex-serviceman's organisation. When she went into exile in Britain, after her release from prison in 1964, she briefly ran South African New Features, then entered academia. Her academic work was always informed by her extensive journalistic experience, but its quality was enriched rather then impaired, by her insistence on empirical evidence to substantiate theoretical propositions.

Ruth First was murdered before she could savour the victory she had worked for all her adult life.

The Cold War and the Corruptions of Stalinism. Ruth First's entry into politics virtually coincides with the commencement of the Cold War. At either end of that great geo-political divide, critical Communists, like Comrade Ruth First, often suffered opprobrium. While she refused to conceal, cover up and concoct alibis for the crimes and horrors of Stalinism, she adamantly would not embrace the even more bloody system of late monopoly capitalism. Ruth First opposed the Soviet-led invasion of Czechoslovakia in August 1968 with the same vigour that she denounced the US war on the people of Vietnam. While she could never be an apologist for the absurd policies pursued by Gomulka and Gierek in Poland, she lent her unstinting solidarity to the British labour movement facing the onslaught of Thatcherism.

For her pains, until quite late in her academic career, she was debarred from the US on the grounds that she was a Communist. And, when the Mozambican Union of Journalists proposed that she be posthumously awarded the Julius Fucik Medal for journalism, their proposal was vociferously shot down by the Union of Soviet Journalists, taking their cue from the leadership of the CPSU.

Despite the terrible reverses, disappointments and broken promises associated with the name of socialism during the 20th century, Comrade Ruth First never wavered in her commitment to socialism as an honourable cause and as a realisable goal. Hers was a commitment not rooted in a complacent and dissembling acceptance that everything from Moscow was gospel; or that pretended that all was truth and light in East Berlin; or that everything that came from Beijing was immersed in incense. Hers was a truly revolutionary commitment in that her solidarity with the socialist countries was always critical. Like the Karl

Marx, from whom she drew her inspiration, she firmly adhered to his favorite adage: 'Doubt and question everything'.

She was, consequently, not afraid to confront the fact that the real-politik socialist countries, including the Soviet Union and China, were compelled to practise, would regularly conflict with the demands of the class and national struggles. But she recognised that it was infantile not to have anticipated these, and churlish not to have accommodated some of them.

Many negative lessons can be drawn from the collapse of the post-capitalist societies of the former Soviet Union and eastern Europe. Like the defeats suffered by revolutionary socialism in Europe on the eve of World War II, the collapse of the Soviet Union has handed one victory after another to the most reactionary elements of monopoly capital. It has, for the time being, also disarmed the working class in the core countries of world capitalism. No amount of sophistry can disguise that this was a major defeat whose ravages it will take years to repair.

THE VISION OF A JUST SOCIETY

Though the 19th century had witnessed the steady incorporation of Africans into the colonial capitalist economy, it was as a result of mining that the overwhelming majority of the African population were drawn into the modern economy for the first time.

The Anglo-Boer War has been characterised as a revolution from outside and from above. Those who subscribe to this view assign to British imperialism the historically progressive role of transforming South Africa from a geographical to a political expression. Yet at the time, J. A. Hobson, the author of 'Imperialism,' expressed the view that it was a war waged.

'... to place a small international oligarchy of mine-owners and speculators in power at Pretoria' and to 'secure a full, cheap, regular submissive supply of Kaffir and white labour. '

There is clear evidence that the war was waged, in part, also to pre-empt the emergence of a non-dependent South African capitalism. To quote Simons and Simons, in 'Class and Colour in South Africa':

'Few agrarian societies were so richly endowed or well equipped as the Transvaal for an industrial revolution. The republic attracted educated and professional men from Holland or the Cape, and was beginning to produce its own specialists. Left to itself, it would have developed an efficient administration, a network of railways and roads, and adequate supplies of water and power.'

The preceding power balance in South Africa had been the outcome of armed conflicts, compromises, relations of clientage and alliances. The destruction of Afrikaner independence and the peace negotiated at Vereeniging opened up new options. The cobbling together of the Colonialism of a Special Type (CST) that became the modus dominandi of capitalism in South Africa was equally the result of new compromises, the redefinition of old, and the creation of new alliances.

The 1905 Native Laws Commission placed the stamp of permanence on these new arrangements by defining all black South Africans, especially the Africans, as a conquered, subject people who would in future have no voice in the manner in which they were governed.

But, perhaps most importantly the Anglo-Boer war resulted in the emergence of a common society, in which Whites and Blacks no longer lived in parallel, mutually dependent, but separate societies.

As they were forced to turn away from the familiar symbolic universe of the family, the clan and the ethnic group, the most advanced elements among the Black intelligentsia adopted the more inclusive concepts of the nation, the African continent, and that continent as part of an international community.

They also embraced as worthy compatriots others drawn from the most recent immigrant communities from Europe and Asia, who identified with Africa's struggles and the aspirations of her people.

But theirs would be an Odyssey characterised by an agonising existential dilemma: either to confidently confront the uncertainties of progress and the future, or cling to the dubious comfort of a disintegrating past. African writers, poets and leaders of thought experienced the modern era as highly ambiguous, combining extremely destructive aspects with constructive elements.

Their dilemma was brilliantly captured in the epic Samuel Mqhayi composed to honour the Prince of Wales (later the Duke of Windsor) when he visited South Africa.

Mqhayi personifies modernity as Britain herself, of whom he then says:

'Ah, Britain! Ah Great Britain!
The Great Britain on which the sun never sets!
She hath conquered the oceans and laid them low;
She hath drained the little rivers and lapped them dry;
She hath swept away little nations and wiped them away;
And today she lusts even for the open skies.
She sent us the preacher; she sent us the bottle;
She sent us the Bible, and barrels of brandy;
She sent us the breechloader, she sent us cannon;
O, Roaring Britain! Which shall we embrace?
You sent us truth, yet denied us the truth;
You sent us ubuntu, yet took away our ubuntu;
You sent us light, yet we sit in darkness,
Shivering and benighted in the bright noonday sun!
Nay, this mighty Britain is confusing the peoples;
Harsh, hard and cold is she, even unto her womb,
What then shall we say of her offspring?!
And, worse yet, what can be said of her father!'

These excruciating ambiguities of modern times grew as urbanisation accelerated. In their distress, many intellectuals were tempted to lend an ear to the siren songs of a backward-looking nativism, which its adherents frequently presented as 'authenticity.'

The colonial intelligentsia in Africa as well Asia often portrayed the dilemma posed by modernity as tragic. The national liberation movement's response was that rather than wallowing in their alienation or seeking refuge in the past, the intellectuals should reintegrate themselves with the common people by active engagement in the political and social struggles for freedom, independence and progress.

The most progressive among the Black intelligentsia consequently evolved an inclusive vision of South Africa, embodied in Rev. Z. R

Mahabane's invocation of: 'The common fatherhood of God, and the brotherhood of man.' From its inception African nationalism in South Africa has preferred inclusivity to ethnicity, and has eschewed racism and tribal particularism. The non-racial national ethos, expressed in the preamble of the Freedom Charter as 'South Africa belongs to all who live in it. ...' is the legacy they left us. In 1924 the left-wing of the then pre-dominantly White labour movement, organised as the Communist Party of South Africa (CPSA), were the first among Whites to accept the notion of a non-racial society. Liberals among the dominant capitalist classes began to see it as the inevitable result of the changes wrought by World War II. White liberalism made its last ambivalent attempt to force this recognition on the rest of White South Africa through the 1946 (Fagan) Commission on Native Laws. The fate of Fagan's recommendations testify to the option the majority of White South Africans chose: excluding Blacks from common citizenship.

Colonialism of a Special Type (CST) thus carried within it two contradictory tendencies – the one, segregationist; the other a countervailing, integrationist thrust. But the empirical fact of institutionalised racism rested like a dark shadow on the consciousness of all South Africans, in instances shaping it to a greater degree than objective socio-economic forces.

INGREDIENTS OF THE LIBERATION ALLIANCE

Marxism requires us to interrogate its own interface with nationalism and to view both nationalism and Marxism as a part of history while we remain alert to their central mission: the reshaping of history.

Though the mission it sets itself is usually progressive, nationalist ideology invariably draws its strength from the past. Marxists regard that as one of the inner contradictions of nationalism. It is however a contradiction inherent in the capitalist mode of production itself. The internationalisation of the capitalist mode of production brought a world market into being, engendering in its wake nationalist responses that may at first appear inherently opposed to capitalism itself. Anti-imperialist movements consequently reflect a rather peculiar historic irony. While anti-imperialist movements were born to resist the transformation of capitalism's periphery by its core, they could only do so successfully by themselves undergoing transformation. The most radical among these movements were not those that strove to restore a pre-colonial golden age, but rather those that had come to terms with the consequences of imperialism, and sought to go well beyond it. In other words, the anti-imperialist struggle is itself a dialectical process. The two poles involved in it continuously modify each other.

For the founders of the African nationalism, operating in the context of the Cape franchise, the aim was the incremental inclusion of the Black majority in the political institutions of the country. The generation of the 1940s recognized that change could only be realised by overturning the existent political arrangements.

They posed democracy, non-racism, non-sexism and equality as the alternative to White minority rule. Democracy in South Africa required that at least two basic conditions be met: adult suffrage and the repeal of all racist laws that institutionalised inequalty. Both the early nationalists and their successors hoped to forge a single South African nation from the diverse elements that make up South Africa. That vision runs like a red thread through a series of political programmes beginning with the 1925 African Bill of Rights, the Programme of the National Liberation League of 1935, the Ten Point Programme of 1943, the Africans' Claims of 1943 and in the Freedom Charter of 1955. These are all infused with a rejection of ethnicity, racism and tribal particularism in favour of a non-racial pan-South African stance captured in the preamble of the Freedom Charter as 'South Africa belongs to all who live in it....'

Without exception, every trend in African Nationalism (including the PAC and BCM) defined the 'nation' not as the Africans or even all the Black people alone, but as the multi-racial, multi-faith and multi-lingual community comprising all the races in South Africa.

But it was not high-mindedness alone that gave African Nationalism this inclusive character. The borders of the country had been decided arbitrarily, with no reference to any of the indigenous communities, throwing together groups of people drawn from disparate communities. The institutions of racial oppression drew few distinctions amongst Africans, they tended to regard them as an undifferentiated mass.

Inclusivity was efficacious for galvanising these unrelated ethnic, linguistic and cultural communities.

African nationalism evolved through continuing political engagement which required it to interact with and learn from a multitude of other political formations in South Africa and beyond its borders. It borrowed freely and adapted to its own purposes the strategies and tactics of the movement for Indian independence. From the workers movement it learnt how to organise strikes. Association with Marxists after 1928 led to the absorption of Marxist analysis. It opened its ranks to like-minded Coloureds and Indians and worked in strategic and loose coalitions with bodies of Whites who were critical of racism. The movement consequently grew as a hybrid that combined a number of intellectual traditions under its roof.

This reality was underscored in the political dynamics of modern South Africa in ways few theorists had anticipated. Having called into being a modern political economy through colonial conquest and rapid industrialization, the White ruling class and its supporters in South Africa, marshalled every political device to evade its socio-political consequences – the emergence of a common society in which Whites and Blacks were not merely mutually dependent, but whose destinies were inextricably intertwined. One of the great ironies of twentieth century South Africa is the desperate attempts by successive White governments, since 1910, to unscramble that historic omelet.

By the cunning of reason, the Black proletariat created by colonial policies of blood, iron and taxes, have been the most consistent proponents of modernity and the multi-cultural, multi-lingual, multi-racial, multi-faith society that is its chief consequence.

Equally, the African nationalism that evolved as a response to the steady erosion of the rights of Black South Africans as the capitalist mode of production in South Africa developed, became the torch-bearer of an open society built on the principles associated with emergence of capitalism. The history of twentieth-century South Africa could thus be characterised as the struggle of Black South Africans to embrace and realise the potential of South African capitalist development vs the efforts of White South Africa to exclude Blacks and if possible undo what history had achieved.

Marxism is unashamedly modernist. It designates the modern proletariat as the key revolutionary agency precisely because the demands and rhythms of capital accumulation require that the proletariat constantly change and adapt itself to technological, cultural and social progress. At the rock face of the capitalist economy, as it were, the proletariat – like the productive forces it operates – is subjected to a never-ending cycle of renewal, improvement and refinement. Such continuity and discontinuity is both a burden and an opportunity. No sooner has the working class experienced the destruction of pre-capitalist modes of existence with the construction of the capitalist mode of production, than it has to pass through the mill of the de-construction of early capitalism and the construction of modern capitalism. Modern capitalism in turn gave way for late capitalism. Conservatism, of any sort, is consequently at odds with the existential situation of the proletariat and can only impair its potential.

South African Marxists have consequently never wrung their hands at the effects of industrialization on pre-capitalist African societies, preferring to accept these because their transformative impact are a necessary baptism to equip the proletariat to assume its historic tasks.

But the birth of a proletariat was itself an extremely painful, bloody process. On the continent, the South African experience was unique only in its extent and societal depth.

The Dialectics of National and Class Struggle

The assassin's hand that reached out from the terrible night of apartheid to snatch away the life of our comrade, hoped by doing so to snuff out a vision. The vision Ruth's murderers hoped to extinguish had been born of a specific moment in South Africa's transformation from a pre-colonial to a colonial society: As Simons and Simons remind us in their magnum opus, 'Class and Colour in South Africa,' hard on the heels of the diamond discoveries:

'British and colonial troops made war on the Hlubi in 1873, the Gcaleka and the Pedi in 1877, the Ngqika, Thembu, Mpondo, Griqua and baRolong in 1878, the Zulu in 1879, the Sotho in 1880, the Ndebele in 1893 and the Afrikaner republics in 1899. The Cape absorbed the Transkei and its peoples in 1879–94. Britain annexed Basutoland in 1868, Griqualand West in 1871, the South African Republic in 1877, Zululand in 1887, Matabeleland in 1894 and the Afrikaner republics in 1900. ...

South Africa's industrial era was baptized in blood and the subjugation of small nations. As from the beginning of the century, the liberation movement took the form of struggles between classes and national communities.' (p. 31)

The history of the national liberation movement is in the main the complex inter-penetration of national and class struggles. That is the explanation for the enduring alliance between the ANC and the Communist Party, and not some sinister, dark conspiracies hatched in Moscow (or Yeoville) as McCarthyists of various stripes have claimed. From very early in their respective histories, the Communist Party and the ANC shared common objectives. In time this matured into a political alliance, with a common approach to their immediate and intermediate goals.

The most visible line of fracture in White-ruled South Africa was race. Power, status, access to wealth and opportunity were apportioned by reference to race. No less important, but perhaps less obvious, was class which intersected and coincided with race in a number of instances. Nationalism proceeded from an uncomplicated unity of 'the people' vs the oppressor/racist regime. Marxism, on the other hand, had to be more sensitive to the real diversity of 'the people' and could ill afford to lose sight of the contradictions among the 'people.' Marxist intellectuals devoted their energies to unpacking the salience of class to the struggle, even as the struggle ensued. Their most important contribution was investigating the symbiotic relationship between racial oppression and capitalist exploitation.

Ruth First was firmly located within the Marxist tradition, and it is that tradition I shall be addressing.

Marxism neither dismisses nor sanctions the divergence of theory from practice. Karl Marx regarded theory and practice as discontinuous. That is: Theory, though different from practice, is not absolutely distinct from it. Theory takes leave of existing practice: i. e. society as it exists; so as to return to it. The struggle to transform the existing society requires an endeavour to comprehend it through theory, so as to lay bare the living relations that undergird it. Theory will thus inform and guide revolutionary practice. In Marx's 11th Theses on Feuerbach, I would underscore the 'only' in order to highlight its latter portion, '... the point however is to change it!' That implies that the kernel of Marxist political practice ought to be the building of political alliances, on the basis of a realistic and concrete analysis of the existing or the potential balance of political and social forces, with the aim of creating a political majority that supports socialist transformation.

In pursuance of that aim, South African Marxists, with a few notable exceptions, have placed great reliance on an alliance with African nationalism. The theoretical practice of those Marxists who preferred to stand outside the national movement, or even in opposition to it, while sounding very learned, tended to be politically irrelevant and divorced from practice.

Ruth First understood the challenge as: evolving a revolutionary practice, rooted in Marxism, that is at once intellectually rigorous and politically engaged. Anchoring herself in both, the Rosa Luxemburg of 'Social Reform or Revolution' had written, '... on its road to development the Social Democratic movement must successfully negotiate a course between two reefs: abandonment of its mass character or abandonment of the final aim; falling into bourgeois reformism or into sectarianism.'

The danger of Marxists isolating themselves on the left margins of society remains very real even today. While sound theoretical practice cannot guarantee success, its principal object has to be striking a balance between these two. South African Marxists have wrestled with that riddle since 1921. Reams of paper have been invested in debating the relationship, if any, between racism and capitalism: to asses which is the determinant and which the dominant contradiction in South African capitalism. There were those who argued that the national and class dimensions were inseparable, and that neither should be stressed at the expense of the other, race and class must be read together. Such a theoretical departure would have had the most profound implications had it been adopted by the liberation movement. Ruth First was among those who contended that racism was relatively autonomous within capitalist relations of production. That approach implied the possibility of intervention through broad-based alliances, around democratic principles, while nonetheless linking the struggle against racism to the struggle for socialism.

[It is, parenthetically, rather amusing to note how these initial Marxist analyses have been rehashed and recycled by subsequent generations of activists. By those who claimed to be 'Trotskyists' and by those mis-named 'Workerists' during the 1980s.]

Comrade Ruth First was among the few members of the South African Communist Party prepared to admit that her party had not always had an adequate appreciation of the dialectics of race, class and gender. She was ashamed that the youthful Communist Party of South Africa had been unable to define an honourable role for itself during the 1922 Rand Revolt. Though she understood why its leaders were very hesitant about allying themselves to the ANC during the late 1920s, she felt embarrassed that even on the eve of its illegalisation, the CPSA still misunderstood the militant nationalism of the ANC Youth League.

Ruth readily admitted that she, herself, was a late bloomer when it came to issues of gender. These are some of the reasons why, unlike many of her comrades in the party, she would not dismiss out of hand the work of younger analysts associated with the New Left.

Ruth First's intellectual activity, both as an editor and as an academic compelled her to confront such issues. When she helped edit Oginga Odinga's study of post-colonial Kenya, 'Not Yet Uhuru,' she had to contend with the reality that the Kenyan liberation movement had in many respects failed the people who had brought it to power. To her dismay, she also discovered that Mzee Jomo Kenyatta, the doyen of the independence struggle and a liberation fighter who had for decades been considered a man of the left, had become the leader of a rapacious indigenous elite, bent of savouring the fruits of freedom on their own, to the exclusion of the mass of the peasantry who had struggled and died for it.

CONTRADICTIONS AMONG THE PEOPLE

It is self-evidently true that the national democratic alliance consists of and contains within itself real and actual contradictions. Marxist dialectics instructs us that the contradictions among the people are not constant. Like all phenomena they are subject to change, mutation and transformation.

Being catapulted into modern times created new options for all within our society at large, adding new facets to old identities while defining new ones.

But the past, unlike the rubble from a derelict building on a construction site, cannot just be carted away for disposal as waste. Entire communities, groups, and individuals have internalised aspects of the past as defining their identities. Yet others, in order to cope with the complexities and trauma associated with rapid change and transformation, tend to cling on to the past, or rather what they perceive to be the past, for security.

This accounts for the tenacity with which some sectors of our society, especially among the African people, hang on to institutions, traditions and practices whose relevance to life in the 21st century may strike one as marginal.

Gender is probably the oldest and most enduring contradiction that bedevils our lives. Even as we speak anachronistic traditions and customary laws regularly undermine the guarantees of legal equality in our Constitution. For the majority of South African women the reality, regrettably, still is inequality in the home and the community. These are not issues that we will resolve by denial. They have to be squarely confronted and receive priority in our national agenda. While the considerations I have mentioned counsel due care and sensitivity, can we afford to allow the dead weight of tradition to thwart the aspirations of more than half of our people?

The de-racialisation of property-ownership has always been integral to the liberation struggle. One dimension of the struggle, after all, entailed creating opportunities for men and women of colour to rise as high as their talents can take them. Representatives of every stratum and class among the Black population probably contributed to the multi-class character of the liberation movement.

Yet it would be correct to say that historically the movement received far greater support from certain classes than from others. Since the 1940s, it was specifically the African working class of town and country who were the movement's main base of support. Historically the movement employed the classic weapon of working class struggle – the general strike – as its principal method of non-violent struggle. The relative weight of the working class and other working people among the oppressed is also reflected in the Freedom Charter's unambiguous tilt in favour of their aspirations.

Despite the momentous political changes South Africa has witnessed, in general terms, the property-owning classes in South Africa are White, while the propertyless, the wage earning classes and the poor are overwhelmingly Black.

The distribution of life chances and skills is similarly skewed. We cannot exclude Blacks from becoming and being capitalists, any more than we can bar them from becoming lawyers, doctors, accountants, engineers, skilled workers, etc.

The opportunities that arrived with democracy can also give rise to new tensions. These will not disappear because of a blind insistence that there is no conflict potential between the director of a corporation and the workers employed by it, merely because both are Black.

But the multi-class bloc, molded to wage the liberation struggle, remains essential for the transformation process. This implies engagement with the emergent Black bourgeoisie rather than leaving them to their own devices. Or worse yet, the devices of others. Such engagement could involve the elaboration of standards of conduct and a business ethic that will speed job creation, the fostering of skills development, the empowerment of women, the strengthening of the popular organs of civil society, and active involvement in the fight to end poverty.

This Black bourgeoisie should also be encouraged to cultivate within their own enterprises and in those where they hold executive positions, the creative management of the conflict potential of industrial relations. Rather than merely pursuing money and hefty profits, the Black bourgeoisie should give the lead within the business community regarding responsible corporate behaviour.

We must accept that there will be instances when the imperatives of service delivery to the working people collide with the claims of one or other section of the working class. But, entrenching the rights of workers must remain central to our ambitious programme of transformation. Efforts to deepen and extend those rights might even conflict with the larger national project of creating a stable economic environment. Taking the easy option of condemning the unionised workers, or alternately, edging towards confrontation with the ANC and the government might make good media headlines, but neither path actually takes matters forward. If the contradictions referred to are grounded in objective reality, the principal challenge is devising a sound strategy for their management.

There is also an unfortunate ethos of entitlement that appears to have taken root among sections of our population, manifesting itself in a refusal to assume responsibility for services or otherwise contribute to the upkeep and maintenance of the very cities and towns we waged the struggle to liberate. This is, regrettably, matched by a culture of indifference towards the needs of the people among many charged with precisely that responsibility. While no one wishes to abridge the rights of teachers and public servants to defend their living standards and fight for improvements, aren't there equally important issues – such as Batho Pele, an ethic of Serving the People – that our Public Service unions should be fostering? At a time when we are all committed to restoring a culture of teaching and learning, is a work stoppage the most creative response that Black teachers can muster to an industrial dispute? There are other contradictions, that one could touch on in passing.

Language:

The constitution guarantees the equality of our eleven official languages. But in reality English has become the dominant language in the economy and in politics. That situation is the result of the unequal distribution of the instruments and means of cultural production. But, can we afford to leave this matter unaddressed? Are there no creative initiatives to be taken to achieve actual equality?

Resources are unevenly distributed among the regions, so that provinces like Gauteng, the Western Cape and Northern Cape stand a better chance of improving the lives of their inhabitants. Does this not pose the danger that in addition to being racialised, poverty could also become regionalised, provoking unexpected tensions within our society?

In allying themselves to the national movement, Marxists hazarded the risk of being reduced to subordinate allies, or allies of convenience, to be dispensed with once the nationalists had attained their objectives. 20th century history offers numerous such terrifying examples. The inordinate fear of antagonising nationalist leaders, sometimes expressed by Communists, is informed by such experiences. But, deliberately muting the class dimensions of the national liberation struggle, as a tactic to nurse this relationship, does not, however, tame the worst impulses of the conservatives.

In Ruth First's intellectual work, both as a journalist and an academic she boldly confronted these issues. Her study of coups in Africa, 'The Barrel of a Gun', portrayed old elites, the emergent propertied classes, and the wa-Benzis, wishing to loot the state's coffers in order to acquire property, emboldened by such tactics, while the ordinary working people were reduced to passivity or disoriented.

The question to my mind should be: what strategy should the Marxist left devise to sustain the unity of the liberation alliance while not suppressing or repressing the actual contradictions within it? Defending and fostering the long-standing ANC traditions of open and vigorous debate, while ensuring unity in action, surely must be a dimension of such a strategy.

THE TRANSITION

By 1988 it was clear that the White electorate would not follow the NP government to the bitter-end. February 2nd, 1990 was not merely an admission that the repression had failed to crush the alternative, it was an acknowledgment that the alternative had acquired a grip on the imagination of the majority of South Africans and was being given serious consideration even by the intellectuals on whom the regime had formerly relied.

Once the legal political space was opened, the different elements of the liberation movement and anti-apartheid opposition came forward and filled it, pegging out their respective constituencies.

But not all the strands in the anti-apartheid opposition had responded to the 30 years of repression with the same degree of resilience.

By 1994 the radical liberalism, personified by the likes of Patrick Duncan, Joe Nkatlo, Randolph Vigne, Jordan Ngubane and Eddie Daniels, that had been dominant in the Liberal Party after 1959, had disappeared from the political landscape. Its place had been taken by a rather pale version, the Democratic Party. While Duncan, Vigne, Brown and others had attempted to root liberalism among the Black majority by building alliances with African nationalism (especially the PAC leadership), the Progressive Party (and its progeny) had chosen to trim their sails to options acceptable to the White electorate. They resurrected Rhodes' bankrupt policy of ' a vote for all civilized men.' The party that by default became the surviving flagship of liberalism was, regrettably, to the right of centre and firmly locked into White electoral politics.

Those who see the 'ironic victory of liberalism 'in South Africa's democratic constitution could well be misreading the situation. By locking itself within the White laager, what remained of liberalism drifted so far to the right, that today the NNP itself feels comfortable under its rubric! The real ironic victory might well be that though the NP lost the political argument, it managed to distort, if not destroy, the soul of liberalism!

By the time of the 1999 elections, a new consensus had become dominant. Its bottom line is democracy, which reduced the White far-right to a marginal political force, isolated on the outer fringes of South African politics. The arrival of democracy had wrought impressive changes. Essential elements of which include :

• ending the colonial status of Blacks – African, Coloured and Indian;
• ending the second class status of the Hinduism, Islam and other non-Christian religions;
• the emancipation of gays and lesbians;
• affirmation of the diversity of South African society;
• and, though we still have a long way to go, setting in motion the emancipation of women.

Democracy also meant that henceforth violence could no longer be a legitimate political instrument. Its eschewal by all parties also signifies acceptance by all of the desirability of stability as the guarantor of our democratic freedoms and as a pre-requisite for economic growth and development.

Peace, stability and security, in the region in general, and in South Africa in particular, are especially important to partisans of the left. It is by growing our economy that we will lay the material basis for the social upliftment of the working people. And, it is by deepening and firming up our democracy that we will secure the gains the working people have made since 1994.

Developing countries have opted for diverse paths to attain political stability and peace. Historical experience has taught us to jettison earlier romantic notions about colonial nationalism and to recognise that nationalist mobilization is determined by the actual form and content and the class nature of the affected societies.

Once freedom/independence had been attained, nationalism has often proved inadequate to sustain the cohesion it had earlier created. Palpable social stratification, evident in the real experience of ordinary people, poses a problem that nationalist ideology cannot resolve. As a result, in many of the societies that are held up as examples we should emulate, nationalist leaders have chosen repressive, authoritarian methods to purchase the stability so necessary for development. In South Africa, however, the consensus expressed in our Constitution is that we value democracy as much as development, and will not trade the one to attain the other.

Political pluralism, the option chosen by our people, underscores the importance of a continuing political dialogue amongst all parties and an ongoing search for consensus. But it also implies the submission of the minority to the majority view. The very fluidity and flexibility of the system however has yet another implication: that today's minority could well be tomorrow's majority, and vice versa.

CONCLUSION

Our nation building project is the outcome of a struggle between two major role players, with divergent political agendas. From their divergent standpoints, at a decisive moment during the 1980s, both sides recognised that negotiation was the preferable option. Forging a single South African nation on the basis of democratic institutions could, however, only be realised by politically defeating the institutions of apartheid and demonstrating the inadequacy of the political programmes put forward by smaller parties.

It is common cause that the negotiated settlement arrived at in Kempton Park was the outcome of a strategic intervention by the national democratic alliance, led by the ANC. That intervention moved political discourse in and about South Africa onto a fundamentally new terrain. Public discourse that had formerly centred on reforming and recasting apartheid in various ways, shifted decisively to the abolition of apartheid and the establishment of true democracy.

On April 27th 1994 the democratic movement won the argument. That victory was further consolidated in June 1999.

The national liberation movement, in all its organised formations, won because it had galvanised an otherwise diverse population, to struggle for freedom and democracy in the first instance. Reconstruction and development, in order to improve the quality of life of our people, is now its rallying call. That must necessarily entail rapid economic growth. It is with respect to the latter, that I want to pose a challenge for the Marxist left.

Marx and Engels described the leadership of the left as '... having over the great mass of the proletariat the advantage of clearly understanding the line of march, the conditions and ultimate general result of the proletarian movement.' Uprooting the legacy of national oppression and delivering on the promise of liberation has not been easy. But there is a slowly emerging consensus that the eradication of poverty should be the priority item on our national agenda. In such an environment, is the left not obliged to make a strategic intervention in order to shift the terrain of the national debate to the issue redistribution?

A creative response to the challenges of today, I submit, would be for the left to elaborate a realistic development model, rather than pointing accusatory fingers at the shortcomings of GEAR. Such a model may well entail re-thinking a number of time-worn assumptions. That will require courage.

Courage is one quality the South African left has always possessed in great abundance.

TWENTY-TWO

The article is a combative reply to one by Stanley Uys. It deals harshly with the Democratic Alliance under Tony Leon's leadership: it became the official opposition 'by stealing the tattered garments of white anxiety', which the National Party had discarded. Uys – charges Jordan – glibly elides the pain and suffering of racial oppression and 'comes perilously close' to an inversion of the truth by suggesting that white South Africans are the victims of racism.

A Future for Whites if They Accept the Past

The Sunday Independent, 29 April 2001

The closest analogy to a semi-literate southern Christian fundamentalist giving an exposition on Darwinism was the caricature of the theory of colonialism of a special type we had from the pen of Stanley Uys (*The Sunday Independent*, April 22). It's hard to believe that so simple a concept could be so spectacularly misconstrued by someone who is obviously familiar with it.

White domination in South Africa was characterised as special because, though similar to colonial regimes elsewhere in Africa, it bore a number of distinctive features rooted in South African history. A white community who had become naturalised over three centuries was but one of these.

Recognition of that reality distinguished the ANC from other movements and imposed a number of policy imperatives. The Freedom Charter states that 'South Africa belongs to all who live in it', a formulation that anticipates reconciliation after a phase of conflict. Thousands of ANC statements, not least those penned by President Thabo Mbeki, foresaw a permanent white presence as one of the elements of a diverse post-apartheid South Africa.

But, it would appear that, to Uys, accepting that millions of whites have made South Africa their home is a Machiavellian device that conceals sinister motives that include 'to quarantine whites, to see them upended in some foot and mouth paddock'.

If not that, Uys alleges, it is some sophomoric ruse to deceive an otherwise restive and discontented working class into racial solidarity with wealthier Africans. Such racial demagoguery, he tells us, would have the added benefit of calming the fears of foreign governments and businesses that are still nervous about leftish projects.

There probably are a number of African capitalists who would plead 'soul brother' in a confrontation with the working class. But the suggestion that the interests of this miniscule stratum of emerging business people drive ANC policy is fantastic.

Perhaps it was unavoidable that the outcomes produced by the political revolution of 1994 would catch the traditionally white parties flatfooted. The National Party (NP) recognised the new political facts too late. Despite a leadership overhaul and an attempt at repositioning, it was decimated in the 1999 general elections. The Democratic Party (DP), so one of its veteran leaders explained to me, seized the opportunity to secure a new following among the huge numbers of post-1997 white 'undecideds'.

That the antecedents of the DP come from the liberal tradition has never been in dispute. But it is equally true that the DP became the official opposition by stealing the tattered garments of white anxiety, which the NP discarded when it tried to reinvent itself as the New National Party. What Uys calls Tony Leon's aggressive style was an unabashed appeal to the worst fears of the white voters. It has been suggested that his less responsible recommendations about Zimbabwe are fuelled by the same consideration.

One would be delighted if the Democratic Alliance (DA) were indeed a liberal party. But its political actions, as its parliamentary voting record will testify, suggest a rather illiberal conservative party. The DA equivocates on the death penalty and still has to make up its mind on the right of women to control their own fertility.

Consistent with contemporary conservative thinking, the DA would like to hand regulation of the economy over to big corporations and their executives, virtually to the exclusion of the state. It has openly stated that it would prefer to see management's powers to hire and fire employees greatly increased and working people made more vulnerable to the fluctuations of the marketplace. It castigates any measures to deliver consistent relief to the poor as creating a nanny state.

When the DP repositioned itself as the party of the indecisive, property-owning whites, it opted to isolate itself from the property-less black majority. Whatever hidden agenda the DP leadership was pursuing, it chose the path of projecting the interests and suspicions of minorities who were unhappy with the new dispensation. How many of the DP's new recruits were motivated by liberal sentiments? How many of them subscribe to liberal values? The jury is still out on whom is teaching whom in the DA.

The DA has deliberately cast itself as the party of business, white property owners and former supporters of the old regime. That such a choice would very likely marginalise it among the minorities on the right of the political spectrum is the stuff of first year political science.

The DA's obsessive reference to the emerging African capitalist would merely be boring if it did not betray residual feelings of white exclusivity. The DA does not even regard these new African propertied classes as current or potential allies and supporters. Because the white propertied classes see them as competitors, the DA regularly denounces them and supports every conceivable device to impede their advancement. Thus in the mouths of DA spokespersons affirmative action and equal opportunities legislation are racial quota systems.

Racism is not merely ideology or human beings behaving badly. Racism is a system of power relations that result in goods and services, collectively produced within a common society, being unequally apportioned with race as the decisive criterion for access. It is neither decreed from on high nor is it programmed into our genes. Racism has always been a matter of conscious political choice by governments, with or without the support of voters. Uys correctly reminds us that this structural violence was sustained by brute force, formal and informal. It is equally true that rituals of subordination reinforced racism. But to mistake these highly visible epiphenomena of racial oppression for racism is like confusing courtly manners with the institution of monarchy.

To uproot racism requires a radically transformative process that entails both reconciliation and justice. To suggest that using political power in pursuance of change is morally equivalent to Verwoerdian social engineering might be cute hyperbolic flutter, but makes little sense.

Uys elides over the immense suffering and pain racial oppression has inflicted on the people of this country with saddening glibness. He even admonishes us to embrace the perpetuity of racism. After all, he opines, even in the 230-year-old United States African Americans, Native Americans, Hispanic and Asian Americans still have to endure it. Perhaps the medical profession should also be closed down; who even remembers how long ago it was that Pandora's box was opened?

Uys's approach is tantamount to suggesting that after resisting racial oppression for centuries, having conducted a struggle that entailed the loss of thousands of lives against racism, now that we have the power to translate fond aspiration into social policy, we should hold back, lest our impetuous haste ruffles the feathers of those who benefited from our degradation.

Uys appears to have a quaint notion of reconciliation. It does not entail working together to arrive at mutually acceptable solutions that will benefit the people of this country, 85 percent of whom are black and the victims of racism. He prefers talking us into coming to terms with being short-changed. The reconciliation we have from his pen is unconcerned with justice. Let white and black get on with their separate and highly unequal lives, he seems to be saying, but in a manner that will not intrude on the comfort zone of white minority, perched atop the unearned rewards of racial privilege.

During a visit to Munich in 1996, one of the city fathers dinned into my ear the terrible suffering experienced by the citizens of Munich as a result of Allied air raids towards the end of the Second World War. He pressed impressive aerial photographs of the ruined city on me. He delightedly pointed out, in the midst of the ruins, the cathedral built by the Bavarian kings, standing almost unscathed. Two hillocks outside the city, I was made to understand, were the rubble of the old city. In winter their slopes are used for skiing, in summer they are lightly forested hills offering walks to the citizenry.

These facts were poured out with an emotionalism designed to elicit my sympathy. After living through weeks of aerial bombardment, the people of Munich had to survive among the ruins of their homes. As members of the human family, the people who had endured all this deserved my sympathy. Yet I felt a sense of shame when I recalled that Warsaw, Rotterdam, Coventry, Leningrad and a host of other cities had been laid to waste by the Luftwaffe acting on the orders of a dictator whose political career had commenced in Munich. I was ashamed because for a brief moment the city father's eloquence had cast the aggressors as the victims. And I had fallen for it.

Warsaw neither invited destruction nor was its bombardment necessary except as an act of Nazi aggression. The destruction of Munich, on the other hand, was the price exacted to put an end to Nazi aggression. Yes, two cities had been destroyed, but for diametrically opposed reasons.

The dreadful suffering of the people of Munich did not diminish the grave responsibility the government of their country bore for waging a war of aggression. It would be inverting the truth if natural sympathy made us cast them as victims. Uys comes perilously close to performing such an inversion by suggesting that in the year 2001, white South Africans are the victims of racism.

TWENTY-THREE

Jordan, having recently visited China, reflects on encounters and developments there. Its main point is that the 'sent-down generation' (younger, educated in the 1960s) had been responsible for the relentless pursuit of economic growth, and that the real challenge they now faced was to democratise socialism – to add 'freedom' to 'bread'.

Observations about
China 2001

It is reported that in the course of one of the heated exchanges in the Central Committee of the Communist Party of China (CPC) during the years of the 'Cultural Revolution' (1967-75), one of Mao's contemporaries challenged him with the taunt:

'Why should we listen to anything these young people have to say?'

Mao, it is reported, replied with the dry yet very suggestive retort: 'Because they will outlive you!'

That the youth of the sixties have outlived both Mao and his generation is self-evident to any visitor to China. Beijing no longer looks like a third world capital. But in Chengdu, in the Sichuan province, some three hours flying time from Beijing, the third world is once again readily visible.

Travel from Sichuan to Shenzhen, established in 1980 just accross the river from Hong Kong, and one enters a new economic zone. Shenzhen was built on the site of a cluster of fishing villages in a wetland created by the waters of the Pearl River. It is a bustling modern metropolis, with a relatively young population. There are contrasts among the various regions of China, among the most jarring is that between Chengdu and Shenzhen.

Modern Beijing, Shanghai, and especially Shenzhen, attest to the achievements of China's Communist leaders. They raised their country, which accounts for a quarter of humankind, from a divided, weak and victimised, semi-colonial society into an industrial power that is ready to take on the world during the 21st century.

Central Beijing is a microcosm of China's transition from its not so distant past to the present. Tien-an-mien Square is bounded by the Forbidden city, the palace built by the Mings. To its right is Zhong Nan Hai, built by Genghis Khan, and now the headquarters of the Communist Party. Mao's potrait looks out on the square, which is flanked on either side by monumental buildings of Soviet inspiration that house the Chinese parliament and a number of museums. At the square's far end stands the mausoleum to the 'Immortals', China's revolutionary leaders: Mao, Zhou Enlai, Liu ShaoQi and Zhu Deh.

The role of the Communists in modern China has been favourably compared with that of the Piedmontese of Italy, who unified an otherwise fragmented country and restored to it a sense of national identity and purpose.

The forced march China undertook between 1949 and the present has been a time of relative stability and peace, punctuated by political upheavals. These tensions have invariably been enacted on Tien-an-mien square. Mao proclaimed the People's Republic of China from this square in October 1949. During the 'Cultural Revolution', Red Guards, waving the Little Red Book, gathered in the square. Shortly before Mao died in 1976, the square was the site of a spontaneous outpouring of grief at the passing of Zhou Enlai. In 1979 the youthful agitators of the shortlived Democracy Wall movement used a wall abutting Zhong Nan Hai to post their polemics and political essays. In 1989 the students of the capital, demanding freedom of expression and democracy gravitated to the square. The Falun Dong cult try to use it in the present.

'Tien-an-mien Papers' published this January, purport to be the minutes of meetings among China's top Communist leaders in 1989. They reveal the anxieties of an aging political leadership, panicked by the outcomes produced by their life's work. The articulate, pushy and sophisticated youth who used the Constitution against the CPC leadership to demand speedier reform, were all educated in China and had shed traditional deference to the old at the instigation of the Communist leaders themselves.

Mass education after 1949, especially of those strata who had previously been excluded, produced a relatively literate society. Jiang Zemin, Li Peng and others now at the helm at Beijing received their tertiary education and training in the former Soviet Union along with hundreds of other Chinese students. Modernity, with its emphasis on innovation and change, privileges youth. When the CPC meets in its 16th congress in 2002, the torch is expected to pass from the post '49 generation, headed by Jiang Zemin and Li Peng, to a generation of younger leaders, educated in China during the 1960s.

Referred to as the 'sent down generation', many were the Red Guards of the late 1960s. During the heady days of 1967 and '68, as young people they sought to catapult China into socialism by the sheer force of their will. When they were 'sent down' to the rural areas to live and work with the peasants, they discovered the yawning chasm between their aspirations and Chinese realities. Experience has taught them that economic stagnation and poverty are not the ingredients of a socialist society. Hence this generation's insistence that China relentlessly pursue economic growth even if it means leveraging investments from overseas Chinese capitalists and western corporations. Their zeal has cast them as ironic allies of one of their principal targets during the 'Cultural Revolution', Deng Xiaoping.

Shenzhen is rightly regarded as a lodestar of China's future. This twenty year old city is the home of China's high tech industries and houses its information technology hub. Its wide boulevards, skyscrapers, overflowing department stores, well stocked supermarkets, and well maintained golf courses point to a prosperous future and a community with leisure time and immense spending power. But, this promising enclave of its future is surrounded by China's past. To preserve it, China operates an influx control system reminiscent of the apartheid regime's Pass Laws.

We were shown what China's youth would be fleeing in a small, wholly privately-owned furniture factory in Sichuan. Working in Dickensian conditions that no South African worker would endure, we saw young people, recently displaced from the countryside, making cane furniture for the international market.

Such sweatshops proliferated throughout China as Deng Xiaoping's reforms took root. Living in a thoroughly mixed economy, in which a host of privately and publicly owned enterprises are competing with each other, the political and social attitudes of Chinese workers have also undergone a metamorphosis. Surveys conducted by the Chinese trade union federation in the mid-1990s discovered a sharp decline in altruistic motivation among workers in industry. A CPC survey among its working class members produced even more alarming findings.

While 32.7% of Communist workers said they were inspired by the desire 'to realize Communism', the comparable figure among members of the Young Communist League was only 7.5%! The same survey also uncovered the rise of religious belief among Communist workers. This probably accounts for the government's heavy-handed response to the Falun Dong cult.

Communist Workers, like their non-Communist colleagues the survey uncovered, believed that the proprietors of privately owned enterprises, followed by managers and administrarors in the state sector, government officials, technicians and peasants, are the principal beneficiaries of the reform process. They saw production workers at the bottom of the list. Most thought that the gap between rich and poor was widening. The de-politicisation of. the working class was also noted in responses such as:

'Politics is the business of the leadership, and it has nothing to do with me.'

Breakneck economic growth has resulted in new problems. In 2000 the state-owned media revealed details of how Shenyang, a city once held up as an example for emulation, was manipulated and corrupted by a gang led by a ranking member of the local Communist Party, Liu Yong.

The Godfather of Shenyang was also chairman of a respected stateowned congolmerate, and boasted personal assets in excess of US$60 million. The reverse side of such corruption is the high speed airport train, whose estimated cost will be US$10 billion, that is planned to connect Shanghai's new international airport to the city centre.

During a very fruitful meeting with the Deputy Foreign Minister, we remarked that in South Africa we do not regard bread and freedom as alternatives. We want our people to have both. The Deputy Foreign

Minister, unfazed, replied that their view was that bread came before freedom.

His attitude captures the dillemma that the 'sent down generation' will have to wrestle with as it prepares for power after 2002.

Until now, both the Chinese leadership and its external critics have treated socialism and democracy as incompatible. As the generation who will have to negotiate the reintegration of Hong Kong, Macau and, hopefully, Taiwan into China, the 'sent down' generation must recognise that the three territories represent significant economic centres with their own large working classes. They have to confront the likelihood that the people of these three territories are unlikely to be attracted to a socialism that is undemocratic and offers them fewer individual rights than they enjoy at present. Unless China regards the 'one nation, two systems' policy as a long term prospect, democratising socialism is the next crisis that awaits China.

TWENTY-FOUR

Although it was published just after the American invasion of Iraq had begun, this piece was written immediately before. It is a powerfully written critique of American foreign policy as it took shape after 9/11 and under the neoconservative hawks. It concludes that the choice facing the rest of the world is not one between Saddam Hussein and the United States, 'but between an international order based on the rule of law or one based on the wild west ethos of 'shoot first, ask questions later'.

US Poses Danger to New World Order

City Press, 23 March 2003

Since the tragic events of September 11, 2001, we have witnessed the elaboration of a new doctrine, as significant to the future direction of US foreign policy as that of 'containment'.

The new US strategic doctrine, shaped by its understanding of this century's international environment, involves the abandonment of containment in preference for a policy of pre-emptive action. As a result for the first time in decades, the naked display of force is being advocated openly by US government leaders. Some even speak of 'a benign American hegemony'.

It is perfectly true since 1991 the government of Iraq has violated numerous UN Security Council resolutions. Unfortunately, Iraq is not the only government to do so.

It is a fact after waging a brutal war against a neighbor, Iran, Iraq invaded another neighbour, Kuwait. For that act of aggression the international community, quite correctly, punished Iraq and drove its invading army out of Kuwait in 1991.

The government led by Saddam Hussein has repressed Iraqi religious and ethnic minorities. It persecutes its political opponent, employing many of methods used in apartheid South Africa.

But, Iraq is not the only country in the Middle East with a government that is intolerant of opposition: that represses a political opponent, religious and ethnic minorities. The authorization of Saddam Hussein's government is, regrettably, all too common in that part of the world.

Nor is Iraq the only country in that region that has produced weapons of mass destruction or attempted to acquire a nuclear capacity.

Why then was the Bush administration so eager to invade Iraq and change its government by force of arms?

Spokesperson and apologists for the new doctrine of pre-emptive action will tell you that is because of the Iraqi government poses a danger to its neighbours and is implicated with the terrorists who attacked the Twin Towers and the Pentagon in 2001.

But there have been a number of bizarre happenings associated with this propaganda for war. British Foreign Minister Jack Straw early last month tried to pass off the Phd thesis of an American student as solid intelligence, gathered by Britain's secret services. While President George W Bush and Defense Secretary Rumsfield were declaring that Saddam Hussein was Bin Laden's ally, the latter issued a televised stamen castigating Saddam as a a 'socialist infidel' and calling for his overthrow- an objective Bin Laden apparently shares with the US administration. All this suggest a hidden agenda, which serves to heighten our anxieties that what is unfolding is something far less high-minded than the war talk from Washington and London would have us believe!

There are disturbing media reports that the spoils of this war have already been divided among of the prospective victors. The Guardian (London) recently reported that a 'select group of companies, including Kellogg Brown & Root, a subsidiary of Halliburton, an oil services company where the vice-president, Dick Chencey, held the position of chief executive from 1995 to 2000, has already won a government contract to oversee fire fighting operation at Iraqi oilfields after any US led invasion, while the other companies also have strong ties to the US administration, including the construction giant Bechtel, the Fluor Corporation, and the Louis Berger group, already involved in the reconstruction of Afghanistan.'

The report continues: 'To speed up the project. The US Agency for International Development (USAid) invoked special authority to solicit bids from just a few companies. The move bypassed the usual rules that would have permitted a wider array of companies to seek the contract.'

Even more troubling is the speculation that the US intends using Iraq as some sort of laboratory to test new weapons systems. A journalist on a military affair, Jim Krane, recently wrote: 'If the United States unleashes a military attack against Iraq, US forces are expected to unleash several new weapons and tactics, including devices still under development.

'US military officials and analysts say the new weapons would target Iraqi armoured vehicles, communications networks and the chemical and biological weapons the Bush administration believes Iraq still holds.'

The charge that it is essentially a war to gain control of Iraqi oil reserves is vehemently denied by the US administration. But the indecent haste with which the entire international community was being pressed to declare war reinforces the suspicion that the proclaimed reason – disarmament of Iraq – is not the real one.

By amazing coincidence (or is it?) virtually all the top echelon in the Bush administration are involved in the US oil and energy sector. Since September last year Bush has told the United Nations to give the US what it wants and, if it does not, the US will take it anyway! Which is probably why a dissident US foreign policy expert, Michael Klare, speculates that the diplomatic round-about Secretary of State Colin Powell set the world on was choreographed to enable the US and its British ally the time to put in place the logistics for a full-scale war. Once these were in place, diplomacy was cast aside and the ultimatum was pronounced.

The actions of the US and Britain this week cannot but have extremely damaging consequences for the international political environment. They have thrown down a challenge to the rest of us to choose. But the options before us are not between Saddam Hussein and the United States of AMERICA. The choices before us between an international order based on the rule of international law, or based on the Wild West ethos of 'shoot first, ask questions later'. If that becomes the new world order, we are all in very serious trouble.

TWENTY-FIVE

This article was published in a special issue – titled 'Two cheers for democracy?' – of a left-leaning Africanist journal. Although it is generally positive, Jordan's article concurred that not all was well in the new democracy, to an extent that might not have been expected of a sitting MP and ex-Cabinet minister. Being in power was 'visibly changing the character of the ANC': political careerism, an appetite for the good things of life, and corruption were troubling symptoms.

The African National Congress: From illegality to the corridors of power

Review of African Political Economy, vol 31, 100 (2004), pp. 203–12.

This article examines both the performance of the ANC in power and the requisites of power which have forced it to redefine itself, experiencing thereby a profound metamorphosis. It argues that radical policy shifts have from the party's birth in 1912, been part of its political reality so that heterodoxy has often become the new orthodoxy. This tradition of change has been accelerated by local and global realities since 1994 – an assumption of office with virtually no power over the civil service and upper reaches of the security forces and a post-Cold War environment which generated a demonised [*sic*] of state intervention. Being in office has also changed the character of the ANC with the party now attracting those seeking a career and the perks of office, a consequence of which has been repeated allegations of the misuse of state funds levelled against ANC representatives. Finally, the paper notes that the ANC's second term has been marked by growing tensions with the Communist Party and a foreign policy with, as its central pillar, the creating of space for Africa to define its own future.

PREPARING FOR POWER

The paths pursued by a reformist National Party (NP) leadership and the African National Congress (ANC) intersected at an awkward historic moment. January 1990 arrived with the ANC at the head of a huge mass movement that had drawn into its slipstream noted public figures. Though it was still illegal, during the 1980s the ANC inspired a significant network of civil society formations, a front of democratic organisations and activists who accepted its leadership. After 1976 the ANC succeeded in placing itself at the head of organised radical opposition inside the country. It had won international legitimacy while isolating the apartheid regime politically from actual and potential sources of support in the international community. It succeeded in having limited economic sanctions imposed on South Africa and at the end of 1989 the international financial institutions refused to extend apartheid South Africa further credit. The ANC's programme, the Freedom Charter, had won widespread support from black (and some white) South Africans and been adopted by both the United Democratic Front (UDF) and the Congress of South African Trade Unions (COSATU). A sustained insurrectionary climate inside the country in the 1980s inspired the ANC leadership to adopt a strategy implemented at the time as Operation Vulindlela.

Explaining his government's decision to legalise the ANC, the Pan African Congress (PAC), the South African Communist Party (SACP) and the other political movements and parties that the NP had banned over the previous four decades, F.W. de Klerk has told numerous audiences that he felt comfortable about it because the collapse of communism in Eastern Europe implied that South Africa would not be overrun by communist states. De Klerk, the constituency of white voters and opinion-makers he represented, doubtless took comfort in that. But it is evident that the Afrikaner political elite had grasped the nettle of reform some years prior to December 1989.

Addressing a meeting of apartheid-regime strategists during the early 1980s, Samuel Huntington of Harvard University decried the absence of 'a Lenin of reform' who would give as 'intense attention' to the strategy and tactics of reform as that which 'Lenin devoted to the strategy and tactics of revolution'. Reform in South Africa, Huntington advised his audience, would be the most effective means of pre-empting revolution. The explicit purpose of reform should be counter-revolutionary, and if properly managed, would place the white minority in a position to co-determine the future of South Africa with its perceived revolutionary enemies.

In Paris, in November 1989, an Afrikaner intellectual with links to the Broederbond announced that it was De Klerk's intention to challenge the ANC on the political terrain. Legalisation, he implied, would create an environment in which credible negotiations could unfold, with De Klerk's prospective interlocutors given the political space to interact with and receive mandates from their constituency. De Klerk's 2 February 1990 speech did not come therefore, as a complete surprise to the ANC leadership. Of greater concern was the limited character of the reforms he had announced. But the ball was now clearly in the ANC's court and it had to respond After the first post-unbanning summit at Groote Schuur, the ANC determined that its key strategic goal was to have power transferred from the NP government as swiftly as possible. Consequently, the strategic debate within the ANC quickly came to centre on the confidence-building steps required for negotiations. Shortly after Mandela's return from a tour of the US, the National Executive Committee (NEC) took the decision to suspend all armed actions unilaterally. Matters might have moved very quickly to discussion of the repatriation of refugees and trained combatants but for the Security Police's arrest of Mac Maharaj, the internal co-ordinator of Operation Vulindlela. Shortly thereafter De Klerk advised Mandela that he had plans to arrest Jacob Zuma and was rescinding the indemnities granted to Chris Hani and Ronnie Kasrils. In briefings to the media Foreign Minister 'Pik' Botha tried to explain De Klerk's actions as a response to a communist conspiracy within the ANC's alliance which had not embraced negotiations but were intent on an insurrection.

The ANC leadership read this as an attempt to sow division between it and the SACP. For its part, once again a legal organisation, the SACP proceeded with plans for its first mass rally in 40 years. (In 1950 when it was banned, the Communist Party of South Africa (CPSA) became the first communist party ever to disband when it was proscribed.) At the SACP's first mass rally, held on 29 July 1990, it became clear that South Africa had inscribed yet another unprecedented occurrence in the annals of communism; at least 50% of the members of the Central Committee it had elected a year previously had resigned from the party once it became legal. With three of its leaders declared virtual outlaws so soon after returning home, it became clear that the course the ANC sought to pursue would not be an easy one. But after that initial hiccup, by June 1991 it appeared that all the hurdles had been cleared and that negotiations could begin in earnest. Both sides had taken the lessons of that first year to heart. There were evidently powerful pockets of opposition to De Klerk's course among both the white electorate and within the security services. The next three years witnessed a wave of unprecedented violence, orchestrated by the die-hard element in the apartheid regime's security services who hoped to derail the negotiation process or precipitate all-out war. In December 1991 the Convention for a Democratic South Africa (CODESA) held its first session. Negotiations stumbled along for the following two years. The ANC suspended talks twice in response to the violence. Even after they resumed as CODESA II, scepticism that they could stay on course continued to dog them. The assassination of Chris Hani in April 1993 concentrated the minds of all the key players on the dangers that could arise from continued uncertainty. The ANC was able to demonstrate its immense moral authority in the tense week that ensued by keeping a firm grip on the seething anger gripping the African townships. For a short while it appeared that a combination of the Inkatha Freedom Party (IFP), the Bophuthatswana homeland government and far-right white formations might prevent a pan-South African general election. But Bophuthatswana collapsed ignominiously when the people of Mafeking and MmaBatho rebelled, and the IFP agreed to participate in the elections at the eleventh hour.

27 April 1994 was the outcome of tough-minded decision making on both sides of the conflict. In order to take on the ANC on the political terrain the National Party (NP) had to change or reinvent itself. Towards the end of 1990, the NP announced that it would open its membership to persons other than whites. As negotiations progressed, the NP also revised its standpoint on two issues. Having amassed power over the years by ruthlessly wielding the instruments of a unitary state, by the 1980s the NP's strategists were expressing a preference for consociationalism.

This option, they argued, was particularly attractive for South Africa as it took account of the deeply fractured character of the society and its multi-racial features. In 1990 the NP positioned itself as the champion of group rights. By 1994 it had abandoned that platform.

On its side, after heated internal debates, the ANC had accepted the idea of a convention of all political parties, including those from the homelands and the tri-cameral parliament. To improve its own representation at CODESA it connived at the farcical resurrection of the Natal and Transvaal Indian Congresses (NIC-TIC), all of whose members were card-carrying members of the ANC. It had also made a major concession to the incumbent state bureaucracy, a key NP constituency, by adopting the 'Sunset Clauses' guaranteeing their jobs for the immediate future. The compromise on an interim constitution was the most significant considering the ANC's prior insistence on a constitution legitimated by an elected Constituent Assembly. A remarkable consensus emerged quite early in the negotiations about making the electoral system as inclusive as possible and on the need for a Constitutional Court. By 1994, a successful transition of power had been achieved and the trappings of a democratic order put in place.

THE ANC IN POWER

For over 90 years, the ANC as a political movement has demonstrated a capacity to adapt to, and remain relevant in the face of, sweeping changes that have taken place not only in Africa, but also in the rest of the world. Originally founded in 1912 as a body of respectable and very respectful black subjects, who regarded their organisation as a loyal opposition designed to give '... expression to representative opinion ...' and to assist the government '... formulate a standard policy on Native Affairs ...', the ANC had evolved by the 1980s into a revolutionary national movement whose principal objective was the seizure of political power. The 1990s required of the ANC that it transform itself again into a party of government able to administer Africa's wealthiest economy but also one of its most diverse societies. To arrive at that point, the ANC underwent repeated redefinition and a profound metamorphosis.

The ANC was shaped by South Africa's 20th century history as much as it helped shape it. Born in response to the racist constitution of the Union of South Africa that excluded Africans, Coloureds and Indians from the country's political institutions, the ANC at first regarded itself as a movement of the African people, pursuing African objectives. In the course of the struggle for democracy, the need for alliances and pacts became evident, persuading the ANC leadership to seek allies and establish ties with like-minded bodies among Whites, Coloureds and Indians; thus was forged the Congress movement of the 1950s. Over and above specifically African aspirations, the ANC repositioned itself as a movement striving for democracy and an end to white racial domination. By 1990, it had become a non-racial movement for all South African democrats, counting amongst its leadership and ranks South Africans of all races.

After the publication in 1960 of Nimrod Mkele's The Emergent African Middle Class, it was generally accepted that, despite differences in lifestyle, life chances and incomes, the shared burden of national oppression would persuade the African petty bourgeoisie and the majority of African working people to make common cause. By extension, the same was assumed to apply among Coloureds and Indians, as well as between Africans and the two black minority groups. These assumptions were the cornerstones of liberation movement strategy and the gravamen of Joe Slovo's 1977 thesis which argued against the likelihood of any accommodation because the disabilities of the black elite would oblige it to seek radical solutions.

When the ANC assumed political office in May 1994, the negotiation process had already disproved one leg of Slovo's thesis. In 1992, Slovo himself had proposed a middle course, the so-called 'sunset clauses', that envisaged the exit of the incumbent civil service by attrition. The elections too, had established that the disenfranchised black population was far more heterogeneous than ANC strategists had realised. Significant segments of the Coloured and Indian working classes had voted for the party of apartheid, and though the majority of Indians had been prepared to follow the ANC's lead by boycotting the tri-cameral elections, that did not translate into electoral support for the ANC in 1994. The election results confirmed the ethnic-regional character of the

Inkatha Freedom Party (IFP) but had also demonstrated its strength in rural KwaZulu-Natal.

The ANC-led government was constituted to take account of a number of tough realities. Though it had won the elections by a landslide, the ANC assumed political office with little power other than control of the majority of ministries. The upper reaches of the security services were still in the hands of apartheid appointees, as was the civil service. Mandela deliberately appointed Derek Keys, a former NP Minister, as Minister of Finance to reassure an uncertain South African and corporate sector. Carefully measured actions and studied moderation, in both rhetoric and action, helped reassure skittish investors and international markets. South Africa experienced a decade of social peace underpinned by political stabilitythanks to such circumspection.

Governing together with the NP and the IFP in a Government of National Unity (GNU), the ANC confounded its detractors with its pragmatism. During his The African Nationual Congress: From Illegality to the Corridors of Power 207 inaugural address to Parliament, Nelson Mandela set the tone for his government by quoting the Afrikaans poetess, Ingrid Jonker. The symbolism of that action was not lost on observers; she had in the 1970s committed suicide in despair about apartheid and the future of South Africa. Mandela was calling on the country to put the past behind it, seize the moment of hope and focus on the future.

The ANC had anticipated the challenges of governing and had drawn up an elaborate Reconstruction and Development Programme (RDP) based on an assessment of what would be required to address huge apartheid-created social deficits. The realities of political office soon made it clear that leveraging the resources for reconstruction and growth would not be easy. The post-Cold War environment brought with it a demonisation of state intervention. The state sector was concentrated in key delivery areas – utilities, posts and telecommunications, and public transport. Though the RDP had called for 'right sizing' of South Africa's hugely inflated state-owned sector, ANC policy makers soon discovered that they were expected to dismember it. The restructuring of state assets thus became a crucial aspect of government policy.

Motivated by an ambitious White Paper, telecommunications is the only sector that has been successfully restructured by inviting the participation of two strategic equity partners. During the last six years, SA Telkom has carried out an impressive rollout of telephone lines into previously deprived and neglected areas. Opinion surveys in 1998 and 2003 indicate that the improvement of communications is recognised as one of the ANC government's most notable achievements.

After two years as part of the GNU and shortly after the adoption of the new Constitution, the NP decided in June 1996 to withdraw from it. The NP's decision signalled a desire to mark out a position to the right of the ANC-led government and its hope to profit from oft-expressed white anxieties about the consequences of democracy. In less than two months, the NP changed both its leader and its name when Marthinus van Schalkwyk was elected leader of the New National Party.

THE REMAKING OF THE ANC AS A PARTY OF GOVERNMENT

Hegel once wrote that a political party becomes real only when it divides. That profoundly dialectical statement will strike many as odd. But, its profundity lies precisely in its paradoxical nature. Provided that it is not brain dead, as a political movement grows, its inner contradictions inevitably begin to unfold. But as these unfold, so too are the movement and its ideas enriched and its political and intellectual life made more vital.

Members of the ANC should take comfort from Hegel's view because it so closely approximates their lived political experience. The tired analogy of the ANC as a broad church can prove useful here in trying to understand the ironies of the debates that have so often taken place in recent years within it and among its alliance partners.

A corpus of religious values holds a church together much as a common programme is the standard beneath which the political faithful are rallied. That programme defines the boundaries of intra-movement debate. Contenders in any dispute each seek legitimacy by an appeal to its authority, but each is expected to respect the bona fides of the others. Episcopates in both the Catholic and the Protestant churches have been prepared to accommodate heterodox thought within their folds, provided it could be contained or co-opted. Thus was many a potential heresy tamed. In the ANC, in contrast, within the living memory of many veterans, heterodoxy has regularly become the new orthodoxy. The dissident voice, the innovative strategy and the critical ideas have won the argument in the movement on several occasions.

While this offers conservatives little comfort, it would be a rash radical who sought to employ it as justification for reckless behaviour. Any serious political movement necessarily requires its adherents to act collectively on the decisive issues. The whips in a parliamentary party are assigned precisely that role. Movements that have been forced to operate illegally place greater emphasis on discipline, because any breach can result in arrests and even the suppression of the movement itself. Theoretically, such discipline does not extend to the inner political life of the movement, but there have been numerous instances when the requirements of discipline have been abused to repress debate and critical thought. Prior to March 1960 when it was banned, ANC practice, as the reams of paper used up in inner-ANC debates will testify, was to encourage optimal debate within its structures until a collective decision had been arrived at. After that, the minority view was expected to submit to the majority. Highly vocal dissenting minorities, like the 'Africanists' of the 1950s, survived for years as ginger groups within the ANC before they walked out in frustration. The communist movement coined the term 'democratic centralism' to describe this practice, which recognised the inevitability of a diversity of viewpoints, but also insisted that they should not impair the movement's capacity for united action.

Security considerations, distances between centres and the dispersal of its membership across the globe severely undermined the ANC's ability to operate in this way during its 30 years of illegal operations. The militarisation of the movement as a result of the armed struggle also tilted the balance away from consultative practices. But even within those limitations, the movement sought to keep alive a tradition of internal debate and discussion that found expression in its publications, conference documents and other records. Feminism, for example, was disdained or derided in the ANC of the late 1960s. But it is firmly rooted within the movement today. Acceptance of same-sex relationships had to be fought for in heated debates.

No strategic shifts came as a surprise to ANC members and supporters because, in most cases, their views had been widely canvassed beforehand. The relative absence of destabilising upheavals that might have led to disintegration attests to the skill with which such issues were managed. While unity was never conflated with uniformity, the crystallisation of factions was also firmly resisted.

Achieving the delicate balance that enables a movement to maintain continuity while remaining open to new initiatives and even heretic ideas is a challenge even at the best of times. Strong leaders are often tempted to assert their wills. There were two occasions post-1990 when even Nelson Mandela was unable to muster the necessary support among the ANC's leadership for his views to prevail. There were numerous other, less publicised, occasions when he was over-ruled by the executive.

Thabo Mbeki initially tabled the central ideas in Joe Slovo's strategic initiative, the 'sunset clauses'. Mbeki lost the argument on that occasion. Despite Slovo's prestige, the initiative he authored was hotly contested and radically amended before it was adopted by the ANC. After its legalisation, the ANC and its key strategic partners, the SACP and COSATU, have often appeared as bodies seething with fractious internal conflicts. But perhaps this capacity, even willingness, to enter into robust debate is a quality to be cherished rather than sneered at. Devoting time and resources to intra-movement debates, arguments and ideological polemics often looks messy and even divisive. But after a decision is taken, most members are confident that every possible option has been examined and they also feel a sense of ownership of the policy positions adopted. The ANC in government sought to re-affirm this aspect of its organisational culture. It reformed the workings of the national parliament by opening up all its plenaries and committee meetings to members of the public and the media. Stressing accountability and transparency, it piloted the adoption of codes of ethics for both parliamentarians and members of the executive. But governing a country has reinforced the centripetal tendencies in the movement's culture, giving countervailing the impression of power centralised in the presidency. Powerful trends are, however, also evident. The NEC meets once every two months, usually according to a pre-determined schedule which permits members to plan their attendance with greater certainty. Participation in its plenaries has also been expanded to include non-elected national government Ministers and Deputy Ministers.

Participating in two general elections and a host of local government elections the ANC has introduced many new concepts to South African electioneering. Compelled to master the skills of modern elections very quickly in 1994, the ANC learnt the use of opinion surveys and focus groups. Borrowing from its own past experience, specifically during the campaign for the Congress of the People in 1955, the ANC introduced the People's Forum during its 1994 election campaign. Such forums were conceived as town hall meetings which would afford members of the general public the opportunity to question ANC leaders on any aspect of its election platform. They proved hugely successful in bridging the social distance between politicians and the citizen. The degree of interaction at such forums increased the sense of identification with a party that was prepared to listen and did not insist on talking to the electorate all the time. The People's Forum has now become part of the ANC's elections repertoire and has been adopted also by the Presidency which refers to its gatherings as imbizo.

But as a party of government, rather than an illegal liberation movement, membership of which entailed risks of imprisonment or even death, membership of the ANC today could open up career opportunities. Apart from the activists who surfaced in 1990 and could now openly affiliate to the ANC, the movement is attracting into its ranks many in search of political careers. The appetites of many old militants for the good things in life have also been whetted after decades of denial. A measure of the problem is repeated allegations of the misuse of state funds levelled against ANC local councillors and government officials. The need to fill civil service posts with personnel loyal to the ANC's vision has inevitably transformed many capable grassroots' activists into state bureaucrats, depriving the movement of the calibre of membership who were the driving force in its local structures.

Being in power is visibly changing the character of the ANC.

Whereas in the past ANC networks linked one to the movers and shakers among organisations representing the disadvantaged, the poor and the disinherited, today they can also give you access to the leading corporate boardrooms, the cabinet, top civil servants and members of the political elite. This was reflected in the ANC's own recasting of its strategy and tactics at its 1997 national conference, that marked the passing of the baton from Mandela to Mbeki. On that occasion, the black middle strata, who had received scant attention in previous strategy and tactics documents, were elevated to the status of one of the motive forces of the National Democratic Revolution. A rather vague Black Economic Empowerment project was also flagged at that conference.

The fleshing out of the project since 1997 has given rise to fears amongst many that the ANC has adopted the creation of a black bourgeoisie as one of its principal objectives for the medium term.

THE ANC's SECOND TERM

The ANC went to the hustings in 1999 very confident of winning by a landslide. The upshot was that it won just one percentage point shy of a two-thirds majority. The most salient feature of the 1999 elections, however, was the collapse of the New National Party, despite its make-over as the New National Party after it walked out of the GNU in 1996. The Democratic Party, under Tony Leon's leadership, emerged as the party of white discontent.

Thabo Mbeki assumed the presidency having acted as de facto President for some years as Nelson Mandela gradually disengaged himself from day-to-day government business. He led the ANC to a magnificent electoral victory that left the opposition in disarray. No other party managed to garner more than ten per cent of the poll and instead of the six opposition parties of the first democratic parliament, there are now ten even smaller groupings. The ANC again offered the IFP seats in the executive though its majority did not require it to find coalition partners. A portent of what has become a feature of Mbeki's incumbency raised its head in the NEC of the ANC during 1994. Reacting rather testily to an editorial in the SACP's news-sheet Umsebenzi, Nelson Mandela castigated the SACP as an unworthy organisation, which owed its place in democratic South Africa to the ANC. Instead of defending the SACP, its former Chairman, Joe Slovo, and its then General Secretary, Charles Nqakula, retreated before Mandela's attack and apologised for the offending article. Relations between the ANC and its communist ally have deteriorated even further and faster under Mbeki's presidency. Neither COSATU nor the SACP had become reconciled to the adoption the Growth and Redistribution (GEAR) strategy piloted through Cabinet during Mandela's incumbency. As the ANC government proceeded with its speedier implementation after 1999, repeated exchanges between the ANC leadership and its allies ensued. These escalated as the policy areas of difference between the ANC and its allies seemed to multiply. By 2001, these included not only the restructuring of state assets, but also the HIV/AIDS pandemic.

Perhaps over-confident that it could win over the rank-and-file members of COSATU affiliates, the ANC leadership took the issues that divided the alliance partners to both COSATU and SACP conferences. The SACP came in for particularly harsh criticism and was repeatedly warned that it was straying from the course pioneered by its previous leaders, J.B. Marks and Moses Kotane, who had been content to allow the SACP to survive as a secret communist network operating within the ANC, but with no independent profile. When the SACP was legalised in 1990, it shed a fair number of its erstwhile members. Consequently there was a massive intake of new members, drawn from the trade unions, the civics and other mass organisations after the SACP's first internal congress in 1992. Buoyed by the popularity of its General Secretary, Chris Hani, the SACP grew fast, reaching a high point of 89,000 paid-up members in 2002. It also underwent a period of intense internal discussion about its future role, especially in the light of the collapse of Soviet socialism in Eastern Europe and the Soviet Union. The outcome of these discussions was a decision that, as the party of socialism, it should begin to carve out an identity distinct from both the ANC and the failed socialist projects in Eastern Europe. To achieve the former, it did not project itself as the vanguard of the second phase of the revolution but instead, spoke boldly about the particular interests of the working class within the alliance. It appealed to the rich vein of indigenous South African radicalism to which South Africa's communists had made a distinctive contribution. Unaccustomed to an SACP that not only differed with, but publicly criticised, positions adopted by the leadership, many in the ANC reacted very negatively to the positions the SACP pronounced. By January 2002 it was not uncommon to hear the epithet 'ultra-leftist' applied to the SACP's leadership. This reached its nadir when two fairly senior ANC leaders, Josiah Jele and Jabu Moleketi, penned a polemic directed against the SACP's leadership. Both sides to this acrimonious quarrel pulled back from the brink towards mid-2002. An ANC policy conference, in anticipation of the national conference, resulted in a wide-ranging consensus on most issues. At the national conference that December, all the delegates from the president down re-affirmed the importance of the tripartite alliance.

There is little dissent within the ANC over the area of foreign affairs where the Mbeki-led government has made its most decisive mark. With an energetic Foreign Minister in the person of Dr Nkosazana Dlamini-Zuma, South Africa has been punching way above its weight. Mbeki's presidency, or rather his foreign-policy profile, has been facilitated by South Africa's assumption of the headship of the Non-Aligned Movement (NAM) and of the Commonwealth. When the OAU changed itself into the African Union (AU) in 2002, South Africa also became chair of that continental body. In addition, in the first three years of Mbeki's tenure, South Africa has hosted four major international conferences – that of the Commonwealth, the World Conference Against Racism, the World Summit on Sustainable Development and lastly the African Union.

South African foreign policy has as its central plank the creating of space for Africa and its people to define their own future by exploring and offering viable, indigenously-evolved, alternative agendas to those imposed on our continent by former colonial powers and their allies. Africa has also adopted new and far-reaching human rights instruments during the past four years. Though the rights contained in these charters are in the main aspirational, they are indicative of and will reinforce the growing trend toward democratic governance on the continent.

Progress towards democratisation on the continent is still very uneven but the struggles of ordinary citizens and political activists have gained momentum during this time and could result in the creation and extension of democratic space in African societies.

The ANC's second term started with a bold foreign-policy initiative in the Congo when Nelson Mandela attempted to arrange a relatively peaceful transfer of power. South Africa became even more deeply entangled after Mobutu fled, and Laurent Kabila assumed power in Kinshasa, backed by Uganda and Rwanda. South African diplomacy at first sought to minimise the capacity of non-African powers to interfere in the Congo so as to give the Congolese and their neighbours a chance to resolve their problems. The upshot was rather different from what had been hoped for.

Uganda and Rwanda had been drawn into the effort to get rid of Mobutu in pursuance of their own interests. Unable to secure these from Laurent Kabilia, whom they had assisted to power, both countries sought to use armed Congolese factions close to them to overthrow Kabila's government. That had inspired President Mugabe of Zimbabwe to seek a multi-state SADC intervention, in support of Laurent Kabila's beleagured government. South Africa, Botswana, Mozambique and Malawi refused to become involved, but Namibia and Angola sent troops and equipment.

From day one of his presidency, Mbeki tried to find a solution to the Congo crisis. After three years of talks, interrupted by outbreaks of terrible bloodletting, the Congo factions agreed to constitute a government of national unity in December 2002. South Africa had invested millions of rands to keep the negotiations afloat but in the end was unable to exclude non-African powers. When the fragile peace in Eastern Congo threatened to unravel in 2003, South Africa was compelled to accept the introduction of French troops to keep the warring factions apart.

As Deputy President, Mbeki had nailed his colours to the mast of an African Renaissance. When he assumed the presidency it was expected that this vision would be further fleshed out. The arrival of the new millennium, six months after he became president, offered a golden opportunity. Working with the Presidents of Algeria and Nigeria, he crafted what was at first named the Millennium African Project or MAP. This was conceived as an ambitious programme for African economic development premised on good governance and rapid economic growth driven by massive inflows of direct foreign investment. The Presidents of Egypt and Senegal were subsequently also drawn in and the projects were redesigned to take account of their contributions. It was then renamed the New Partnership for African Development (NEPAD) with roughly the same features. Mbeki took the lead in canvassing and winning support for NEPAD among the political leaders of the developed world. Despite extremely parsimonious commitments from G8 summits in Canada and France, there is still optimism that the developed economies will come to the party.

CONCLUSION

During its first five years under Mandela's presidency, the ANC's main aim was the consolidation of the democratic breakthrough and ensuring that the majority of South Africans bought into their newly-won democracy. The 1999 elections seemed to confirm that it achieved that objective.

27 April 1994 completely transformed the South African political landscape. The African majority – some 77% of the total population at last count – are now the decisive factor in electoral politics. No political party can hope to prosper except by addressing the needs and aspirations of that majority. Reducing the gap between rich and poor remains the priority issue on the national agenda. Apartheid, and not the ANC's rhetoric, has determined that this line of cleavage will in large measure coincide with race. Addressing a graduating class at Howard University in Washington, DC, in June 1965, President Lyndon Johnson, declared:

But freedom is not enough. You do not take a person who, for years, has been hobbled by chains and liberate him, bring him up to the starting line of the race and then say, you are free to compete zwith all the others, and still justly believe that you have been conipletely fair. Thus it is not enough just to open the gates of opportunity. All our citizens must have the ability to walk through those gates.

The extent to which it succeeds in giving the previously disadvantaged the capacity to walk through those gates is the measuring rod South Africa will use to judge the ANC's ten-year stewardship.

TWENTY-SIX

This well-crafted, sincere and moving tribute to 'MaBrrr' was delivered by Jordan at Brenda Fassie's graveside, in Langa, in May 2004.

A Tribute to Brenda Fassie

This Day, May 2004

We are here to celebrate the life of Brenda Fassie.

Langa township was her home and the home of many who have gathered here today. Langa, like so many other places on the Cape Flats – Athlone, Bonteheuwel, Mitchell's Plain, Hanover Park, Mannenberg, Nyanga, Gugulethu and others – was not placed here by accident. The position of this township bears testimony to the human geography and the spatial planning that colonialism and apartheid foisted on this country and its people.

We know that to be surrounded by the beauty and splendour that is the Western Cape – to live in the shadow of these mountains, to breathe and hear the rhythms of the two seas, to feel the cooling shade of the valleys – can inspire great creativity and light up the soul of a poet. We also understand the pain of knowing that yours was to look upon all this, but know that it did not quite belong to you.

Brenda first saw the light in this township in 1964. It became her home, as it was to her parents before her. Yet at the time she was born, Africans were not allowed to own property here. During those years it was written into law that Africans did not belong in the Western Cape and everything was done to make them know that they were unwelcome.

Their home, so the apartheid government said, was in the Ciskei or the Transkei. Thousands of Africans were thrown out of this province to ensure that even those whom the regime allowed to remain got the message: you are not wanted here.

Yes, Langa was Brenda's home, but she was told – as was every African at that time – that it was not her home. She was made to feel like an alien in the very place she was born. That sense of not belonging, of not being rooted anywhere was dinned into the consciousness of every African child born in the Western Cape.

But we all know that Brenda was rooted in Cape Town. We all know this was her home, which she always laid claim to with a singular passion. Yet we know too the extent to which the structure of township life, that feeling of being excluded, impacted on her life, contributing to her creativity and to the pain that she so melodically sang of in her music.

When we recall the body of her creative work, two things stand out. The first is the gift she had – her beautiful voice.

The second is her authenticity. Brenda never was and never sought to be a poor carbon copy of some imported American singer. She sang as a uniquely South African original, a Cape Town original, a Langa original. She sang of the experience, the hopes, the joys and sorrows of the people she knew so well.

If there is [a] secret to her ability to communicate, it is that.

And, as she laid her soul bare in her songs, so too her life – with its triumphs, its ups, its downs and its tears – was laid bare for all to see.

Those who wish to suppress and suffocate the human spirit speak of 'tough love'. There is no such thing. What there is, and Brenda told it like it is in her song, is the fact that loving is tough.

When Brenda sang about love, it was not the sloppy sentimental drivel you hear, what some used to call 'muzak'.

Her songs were always provocative, with a defiant tinge that spoke directly of the multifaceted thing we call love – of its complexities, of its intricacies, its intimacies, its enigmatic character, its laughter, its tears, the anger it can bring out, together with a tenderness that is unequivocal, honest and pure.

All these were aspects of her own personality. Like she used to say: 'Indaba yam[i] istraight, ayifu ruler' (My situation is straight, it's not crooked, does not need a ruler).

Perhaps it was providence that ensured that the song that won her acclaim was called Weekend Special. The lyrics might seem rather indifferent but they speak eloquently of the experience of young women, not only in this country, but probably everywhere.

Perhaps Brenda was less fortunate than most in matters of love, especially with men. Yet there was no mistaking in her life – the way she lived it – and in her song that this was a strong, independent woman who was not going to be taken for granted.

Brenda – like all of us – bore the scars of the oppression we had to endure. But she was never submissive. A born extrovert, she must have known that she had these special gifts, and she was not about to hide them under a bushel.

We have, over the past weeks, seen and read a great deal about [the] life she lived as a pop diva. Yet there was [a] dimension of Brenda that was deeply spiritual. These are themes that she returned to again and again in her songs and in the way she led her life.

Brenda never lost touch with her roots. She said it over and over again, in so many different ways: 'Others helped me when I had nothing. Others shared the little they had with me when I had nothing. How can I now not wish to share with others what I have?'

Perhaps it was that generosity of spirit which laid her open to abuse and exploitation by those who read it as vulnerability and weakness. Like all of us, she was very vulnerable. Like all of us, she had her weaknesses. Like all of us, she made her fair share of mistakes. But in all that, what we see always gleaming through is her humanity.

Brenda Fassie, the living, breathing earthly being, has passed on. But Brenda Fassie lives. She lives in the hearts of the millions of people of this country and beyond, to whom she brought hope and joy with her music.

TWENTY-SEVEN

There are actually two newspaper columns below, but they are presented as a single document providing interesting commentaries on historical and contemporary Zimbabwe. In the first, Jordan argues that moral claims by Africans to land in Zimbabwe were unimpeachable – but could not justify the abuses perpetrated by Mugabe's government. The second column elaborates on the shortcomings of ZANU-PF in power. Social justice and democracy are not alternatives: Zimbabwe will not have one without the other.

Sorting out the Legacies of
Rhodes and Hitler

This Day, 2004

SORTING OUT THE LEGACIES OF RHODES AND HITLER

In 1993 an Austrian ex-corporal by the name of Adolf Hitler was made the chancellor of Germany after his party won a convincing majority in the general elections.

Terrified at the prospect of living in a country ruled by Hitler and his henchmen, the Rosenthals, a Jewish family which had made its wealth in the laundry business, fled their homeland and sought refuge in Holland. In their haste the Rosenthals left behind many of their valuables, including art works that they had acquired.

Four years later Hitler annexed his homeland, Austria, to Germany. In Vienna another wealthy Jewish family, the Grafs, hurriedly fled their hometown, leaving behind valuable art works.

The possessions of the Rosenthals, the Grafs and millions of other Jews in Germany, Austria and the other countries invaded by Hitler's legions, were seized. Some of the loot was divided up among the Nazi leaders; some was sold off; some was stored away for later disposal.

When the Second World War ended in 1945, property valued at millions of dollars was recovered. Many of its rightful owners had been murdered by the Nazis and these items remained unclaimed. Others had survived the Holocaust and were able to begin a search to try to recover what had been stolen from them and their families.

Art collectors, auction houses and dealers co-operated in establishing a register of looted art that aimed to help the victimised families recover their property.

In recent weeks the British press has reported that a well-known auction house knew of two such art works, the property of the Rosenthal and Graf families respectively, that had fallen into the hands of two of the auction house's clients.

From the reports it would appear that rather than acting honourably and assisting the descendants of the two families, the auction house has opted to conceal the identities of its two clients who now possess the looted art.

The fate that befell the Rosenthals, the Grafs and about six million of their co-religionists was the most horrific outcome of the dogmas of racial superiority propagated by Hitler and his henchmen.

In 1890 a wealthy Englishman by the name of Cecil John Rhodes financed a column of European invaders which crossed the Limpopo and took possession of the unconquered territories north of it.

Inspired by racial dogmas not too dissimilar from those that inspired Hitler, Rhodes' column seized the lands of the Ndebele and Shona kingdoms and reduced their inhabitants to virtual serfdom.

By the time of his death in 1901, Rhodes had renamed the territories he had seized after himself – Southern and Northern Rhodesia – both of which became British colonies, to be settled by whites from Britain and other European nations.

When Hitler went on the rampage in Europe, the European settlers in Rhodesia had seized the best agricultural land. And though they never numbered even half-a-million souls, the settlers had reduced the indigenous African population of about three million to rightless Helots dependent on the wages earned for labouring on the farms that were carved from their ancestral lands.

Hitler's actions in Europe sparked the Second World War. An alliance led by Britain, the Soviet Union and the US crushed Hitler's regime. At the end of the war the British government seized even more fertile land from the indigenous Africans in its colony, Rhodesia.

This land was virtually given to white ex-soldiers, further compounding the landlessness of the Africans. By the time the African majority took up arms against colonial rule in the 1960s, the best land in Rhodesia was in white hands.

There are not many who would dare contest the moral right of the Rosenthal and Graf families to the paintings plundered from their grandparents. Indeed, the register of Nazi-looted art is a token of the world's recognition of the morality of the victims' claims.

I have consequently found it odd that so many who readily recognise the victimisation of those persecuted and robbed by the Nazis have such great difficulty in applying the same standard when addressing the land issue in Zimbabwe.

For the African victims of Rhodes's invasion, the distinction between looting and plunder perpetrated by German Nazis and by English adventurers must be very obscure indeed.

I have yet to find the person who can explain the difference between the forced sale or seizure of Jewish businesses, land, homes and personal possessions and the seizure of the lands and home of Africans by colonial regimes. And, if there is no essential distinction, why are the two cases handled so differently?

Reclaiming the land was at the core of the struggle for liberation in Zimbabwe. The moral claims of the African majority to the land are unimpeachable. In that respect I have no quarrel with the Zanu-PF government.

However, the morality of the land reform programme cannot justify the 'in your face' abuses that the Zimbabwean government has perpetrated against citizens of that country. Employing immoral means to attain perfectly legitimate social goals compromises both the morality and legitimacy of those goals.

Democratic rights are not privileges, to be extended or withheld at the discretion of the political party in power, no matter how honourable a liberation track record it has.

Perhaps it is important to remind ourselves that it was the people of Zimbabwe who waged the struggle to attain democracy, accountable government, the rule of law, an independent judiciary and freedom of expression, along with the land that had been seized by the colonial regime.

These are the rights the people won, at great cost, through decades of struggle. The British colonial authorities never respected these rights when they held sway in Zimbabwe.

The suggestion that our insistence that Harare nurture and respect these rights is part of an elaborate British imperialist conspiracy is not merely utter nonsense, but amounts to a repudiation of the very struggle Zanu-PF led to victory in 1980.

The pressing need for a national dialogue among the key political players in Zimbabwe should be self-evident.

TWENTY-EIGHT

Zimbabwe Must Seek the Kingdom of Social Justice

It was not until 1980 that all adult Zimbabweans had a chance to choose their own government. Unlike South Africa, Zimbabwe's first democratic elections were run on two electoral rolls: One for African majority, who elected 80 percent of the public representatives; and another for whites and other minority groups, who elected the remaining 20 percent.

That was not an arrangement of Zimbabwe's choosing. It was one of the compromises reached at Lancaster House, a temporary measure– a 'sunset clause' if you like – that would apply for the first 10 years of independence that would ease the white minority into majority rule.

Every colonial power tried to remake its colonies in its own image. The history of the colonized people was invariably the first causality.

In Zimbabwe, for example, successive colonial and white minority regimes desperately cast about for some non-African explanation for the magnificent ruins, old mines and other remains of the ancient African civilisation whose centre had once been Zimbabwe.

As a boy I read H Riders Haggard's novel *King Solomon's Mines* which purportedly offered such an explanation.

But there were even more fanciful ones. Any explanation seemed worthy of examination, except the rather obvious one that the ruins were the word of the indigenous people. As recently as the 1970s Ian Smith and his cronies drove a distinguished scholar from his post because he dared to suggest that Zimbabwe had once been home of an advanced African civilisation.

In Zimbabwe the colonizers not only dispossessed the indigenous people, they added degrading insult to this injury but renaming the country Rhodesia, after the arch-imperialist Cecil John Rhodes. The Emotive character of the land question in Zimbabwe is rooted in this past. When Ian Smith pronounced that majority rule in Zimbabwe would not be attained for a thousand years, his words expressed the white minority's perception that the African majority's perception that the African majority did not have a claim to the country, and no sensibilities worth respecting.

The tone of governing Zimbabwe had been set in Berlin, six years before Rhodes' column entered the country, at a conference of the leading European powers.

By 1890, with the exceptions of Ethiopia ad Liberia, every other part of the continent was under foreign rile. With the collective decree of the European powers, Africans had collectively been reduced to a subject people.

Colonisation in Zimbabwe did not merely involve the imposition of a foreign government. Colonist settlers and administrators arrived who set about dismembering the economic independence of the indigenous people.

Taxes were imposed both to sustain the colonial administration and to separate tillers from their land to create work-force to serve colonizers. A regime of forced labour, not dissimilar to the medieval corv e – enforced with the sjambok and the gun – was established to build public works.

Africans were not citizens, they were colonial subjects, governed in terms of a distinct system of law. Incalculable mischief was wrought by the so-called experts in 'native culture' and 'customary law' who corrupted indigenous legal systems to suit the needs of the colonial administration. Unaccountable, arbitrary power was the hallmark of the colonial administration.

But colonization had a dialectical character. While it did terrible violence to the colonized, their society and their culture, it nonetheless cries a modernizing impulse. To administer its colonies more effectively and to maintain military control over the territory and its people, the colonial power built roads, railways and introduced modern communications, imposing a degree of unity on the country.

Colonial domination also pawned a number of centripetal forces that conspired to create a common society. The leadership of the Zimbabwean nationalist movements shared a number of common values with the colonisers. They invariably were also modernist who wanted to give their own country and people access to modernity. It is striking that none of the nationalist leaders sought to restore some romantic pre-colonial medievalism.

Kwame Nkrumah, the founder president of Ghana, declaimed: 'Seek ye first the political kingdom...' Seeking the political kingdom in a colonial context required that two basic conditions should be met. Government should be based on the consent of the governed, and all the adults should have the right to participate in lawmaking bodies.

It is an incontrovertible historical fact that democracy and all the institutions associated with it – regular elections, the rule of law, separation of powers, an independent judiciary, freedom of the expression and so on – came to Zimbabwe through the agency of the national liberation struggle. It was to attain these that the national liberation movement waged a war, employing whatever means were deemed necessary.

Colonial regimes were notoriously averse to criticism, whether expressed by their subjects or by citizens of the colonial power. In the past, the leadership of Zanu PF stood by and fought alongside those who were silenced by white minority government because their views had incurred the wrath of some minster or pretty official. Editors, writers, musicians and other whose work was suppressed and banned had received the support of Zanu.

It is precisely because of these values Zanu-PF once held in such high esteem that I am shocked at the manner in which it so impudently is violating them today.

In Zimbabwe the political kingdom was attained in 1980. It is in pursuance of the second kingdom, social justice, that Zimbabwe has run into serious problems.

No Zimbabwean political leader worth his or her salt can afford to ignore the legacy of colonialism. That applies equally to Zanu-PF and the MDC leadership rigorously about the views on the land question. They all agree that it has to be addressed.

The challenge facing Zimbabwe is how to enter the kingdom of social justice without doing violence to the fundamental principles of democracy. Zanu-PF can keep faith with the best of its own traditions only by respecting democratic principles in the pursuance of social justice.

Social justice and democracy are not alternatives. Zimbabwe will not have one without the other.

TWENTY-NINE

This is an intriguing and important piece. It was presented as an address to the Platform for Public Deliberation at the University of Johannesburg on 8 November 2008. The 'problems facing the ANC' were, immediately, the breakaway of the Congress of the People (COPE); but also, as becomes clear, issues that had been much longer in the making. Jordan argues that social changes in South Africa – especially capital accumulation and political advancement by a new elite – were reflected in the ANC itself; but that the organisation had wilfully resisted acknowledging or examining the contradictions generated by its own policies. The appearance of COPE ('sprung from the very loins of the ANC') represented a collective failure of the leadership corps.

A Letter to Comrade Mtungwa, an old comrade and dear friend

November 2008

Rather than give a conventional address, I have put my thoughts together in what I call:

A Letter to Comrade Mtungwa, and old comrade and dear friend.

Mtungwa is an abstract comrade but also a real person who has been my interlocutor on these matters for some weeks now. The letter reads as follows:

Khumalo,

I have thought it wiser to approach the problems facing the ANC from a very different angle than that employed by others. The temptation to cast the problems in terms of a Shikota vs Zuma camp is the intellectually lazy way out. We both derive from a specific political and intellectual tradition and, unless I am mistaken, subscribe to a number of propositions associated with it. Among these is one taken from Karl Marx's third theses on Feuerbach:

'The materialist doctrine concerning the changing of circumstances and upbringing forgets that circumstances are changed by men and that it is essential to educate the educator himself.'

The urgency attached to a critical examination of what amount to seismic shifts in the political economy of South Africa post 1994, somehow failed to impress itself on the ANC leadership. Repeated appeals for such a discussion, inside and outside of the NEC, were studiedly ignored. In that respect, there was a serious failure of leadership on the part of the ANC.

Is what we are witnessing in the ANC today the chickens of such evasion coming home to roost?

One of the ironies of the current division in the ANC is that both sides to the quarrel claim the Freedom Charter. The even deeper irony is that both sides can claim it with equal justification.

The question has often been posed, what then is the Freedom Charter if the antagonists in a dispute can claim it with equal conviction.

The Freedom Charter, like all great historical documents, must be viewed dialectically. For the socialists, communists and others on the left, the Freedom Charter was a minimum programme, similar to that proposed by Marx and Engels in the Communist Manifesto. The realization of its objectives, it was assumed, would create political conditions in which an advance to socialism would be possible. Equally, for those who sought only to remove the racial barriers to their advancement and bring about democracy, the Freedom Charter embraced all they sought – it was a maximum programme.

I find the leftist view very well expressed in an essay Joe Slovo wrote in 1988, in which he says:

'The South African Communist Party, in its 1984 constitution, declares that its aim is to lead the working class towards the strategic goal of establishing a socialist republic 'and the more immediate aim of winning the objectives of the national democratic revolution which is inseparably linked to it'. The constitution describes the main content of the national democratic revolution as '...the national liberation of the African people in particular, and the black people in general, the destruction of the economic and political power of the racist ruling class, and the establishment of one united state of people's power in which the working class will be the dominant force and which will move uninterruptedly towards social emancipation and the total abolition of exploitation of man by man'.

The national democratic revolution – the present stage of struggle in our country is a revolution of the whole oppressed people. This does not mean that the oppressed 'people' can be regarded as a single or homogeneous entity. The main revolutionary camp in the immediate struggle is made up of different classes and strata (overwhelmingly black) which suffer varying forms and degrees of national oppression and economic exploitation.

I have recourse to our characterization of White domination in South Africa as a 'Colonialism of a Special Type'. In a document the ANC produced for a meeting amongst the Frontline States in 1987, one reads:

'Because the undemocratic colonial, white minority state occupies the same territory as the people it dominates, there can be no question of a hand over of power from an externally-based colonial state and its agents, to an internally located national government. The struggle of the South African people has therefore centred on the abolition of the colonial white state and the creation in its stead of a democratic state based on the principle of majority rule.

Because of the special circumstances in South Africa, the constitutional modalities through which this can be accomplished necessarily entail the acquisition of political rights by the Black majority, that is, the abolition of the monopoly on political power by the whites. That monopoly is effectively maintained with both the Bantustan system and the tri-racial parliamentary system.

In addition to the racist and undemocratic character of the White state, we also spoke of its other essential features: Its role as the engine of an accumulation path evolved by British capital in the late 19th century and elaborated in alliance with Afrikaner agrarian capital during the 20th century. The 19th century German Social Democrats referred to an alliance between 'iron and corn' as the drivers of the modernization of Germany, so we in South Africa spoke of the alliance between gold and maize. As Thabo Mbeki expressed it in a talk delivered in 1978:

'The historic compromise between the British bourgeoisie and the Boer peasantry represented hence not an historical aberration, but the continued pursuit of maximum profit in conditions of absolute freedom for capital to pursue its inherent purposes.'

The Marxist tradition in our movement regarded the White racist state as both the product and the agency of a path of capitalist accumulation that entailed the colonial conquest and dispossession of the African people of their land and its wealth. Apartheid was not merely a system of segregation, but rather a comprehensive system of colonial domination.

The ANC's 1987 document explains:

'This is why the ANC has always considered the two economic clauses of the Freedom Charter : 'The People Shall Share in the Country's Wealth' and 'The Land Shall Be Shared Among Those Who Work It' to be the very core of its programme. These clauses envisage the seizure of economic assets, presently owned and controlled either by individual capitalists or capitalist companies drawn exclusively from the white minority or trans-national corporations.'

Yet in a strategy document that served before the Kabwe Consultative Conference in 1985, the ANC explicitly states :

'Though the Freedom Charter is not a programme for socialism, it must, nevertheless, be distinguished from a conventional bourgeois-democratic programme. In its third and fourth clauses, the Charter projects the seizure of economic assets presently owned either by South African capitalist firms or trans-national corporations. Such measures will strip the present ruling class of the actual substance of its power, by seizing hold of the commanding heights of the economy. People's power, as conceived within our movement, will therefore entail a democratic revolution of a new type, in which the interests of the working people, of town and countryside, will be pre-eminent. At the same time the democratic state will secure the interests of the small property-owner, the petty commodity producer, the artisans, traders and professional strata.'

Thus, as Slovo would have it, the immediate goal of socialists and communists is the liberation of the Africans in particular and all Blacks in general, in order to throw open the road to an uninterrupted march to socialism. While the ANC also speaks of the seizure of economic assets in order '...to strip the present ruling class of the actual substance of its power, by seizing hold of the commanding heights of the economy', the ANC does not regard these measures as preparing the ground for socialism.

I fear what we have seen over the last eleven months is the outcome of the failure of ANC leadership or its inability, during this phase of the national democratic revolution, to map out the relationship between the minimum and the maximum. After all minimum and maximum are the two extremes of a continuum, which means they are not necessarily contradictory. I shall have recourse to Marxist theory in this letter because, in my view, it is the only theoretical system with the capacity to unpack and dissect the problems that have arisen in the ANC, culminating in the so-called Convention held in Sandton two weeks ago.

Writing prior to the 1905 Revolution in Russia, V.I. Lenin once said that 'every movement of the people is necessarily fraught with contradictions'.

In an appreciation of our former President, Oliver Tambo, inter alia I remarked:

'Because of the nature of the oppression suffered by the people of this country, the ANC was necessarily a broad movement, drawing support from a wide spectrum of social and economic forces. There were people who were drawn to the ANC because freedom from apartheid offered them the opportunity to ' realise their dreams on the Johannesburg Stock Exchange', as one recent headline put it. Yet others joined and supported it because freedom would open up the chance to rise to the heights to which their talents could take them. Others sought the restoration of the right to the land that had been seized or from which they had been driven by racist laws. Others hoped to restore the dignity and grace of African culture. The movement counted amongst its supporters members of the middle classes, the working class, the rural working poor, aspirant capitalists and entrepreneurs, as well as militant socialists and communists.'

The ANC has since its inception been one of the best testimonies to Lenin's assertion concerning the contradictory nature of popular movements. Oliver Tambo's genius was understanding how to manage the contradictions inherent in such a broad movement. The feat of reconstructing the movement, was something akin to repairing a skoro-koro in motion through heavy traffic! Unlike other liberation movements that were plagued by internal divisions, schisms and splits, the ANC enjoyed relative stability thanks to his leadership qualities. (Compared especially with its prodigal off-spring the PAC!!)

In yet another context I had occasion to write:

'No serious person, even from among our opponents, could pretend that South Africa today is not a country of far greater opportunity than it was ten years ago. The opening up of new opportunities for many who never had a chance to pursue their own ambitions, aims and individual aspirations before, has created an environment conducive to the emergence of a class of Black capitalists, a stratum of very senior Black managers and business executives, a stratum of senior Black civil servants and bureaucrats, a stratum of Black professionals, as well as a Black lower middle class. ...

After all the struggle for democracy was also a struggle to create opportunities for Black women and men to rise as high as their talents can take them. Obviously, the ANC cannot bar Blacks from becoming and being capitalists, any more than it could debar them from becoming lawyers, doctors, accountants, engineers, skilled workers, etc. The high visibility of these strata should not however deceive us. In absolute terms they number far, far fewer than their equivalents among Whites.

The vast majority of Blacks, however, remain workers and other working people.'

In that same piece I also said:

'Since 1994 the multi-class character ANC itself has of course changed. Whereas in the past there were no captains of industry in the leading organs of the ANC; today an NEC member heads one of the largest conglomerates trading on the Johannesburg Stock Exchange. This corporation, moreover, employs thousands of other ANC members as well as ANC supporters! Prior to 1994 Transnet, one of the biggest state-owned corporations which employs thousands of ANC supporters and members organised in SARHWU, was headed by one Johan Maree. Today its MD is a member (of the ANC.) We will neither handle the tensions this new situation can give rise to by denial nor by a blind insistence that there is no conflict potential between the director of a corporation and the workers employed by it.'

Since the October Revolution, we on the left have tended to polarize all discussion on developmental paths. One either took measures to seize control of the productive assets of society from the capitalist and other propertied classes or one tinkered with the worst excesses of the system but otherwise was content to administer the capitalist system and not tamper with property relations, as the Social Democratic parties have done.

I think we can agree, that sort of Manichaeism is no longer relevant in a world where the Communist Parties in China, in Vietnam and now, also in Cuba, are finding new ways of harnessing the capitalist class's drive to maximize profits for the socialist project. The leadership corps of the South African Communist Party these days speaks of a '1996 Class project'. This posture, to my mind, is the one pole of the un-dialectical discourse that has dominated the tri-partite alliance for the past decade The un-dialectical either/or posture of the SACP's leadership corps seems unable to appreciate, and is unwilling to explore possible synergies between '...the 1996 class project' and that of the working class. In equal measure, the ideological opponents of the SACP's viewpoint, perhaps best expressed in the Moleketi/Jele pamphlet of a few years ago, can only imagine growing the economy as a process presided over by a supervised capitalist class. As with their opposite numbers, the developments of the past twenty years appear beyond their ken.

Consequently the opposing sides in this argument have each hunkered down in their respective trenches, leaving little space other than for a dialogue of the deaf.

POST-APARTHEID SOUTH AFRICA AND THE
EMERGENCE OF NEW CLASSES

According to the 'Fifteen Year Review', recently published by the Government Communications and Information Service (GCIS) the South Africa we inherited from the racists was a society characterized by extremes of White wealth and desperate Black poverty. Apartheid had managed to disguise these realities with its homeland policies and other devices for decades, but they burst forth during the 1980s resulting in the proliferation of huge informal settlements around all urban areas. The pace of urban migration has increased exponentially since 1994, supplemented by evictions from White-owned farms.

However, since 1994, and the census figures will bear this out, a portion of the Black community have seized the opportunities created by the end of apartheid and are emerging as a well-to-do upper middle class and capitalist class ensconced in the state and in business. I see no need to recount the emergence of the so-called 'black diamonds'. One can read it in every newspaper and magazine. One consequence of their appearance is a very partial de-racialisation of the wealthy classes in South Africa.

The same, however, is not true of the other end of the class spectrum. Yes, there are some poor Whites, but every census demonstrates that poverty is a Black condition, specifically affecting Africans and Coloureds. Studies also testify to the fact that the gap in earnings amongst the Blacks has widened at a rate few had anticipated. The geni co-efficient in South Africa is amongst the highest in the world! Thabo Mbeki tried to capture this in his thesis about two nations, one White and wealthy, the other Black and poor.

The 'Fifteen Year Review' reveals that a handsome 'democracy dividend' accrued to the wealthy classes, White and Black. The South African economy has experienced more than a decade of steady growth while business has prospered as never before since 1994!

The wealthy have benefited disproportionately since 1994. The poor have benefited somewhat because, for the first time in the history of this country, the ANC government has put in place a social safety net for the poor of all races. Yes, it is very inadequate, barely keeping peoples noses above water, but it is there and better than what the poor had before 1994.

In many senses excluded, those who have seen the least improvement in their material situation, are the ordinary salaried and wage-earning people – teachers, nurses, workers in industry, on the land, in the lower professions, in the service sector, etc. These are specifically the occupation groups organised into the trade unions, most of whom are affiliated to COSATU.

Stripped to the bone, one could say, the burdens of building the new South Africa are being borne, disproportionately, by these sectors of our society. The implications of such developments for the ANC as a multi-class movement, the likely impact of such changes on the Tri-partite alliance, are issues the NEC of the ANC has studiously avoided discussing for the past nine years.

Over the fifteen years post-1994, the ANC itself has also undergone a metamorphosis that finds reflection in a number of organizational reports the Secretary-General has placed before ANC conferences in Stellenbosch, (2002) and at Polokwane 2007. Symptomatic of this change was the need the ANC leadership felt to prepare a document, 'Through the Eye of a Needle', in 1998, setting out criteria for election to public office. To reinforce what that document says the ANC also pioneered, then piloted through parliament, a host of measures to curb corruption and as a deterrent against the temptations of corruption.

The remarks of the Secretary-General in his report to the Stellenbosch conference bear repetition because they most eloquently demonstrate the dilemma facing the movement.

Para 102. We have also reported to the NGC on the challenges being in power has on the structures of the movement. *We found that the issues dividing leadership of some of our provinces are not of a political nature, but have mainly revolved around access to resources, positioning themselves or others to access resources, dispensing patronage and in the process using organisational structures to further these goals. This often lies at the heart of conflicts between constitutional and governance structures, especially at local level and is reflected in contestations around lists, deployment and internal elections process of the movement. These practices tarnish the image and effectiveness of the movement. Yet when we decide to act firmly, we have seen an overwhelmingly positive response from members and our people. A good example was the positive response to our undertaking in the 2000 local government manifesto and campaign to act against corrupt councillors.* (My italics)

Earlier in that same report, the Secretary-General posed the matter in these terms:

Para 79. The 1994 breakthrough opened up new opportunities for material and social advancement through positions in the public and private sector and for economic empowerment. With the dismantling of apartheid career barriers, the availability of much greater choice of career paths and scope for the realisation of individual preferences and ambitions became possible. The occupation of positions of power and the material reward this offers could create some 'social distance' between individuals and constituencies they represent, particularly in the context of the legacy of inequality, large scale unemployment and poverty that still plague us. This could render some in the revolutionary movement complacent, concerned with maintaining their positions and even indifferent to the conditions of the poor.

We who are materialists know that the explanation lies in the nature of the society we live in. Or as Marx put:

'In its reality it is the ensemble of the social relations'.

As the Secretary-General's report makes clear, the democratic breakthrough of 1994 also entailed the opening up of as yet unexplored career paths for thousands of Black South Africans. The growing middle strata and capitalist class are a direct consequence of democracy. Many who aspire to that lifestyle do not necessarily possess either the educational qualifications or the capital to enter it. The quickest route into the middle class is often public office, which offers a steady salary, sometimes with perks, but above all, access to resources which can be manipulated to personal advantage. The changing character of South African society is necessarily finding reflection in the ANC itself.

Regrettably, in its negligence, the ANC leadership chose to

discuss this issue solely as a problem of corruption, down-playing its essential dimension as a short-cut in the race to accumulate capital. The social and economic realities in whose context this race occurs are laid bare in the most recent UN habitat report. It tells us that South African cities are among the most unequal in the world. I think most of us are vaguely conscious of this, knowing as we do that Clifton-on-Sea is in the same city as Delft and a few bends along the highway away from Imizamo Yethu! That, lower Houghton is a stone's throw from Alexandra township! Despite the changes I have noted above, these divisions are highly racialised.

CREATING NEW OPPORTUNITIES ON THE BACK
OF MISSED OPPORTUNITIES

Writing about early twentieth century Russia, Lenin said:

> 'The progressive historical role of capitalism may be summed up in two
> brief propositions: increase in the productive forces of social labour, and
> the socialisation of that labour.' [Lenin. 'The Development of Capitalism
> in Russia.']

Capitalism has been the agent of cataclysmic social change which has nonetheless given birth to a modern industrial society in South Africa. Prior to 1994 the political institutions restricted access to its benefits and its potential to the White minority. The end of statutory racism opened up new opportunities to Black South Africans, which a tiny minority have been able to seize. In addition to growing 'the productive forces 'this emergent class of Black capitalists could be a creative force in the boardrooms of capital. A growing economy promises a higher standard of living for all South Africans.

The ANC evolved from a body of loyal second class citizens into a revolutionary national movement because of its ability to critically examine its experience and because of its capacity to absorb and integrate into its own practice lessons derived from other struggles. The perspective of the ANC's founders was essentially to reform the colonial state by incrementally de-racialising it. Experience however demonstrated that the white supremacist state was structurally not conducive to reform, the only option was its overthrow or dismantling.

But, even as it embarked on the armed struggle the ANC and its allies did not paint themselves into a strategic corner. In MK's founding manifesto the option of a negotiated settlement was posed. The same tactical flexibility was demonstrated in the late eighties when insurrection became a realistic possibility, but the ANC nonetheless signaled a willingness to forgo the military option provided that negotiations in earnest, with the realistic prospect of success, commenced.

The ANC's negotiating posture displayed the same strategic firmness combined with a tactical flexibility that recognised that securing the beach-head of democracy, at the price of less significant tactical retreats, would be an irreversible strategic advance. That capacity to define and act on the linkages between minimum and maximum seemed to disappear once the ANC attained political office and became government.

What I suggest is that the divisions within the ANC are rooted in the real material conditions of life of the various strata of our society; they arise in an environment of exciting flux in both South Africa, the continent and the world; and they reflect the outcomes produced by the new avenues of social mobility among Black South Africans. That these tensions have resulted in a splinter group, politically positioned to the right of the ANC, is a direct consequence of a failure in leadership on the part of the ANC. Because the movement neglected a scientific study of the transformations freedom had brought about, it was unable to anticipate potential points of tension and conflict, and proved unable to manage the contradictions its own policies had generated. It is the leadership's failure to examine, analyze and scope the new points of actual and potential conflict its own policies produced, that resulted in an incapacity to manage them within the movement, within the alliance and within the ANC's broader constituency.

Understood in those terms, the appearance of an opposition formation sprung from the very loins of the ANC and led by former ANC leaders reflects neither a failure on Zuma's part, nor Mbeki's part, nor Shilowa's part, nor Lekota's part. It reflects the collective failure of the leadership corps to whom the ANC membership had entrusted their movement in 2002.

Neither side in this quarrel can with conviction claim to be exclusive custodian of the Freedom Charter, the Congress of the People, nor any subsequent ANC strategic document. Both can legitimately lay claim to them all. A reconciliation will require that each side recognizes the legitimacy of the other, and that both sides explore and pursue the synergies possible between the minimum and the maximum.

What the media have dubbed the Shikota splinter group has decided to strike out on its own, as a party in opposition to the ANC, and that is their right.

- Will this splinter coalesce into an effective opposition to the ANC, perhaps even displacing the DA as the official opposition?
- What consequences will arise from the emergence of an ex-ANC opposition formation? Is majority rule undermined or strengthened by the appearance of this new formation?

These are all matters for speculation. But I will hazard one guess. If this ex-ANC splinter group does not displace the DA as the official opposition, it has no future in South African politics.

As for myself old friend, I am sticking with the ANC. To plagiarise the words of Brecht, 'with this one, there is at least the possibility of conception'.

Meet you in the whirlwind!
Amandla!

Fraternally,
Z Pallo Jordan

THIRTY

As a back-bench MP, Jordan was willing to write this frank and spiky critique of ANC foreign policy, as reflected in its refusal of a visa to the Dalai Lama to attend Archbishop Emeritus Tutu's 80th birthday celebrations.

The Dalai Lama Dilemma

'Our government is worse than the apartheid government, because at least you were expecting it from the apartheid government,'

'We were expecting we would have a government that was sensitive to sentiments of our Constitution,' ...

'People were opposed to injustice and oppression and people believe that we South Africans would be on the side of those who are oppressed. Tibet is being oppressed,' ...

'Our government, representing me, says it will not support Tibetans who are being oppressed viciously by the Chinese.'

These were the tones in which Archbishop Emeritus Desmond Tutu denounced the government's indecision regarding the Dali Lama's visa application to attend Tutu's 80th birthday celebrations.

To many of us withholding of the visa seemed strange because this would have been the Dalai Lama's fourth visit to South Africa since 1994. On each of those occasions his arrival in this country raised eyebrows in Beijing. South Africa was as aware of Chinese sensibilities on the matter then as it is today. Yet visas had been issued and the visits proceeded without incident.

In 2009 when the Tibetan monk was first refused a visa, South Africa had earned itself international opprobrium. On that occasion the government explicitly stated that its decision was informed by China's concern around the anniversary of the 1959 Tibetan rising. There was a well justified fear that the visit might be used to promote the Tibetan cause from South African soil and the Dalai Lama's visit might be interpreted as South African support.

No government would deliberately invite international condemnation over the small matter of a birthday party. So there must be an explanation for the government's decision.

Ironically, Archbishop Tutu unpacks precisely the reasoning undergirding this decision in his scathing remarks.

> '...people believe that we South Africans would be on the side of those who are oppressed. Tibet is being oppressed ...
>
> 'Our government, representing me, says it will not support Tibetans who are being oppressed viciously by the Chinese.'

By putting that construction on both his invitation and the South African government's consent to a visa application, the Arch confirms the worst fears of the China desk at the Department of International Relations and Cooperation (DIRCO). If by granting the Dalai Lama a visa the South African government is affirming that the Tibetans are an oppressed people and the visa signals South Africa's support for the struggle of the Tibetans, the government of China would read that as an affront.

A related question, which everyone assumes can elicit only one answer, is : is the position of the Tibetans any different from that of other ethnic national minorities in China? If it is different, in what respects does it differ? If it is no different, why does the issue of Tibet have such a high profile whereas the others are unseen and unheard?

Few people in South Africa realise that in addition to the majority Han ethnic group, China is also the home of fifty-five other ethnic minorities, including the Tibetans. How these various peoples were absorbed into the Chinese state is a complicated story stretching over centuries. The Mongol minority at one time conquered and ruled China for a century. The Manchurians gave China her last imperial dynasty after overthrowing the ethnic Han Ming dynasty during the 17th century. Tibet was incorporated during the Yuan dynasty, a century of the Mongol rule established by Genghis Khan. In their baggage these plains horsemen brought Mahayana Buddhism to the Tibetan plateau. The title 'Dalai Lama' comprises a Mongolian term, borrowed by the theocracy who governed Tibet until 1949, plus the Tibetan word for guru.

From the 13th century, though it enjoyed a measure of autonomy even under the pre-1911 imperial system, Tibet fell within China's historical borders. Even during the 19th and early 20th centuries when there were concerted Western, Russian and Japanese violations of China's sovereignty, none of these other governments ever contested Tibet's status as part of China. The re-assertion and defence of China's historic frontiers is an important dimension of the nationalist narrative subscribed to by Chinese Nationalists and Communists alike. Beijing is as prickly as Taipei on that particular issue. China reads even the suggestion of revisiting its internationally accepted borders as a call for the return of the bad old days when outside powers came close to dismembering the country. China regards the advocacy of secession or support thereof as an act of hostility. Even the USA explicitly recognises China's sensibilities on this matter, while maintaining a strong relationship with Taiwan.

The Buddhist monasteries appear to have been the organising centres of the secessionist 1959 uprising that culminated in the Dalai Lama's flight and exile in India. The Dalai Lama has since renounced secession, but China clearly remains mistrustful and tends to treat hosting him as an unfriendly act. Archbishop Tutu's words unwittingly confirm their suspicions and that interpretation.

It is incontestable that there is a powerful sense of national grievance among Tibetans. During a visit to China, leading a delegation of the Parliamentary Portfolio Committee on Foreign Affairs in 2001, we raised the issue of Tibet very sharply with our Chinese counterparts and with the Chinese Foreign Ministry. To our surprise, the Chinese parliament invited us to visit Tibet to see for ourselves. Unfortunately that visit did not materialise because our committee had other fish to fry. It might be worthwhile for the incumbent committee chair to investigate whether that invitation still stands.

DIRCO is obviously very attentive to China's view on Tibet and the status of the Dalai Lama. At this moment South Africa is caught between the rock of Western insistence on regime change in Libya and the hard-place of a disunited African Union's position requiring an inclusive government. As a member of the United Nations Security Council, China's diplomatic support for South Africa's posture on this matter could determine whether it succeeds or fails.

Among her newly acquired partners in BRICS, it was China's support of South African membership that made the difference. South Africa's fraught relations with the Western powers on a host of issues, compare badly with an expanding and increasingly warm relationship with China.

But the question still stands. How should the South African government have responded to the Dalai Lama's visa application?

To those who regard the Dalai Lama as Tibet's Spiritual leader and as an exiled political leader akin to Oliver Tambo, the answer is simple: As the Archbishop argues, South Africa should support the struggle of an oppressed people on principle, regardless of whom that upsets or annoys; by apparently bowing to perceived or actual Chinese diplomatic pressure, our government has let the side down and betrayed the values in our Constitution.

The protestors who took to the streets from the campus of Wits and other tertiary institutions, say our government was doing the dirty work of the Chinese government by silencing a critical voice and offering moral support to China's governance of Tibet.

An agnostic, like myself, is highly sceptical about the value of spiritual leaders be they Buddhist, Anglican, Catholic, Muslim or Hindu. And, just as I would have difficulty in embracing a theocracy led by the Archbishop of Canterbury, the Pope or a Shi'ite Imam, I have difficulties with those led by Buddhist monks. Consequently, I do not see an Oliver Tambo in the Dalai Lama, but rather a figure closer to the late Imam Khomeni.

Should our government have denied him the opportunity to visit South Africa to celebrate a fellow Nobel Laureate's 80th birthday? The answer to that is no; on two counts.

When Clinton visited South Africa during the Mandela presidency, though the two were on extremely good terms, Mandela did not mince words telling him that our relationship with Cuba was based on our understanding of the history of that Caribbean country and the role Cuba played in the liberation of southern Africa. We would not abandon an old friend, Cuba, to accommodate American sensibilities.

Surely China can be told the same thing? Tibet, is not like Cuba, but the principle that South Africa defines her own path in international relations is fundamental.

If pragmatism dictated government's course of action, it has backfired miserably. As a result of this decision, Tibet and its status in China, has a far higher profile in our media than otherwise. Neither South Africa, nor China has come out of this incident looking good.

THIRTY-ONE

Jordan recalls that Chris Hani was a 'close and very dear friend', and his commemorative lecture has three main themes. There is a description of the Cape Town political climate ('one found every political trend, current and body of opinion there was in the modern world') where both men began their political activity; there is an important section on the crisis within the ANC in the late 1960s, the Hani Memorandum, and the Morogoro Conference; and a conclusion on the 'challenges of the day'. These included the 'emergence of a rapacious indigenous elite – the wa-Benzis of South Africa' and the 'abuses and corruption that seem at times to besiege our movement'. These would have earned Hani's 'critical appraisal and round condemnation' – and Jordan's own distaste is clearly audible.

Chris Hani Memorial Lecture

10 April 2012

Ladies and gentlemen,
Comrades and friends,

Allow me first to thank the City of Ekuruleni and its municipal council for inviting me to deliver this Chris Hani Memorial lecture. I consider it a great honour to have been chosen for this task because Comrade Chris was a close and very dear friend of mine.

What we are marking tonight is not a pleasant moment in the annals of the liberation struggle. We must at all times recognise, even as we celebrate the life and times of Comrade Chris Hani, that we are in fact marking a dastardly act of murder! What is more, we must always remember that this was not merely one more act of violence, in the history of a violent society during a very violent phase of our recent history. No! This was an act of murder intended to unleash a wave of violence! It was an act of murder designed to generate many more deaths! That the perpetrators of this crime failed in their inhuman objective was not for lack of trying on their part! Had it not been for the level-headed, responsible and extremely measured response of the ANC and its leadership, Clive Derby-Lewis and his co-conspirator Janusz Walus, might well have succeeded in derailing the negotiated transition and detonating blood-letting on an unimaginable scale.

We remind ourselves of these facts because there is a tendency to treat these two murderers like any other killer in prison. When the issue of Derby-Lewis' eligibility to parole is discussed these facts are conveniently forgotten and it is handled as if he were just one other misguided soul who has taken the life another.

Those who planned and executed this act of violence were intent on mass murder! Murdering Comrade Chris, in their plans, was merely the detonator! Had they had their way, we would be marking the deaths of many more people than Chris Hani.

I feel particularly honoured to be the chief celebrant at this memorial because Comrade Chris Hani embodied the finest traditions of our revolutionary alliance. When we cast our eyes back over his political biography it captures some of the most crucial moments of the liberation movement's history after the ANC was banned in 1960. Like many of his generation, Chris Hani came into liberation politics during the late 1950s and the early 1960s. Ours was the generation that grew up under the first decade of National Party rule. Ours was the generation who experienced the steady and incremental elaboration of a comprehensive system of national oppression based on the dispossession and complete disenfranchisement of Black South Africans.

We were consequently called upon to make our contribution during three of the most challenging and trying decades of the ANC's history. Decades during which the movement faced the threat of near complete destruction; faced a crisis of leadership; faced massive infiltration of its ranks by enemy agents; was forced to confront and put down a mutiny in its army; and yet was able to overcome all these challenges, rebuild its strength, make an impressive resurgence and was finally able to lead our people to victory over the racist enemy and bring democracy to South Africa.

It has become fashionable in certain academic circles these days to carp on and make snide remarks about 'authoritarian tendencies' in the ANC; some even speak of 'an authoritarian practice' in the ANC. While it is wise not to romanticise the 30 years of the ANC's illegality; not to romanticise the experience of exile and the 28 years on MK in Africa and beyond, it is reckless to imagine rank outsiders will ever be able to appreciate the complex nature of the exile experience and especially that of combatants in the liberation army. If there is a political biography that gives the lie to all the scribblings of these pundits, it is the political biography of Chris Hani.

Many who prattle about the ANC's thirty years of illegality have never belonged to a political organisation, let alone a revolutionary movement. Usually they have no practical experience of involvement even in ordinary day to day political work, and have even less knowledge of what illegal, underground political activity requires or entails.

Chris took up political activity in earnest after leaving college. He arrived in Cape Town in 1961 to join the firm of Schaefer and Schaefer as an articled clerk preparing for his attorney's admission. The previous year, 1960, Langa Township in Cape Town, alongside the more notorious Sharpeville, was the other site of a massacre. Cape Town's two main African townships, Langa and Gugulethu (then called Nyanga East), had held out in a month long general strike after March 21st. This demonstration of solidarity was reinforced in a mass procession of some 30,000 township residents into the city centre on 30th March. The regime responded by laying siege to the African townships. It was in the context of that siege that a baby, memorialised in Ingrid Jonker's poem, 'Die Kind', was shot by police. The residents of the townships were able to hold out thanks to the support networks amongst Coloured and Indian traders and professionals.

In his biography, 'Freedom in Our Lifetime', Comrade Archie Sibeko describes how a close knit ANC leadership, made up of trade unionists and civic activists, was able to implement to 'M' Plan in its strongholds in Langa and Gugulethu well before the banning in 1960. Adapting to operating as an underground movement was relatively easy for an ANC leadership accustomed to communicating in secret along its own networks in townships and workplaces.

In the past, the occasional African student at the University of Cape Town (UCT) had joined the ANC Youth League in Cape Town. A case in point was Nana Nelson Mahomo, who arrived in Cape Town from the Transvaal in 1957 to study law at the UCT. He quickly became the central figure amongst the Africanist faction in the youth league, winning the support of long time members like Bam Siboto, Gleg Ntshokoma and a few others. When the Africanists walked out of the ANC in 1958, Nana Mahomo was among them and he became a prominent figure in the Pan Africanist Congress (PAC) when it was formed in April 1959. In 1960 Mahomo was the PAC's Secretary for Culture.

Mahomo's subsequent political career speaks for itself and need not detain us here.

But the league's experience with him left an air of dubiety about intellectuals. The Hani family's political activism in Cape Town facilitated Chris's own involvement and swift integration. Gilbert Hani, Chris's father, was an ANC member who had been active in the Langa Vigilance Society for many years. His sterling record of civic service had earned him the chairmanship of that body. In the nearby town of Stellenbosch, other members of the Hani family belonged to the ANC branch. Chris was amongst the few African graduates in Cape Town to join the ANC Youth League. Most of Cape Town's African professionals, with a few exceptions, kept a safe distance from politics. Teachers who had once been active in opposition to the introduction of Bantu Education were being systematically hounded out of their jobs intimidating those who remained into a sullen silence. The handful of African students at UCT were divided between the Unity Movement's two factions and the PAC.

Chris was preceded by his track record as a student at Fort Hare, where he had been an ANC Youth League member since his freshman year. He was drawn into the leadership structures shortly after his arrival in Cape Town mainly because of the skills he brought to that collective as an educated person.

The Cape Town Chris Hani arrived in was the mother city of modern South Africa. It had a distinctive history as a port of call along one of major sea routes and was influenced by every important intellectual and cultural development at either end of that trade route it straddled. Consequently in Cape Town one found every political trend, current and body of opinion there was in the modern world. Cape Town also had its own local political traditions, some dating from the 19th century. On the left of the political spectrum, besides the liberation movements, were a mixed band of socialists, including the Communists, about three or four factions of Trostkyists, the remnants of the stillborn Socialist Party, and a host of other non-conformists. In the centre were liberals of various stripes, ranging from the erstwhile supporters of Jan Hendrik Hofmeyr who constituted the Progressive Party in 1959, to the radical liberals found amongst the ex-servicemen in Alan Paton's Liberal Party. The right was peopled by the Broederbond-led Nats at the extreme and the Anglo White supremacists of the United Party closer to the centre.

Liberation politics in Cape Town had for decades been impacted upon by all the trends represented in this spectrum. The peculiar political history of the Cape Province, where Africans and Coloureds exercised the vote in one form or another into the early 1960s, in turn enabled liberation politics to act on white politics as well.

It was in Cape Town that Chris was recruited into MK in 1962. The history of those early units still needs to be written and it remains our hope that some diligent student will find the energy and drive to do so. With the benefit of hindsight one might criticise the rather rudimentary security measures those first volunteers employed. But, let us remember that these were pioneering efforts in terrain the movement had never before explored. Disguised as judo clubs, hiking clubs and mountaineering clubs, the first MK units in the Western Cape began in earnest in 1962. Venues that might one day be revealed hosted them for their meetings. Later a farm outside Mamre was acquired to serve as a training site.

HANI, THE MK COMBATANT

By the time Comrade Chris Hani met his untimely death, he had risen to the rank of Chief of Staff of MK having served as National Commissar for a number of years after 1985. For a number of objective and subjective reasons his career path to that rank was destined not to be a smooth one.

Among the objective factors was the crisis of leadership that the ANC experienced as a result of the Rivonia arrests and the repression that followed. That had brought to light a crisis in strategy that the ANC had applied during the Wange and Sipolilio campaigns of 1967/8. The third objective factor was the codification of a military culture as the dominant culture in the movement.

Among the subjective reasons we can count the revolutionary impatience of a generation of militarily trained cadres and Comrade Chris's own consistent radicalism and highly motivated revolutionary optimism.

To appreciate these factors let us recall the situation during the 1960s.

The leadership of the movement had established MK as the nucleus of a liberation army during 1961 and began to build it into a fighting force during 1962. As we know, Comrade Nelson Mandela's trip through Africa entailed a search for training facilities for MK and he himself underwent training in Algeria. The first MK units received their training in China and the former GDR. In later years training was offered in a number of African countries, including Egypt, Morocco, Algeria and Ethiopia. Tanzania gave the ANC land to build its own camps to house trained fighters and to train recruits.

Piecing together what our leadership planned for from the Rivonia and subsequent political trials, we can surmise that it was planned for the units sent to train outside to be infiltrated back into South Africa using various means, to be received inside South Africa by underground cells responsible for servicing them and for their security. It was envisaged that such an embryonic fighting force would reproduce itself by training others and by such progression create a network of combatants with the capacity to engage the regime militarily.

The High Command executing this strategy was surprised at a secret meeting at Rivonia in July 1963. Among them were one of the first batch of MK fighters trained in China, Raymond Mhlaba. Elias Motsoaledi and Andrew Mlangeni who were part of that group had been arrested a few days earlier. The Rivonia arrests were followed by a wave of repression characterised by the most brutal mind-breaking tortures and murders in detention that virtually dismantled the underground structures the movement had hoped could sustain trained combatants. Mini-Rivonia, involving Wilton Mkwayi, John Matthews, David Kitson and Mac Maharaj represented the winding up of the underground creating a bottleneck for the trained cadreship of MK, completing their training in camps in Africa and military academies in the USSR.

The situation the movement found itself in was a function of both its own optimism in the wake of the first successful national liberation war, Algeria, on our continent. At its 1962 Lobatse Conference the ANC had been reluctant to take ownership of MK and the legend that MK was a separate organisation was maintained. The movement's external mission was completely oriented towards diplomatic work and regarded itself as the agent of a leadership inside South Africa, to whom it accounted in the last instance. The disastrous breech of security at Rivonia in July 1963 made all that irrelevant.

After July 1963 there was in effect no leadership to report to inside South Africa.

The task of leading the movement had, by default, been passed on to those members of the movement leadership who had been posted outside the country or had escaped the dragnet of repression in the wake of Rivonia. But, the external mission was neither designed for, nor did it quickly adapt to the new situation that had arisen. In a candid appraisal during 1969, 'Mayibuye', the ANC's newsletter commented:

'The External Mission had, however, been sent out to undertake certain specific tasks, vital but supplementary to the internal struggle. The total command of the people's army and the prosecution of the armed struggle was not, initially, one of these tasks. The leadership vacuum resulting from the destruction of the internal military structure saddled the External Mission with this additional task. In the course of time and by an accumulation of experience it became clear that the External Mission as then constituted was not organisationally geared to undertake the urgent task of undertaking the People's War. As the External Mission attempted to play this vital role many weaknesses began revealing themselves, weaknesses inherent in the contradiction between organisation and method of struggle. Gradually these weaknesses became magnified and harmful affecting discipline and morale, and unhealthy tendencies crept into the Congress.'

Though it took a very long time for it to realise it, the ANC leadership was facing a crisis it had neither anticipated and nor planned for. The countries that hosted MK's trained fighters were keen to see them depart to take on the enemy in South Africa. Those countries that offered training also wanted to see the resources they had so invested properly utilised on the battlefield. And, the trained combatants who had left South Africa in high spirits were eager to reach home where they were confident their training would enable them to meet the enemy on equal terms.

It was in that sort of charged political environment that the ANC/ZAPU military alliance was forged and the joint MK/ZIPRA Wange and Sipolilo military operations were planned and executed. Today we can judge the morale and spirit of the MK combatants from some of the poetry that moment produced:

FRONTLINE, front – line

Where manhood and consciousness is tested,
The only place to bury persecutions and the burden of ages,
The only place to declare names immortal,
Trust me brother you will not be alone there.

FRONTLINE, front – line,
Where bullets will graze on man and grass,
Where man will make his own lightning and thunder,
Where the enemy will fall and never rise,
Brother truly my shadow will be next to yours.

FRONTLINE, front – line,
I know it is bitter but I like it,
I like it particularly because it is bitter,
I like it because it is where I belong,
For out of bitterness comes equality, freedom and peace.

I will be in the frontline when the roll is called
Frontline! – valleys and plains of events and history
Frontline! Frontline! Take me to the frontline!!

There can be little doubt about the heroism and skill of the MK/ZPRA columns that entered Zimbabwe in 1967 and '68. But what we had always preached and sought to impart to all our fighters proved all too true during those incursions. It was central to the military and combat strategy of the ANC that no group of armed combatants, no matter how heroic or skilled, could hope to make a revolution without the organised support of the people. Wange and Sipolilo were doomed to failure from the onset. Contrary to the extravagant claims of its ZAPU ally, the columns found there were no political structures on the ground to link up with in Zimbabwe. Worst yet, because there had been no prior political mobilisation of any sort, it proved easy for counter-insurgency forces to stage provocations by disguising themselves as freedom fighters and ensnaring potentially supportive rural communities in this fashion, thus sowing confusion amongst the people. Some population centres were even subjected to attack as a means of alienating them from the genuine freedom fighters.

The plan undergirding the campaigns aimed to create a corridor through Zimbabwe into the northern Transvaal, the North-western Cape and possibly into Natal. After splitting into two columns, one headed east towards the Zimbabwean interior, the other west, towards Matabeleland, where ZAPU had a long-standing following. Comrades John Dube and Wilson Msweli [Zolile Nqose] commanded the westward column, with Chris as its Commissar. The second column was commanded by Comrade Ngwenya of ZIPRA, with Freddie Mninzi of MK as his Deputy.

Under pressure from joint Rhodesian/SADF forces, the columns were forced to retreat into Botswana in the west and back into Zambia in the east.

The recounting of these campaigns is a task for another day. Our concern tonight is how these developments impacted upon the political biography of Chris Hani, and how his actions, in the context of these developments shaped not only events but also his own future.

The Wange and Sipolilio campaigns brought to light the second dimension of the crisis the ANC confronted: a crisis of strategy! This was to prove the most intractable dimension of the post- Rivonia crisis and the most difficult to resolve.

I mentioned a third objective factor: the codification of a military culture as dominant within the movement. The national liberation movement operating inside South Africa, whether as a legal or illegal organisation, had evolved a set of norms and practices that enabled the membership to engage the leadership on issues of movement strategy and its day to day tactics. When the movement was legal the branch, the region, the province and the national conference were the arenas for such engagements. In the illegal post-1960 ANC, though the space for such engagement was greatly reduced, the regular interaction between higher and subordinate leadership layers theoretically offered opportunities for such exchanges.

The overwhelming majority of the movement's membership outside the country were military personnel or otherwise integrated into its military structures. By default, the ethos of the military, which requires the subordinate to follow orders and never question them, had begun to take root in the movement.

That was the third dimension of the crisis in the ANC during the late 1960s.

THE MEMORANDUM AND SUSPENSION

The now famous 'Memorandum', usually attributed to Chris Hani by supporters and detractors alike, was in reality the product of a number of minds. By all accounts it was collective view of a large section of the MK combatants, but was informed by the Wange-Sipolilo experience, hence the appearance of the names of many who had fought in those campaigns among the eight signatories.

It is perhaps ironic that it was the MK combatants who were the first to articulate the central issues relating to the crisis the ANC faced. Though it identified the symptoms of the crisis, the Memorandum was weak in a number of other areas, perhaps owing to its attempt to cover as many issues of contention as the MK fighters had identified. But, that Memorandum cannot be faulted on the seminal issue of the need for the movement, its leadership and all its structures to be re-oriented towards the pursuance of the struggle inside South Africa. The memorandum correctly charged that the leadership were in a state of denial that refused to accept the challenges of the day – leading the liberation movement by rebuilding its organisational capacity inside South Africa.

Regrettably, because of the codification of the military culture by default, many regarded the writing and submission of the Memorandum as an act of gross insubordination. The details surrounding these events will likely remain in dispute for a number of years. What is clear though is that Chris Hani was regarded as the inspiration of the Memorandum by persons as diverse as Duma Nokwe and Tennyson Makiwane. Together with the other signatories, he was suspended from ANC membership after appearing before a Commission of Inquiry

Despite the hostile reception of the Memorandum, there was a sufficient spirit of introspection and self-criticism in the ANC leadership to persuade it to address the crisis politically. The Morogoro conference of 1969 was the outcome.

Chris and his comrades who had signed the Memorandum were unable to attend the conference because they were under suspension. But it is only the short-sighted who could refuse to recognise that Morogoro was in many respects the outcome of their courageous intervention.

There is an important lesson we can adduce from that interesting episode in the life of Chris Hani. It took a great deal of courage for Chris and the other comrades to put their signatures to that Memorandum. But over and above courage it required commitment: commitment to a cause; commitment to a movement as the most effective instrument for the pursuance of that cause; and a commitment to the hard and bitter truth, which a leadership in a state of denial was not yet ready to recognise.

The lesson I want to underscore is that of commitment. When we join the national liberation movement we commit ourselves to it; we commit our very souls to the cause of liberation freedom and democracy. We make that commitment not to a particular leader, no matter how eminent that leader may be! We make that commitment, not to a group of leaders, even if it is the wisest group leaders! We make that commitment to the cause of freedom and to the movement whose track record demonstrates that it is the most effective instrument for pursuing the cause of freedom.

The second lesson to underscore is that of perseverance. There were those who thought that the comrades who signed the Memorandum would leave the ANC and MK in disgust after the cold reception given a

Memorandum whose purpose was to correct. I daresay there were even some who hoped they would. All such thoughts and fears were sadly disappointed. Instead of parting company with the movement and by so doing leaving it to the un-tender mercies of those in denial, the comrades stayed in its ranks to wage new and perhaps more difficult battles in the years ahead.

THE MOROGORO CONFERENCE AND CHARACTER OF OUR STRUGGLE

The 1969 Morogoro Consultative Conference was convened to resolve the friction that had developed between an exiled leadership and the armed combatants under its command. The Memorandum had not only identified a fundamental strategic flaw, but had also brought to light the depth of social distance that was growing between the leadership of the ANC and cadreship of MK. The latter was recognized as a function of the external orientation of the leadership at a moment when its focus should have been South Africa.

The Morogoro Consultative Conference restructured the entire national liberation movement and created an additional layer of leadership to be drawn from the ANC's allies in the Congress Alliance. This now superseded the Congress Alliance and formalised the alliance between the ANC and SACP. The Revolutionary Council established at Morogoro, chaired by ANC President Oliver Tambo, was specifically charged with active prosecution of the struggle inside South Africa and the re-orientation of the entire movement to focus on the internal reconstruction of the movement. The decision to open membership to all South African revolutionaries, irrespective of race, proved to be the most contentious.

From the conference the movement emerged with a more coherent strategy, aimed at achieving four inter-related goals:

- Making the ANC an organised presence among the people of South Africa while generalising among them an appreciation that revolutionary violence was not only necessary but could be successfully deployed against what appeared to be a formidable enemy;

- Inspiring self-organisation through every form of mass organisation for active engagement in the struggle to overthrow the apartheid regime;
- Stimulating among the people an understanding that without their active support and protection the armed cadres of the movement could not hope to survive in the country; and
- Creating secure lines of communication between units on the ground and the leadership for purposes of intelligence and counter-intelligence.

To succeed, the conference concluded, the armed liberation struggle would have to be built on four interdependent pillars. The first of these was

- an effective underground ANC organisation capable of galvanising the people. Such an underground could in turn stimulate
- mass political mobilisation to create an environment in which the
- armed struggle could be effectively conducted by militants who enjoy the support and protection of the people. The last pillar was
- international solidarity to isolate the racist regime from possible sources of support in the international community while mobilising material and moral support for the forces of liberation.

The Morogoro conference and the Strategy and Tactics statement it adopted identified the rebuilding of the ANC and its organisation inside South Africa as the most important challenge facing the movement. This required a de-emphasis on the military aspects of the struggle and greater attention to grassroots matters around which small scale and ever widening struggles could be waged. The reconstituted ANC underground itself would have to refocus by transforming itself into the tribune of the people, offering leadership and coordination of local struggles so that to they assumed national dimensions.

As one amongst those who had diagnosed the crucial problem of the absence of organisation, when his suspension was lifted Chris Hani turned his attention to the reconstruction of the movement inside South Africa. In about 1973/4 he crossed South Africa from Botswana and located in

Lesotho from where he worked with others to rebuild the movement's structures in the Cape, the Free State and the Transkei. The involvement of the woman who later became his wife, a Lesotho national, Limpho, in these efforts is perhaps not as well known as it should be. Exploiting a passport she carried by virtue of being an employee of the national airline, Comrade Limpho repeatedly travelled to various parts of the eastern Cape. Her missions helped revive long dormant ANC structures and activists. On one such mission, she was detained with Comrade Kati (Kit-Kat) of PE and as a result suffered a miscarriage.

Reconstituting ANC structures that had been battered by arrests, executions and the treachery of informers was painstaking work requiring patience and tact. A note of urgency was unexpectedly introduced as a result of the Soweto Uprising in 1976, bringing with it a new crop of youthful future combatants for MK and militants for the mass struggle inside the country.

Your worship, ladies and gentlemen,
Since the late 19th century, the national project – a conception of and the pursuance of the vision of a non-racial South Africa, defined territorially rather than by racial or ethnic identity – has been the national liberation movement's agenda. During the twentieth century it was taken up in earnest by all African political formations, except those associated with homeland politics, beginning with the ANC in 1912. All subsequent national movements were required to at least measure up to that vision.

In contrast all the White political parties subscribed to a settler-colony vision of the nation. I include here too the liberal formula of 'equal rights for all civilized men', which did not depart from that conception since the terms 'civilized' and 'white', in their mouths, were virtually synonymous. The liberals pursued an essentially integrationist agenda that envisaged 'suitably qualified' Blacks being absorbed and integrated into a national polity defined, designed and dominated by the White minority. That was the essence of 'Cape liberalism' before Union in 1910; it was at the core of the Liberal Party's programme in 1953; the Progressive Party's programme in 1961 actually excavated it. It is such considerations that inspire the federalist pretensions of the DA in the present day. What gives the game away are the Freudian slips of Frau Zille, the offspring of refugees from Germany, who has the audacity to refer to African residents of the Western Cape as 'refugees from the Eastern Cape'!

Throughout the ANC's very checkered history its commitment to a non-racial nation state has been a constant. Even the PAC was compelled to go into elaborate sophistries in an attempt to demonstrate its adherence to that modernist vision.

Historically the central strategic challenge for Marxism in South Africa has been the relationship between the national and class struggles. Since the first decade of the 20th century various political theorists have denied such a relationship. Some asserted that the class struggle superseded or even rendered irrelevant the national struggle. Others have argued that the national struggle is fatally doomed to degenerate into an accumulation path for an aspiring Black bourgeoisie. The experience of the South African left is that formations that either denied or tried to ignore the national struggle have become politically irrelevant or have isolated themselves on the left fringes of the movement for liberation.

Marxism was brought to South Africa by the waves of European immigrant workers and artisans who arrived in South Africa in the wake of the opening of the goldmines in 1883. The South African labour movement was initially based on the struggles and the unions of the skilled White workers in the mines and related industries. As Black, especially African, workers were increasingly drawn into the industrial working class the labour movement was compelled to respond to the living experience of Black labour. While it was pre-occupied with winning support amongst the White workers, the movement inspired by Marxism made little progress. It was only after the Communist Party of South Africa (CPSA) adopted the objective of establishing a Black Republic in 1928 that it was able to root itself amongst the African working class and Communists were more widely accepted as committed participants in the liberation struggle.

After 1928 the Communists interpreted the system of racial oppression in South Africa as the function of a capitalist system that developed in a colonial environment. Decades of ideological struggle in the Communist movement finally drove it to the conclusion that what was prevalent in South Africa was a system of colonialism, essentially no different from others, except for the fact that the colonial power and the colonised people lived within the borders of the same country. In its programme, 'South Africa's Road to Freedom', adopted in 1962, the South African Communist Party came forward with the theory of 'Colonialism of a Special Type', declaring that Black South Africa was the colony of White South Africa. The class struggle in South Africa, the SACP said, would therefore proceed in tandem with the national struggle against colonial domination.

By 1962 Chris Hani was already a member of the SACP and actively engaged in its underground regional structures in the Western Cape. The SACP programme confirmed the strategic option he had chosen of being an ANC activist, but also gave him a theoretical framework within which to conduct the political work he was engaged in.

The decade of the '70s was inaugurated by a wave of strikes amongst the African workers of Natal. That strike wave gave rise to a renewed effort to organise the unskilled and semi-skilled Black workers into unions. It was during that decade that the class dimensions of the liberation struggle, so often concealed behind national issues, began to assert themselves as never before. One outcome of the re-emergence of class as one of the key aspects of the liberation struggle was the appearance of a host of 'socialist schools of thought' that contested the relevance of the national struggle, questioned the role and the credentials of the ANC, and usually by extension, that of its allies the SACP and SACTU.

Rather than entering into a sterile debate with many of these new 'theorists', comrades like Chris chose to demonstrate that they were wrong through revolutionary political practice. Employing the tactics of 'a united front from below' where appropriate, they cooperated with the unions and unionists in FOSATU and CUSA when necessary in order to build workers' organisations that would through experience learn and appreciate the relationship between the class and national struggles. That approach was vindicated when COSATU emerged as the leading Black union federation after 1985, winning the support of powerful unions that had at one time been the mainstays of CUSA and FOSATU. As Lenin had stressed, reference to ' ... the people's revolution' does not require '... cover(ing) up ... class antagonisms amongst the people ...'

> '... However, it does not divide the 'people' into 'classes' so that the advanced class becomes locked up within itself ... the advanced class ... should fight with all the greater energy and enthusiasm for the cause of the whole people, at the head of the whole people.'

In other words, it is only by offering leadership to all those oppressed and degraded by national oppression that the Marxists would earn their support and place themselves in a position to lead the charge for freedom and democracy.

That is a view that resonates with that of the founders of the modern Communist movement, Karl Marx and Friedrich Engels. Marx and Engels argued that the Communists within the democratic movement should play a very special role. In the Communist Manifesto they describe the Communists as :

> '... on the one hand, practically, the most advanced and resolute section of the working class parties of every country, that section which pushes forward all others; on the other hand, theoretically, they have over the great mass of the proletariat the advantage of clearly understanding the line of march, the conditions and the ultimate general result of the proletarian movement.' What did Marx and Engels mean by '... understanding the line of march ...'? What exactly does '... understanding the line of march ...' entail?

It is my suggestion that it implies that the Communists should have a firmer grasp of the overall strategic tasks and challenges facing the democratic movement; and that their theory should equip them with a clearer vision of the immediate, the inter-mediate as well the long range objectives of the movement they are involved in, enabling them to dis-aggregate how these objectives are inter-related.

In other words there are no pre-set formulae and infallible quotations strategists can appeal to for guidance without due regard to the concrete situation. That in every situation the challenge facing Communist activists is to be concrete: To examine the realities of their society at that particular moment and to act in accordance with their comprehension thereof.

Comrade Chris Hani, through his actions demonstrated that the role of a revolutionary is not to go along in order to get along. That there are times when revolutionary commitment requires that one challenge complacency and self-satisfied business-as-usual postures. But his willingness to swim against the current should not be read as lack of discipline or recklessness. When mischievous elements exploited justifiable grievances amongst MK fighters to organise a mutiny in Angola in 1984 it was Comrade Chris Hani who took up the challenge of confronting them and putting it down.

CHALLENGES OF TODAY AND THE LEGACY OF CHRIS HANI
Ladies and Gentlemen, comrades and friends,

In her famous pamphlet, 'The Mass Strike, The Political Party and the Trade Unions,' Rosa Luxemburg, one of Marx's ablest disciples with reference to proletarian class consciousness emphasised:

'And what it is, that should it dare to appear.'
Rosa Luxemburg's formulation captured a classic construction of dialectical reasoning, that appearance often contradicts essence.

Comrade Chris Hani was a Marxist and a card-carrying Communist all his adult life. While many short-sighted people find difficulty in understanding why he spent all those years in Mkhonto weSizwe and in the ranks of the African National Congress, the answer is rather simple. Comrade Chris never mistook revolutionary consciousness for clever, radical-sounding slogans. While he continuously interrogated the relationship between nationalism and Marxism, he understood that both were part of an existent historical reality. A meaningful Marxist political practice required the steady mobilization of the necessary class, social and national forces that could be yoked to build the political alliances capable of striving for and achieving freedom and democracy. Given the interface between national oppression and capitalist exploitation, an alliance between Marxism and African nationalism was essential for such a project. To Comrade Chris, Marxism was not an abstract theory. Its principles had to be applied to concrete revolutionary practice. And while these principles remained unchanged, their translation into practical programmes that galvanised the working people and the oppressed is what made these principles meaningful.

The theoretical practice of those Marxists who have preferred to act outside of and in opposition to the national movement has always sounded very learned and erudite. But it has in fact been politically sterile and divorced from actual practice. The historic decline of a number of far-left groupescules into political irrelevance testifies to this. The Cape Town, where both Chris and I began our serious political activity, was awash with such groups!

What then are the challenges that face the revolutionary forces of South Africa today. Comrade Chris Hani was among those South African Communists prepared to accept that the party had not always had an adequate appreciation of the dialectics of race, class and gender. Unlike many others who served in the leading bodies of the SACP he did not arrogantly dismiss the views of non- party Marxists but gave their views and arguments the serious attention they deserved. Many of his SACP comrades could not, for example, understand his longstanding and profoundly comradely relationship with the late Livingstone Mqotsi and his friendship with certain leaders of the PAC, the Unity Movement and other bodies outside the ANC alliance.

Within the ANC alliance too Chris refused to keep silent about the abuse of power and incipient corrupt practices. As we have seen, there were occasions on which he personally suffered for having the courage to speak up on issues others thought it better to maintain a silence about.

The emergence of a rapacious indigenous elite – the wa-Benzis of South Africa with their life-style of conspicuous consumption – from amongst our own ranks would have earned his critical appraisal and round condemnation. While no one should concoct and offer up alibis for the abuses and corruption that seems at times to besiege our movement, let us not forget that the accumulation path of grasping hold of the state in order to leverage economic advantage through control thereof was pioneered first by the Anglo-capitalist Randlords of the late 19th century, then perfected by local capital and especially its Afrikaner component after 1948. Of course, their actions were not described as corruption! They were the elaboration of a consistent and sensible 'native policy'. That its effect was to rob the African and other Black property-owning classes of what little property they possessed is considered purely incidental: a form of political 'collateral damage' as it's called these days.

I have for some time been arguing that despite the essentially conflictual relationship between capital and labour, there are a number of places where the interests of the emergent Black capitalist classes and the working class intersect. And, since no one suggests an immediate transition to socialism at this juncture, it is wise to explore such intersections to the mutual advantage of both classes and for the benefit of the nation as a whole. While accepting the need for such exploration, I do not want to sow the illusion that private capital is altruistic. The business of business, White or Black, is business. And there is no free lunch! But, there are times precisely in their pursuit of profits, that the private sector can be spurred to create or expand badly required services. There are in fact instances when the private sector's drive for profit can be harnessed to develop and expand South Africa's productive forces. There will be instances when the resources in the hands of the capitalist classes will have to be harnessed for purposes of the national project, but fully conscious that their motive is to maximise profits.

An instinctive democrat and committed Communist, Comrade Chris Hani sought to build the SACP as a powerful and independent voice of the working class within the Tripartite Alliance. But he never projected that as the SACP acting and speaking like an antagonist of the ANC. The role he defined for the SACP was that of a concerned ally, pursuing a shared agenda, but each party always conscious of the other's sovereignty.

The people of South Africa waged a century-long struggle – making great sacrifices – to put an end to colonial domination and to assert their rights to govern themselves. Chris understood that democracy, the civil liberties and human rights that sustain it, and which makes the pursuance of social justice possible, are not privileges to be dispensed or withheld at the discretion of power wielders. These are the inalienable rights for which we all struggled. And, if anyone has earned them, it is the ordinary working people of town and country who did the struggling, the fighting and the dying so that we can enjoy them today. He would have dismissed as arrant nonsense the characterisation of the struggle for democracy in post-colonial societies as an imperialist agenda.

As South Africa approached the dawn of democracy, Comrade Chris was amongst those within the alliance leadership who fought for recognition of the pluralism of South African society. Such pluralism, he hoped, would be sustained by a continuing dialogue amongst the people, the government, the ANC, the Tripartite alliance and all other political parties.

What then is '... the line of march ...' of our South African national democratic revolution today? Is it to create an environment conducive to job creation by those who control the country's resources? Is it to radically improve the productivity of the South African economy? Is it to radically transform the character of our economy to break the cycle of reproducing the template of 'colonialism of a special type' and take the economy on a different and radically new growth path? If we say the challenge is to do all these three, can and should the working class undertake that challenge alone? Or will the attainment of these objectives require the working class to act in alliance with other class forces? If these challenges require the building of new alliances, which class forces and fractions are the most likely to be mobilised for such an undertaking?

I raise these questions by way of suggesting a new '... line of march ...' that entails the continuity of the Tripartite alliance and a policy of active engagement with the emergent Black capitalist classes to assign them a set of national objectives to pursue in both their own class interest and to attain agreed national goals.

The elaboration of a new national agenda will also require the Tripartite Alliance to clean up its own act. The growing perception, true or false, that we are presiding over a regime of galloping corruption and skimming from the top will not be eliminated except by resolute and tough action against the corrupt in our ranks. The Tripartite Alliance will retain and expand its credibility amongst our people if we take up the call for clean government and a clean ANC that has a demonstrable commitment to rooting out corruption.

The days we are passing through are in many respects much easier than those we faced during the late 1960s. Yet there are challenges facing the movement today that pose far more profound dangers to its existence than the threats we overcame in the past.

Fighting for sound policies that will take the movement and our people forward has never been a task for the faint-hearted. Speaking up against wrongdoing within and amongst ranks sometimes requires more courage than facing the enemy. Comrade Chris Hani repeatedly demonstrated the courage to do precisely that when it was necessary.

Writing a letter to Adophe Sorge the day after the death of his old comrade, Karl Marx, Friedrich Engels ended it with the words:

'The struggle of the proletariat continues. That victory is certain. Well, we must see it through. What else are we here for? And we have not lost courage yet.'

Courage was one quality that defined Comrade Chris Hani. We honour him best by emulating his courage, his honesty and integrity.

THIRTY-TWO

This (untitled) lecture was an address to the Eastern Cape legislature in September 2012, the tenth anniversary of the Bisho shootings, but also just weeks after the Marikana massacre. The march to Bisho on 7 September 1992 is remembered respectfully; but for those present the main impact of Jordan's address must have been his dismay – anger, even – at the Marikana shootings. 'What words capture the criminality of actually shooting African miners during a protest?' he demanded, adding that the event represented a crisis of conscience for the liberation movement and for South African democracy. His concerns about the nature of the state included Mbeki's AIDS denialism; an environment of corruption 'encouraged by a pervasive attitude of connivance and impunity'; and the loss of legitimacy by the ANC at local government level. He concludes by asking whether Marikana was South Africa's 18th Brumaire, its Kronstadt, its moment of truth.

Remembering Bisho
– and Marikana

September 2012

Madam Premier of the Eastern Cape,
Members of the Provincial Legislature and Government,
On the 8th September 1992, then President of the ANC, Comrade Nelson Mandela's issued a public statement on the Bisho Massacre. The message read in part:

'Each one of the people who lost their lives at Bisho yesterday, 7th September, was a unique human being. The daughter or the son of some mother; the father or mother to some child; a person linked to a home, to a community of relatives and friends who had loved, cherished and nurtured her or him for many years in the hope of a continuing and shared future.

Thousands marched full of hope for a better tomorrow. Dozens did not return.

Those fateful four minutes of gunfire, that reverberated through the length and breadth of South Africa, snuffed out those lives as if they were of no consequence. The staccatto of those automatic weapons added one more grisly episode to the already bloodstained annals of twentieth century South Africa.

The facts of what occurred have been established by the international media and eyewitnesses representing local and international agencies whose reputations are beyond reproach. The shootings were unprovoked and were not preceded by any warning. Lethal force was employed as the first option of the Ciskei Security Forces in circumstances that did not even remotely warrant its use.

We condemn these killings in the strongest possible terms!

To the bereaved families; to the relatives and friends who have lost their loved ones we offer our heartfelt condolences. The words of comfort and sympathy we pronounce can however do nothing to restore the lives that have been so brutally cut short. We can but hope that these few tokens of our deep concern will lend them the support to alleviate their sorrow. We mourn with the communities of the Border region that continue to bleed even while our country makes its troubled transition from the autocracy of apartheid to democracy.

From this day, Bisho will rank alongside Boipatong on that roll call of infamy that recounts the past two years of F.W. de Klerk's incumbency. The authors of yesterday's massacre already stand condemned in the eyes of the nation and the world for their criminal actions.'

Twenty-eight people were killed on September 7th 1992, two years before South Africa's first democratic elections. 200 more were wounded in a fusillade that lasted more than 1 minute. The massacre at Bisho followed close on the heels of the Boipatong Massacre of 17th June 1992, when armed assailants organised by the Third Force attacked a small township, killing 45 people and injuring scores. It was later revealed that the attack was an aspect of 'Operation Marion', run by the generals of military intelligence to destabilise the country and thwart progress to democratic elections. Though Dr Mangosutho Buthelezi strenuously denied any involvement by his party or supporters in that murderous incident, at the TRC six members of the IFP applied for amnesty for their involvement in the Boipatong massacre!

During the centenary year of the ANC, on 16th August 2012, thirty-four mineworkers were killed. Eighteen years into South African democracy, the post-democracy state massacre occurred under circumstances that still need to be unpacked and closely investigated by a judicial enquiry.

The circumstances and the environment in which these two massacres took place does make them vastly different events. Yet,

Who is here so bold as to say the tears shed for those who died on September 7th 1992 are less bitter than those shed for the fallen of August 16th 2012?

Who is here so callous as to suggest that the death of a father, a husband, a brother, a son, a relative, a neighbour – is less painful because those who fired the shots came from a different government?

Who is here, so heartless as to suggest that the lives lost at Marikana are less valued, less precious, less important than those of the victims of Boipatong and Bisho?

Who is here so cold-hearted, insensitive and cold as to suggest that our humanity, the humanity of our community, of our people, of all South Africans was not violated by the live ammunition fired into a crowd of protesting mineworkers?

Who is here so unfeeling as not to recognise that this massacre and the blood of the fallen cry out for a thorough and intense investigation to get to the root causes of this terrible tragedy and to deal with those responsible?

We are here today to mark one of those terrible moments in South Africa's march to democracy. In the euphoria that accompanies so much of our celebration of our democracy we too often forget the price that was exacted from our people to arrive at 27th April 1994.

In our enthusiasm for the wonderful democratic order, our Constitution and the democratic institutions we have today, we all too often forget that those last four years of apartheid, between February 2nd 1990 and 27th April 1994, witnessed some of the worst bloodletting, overt state violence and covert-state-sponsored violence South Africa had yet witnessed in a century.

It is absolutely necessary that we recall that the much praised 'peaceful transition' was peaceful only to the oppressor! The sacrifices of the numerous families who lost their loved ones during those fateful four years demand that we acknowledge that our 'peaceful transition' was only peaceful in that the people and their armed combatants did not once retaliate against the apartheid state apparatus or its agents for the murders they visited on entire communities, in Natal, in Gauteng, in

Mpumalanga and in the Free State.

One of the most diabolical aspects of racist repression was the regime's ability to outsource it to puppet regimes like those of Matanzima, Oupa Gqozo and other 'homeland leaders'.

The massacre at Bisho in September 1992 was one such instance.

After de Klerk announced the unbanning of the ANC, PAC the SACP, BCM and other organisations on 2nd February 1990, it was very clear to all of us in the liberation movement that his actions were inspired both by the pressure from below in the shape of mass struggles and international isolation, as well as a hard-nosed realism on the part of the NP leadership who opted to negotiate before they had lost everything/ before total defeat/ to avoid total defeat.

South Africa's transition consequently would have two features. One was the attempt by the then dominant White minority to save what they could by accommodating some of the demands of the oppressed; the other would be continuing pressure from below, driven by the people's own desire to realise a freedom that was meaningful and gave democracy real content.

Within the ranks of the liberation movement itself there was an ongoing ndebate about the best tactics to employ. I think comrades will recall what was then called the debate about the 'tap, the boat and the Leipzig option' – during which some comrades argued that mass action could be turned on and off, like a tap, as and when the occasion demanded. Others at the same time argued that de Klerk and his supporters in the NP were not necessarily fully in charge and for us to rock the boat might well assist the more intransigent elements amongst them who were opposed to change. There was the third point of view that advocated sustained pressure on the de Klerk government on all fronts, similar to the mass demonstrations in Leipzig and other places that finally forced Erich Honecker and his colleagues to resign in 1990.

The eigthty thousands who marched on Bisho that day to demand the dissolution of the puppet state called the Ciskei and its reincorporation within the official borders of South Africa were participants in a campaign of mass action, inspired by the ANC and its allies. We regarded that as one of many levers to break the log-jams in the negotiating process and to maintain popular pressure that was so necessary to compel the De Klerk government to negotiate in earnest.

Let us recall too that the ANC had withdrawn from CODESA in protest against the Boipatong massacre, three months previously. The Bisho Massacre in many respects was the high-point in a continuing campaign of mass action, responded to in bulkers by the regime and its surrogates.

The poignancy of this moment, in 2012, when we our people are once again mourning, is that it does perhaps throw into very sharp relief that contradictions arising from those two dimensions of our transition.

Because the midwives of democratic South Africa were both mass pressure and elite accommodation, the property relations of the old South Africa were carried over into the new. Yes, to be sure, democratic law has made it illegal to deny any South African access to or the right to own property on grounds of race, but those who had in the past acquired their property precisely on grounds of their race, were allowed to keep it. In effect what the outcome has been is that we re-racialised property-ownership; we de-gendered property-ownership; but at the same time we doubly racialised poverty and propertylessness! We racially gendered poverty! Using any index one might want, poverty in South Africa is a condition suffered by Africans, and is concentrated specifically among African women!

The arrival of democracy has opened the path to property-acquisition and capital accumulation to a small minority of Africans who have since 1994 become capitalists engaged in mining, agriculture, secondary industry, finance management and banking but it has left largely un-changed the poverty that compels thousands of other Africans to descend into the bowls of the earth to extract the minerals that go to enrich a few.

The system of 'bantu homelands' stood at the centre of a migrant labour system devised in 1905 specifically to produce and reproduce an easily exploitable labour force from amongst landless peasants forced to join the working class. After 1948 when the NP first won a majority in Parliament, the system was further refined by delegating a number of policing functions to 'homeland governments', four of whom even opted for the cynical 'independence' that the NP imposed on them.

From the inception of mining in this country, the Eastern Cape, like many of our impoverished rural areas and those of South Africa's immediate neighbours have annually supplied thousands of men to work on the mines. We need not detain ourselves here recounting the apalling, concentration-camp-like conditions under which African mineworkers were forced to live.

During our campaigns to improve the lot of the African miners we declaimed to our country and to the world, that:

It is a crime to place the African peasant in circumstances compelling him to seek work on the mines!

It is a crime to monitor, control and oppress African miners with dompasses and permits;

It is crime to house African miners in unhealthy compounds under prison-like conditions!

It is a crime to pay African miners starvation wages while mining corporations and bosses got rich;

What words can we pronounce today?

What words capture the criminality of actually shooting African miners during a protest ??!!

The massacre at Bisho, here on 7th September 1992 was an unprovoked act of repression carried out by a desperate puppet regime, run by a drunken maniac and sustained by mercenaries and a repressive police force.

How will future generations account for the first post-democracy massacre?

How do we, as the militants of the liberation movement

- that brought this country democracy;
- that helped craft a much-envied democratic Constitution;
- that has created the legal framework enabling thousands of Africans to become socially mobile;
- that transformed South Africa into a land of hope by casting open the doors of opportunity for millions:

What meaning do we read in this post-democratic massacre??

How do we account for this post democracy state massacre?

If ever there was a moment for us all to take stock, it is now!

Marikana is a terrible tragedy as the first post democracy massacre, but we can also turn it into a moment for collective introspection as a nation. I consider this one of those moments that represent a crisis of conscience : A crisis of conscience especially for the liberation movement but also for South African democracy.

It raises serious questions about the quality of our police service that in 2012 its response to public manifestations is live ammunition.

It raises serious questions about the quality of our democratic state that we have not after eighteen years been able to train our police service to handle crowd control other than by repressive means.

It raises serious questions, especially after the death at the hands of the police of Andries Tatane, about the standing orders on public order policing within the SAPS.

On coming into office in 1994, the democratic government set about reforming what had in the past been a repressive apparatus into a police service. We demilitarised the Police Service as one means of re-orienting it to serving the people of the country. Perhaps such reform has not proceeded far enough or has been arrested too soon by the exigencies of the present.

Notwithstanding the unfavourable international economic climate, the democratic government has kept the ship of the South African state on course. It is only those who are wilfully blind who can deny that our government has delivered a democracy dividend to the people of this country.

The democratic government has restored and given rights to a host of communities, defined by faith and by chosen lifestyle.

The democratic government has delivered new housing units at a rate of over 1000 units per day since 1994.

The democratic government has multiplied the number of South Africans who cook with electricity by 130%.

The democratic government has multiplied the number of South Africans who have clean running water in their homes by 71%.

The democratic government has multiplied the number of South Africans who have access to schooling.

The democratic government has brought health and social services to all South Africans.

Our undeniable successes, I think, have led to an attitude of complacency and postures within the movement itself of 'let's go along to get along' if not 'to get ahead'. We have seen the ravages that denialism on the part of the ANC and its leadership has led to in the past.

We have in the past observed the leadership of the ANC, in and out of government, go along quietly as the denialism of a President played havoc with the lives of millions!

It is at moments such as these that the mettle of our leadership and the quality of our movement are tested.

Those among us who want to close their eyes to reality might not like facing up to the widely held perception that we live in an environment of corruption.

A perception that this corruption is sustained and encouraged by a pervasive attitude of connivance and impunity.

A perception that the ANC, as a movement and as a government is very permissive about corruption.

A perception that the ANC's permissiveness is the outcome of deep implication of both its leaders and members in such corruption.

Over the past eight years were have seen the escalation of local protests over perceived corruption at local government level. Though many of these protests are fuelled by rising expectations, there can be no doubt that in many instances this has led to the ANC losing legitimacy among the people. It is only a matter of time before that loss of legitimacy percolates upwards – to the provincial and national leadership.

The successes the democratic government has registered over the past eighteen years are the direct result of the strategic vision our movement has pursued over the years. It was that strategic vision that had enabled the ANC to raise itself from the near-dismemberment of the post-Rivonia years to the status of effective leader of all the democratic forces of the country during CODESA.

It was that strategic vision that took us from the doldrums of Bisho in September 1992, to April 1994.

The strategy that our movement had devised and tested in the crucible of struggle, over decades, was to mobilise all those who could be mobilised against the common enemy. The strategy of our movement was to isolate the main enemy. And, we did this by winning to our side all those political and social forces who sought change in earnest. There were also those whom we could not organise. If it was possible we sought to neutralise such forces rather than drive them into active opposition.

Can any of us claim that our movement is applying such a strategy today?

It is true that we left twenty-eight of our fallen in Bisho on that day. But it was Oupa Gqozo, the collaborationist stratum he led, the De Klerk government and the third force they claimed they could not control who lost on that day. The movement was able to return to CODESA II having extracted firm commitments to negotiate in good faith from De Klerk.

The outcomes produced by the actions of the ANC and the government it leads are not a widening network along which influence radiates, but rather increasing isolation as the sphere of influence of the movement shrinks. The credibility of the ANC is probably the lowest it has been since 1990! The leadership has been stripped of its dignity! The best advice one can offer our movement caught in a hole is: 'stop digging!'

How we emerge from this terrible tragedy will depend on how seriously we take the challenges it has placed before us.

It demonstrates the determination of the government to get at the truth that the President appointed a Judicial Commission of Inquiry within days of the shootings. Commendable as the appointment of the commission is, its primary concern will be to establish legal matters of fact relating to the specific events of that fateful day, August 16th. We are confident that the Judicial Commission of Inquiry will conduct its investigations with the appropriate rigour and uncover all the relevant facts.

But Marikana is symptomatic of a much deeper malaise. The all too easy recourse to lethal violence on the part of the Police tells its own terrifying tale. Besieged by new forms of violent crime perpetrated by criminals armed with military hardware, the South African Police Service has been exhorted to meet fire with fire by more than one minister and

National Police Commissioner. This might have had the unfortunate consequence of encouraging the use of lethal force.

The sources of the tensions that led to bloodshed on August 16th go far deeper than the specific events that unfolded that day. I want to use this platform to call upon the leadership of the Congress of South African Trade Unions to organise a Workers' Commission of Inquiry into the Marikana tragedy. COSATU should invite the other two union federations to participate in such a Workers' Commission that should investigate, amongst other things, the return to South Africa's mining industry of the 'native labour touts', who pitted workers against each other for their own profit in yesteryear, in the shape of labour brokers. The 'outsourcing' of recruitment was through labour brokers prevalent in Marikana played a notorious role in piling up the dry tinder of conflict. It should also shed light on the manner in which the mining industry is evading its responsibilities to its work force who live in shanty-towns around the mines.

A Workers' Commission should also be tasked with investigating the shockingly high levels of violence in our society. An aspect of this violence is the alarmingly high incidence of private gun ownership in this country. The close correlation between high levels of gun ownership and gun-related crime is now well established. The best way to curb gun related crimes is to move towards a gun-free society. The police service in a gun-free society will have no need to carry firearms.

Madam Premier,

Ladies and Gentlemen,

Comrades and friends,

Does it sit easily with the membership of the ANC? Does it sit easily with the millions of ANC supporters here at home, and in the world at large that during its centennial year, the government, led by the ANC presided over the first post-democracy state massacre?

How do we explain to the shade of Uncle J.B. Marks that today it is bullets fired from the automatic weapons of our democratic police service that are creating widows and orphans in the villages of the eastern Cape, of Lesotho, of the North-West province?

Who will explain to the martyrs of Bisho that the Police service they laid down their lives to create, also fires live ammunition at demonstrators?

The tensions that erupted in the continuing strike that led to the events of August 16th are in many respects the result of the compromises the movement made to attain the beach-head of democracy in 1994. We substituted BEE for wealth redistribution; we persuaded ourselves to be content with less than what we had fought for, because it was much more than what we had had.

In another context I once raised the question: Will our Black captains of industry behave like the Randlords who incited the Anglo-Boer war and the atrocities of the Concentration Camps? Or will they behave like the latter-day White monopolists who mouthed liberal sentiments, voted for the UP while they profited handsomely from collaborating with apartheid? or would pioneer a new path of corporate responsibility by promoting better working conditions and wages for workers?

Regrettably, it would appear the emergent Black capitalist class have bought into and are being incorporated into the culture of White capital.

It might be unpleasant, but the current ANC leadership and the government it leads must accept that it has probably presided over the years of the ANC's most profound crisis. Which poses the matter of the quality of the movement's leadership at this moment.

Every movement for political transformation has arrived at this moment of truth sooner or later. During the French Revolution it came on the 18th Brumaire; during the Russian Revolution it was Kronstadt. Has that moment also arrived for South Africa in the shape of Marikana?

Let Marikana be the moment when to once again take hold of the movement of our people and steer it again towards the sound and sober strategies of the past.

The elective conference that the ANC holds at the end of this year must rise to the challenge of producing a leadership corps that has the will, the moral courage and moral standing to take on task of cleaning the Augean stables of corruption!

The elective conference of the ANC must rise to the challenge of producing a leadership corps that will restore the credibility of the movement amongst its friends and opponents.

The elective conference of the ANC must rise to the challenge of producing a leadership corps that will restore the movement's reputation and record of compassion.

Only by correcting itself in that manner will the ANC regain the confidence of the democratic forces of this country and take us all on a higher trajectory to a better life for all our people!

THIRTY-THREE

Commemorating Zwelakhe Sisulu, who had died two weeks earlier, Jordan reflects on the history of black journalism since the 1950s. Although it is not spelt out, the concluding call for the ANC to reclaim its commitment to media freedom suggests that such commitment has failed.

ANC Must Reclaim Media Freedom Sisulu Punted

New Times, 18 October 2012

Reflecting on the life of Zwelakhe Sisulu once again underscored the integral relationship between the liberation struggle and media freedom. It is appropriate that we remind ourselves that among those who gathered at Mangaung in 1912 were at least three founder editors, who consistently fought the good fight for a free press.

Receiving the sad news of the passing of Sisulu made me recall my encounters with the man. I knew him by the reputation he had earned as a courageous journalist and liberation activist. Besides his pedigree as one of the sons of a distinguished family in the liberation struggle, Sisulu had crafted his own identity over many years of persecution at the hands of the apartheid regime.

Our eyes immediately fell on Sisulu when filling the office of the first post-apartheid CEO of the SABC. Tension between those tasked with governing and the media, as purveyors of information and opinion, is inevitable, even in a democracy. Accepting this tension does not betray a temptation to censor. As a seasoned journalist, Sisulu brought to the job an integrity honed in the struggles he had waged in the local media and against a repressive regime. He left the SABC with his reputation untarnished.

One day, the story of the struggle on two fronts that black journalists were compelled to wage will be told. Newspaper proprietors insisted on a staple of crime, gossip, celebrity and sport, pandering to the worst vices of tabloid journalism to realise profits.

That is where most black journalists cut their teeth in the 1950s and 1960s. The 1976 Soweto uprising compelled editors to treat news about the urban black community more seriously. Sisulu was among the black journalists who drove that transformation through interventions in the profession.

The apartheid regime exacted a heavy price from those who opposed it in earnest. Beginning with the banning of the Guardian, a leftwing weekly edited by communists Brian Bunting and Ruth First in 1952, it also banned the Guardian's successors, People's World; Advance, New Age and Spark. Banning orders served on the papers' editors in 1962 prevented them from working as journalists. The Torch, aligned to the Unity Movement, fell before their axe too, in 1963.

A multifaceted censorship regime, which Lawrence Gandar and Benjamin Pogrund were prosecuted for violating by publishing the prison experiences of Harold Strachan, was also in force. Strachan was sent back to jail for the 'crime' of discussing his experiences with the journalists.

It was in that authoritarian environment that a young Sisulu learned how to navigate the repressive laws of the time. Some editors had the courage to employ black journalists. When trouble came, they stood by them. But the print media's record was inconsistent. Anthony Holiday lost his job the day after he was detained by the security police. No Afrikaans editor ever criticised these overt repressive measures. Some even supported the state against the media.

The mere act of reporting accurately on the lives and experiences of black people constituted a political action during those decades of white minority rule. The indefatigable Henry Nxumalo, 'Mr Drum' of the early 1950s, deliberately engineered a week's imprisonment by violating some degrading curfew law and brought out a harrowing report on prison conditions. But rather than improve its prisons, the apartheid regime passed the Prisons Act, making it illegal to report on any South African prison – the law Gandar and Pogrund fell foul of. Yet imprisonment for breaking one or other of the hundreds of laws and ordinances that regulated the lives of black people was the experience of thousands in urban areas.

Sisulu and the generation of black journalists who helped to found the Media Workers Association of South Africa faced the more daunting challenge of telling these stories in an environment of intense repression by a regime facing the active hostility of the majority. Though never charged, tried and convicted of breaking a single one of their repressive laws, Sisulu served repeated bouts of detention without trial. Undeterred by these persecutions, he returned to the trenches to take up the fight after each. It was these qualities that recommended him to the Southern African Catholic Bishops' Conference when they sought an editor for their newspaper, The New Nation.

Under Sisulu's stewardship, the paper became the pioneer of the 'alternative press', offering accurate information and servicing an ever-widening network of democratic activists. Working together with others, they mentored a number of aspiring black journalists, some of whom now hold senior positions in our print media. They had the good fortune of training in environments far more friendly and supportive than previous generations. But making the country's media demographically more representative proved as great a challenge as freeing it from repressive laws.

Sisulu was a journalist in the tradition of the founders of the African National Congress (ANC).

It is by reclaiming its historic standards, such as media freedom, that the ANC will renew itself and restore its credibility. Lala ngoxolo Xhamela!

THIRTY-FOUR

Jordan cites Mamphela Ramphele's complaint that liberalism was increasingly being demonised, and uses this for a brisk exploration of the 'love–hate relationship' between African nationalism and liberalism in South Africa. The victory of liberalism (as in the 1996 Constitution) was paradoxical, as it had been secured by a nationalist movement which had had a troubled relationship with liberals.

Disdain for Liberals is Not Because of Intolerance

New Times, 22 November 2012

In her book *Laying Ghosts to Rest*, published about five years ago, Mamphela Ramphele complains of 'an increasing tendency to demonise liberalism as a political orientation. There is a dismissive view about the role of liberals in our political history, although many fine South Africans made a significant contribution to the anti-apartheid struggle from the platform of liberalism'.

I found her comments ironic considering the scathing critique of liberalism that came from the Black Consciousness movement during the 1970s and 1980s, particularly from Steve Biko, who explained the movement's break with the National Union of South African Students thus: 'Blacks are tired of standing at the touchlines to witness a game that they should be playing. They want to do things for themselves and by themselves.'

In the climate of political quiescence after the Rivonia trial, Biko was not only underscoring the spirit of black self-reliance but he was also rejecting the paternalism evident in the words and deeds of the liberals.

Black political elites did not always have a negative attitude to liberalism. As fellow advocates of liberal democratic institutions, the black elites viewed liberals as their allies. Both the African and coloured political elites considered the retention of the Cape colonial franchise as an entrenched clause of the 1909 Union Constitution as in-principle recognition of the aspiration to common citizenship. The complete disenfranchisement of Africans in 1936 represented the repudiation of both the aspiration and the principle. African politicians in the Cape had campaigned in defence of the Cape franchise through the 1920s in the expectation that their liberal allies were doing likewise among whites. The upshot was that white women were enfranchised in 1930 but, five years later, by merging into the United Party, Jan Smuts and JBM Hertzog mustered the two-thirds majority to amend the constitutional clause protecting the Cape franchise.

Instead of raising their voices in defence of the principle of common citizenship, the liberals compromised. A basic principle of liberal democracy was sacrificed because white voters would not accept it.

The African political elite of the 1940s and 1950s censured the liberals for being too deferential to white racism and for selling out fundamental liberal values to accommodate it. After 1943, every trend in African nationalist politics unapologetically demanded majority rule, expressed in the principle of government by the consent of the governed. The black political elites led the charge in the struggle to establish it in South Africa.

South African liberals could not reconcile the elementary liberal principle of government of the people and by the people with their political strategy that relied on white support. Liberal democratic principles never gained much traction among white South Africans. But, the liberals opted to retain a political foothold within that illiberal white community by compromising basic principles. Perhaps this accounts for Robert Sobukwe's wickedly facetious 'umlungu osithandayo' — the whites who love us (but not enough to affirm our humanity). Even the Liberal Party of Alan Paton proceeded from the assumption that the country's political institutions should be under white control.

As recently as the 1970s, liberal scholars David Welsh and Frederik van Zyl Slabbert decried 'majoritarianism' and admitted that their advocacy of federalism was a device to evade it. Hidden behind the appearance of mere prejudice are the palpable material interests white power established and defended. Liberal political and social values arrived in South Africa with settlers from Europe but they were repressed and subverted by state practice. When European settlers were not agents of that colonial state, they were the direct beneficiaries of its oppressive policies. The advocacy and defence of liberal democratic values usually devolved on the African nationalist movement. The victory of liberal democracy in South Africa is paradoxical because its midwife was an African nationalist movement with a history of a troubled relationship with liberals but which had nonetheless consistently defended basic liberal democratic principles. It was the parties associated with that movement that upheld the universalist vision at the core of the liberal democratic tradition during our constitutional talks.

The antagonism between the universalism of the liberal political tradition and the reality of aggression, dispossession and domination was the material undergirding of all nationalist intellectual traditions in the colonies. In some places, nationalist intellectuals retreated into the cul-de-sac of 'authenticity'. South Africa is fortunate in that the majority preferred the universalism of the liberal tradition.

To return to Ramphele's complaint: the love/hate relationship that evolved between all schools of African nationalism and liberalism in South Africa is not a result of political intolerance. Its cause is the liberals' perceived betrayal of the principles that they claim to uphold. The assertiveness of Biko and his generation was indispensable for the revival of mass politics during the 1980s. Democratic Alliance leader Helen Zille's toyi-toyi tells me that it was right on the money.

THIRTY-FIVE

This column is by Jordan in his teacherly mode. It is a trenchant and well-informed overview of the role of Britain and France in shaping the contemporary Middle East: the war on Iraq, civil war in Syria, and the issue of Palestine can all be traced back to the dismantling of the Ottoman Empire in 1918.

France and UK are Culpable in Middle East Conflict

New Times, 29 November 2012

Our images of the dismemberment of the Ottoman Empire are a heroic TE Lawrence, brilliantly played by Peter O'Toole, leading bands of Arab guerrillas against Turkish lines during the First World War.

We know less about the intrigues of the Entente Powers, specifically the UK and France, which orchestrated aspects of that Arab revolt, and their culpability for the tension that plagues the region today.

In November 1917, the UK's wartime cabinet effectively endorsed the establishment of a national homeland for the Jews in Palestine. A letter addressed to Baron Rothschild by UK foreign secretary Arthur James Balfour gave the Zionist movement the assurance that it could expect the support of the UK in the pursuance of its objective of establishing a Jewish national state.

It might come as a surprise that the only Jewish member of David Lloyd George's cabinet, Edwin Montagu, objected strongly to a Jewish state, underscoring that since the French Revolution, the Jews of Europe had fought their way out of the ghetto. A Jewish state amounted to recreating, rather than abolishing the ghetto, he said.

Montagu's words were partially true. In the 19th century, Benjamin Disraeli became Europe's first Jewish prime minister. As European nations extended civil rights to Jews, Jewish communities seized new opportunities, and some prospered.

While Balfour made these undertakings to the Zionists, other agents of the same war cabinet were cutting deals with their French counterparts about dividing the Ottoman Empire between themselves, while others undertook to support Arab nationalists.

It would indeed be an extremely hard heart that could not appreciate the communal trauma the Holocaust represents for the Jewish communities of the world. The Jews of Europe had attained near equal rights with their gentile fellow citizens by 1914. The rights of Europe's minorities expanded exponentially after 1918, especially in the former Prussian, Austro-Hungarian and Tsarist empires. Yet, during the third decade of the 20th century, a fanatically anti-Semitic movement transformed Germany and Austria, among Europe's more enlightened nations, into a 'Herrenvolk' that gloried in the industrial slaughter of fellow humans.

Monuments in the towns, villages and hamlets of Belarus, the Ukraine, Poland, the Baltic states and elsewhere bear testimony to the depravities inspired by racism. Whereas the majority of the world's Jewish population had treated Zionism with scepticism in the past, it acquired an emotional appeal few ever question. In his book, Beyond Chutzpah, Norman Finkelstein argues that the state of Israel and the Zionists debase the Holocaust by using it as an alibi for the Israeli aggression against the Palestinians.

Israel has indeed extended its borders since its founding in 1948. The Palestinian people have now lived under military occupation for more than 60 years. In the past 20 years, Israeli colonists have systematically settled territory once designated as part of a future Palestinian state. Such settlers then receive Israeli military protection. With Israel's proven military capacity, unmatched by any of its Arab neighbours, the military capacity of the Palestinians amounts to pitting a slingshot against helicopter gunships. In this David and Goliath contest, Israel, with its nuclear arsenal, cannot be cast as David.

At an international airport this past weekend, I watched an Arab air traveller subjected to a virtual strip search. That is the price that the double standards of the West exact from the international community. To bring their plight as a conquered and dispossessed people to international attention, militants of the Palestinian liberation movement began hijacking international flights in the 1970s, metaphorically declaring that the front of their liberation war would be everywhere there was air travel, as long as Israel was allowed to act with impunity. Rather than address the root cause of this problem, the international community prefers the inconvenience of metal detectors and body searches at airports – international air travel in a siege environment.

The ashes in the mouths of Tony Blair and French President Francois Hollande recall the role their two countries played in creating the unstable conditions in these former provinces of the Ottoman Empire. Their response to Israeli Prime Minister Benjamin Netanyahu's brinksmanship highlights the cynicism of these powers. The pretence that the actions of a Palestinian resistance to an occupying power are morally equivalent to aggression by another state plumbs the depths of hypocrisy. Instead of encouraging restraint, their words fuel Israeli impunity.

The manner in which the victors carved up the Ottoman Empire in 1918 has produced one of the most militarised regions in the world. The war on Iraq, the continuing Syrian civil war and the issue of Palestine can all be traced back to that fateful year. Palestinian and Israeli families have all lost loved ones in this tragic conflict.

Is it paranoia that makes me wonder whether the Israelis and the Palestinians are pawns in someone else's power game?

THIRTY-SIX

Jordan makes some deft historical comparisons between the National Party's and the ANC's use of state employment as 'a gateway to social advancement' of their followers. He hopes that Ramaphosa, recently elected as Deputy President of the ANC, might lead black capitalists to play a more positive social and political role – the vision of a 'patriotic bourgeoisie' flickers in and out of articles in this collection.

Ramaphosa's Role in Harnessing Black Capitalists

New Times, 20 December 2012

One of the less discussed aspects of white domination and apartheid was the destruction of the African property-owning classes after 1910. The 1913 Natives Land Act, which denied Africans the right to own land, set in motion a process of systematic destruction. First affected were Indians, then all black property owners, including coloureds, with the passage of the Asiatic Land Tenure Act of 1946 and the Group Areas Act of 1951.

Africans in the Cape Province managed to hold on to their property rights into the 1960s after a Supreme Court decision in 1918 overturned the implementation of the Natives Land Act in the Cape. In the rest of the country, an African was required to apply to a native commissioner with the discretionary power to determine whether the applicant was worthy of that 'privilege'. In addition to the symbolism associated with it, the destruction of Sophiatown in the 1950s and of District Six in the 1970s has real, material significance – the destruction of black property rights.

Census 2011 shows a measurable increase in property ownership among Africans and the emergence of a middle stratum, including high-earning public servants, professionals and business executives, since the early 1990s.

There are striking similarities with the outcome of the National Party's 1948 election victory. Between 1948 and 1960, the numbers of Afrikaners employed by the state grew exponentially. By 1994, when the African National Congress (ANC) took office, the 'shop-floor' language in the public service was Afrikaans. Whereas Afrikaner bankers could be counted in their hundreds in 1948, by the 1960s they numbered thousands. In 1957, Senator Leslie Rubin complained about the politically motivated elevation of junior Afrikaner jurists, while highly qualified non-Afrikaner barristers were deliberately overlooked. Each of the ethnic elites that has become politically dominant has employed control of the state for purposes of capital accumulation and for its own social advancement.

British cannons and concentration camps imposed the political domination of the white English-speaking minority between 1899 and 1902. To throw off English domination, the Afrikaner elite devised its own political strategy to attain political dominance. The condition for Afrikaner political domination was the disenfranchisement of the black majority, which the Afrikaner nationalists attained incrementally. Step one was the Union Constitution. Step two was the Hertzog bills of 1935. Step three was the Separate Representation of Voters Act of 1951.

Like the English and the Afrikaners before them, the African political elite is today using control of the state as a gateway to social advancement. At the lower reaches of the government, election to political office means a job and a salary. With political office come opportunities for patronage; often the thin edge of corruption.

An elite with no property but with a number of technical and professional skills has employed its political dominance to deracialise property ownership in South Africa. Despite the visible progress so far, Census 2011 tells us that white males still dominate the economy. Although a handful of Africans have become very wealthy, poverty in South Africa remains highly racialised and gendered, with African women at the bottom. Although the Gini coefficient is widening, the poor in South Africa are not getting poorer and government policy has positively affected the quality of people's lives, according to these findings.

The emergence, growth and development of this propertied African elite is also littered with scandals – the abuse of public funds, abuse of public office and the occasional salacious sex story. Barney Barnato's suicide is echoed in the arranged murder of Brett Kebble. Rhodes was the living embodiment of political power intersecting with immense economic power. It is an open secret that it was the scheming of Rhodes and his cronies that precipitated the Anglo-Boer War.

Does the election of Cyril Ramaphosa as deputy president of the ANC signal the arrival of the post-1994 African capitalist classes?

Ramaphosa brings talents and skills acquired in a working life that includes legal practice, leadership of a union, negotiating our democratic constitution and being a business leader. Having seized the opportunities that came with democracy, we expect Ramaphosa to lead the charge in defining a more positive role for black capitalists. Instead of being passive earners of dividends, they must be pressed into tackling the challenges facing our democracy.

It required the social and political shake-up of China to galvanise and release the latent energies of the Chinese capitalist classes that have made China the world's second-largest economy. The emergent African capitalists should address the social deficits inherited from the past. Is it asking too much to hope that, having been afforded this opportunity, Ramaphosa will make yet another sterling contribution to the development of South Africa by leading them in making such a commitment?

THIRTY-SEVEN

Jordan uses South Africa's provision of funds, training, conferences and translation of medieval Islamic documents in Mali to express his horror at the way in which fundamentalist Islamists were threatening the destruction of the heritage of Islam's golden age.

Rich Irony in Islamic Threat to Mali's Treasures

New Times, 7 February 2013

Under my stewardship as minister of arts and culture, SA funded the construction of modern archive facilities at the Ahmed Baba Library, trained several Malian archivists and provided the storage boxes to help preserve the fragile medieval paper. The department also sponsored conferences and a task team bringing together North African, West African, South African and European scholars to translate and study the manuscripts. Translation, under the leadership of Shamil Jeppie of the University of Cape Town, will teach us much about the late Middle Ages in Africa.

I was, consequently, filled with intense anxiety when unconfirmed reports about the pillage of that library reached us last week. I was equally relieved watching French President Francois Hollande inspecting it in the presence of TV cameras.

The emergence and rapid growth of the new religion founded by the prophet Mohammed in the 7th century was probably one of the more important transformative movements that shaped world history. Islam left an indelible impression on what was then known as the 'old world' of the Middle East, Central Asia, Europe and Africa.

Its effect on these societies may be measured by the extent of the empire the Muslims established. Within 50 years of the prophet's death in 632 CE, Islam spanned two continents, from the shores of the Atlantic in the west to the borderlands of India in the east. Contrary to a view prevalent in the West, Islam's abiding historical influence owed more to its cultural effects than to the sword. The speed with which it was adopted betrays the moribund character of the societies it penetrated. Islam was the religion of thriving urban-centred communities inhabited by merchants, guilds of craftsmen and artisans, scholars, jurists, poets and writers.

The teachings of the prophet extolled industry, thrift, cleanliness, imposed a number of disciplines and enjoined charity among his followers. The Muslims were also avid traders who dominated both the Indian Ocean trade routes as well as the land routes across Asia and Africa into western Europe. The Mediterranean, once dominated by the fleets of Rome and Byzantium, was transformed into a Muslim lake for 500 years. The opulence of the courts in Andalusia, Spain and those of the sultanates of Indonesia were possible thanks to indigenous artisans but also to the rich transcontinental trade routes controlled by Muslim merchants. Africa is the site of one of the earliest Muslim communities, predating the prophet's emigration from Mecca to Medina. Many more African lands, north and south of the Sahara, came under the sway of Islam during its westward expansion. The Maghreb became the staging post for the invasion of the Iberian peninsula, Sicily, Corsica and parts of Italy. From 711 CE until late into the 1400s, Spain and various parts of the Iberian peninsula were under the domination of the Moors from Africa.

During its golden age, the community of the faithful embraced blonde Caucasians from Europe, North Africa and parts of Asia; Africans of a multitude of hues from pitch black to tan; Mongoloid Uighurs, Indonesians and Malays; Indians, Persians as well as the Arabs. The peace, prosperity and progress of these Muslim territories was disrupted by Christian aggression, orchestrated from Europe, during the Crusades in the 12th century. It was armies drawn from this tapestry of humanity that faced the equally diverse Crusader armies at the gates of Jerusalem.

As part of this multiracial, cosmopolitan Muslim world, the intellectuals of the kingdoms of Africa, including Mali and Songhay, contributed to its scholarship and research in astronomy, mathematics, chemistry, zoology and botany. They engaged in its philosophical debates and participated in the jurisprudential disputes amongst Muslims scholars.

Situated at the crossroads between the eastern and western savannah and along the camel routes that connected the Mediterranean with the Gulf of Guinea, Timbuktu, in the Songhay Empire, grew into a prosperous centre of learning, where scientists, mathematicians, physicians, jurists and philosophers congregated to practise their craft and hone their skills. They preserved their ideas, the results of their work and their thoughts in leather-encased manuscripts, which have survived the ages. These manuscripts are a small sample of wealth of human knowledge debated, studied and stored by the intellectuals of West Africa during a gilded age.

These historic manuscripts from the Ahmed Baba library of Timbuktu came to international attention thanks to the intervention of former president Thabo Mbeki, who launched an international appeal for funds to rescue these treasures from Africa's past from the termites and the elements that threatened to reduce them to a pile of dust.

Because he immediately recognised their significance both to Africa and to humanity at large, Mbeki committed SA to the preservation and dissemination of these writings as one of the first projects of the New Partnership for Africa's Development.

An outer veneer of piety conceals the barbarism latent in all religious fundamentalism. 'Ironic' does not capture the paradox of a secular South African government spending millions of rand to preserve the best examples of Islamic scholarship in Africa against threats from a movement that claims to advance an Islamic agenda.

THIRTY-EIGHT

The argument of this terse, angry column is summed up in its title. Jordan contends that the American invasion of Iran and toppling of Saddam Hussein have not only left Iraq a divided, feeble state but a region beset with instability.

Mideast Will Pay the Bill for US Failure in Iraq

New Times, 4 April 2013

Ten years ago, TV viewers across the world watched US President George Bush demand the unconditional surrender of Saddam Hussein, his sons and the government he led. By the next day, these TV audiences could watch in awe as the US unleashed its digitised war machine on Iraq. Within two weeks, Bush could land on an aircraft carrier and proudly declare, 'Mission accomplished!' to the soldiers assembled for the purpose.

We could be forgiven our confusion about the exact nature of the accomplished mission, but a number of things were clear. First, Iraq's infrastructure had been well-nigh destroyed by US aerial bombardment. Second, thousands of non-combatant Iraqis had perished. Third, although Bush sounded extremely confident, the conflict he had ignited in Iraq was far from over.

The war that finally arrived in March 2003 had a long incubation in the planning rooms of Washington, DC. Like all modern wars, it was preceded by a lengthy propaganda campaign to convince the US public of the justice of the war and to persuade international opinion that the US was acting in everyone's best interest.

Even before Bush assumed the presidency, many who then took up official positions in his administration had advocated the invasion of Iraq.

Using the repetition of misinformation, they created the false impression that Iraq was behind the September 11 2001 attacks on the US. Every possible inducement was also used to persuade the Central Intelligence Agency (CIA) to link those attacks to Iraq. An alleged meeting between one of the hijackers, Mohammed Atta, and Iraqi intelligence officers in Prague turned out to be a lie. A front group, named Citizens for a Free Kuwait, was established with the assistance of one of the largest public-relations companies, Hill & Knowlton. Another group, called the Council of American Muslims for Understanding, launched the Open Dialogue website, funded by the US state department. Even the much-touted Iraqi National Congress, whose spokesmen unashamedly called for the invasion, turned out to be little more than a front organisation funded by the US government.

The invasion was ostensibly to uncover and destroy the weapons of mass destruction Saddam had allegedly amassed. Throughout the build-up to the invasion and during the war itself, the huge elephant in the room was the nuclear power in the region, Israel.

The first casualty in all wars had already been ruthlessly mutilated by a compliant US media even before US boots hit the ground in Baghdad. Their Goebbelsian style was shamelessly emulated by virtually every media organisation in the West, including our own. Within days of the initial US aerial assault, they had invented a name with a profoundly racist undertone, 'Ali', as a kind of 'one name, fits all' for all Iraqi officials.

Ten years later, about 5,000 US soldiers, most of them young men and women who went into the military for lack of opportunity, have died in Iraq. The Iraqi dead are numbered in the hundreds of thousands; the wounded in the millions. Not one weapon of mass destruction was found and disarmed.

Many of the trailer-park lads and lasses who fought the war will come home minus a finger, a leg, an arm or an eye; 200,000 have already returned home with post-traumatic stress disorder; 5,000 will never see their homes again. The stated aims of the war – to restructure Iraqi political institutions and unseat a dictator – have been only partially achieved. The US invasion has left the country and the region less stable and its future far less certain than before. The armed US presence next door has fuelled Iran's drive to acquire nuclear weapons as a deterrent.

Clearly Saddam's 'weapons of mass destruction' were a pretext for the invasion. Had the CIA been less rigorous, September 11 would have served the Bush administration equally well. Iraq has now been reduced to a divided nation state, its military capacity destroyed and its infrastructure in ruins. Thanks to the US war, there are now only two regional powers, Israel and Iran. Of the two, Israel is the nuclear power.

To his credit, while serving as a senator for Illinois, US President Barack Obama denounced the war as 'dumb'. Ironically, he is now obliged to clear up the mess made by his predecessor and to salvage what he can of US dignity. Obama has slapped down Israeli Prime Minister Benjamin Netanyahu's invitation to a confrontation with Iran and twisted his arm to apologise to Turkey. As he disengages US forces, the question arises: what did the US war in Iraq achieve?

The war has demonstrated the limits of US power. Instead of bringing a new order to the Middle East, it has stimulated instability. The 'new American century' Bush and his neoconservative backers had hoped the war would inaugurate has lasted less than a decade. But the price for that failure will be exacted in the Middle East, not in the US.

THIRTY-NINE

This is a brief but punchy critique of American foreign policy as experienced in Latin America, using the CIA's role in the overthrow of Chile's Allende as a key instance.

Chile's 9/11 Hints at Real Intention of US Administration

New Times, 12 September 2013

On the morning of September 11 1973, exactly 40 years ago on Wednesday, a military junta led by Gen Augusto Pinochet overthrew the democratically elected government of Salvador Allende. Allende had led a coalition of socialists and community activists, the Popular Unity Front, to an electoral victory in Chile's 1970 presidential elections. In a three-way contest, Allende won 36% of the vote and was elected president by the Chilean parliament in November 1970.

The US Central Intelligence Agency (CIA) tried to pre-empt Allende's assumption of office by staging a coup. Chile's chief of staff, Rene Schneider, refused when approached. On October 22 1970 his car was ambushed. He died in hospital three days later. The failed coup rebounded to Allende's advantage and he was installed as president.

CIA director Richard Helms later reported that his orders from the White House were to 'make the (Chilean) economy scream'. A campaign of covert activities to destabilise Chile was set in motion. Opposition political parties were funded and secret contacts established with far-right paramilitary groups whom the CIA trained in sabotage. US corporations with interests in Chile financed covert CIA operations to back opposition media.

There was also a decisive chilling of relations with the newly elected leftist government. Acting in concert with US corporations, the US government orchestrated the denial of loans by the Inter-American Development Bank, the termination of existing loans and the blocking of funds from multilateral institutions.

The Popular Unity Front government had taken measures to uplift the most vulnerable in society. It instituted a programme of free milk for all school going children up to the age of 15; stimulated wage increases in every sector of the economy; lowered taxes for middle-income earners and exempted small property owners; launched literacy and adult education projects; and increased the social wage for the working poor. Its legislative programme initially enjoyed the support of the Christian Democratic Party. But during the government's second year, the external pressures converged to produce an economic downturn. The government could not raise the loans to finance its ambitious reform programme. The government's opponents had successfully engineered a fiscal crisis.

In contrast to its frosty attitude towards Chile's government, during 1972 and 1973, the US increased military aid and stepped up the training of Chilean military personnel in the US and Panama. Saboteurs trained by the CIA also went into action, staging a number of arson attacks in late 1972. A strike by truckers in early 1973 threatened to bring the country's road-transport system to a halt. Middle-class housewives, incited by CIA-funded radio stations, also took to the streets in noisy 'empty pot' demonstrations.

Both sides hoped the congressional elections in March 1973 would resolve the political impasse. The Popular Unity Front coalition increased its share of the vote from 36% to 42%, dealing a serious blow to the opposition and its US backers. They turned to armed force. In June, tank commanders tried to stage a coup, but were disarmed by troops loyal to the government. In July and August, tension mounted as the opposition took to the streets again – joined by professionals and employers. As winter turned to spring, the first signs that the military had begun preparations for a coup became evident. They raided for arms against working-class neighbourhoods, the Popular Unity Front's key constituencies, and compiled lists of activists for arrest. Allende and the leadership of the Socialist Party hoped to break the political deadlock by calling a referendum for September 11 1973. The newly appointed army commander, Augusto Pinochet, ordered an attack on the presidential palace and the overthrow of the government that very morning. Allende was killed during the assault.

Even by Latin American standards, the Pinochet dictatorship was brutal. In addition to arbitrary arrests, detentions and torture, it carried out executions in football stadiums. For 17 years, the Chilean junta acted with impunity. Last week, members of the Chilean judiciary redeemed themselves by admitting its connivance in that repression.

Since the Spanish-American War, the US has regarded Latin America as its dominion in whose politics it has the moral right to intervene. It either sent in the marines or incited generals to overthrow liberal and left-inclined governments. Chile in 1973 was but one of many coups.

At a time when a US administration is rattling its sabre in the presumption that it has the right to impose and depose governments 'from the halls of Montezuma to the shores of Tripoli', it is helpful to remind ourselves of this other 9/11. The proof of the US's real intentions is written in the Latin American experience.

FORTY

While unstinting in its praise for Mandela – Jordan is 'eternally grateful for having served under the leadership of a world historical figure – this column is very different from the hyperbolic rhetoric of so many tributes and obituaries. It notes wryly that a revolutionary figure had been appropriated by the global establishment, and also comments on how Mandela's life has been airbrushed and mystified.

South Africa Basks in Hard-earned Glory of One Long Walk

New Times, 12 December 2013

Watching the arrival of foreign delegations at FNB Stadium to attend Nelson Mandela's memorial service, I could not help noting how one of the 20th century's revolutionary leaders has been appropriated by the establishment. Former US president Jimmy Carter, now counted among the world's elders, ambled in with shoulders now slightly stooped by age. Three other US presidents, two Democrats, including the incumbent, plus a Republican were also present. The incumbent British prime minister and his predecessors, a former president of France, the presidents of Brazil and Cuba all arrived to pay their last respects to a deceased liberation fighter born in a tiny village in the Eastern Cape.

The pushy young man who had arrived in the humming urban environment of Johannesburg from the Transkei, fleeing an arranged marriage, had indeed arrived!

The passing of no other African former head of state has been marked by flying the US flag at half-mast. It seems that, except for the sheriff of some small town in South Carolina, President Barack Obama's instruction was universally observed. No African politician's passing occasioned a special sitting of the British House of Commons.

The funerals of few heads of state attracted so many foreign dignitaries. It could easily have been mistaken for a mini-summit.

South Africa will not experience such a proud moment for a lifetime or two! Not only does this moment demonstrate the tremendous goodwill South Africa enjoys, thanks to Mandela, it is also a symbolic expression of the world community's unmistakable endorsement of the achievements of South Africa's democracy.

The procession brought home the ironies of Mandela's life. In the past, collecting signatures for the hundreds of 'Free Mandela' petitions circulating in the capitals of the West one was constantly reminded he was an outcast. Mandela and the South African people's struggle for freedom and democracy were causes championed by the left. In one or two countries, parties and nongovernmental organisations of the centre could be counted among anti-apartheid forces, but in the main, our supporters were social democratic and other socialist parties, the trade unions and a handful of very conscientious clerics. During the 1970s, the ecumenical community also found ways of relating to the struggle.

Mandela represented the millions enslaved by the shackles of racism. Compelling the Pretoria regime to release him would constitute symbolic recognition of the justice of his cause and create opportunities for a resolution.

One can already recognise the mystification of this historic figure. His role as a man of action and one of the initiators of the armed struggle is being suppressed. When his statement from the dock is quoted, they underscore his readiness to make the ultimate sacrifice, understating his willingness to employ force. Everyone reminds us of the ideas and ideals Madiba taught. Far too few say that he also taught us that it was proper, when necessary, to fight to realise them.

The international movement demanding freedom for Mandela was one of ordinary citizens. Its charm was that it was a loose coalition that could appeal to every shade of political opinion, this side of the ultraright. But political parties of the centre and right and the governments they constituted at various times during the 28 years of Mandela's imprisonment responded negatively to our campaign. Conservative politicians in the UK, France, Germany and the US gave apartheid leaders Hendrik Verwoerd, BJ Vorster and PW Botha support. Their presence at Madiba's funeral means that we have won the argument.

We have convinced ice-blue Tories that taking up arms in pursuance of freedom is not only morally right, but an obligation when there are no other options.

It took years of hard slog to bring greater awareness of South Africa's struggle to people in countries that faced their own problems. Thousands of unknown activists contributed to the impressive farewell by the world on Tuesday. It was that international grassroots movement, capable of bridging the political divide between left and right, that made Mandela the 20th century's best-known political prisoner. The movement was fortunate to crest at a moment when there was a highly socially conscious artistic community. But there were many demands on such people from a host of worthy causes. Many willingly lent their names and talent to demand his release.

The words of Raul Castro: 'Eternal glory to Nelson Mandela, the heroic revolutionary!' captured the day.

Madiba, with his legendary modesty, would probably have rejected the laurels of eternal glory. Glory does indeed attach to Mandela's name and his long walk to freedom. And there can be no doubt that he earned it. South Africa basks in the hard-earned glory of an extraordinary life spent in the frontline trenches of the freedom struggle. Mandela has truly done his people, his country and our continent proud.

It is a rare privilege to work with and serve under the leadership of a world historical figure. I shall remain eternally grateful that I was afforded that opportunity.

Lala ngoxolo Ngub'engcuka!

FORTY-ONE

The apparent union between Helen Zille's Democratic Alliance and Mamphela Ramphele's Agang was 'only a highly publicised one-night stand or, at best, a naughty week of exhibitionist love-making' – this opening sets the tone for a shrewdly witty analysis of a failed 'realignment'.

DA, Agang Won't Recover Easily from Fiasco

New Times, 6 February 2014

The upshot is that this was merely a highly publicised one-night stand or, at best, a naughty week of exhibitionist lovemaking, instead of a happy union. Given the media hype and the gushing editorials celebrating the unlikely union among Black Consciousness, white liberals, old Nats and disillusioned African National Congress (ANC) voters, I suppose that, like so many others, I was also fooled.

My serious misreading of the politics of the moment was reinforced by the Sunday press, which carried articles by and interviews with Mamphela Ramphele explaining her decision to serve as the Democratic Alliance's (DA's) presidential candidate. Considering the enthusiasm with which the good doctor expressed herself, the last thing one expected on Monday were the media conferences at which the former partners attacked each other in emotive language.

'By going back on the deal … just five days after it was announced, Dr Ramphele has demonstrated – once and for all – that she cannot be trusted to see any project through to its conclusion,' Helen Zille told the media. 'It is not clear what her objective is, but whatever it is, it is not in the interests of the South African people.'

Not to be outdone, at her media briefing, Ramphele explained her withdrawal from the five-day-old political merger, saying: 'I believed that we had the opportunity to transcend party politics and engage South Africans in a conversation about the future. Some cannot or will not transcend party politics. We see people trapped in old-style race-based politics.'

Most adults probably know that the most pleasant sexual encounters can, on reflection, sometimes be seen to have been unwise.

But this was not some casual bar-room pick up. According to Zille: 'We worked very hard to get this together over a very long period of time. It didn't happen in a week, I can assure you. Since 2010 I have been talking to Dr Ramphele about this.'

So two old friends climbed into bed together only to discover later that it might have been wiser not to. Such instances end in mutual regret but rarely with so much recrimination.

Since our first democratic elections, close to two-thirds of the voters have consistently supported the ANC at the polls.

The remaining one-third has been shared among a number of smaller parties.

Our constitution was deliberately designed to create as much political space as possible for small political constituencies as a way of ensuring inclusivity. The threshold for entry into our legislature was set exceedingly low to facilitate the participation of such interest groups.

At the Convention for a Democratic SA, all parties shared Lyndon Johnson's view that it was better to have them inside the tent.

At that time, the Democratic Party (DP) agreed with the rest of us. As one of the smaller parties, the DP readily recognised the virtues of a system that rarely resulted in outright majorities, thus encouraging coalitions that could contain the ambitions of larger parties.

Now that it has evolved into the largest opposition party, it would appear DA strategists would be more comfortable with less representative legislatures in which these smaller constituencies are excluded outright or are swallowed up by the bigger parties. Stripped of Zille's flowery rhetoric, her much-touted 'realignment' of South Africa's politics masks a longing for a return of the two-or three-party system Anglophone democracies grew accustomed to. The effect would be to rob our political landscape of its rich diversity and to disenfranchise the voters who make up these small constituencies.

The indecent haste with which they announced their marriage, this recently divorced couple explain, was driven by the tension in the ANC's alliance.

Both saw this as a propitious moment to offer the voters an attractive alternative that would also consolidate an otherwise fractured opposition. The prospect of the ANC contesting an election without the unequivocal support of a big union like the National Union of Metalworkers of South Africa and facing a challenge from the Economic Freedom Fighters, according to Ramphele, signalled the possibility of a radical political realignment.

The appearance of Agang SA was a sign of the growth of a constituency of voters, most of them probably African, who do not feel comfortable voting for the ANC or any of the other parties associated with the liberation struggle. As Ramphele explained on Monday: 'There are millions of South Africans who will never vote for the DA, but they want a home, which Agang will give them.'

The five days this marriage lasted suggest that neither the DA's federal executive nor Ramphele understood the other's intentions. In business, a merger is preceded by a due diligence study to gauge what each partner brings to it. It would appear that neither party thought one necessary. The pellets in their aching feet will make it hard for either to quietly walk away from this fiasco.

FORTY-TWO

A heartfelt salute to Epainette Mbeki. Although she was wife of a Rivonia triallist and mother of South Africa's second President, Jordan concentrates instead on her family background, her political steadfastness, and the 'thousands of unnoticed interventions' that she made in the Transkei.

MaMbeki's Passing Marks the End of an Era

New Times, 12 June 2014

Mme Mofokeng, Aunt Piny, MaMbeki and many others are the expressions of affection she earned in a life of service. The passing of Epainette Moerane-Mbeki on June 7 truly marks the end of an era.

Born in February 1916 to a family of African teachers, who had migrated from Lesotho, she grew up as a member of the tiny landowning African elite made up of peasant farmers, professionals and clergy. Like others of their stratum, the Moeranes invested in the education of the children.

The Moerane family, like thousands of others in the colonial world, was the outcome of events unfolding thousands of miles from the tiny village of Mount Fletcher. Like many modern African peasants, the family were practising Catholics, and consequently lived in two worlds. One was the traditional setting of the rural Eastern Cape, before the collapse of the peasant economy in the 1930s. The second was an international faith that linked them not only to millions of co-religionists throughout the world but, through the written word, to the rest of humanity as well.

Thus it was that one year after her birth, in February 1917, a women's demonstration on the streets of Petrograd escalated first into a citywide uprising and then into a revolution that was to have a decisive effect on her life and that of her family.

Mme Mofokeng, Aunt Piny was the sort of activist movements dream of. Possessed of a singular dynamism, she was the initiator and supervisor of developmental projects within her community. She was active within the village she had made her home in 1941 until the eve of her admission to hospital.

She joined the Communist Party of SA in 1938 and remained committed to its vision until her passing.

Like the Catholicism into which she was baptised, communism was an international movement, but one committed to the emancipation of all humanity from oppression and exploitation. In SA, the Communist Party was the only one that admitted people of all races as equals.

Perhaps providentially, the week during which the mortal remains of this outstanding heroine are laid to rest coincides with the 50th anniversary of one of the great turning points in her life and the life of her family. All too often we focus on the heroic dimension of the struggle, sparing little thought for the toll that such commitment takes on the individual lives. Moerane married her fellow teacher, Govan Mbeki, in January 1940 and bore him four children, a daughter and three sons, between 1941 and 1948.

The political commitments of the Mbeki parents conspired against family life. After Govan took up the editorship of the New Age in the mid-1950s, they virtually lived apart. The intensification of the struggle finally led to a life sentence on June 10 1964. Like many others, Aunt Piny became a struggle widow for the next 27 years.

Epainette Mbeki initiated community development projects in Idutywa from the year she and Govan settled there. Using a shop as her base, she built up co-operatives of peasant producers and crafts workers that remain active till today. But she was trying to do this in a Transkei radically changed since her youth. Her second son, Moeletsi, characterised the ancestral homestead in Mount Fletcher during the 1960s as having the 'Chekovian air' of lost wealth.

The destruction of the landowning African middle class was indeed one of the objectives pursued by the National Party of DF Malan, JG Strijdom, Hendrik Verwoerd and BJ Vorster. Alongside others, the Mbekis had organised to fight this onslaught through the Transkei African

Voters Association, of which Govan became secretary in 1941, and the Transkeian Organised Bodies, a federation of local peasant bodies. The thrust of national government policy, supported and administered by a corrupted traditional hierarchy, led to the peasant uprisings of the late 1950s and early 1960s that Govan Mbeki so ably reported in New Age.

Mme Mofokeng leaves behind a country, a continent and a world that has been completely transformed from the one into which she was born. In thousands of unnoticed interventions she made her own singular contribution to that change. In February 1916, the great powers of Europe were engaged in the first international conflict of the industrial age, to reorder the world's geopolitical hierarchy. The disequilibrium that conflict produced resulted in a revolution in Russia the following year.

The new power that revolution gave birth to inspired a global movement committed to ending oppression. Like thousands of her generation, Aunt Piny heard its call, and she responded. Her impressive track record in the struggle derived as much from a passionate commitment as from her profound grasp of the social forces required to make change possible.

Tsamaya hanthle Mme Mofokeng.

.

FORTY-THREE

The tone of this column is regretful and compassionate. It recognises Ramphele's place in the history of the Black Consciousness Movement – but wonders whether the end of her political career is a metonym for the political demise of black consciousness.

Mamphela Ramphele Reflects the Tragedy of Black Consciousness

New Times, 10 July 2014

Though it came as no surprise, I was nevertheless a bit saddened by the announcement this week that Mamphela Ramphele was leaving politics after being expelled from Agang SA, the political party she founded. Ramphele was among a generation of young black intellectuals who came to the fore during the political ice age that descended on South Africa in the aftermath of the Rivonia treason trial.

The thaw that came after they parted ways with the National Union of South African Students owed much to their youthful courage that rejected both the repressive racism of the National Party government and patronising liberalism. After establishing the South African Students Organisation, inspired by black consciousness, they mobilised students at tertiary institutions established in pursuance of Hendrik Verwoerd's grand apartheid, turning many into bastions of the liberation movement. Ramphele's personal contribution earned her the wrath of the apartheid authorities and a deportation order.

When launching her political platform last year, Ramphele announced that her intervention was to bring about a realignment of South African politics and to recapture the mood of optimism that animated the country in 1994. Those of us who recognised in her launch the voice of a substantial number of people who were alienated from existing political parties welcomed her initiative as enriching the healthy mix of political opinions in our institutions. The formal launch of her political campaign a few months later seemed to indicate that she was earnest.

In an act that betrayed inexplicable political folly as well as a willingness to front for others, early this year she accepted nomination as the Democratic Alliance's (DA's) candidate for president. Within a week what had been marketed and appeared to be an ardent political love affair ended. The 'couple' parted amid bitter recriminations. Apparently Ramphele had not consulted her party and had made undertakings she could not honour to DA leader Helen Zille.

After the lacklustre election campaign it ran, it is difficult to assess the extent of the damage Ramphele inflicted on her party and her own political credibility by offering to serve as the DA's election poster girl. The electorate was clearly unimpressed and returned only two Agang members to the National Assembly. A leader whose party fared that badly should usually step aside.

The electorate has responded rather cautiously to the new parties that came on the scene after 1996. Bantu Holomisa's United Democratic Movement (UDM) was able to make its mark in the 1999 elections thanks to powerful regional loyalties and his charisma. Floor-crossing before the 2004 elections decimated the UDM and it came to Parliament with its numbers depleted.

The founding of the Congress of the People (COPE) by those elements of the African National Congress (ANC) leadership who were dissatisfied with the outcome of the Polokwane conference was accompanied by excitement in our media. Pundits, columnists and commentators gleefully announced that an effective challenge to the ANC had at long last arrived. At first, COPE appeared to perform much better than the UDM.

But, by the time the date of the 2009 elections was announced, it was clear that all was not well inside COPE. It emerged from the elections as the third-largest party in the National Assembly, then became embroiled in a self-destructive faction fight waged in the courts. Endless litigation prevented it holding its inaugural conference. During this year's elections, the voters punished COPE, returning only three of its members.

This year's elections did realign South Africa's politics to some degree, but not in the manner Ramphele had hoped for. Opposition benches that at one time reflected the rich tapestry of political opinions in this country are today dominated by two parties, the DA and the Economic Freedom Fighters (EFF). Judged on the basis of parliamentary representation, South Africa is drifting towards a three-party system. While the ANC has maintained its dominant position, commanding more than 60% of the vote, between them, the DA and the EFF have virtually wiped out the smaller opposition parties. It is the opposition that has been realigned, in effect reduced to two parties.

The great tragedy of the Black Consciousness Movement (BCM) was that it was never able to gather and retain much support beyond a narrow band of African intellectuals. After initially leavening liberation politics in the late 1960s and early 1970s, the BCM lost momentum as many of its adherents joined the ANC after 1976.

While the radical posture it had adopted at its inception served the cause well, when radicalism per se ossified into inflexible political practice, it tempted the BCM into grave tactical errors. The BCM turned down participation in the Convention for a Democratic South Africa and boycotted the first democratic elections in 1994, marginalising itself on the fringes of politics. Is the end of Ramphele's political career emblematic of the political demise of black consciousness?

FORTY-FOUR

---

*The political points made in this article were hinted at in a discussion document submitted by Jordan to the ANC in 1999 (**Document 15**); amplified in September 2008 into what was effectively a draft of this version – and finally published only in 2016. It offers an expansive overview of monarchy as an institution; discusses South African monarchies in historical perspective (emphasising that monarchic status had secular origins, not divine right); notes that 'traditional leadership' was compromised by its association with segregation and apartheid; and discusses the ANC's involvement with monarchies over the decades. He concludes that during negotiations the ANC was 'compelled' to enter a tactical alliance with traditional leaders in Contralesa; but asks 'how flexible are we prepared to be in accommodating them?' – having earlier identified the institution of monarchy as fundamentally anti-democratic. The article tackles a major issue that is hardly acknowledged, let alone discussed, at present. Jordan's views are in stark contrast to the increasing closeness since 2009 of the Zuma presidency to traditional leaders.*

On the Institution of Monarchy in South Africa

African Communist, March 2016

Since January 2008 there have been sporadic outbreaks of violence against foreign-born Africans in a number of informal settlements close to Pretoria, Johannesburg and Cape Town.

This violence also escalated sharply in the informal settlements near Alexandra, Diepsloot, Reiger Park and in Jeppestown. Within days of the pogrom's outbreak they took an ethnic turn, with attacks even on other South Africans, especially those speaking Tsonga and Venda. When the final tally of those killed was completed, it was clear that the majority of people killed were South Africans, 22 in all!

There are indications that much of the violence was orchestrated. But the brutality of the attacks and the willingness of even relatively small numbers of South Africans to constitute these violent mobs suggests that feelings of antipathy towards those cast in the role of 'others' are relatively easily mobilised among the poorest section of the African people, such that they can be incited to mount violent attacks on neighbours and strangers.

Are the events we have witnessed evidence of a resurgence of ethnic identity? The urban African tends to identify less with the ethnic group than his or her rural cousin, yet it was in the urban areas that the xenophobic violence took place.

Can we in earnest assert that 104 years after 1912, the traditions of anti-tribalism, of a progressive African nationalism and internationalism are firmly rooted in our society? Can we be absolutely certain that they are secure even within the ANC?

In his call convening the inaugural conference of the ANC, Cde Pixley ka Isaka Seme wrote: 'We are one people, these divisions, these jealousies, are the cause of all our woes today.'

Writing in Govan Mbeki's 'Inkundla yaBantu'in May 1946, Cde Anton Lembede expressed it as follows:'Africans are one: Out of the heterogeneous tribes, there must emerge a homogenous nation.' In 1948, the ANC Youth League's Basic Policy of the Congress Youth League declared: 'The African people in South Africa are oppressed as a group with a particular colour. They suffer national oppression in common with thousands and millions of oppressed colonial peoples in other parts of the world.

'African Nationalism is the dynamic national liberatory creed of the oppressed African people. Its fundamental aim is:

- The creation of a united nation out of the heterogeneous tribes;
- The freeing of Africa from foreign domination and foreign leadership; and the
- The creation of conditions which can enable Africa to make her own contribution to human progress and happiness.

'The African has a primary, inherent and inalienable right to Africa which is his continent and Motherland, and the Africans as a whole have a divine destiny which is to make Africa free among the peoples and nations of the earth.'

That an ethnic consciousness is still quite pervasive amongst sections of the African people casts doubt on our attainment of the objectives that the visionaries of our movement inspired us to strive for. Though it is highly differentiated and can often be correlated with urbanisation, class and region, ethnicity is a political reality our movement is pledged to oppose.

A question we have to pose to ourselves is: has there been a resurgence of ethnic consciousness among the African people, and indeed amongst other South Africans?

The ANC was founded to nurture a national, as opposed to an ethnic, consciousness among the African people. As the pioneer national movement in Southeastern Africa, the ANC also embraced a pan-African vision that linked us in South Africa, not only to the rest of the continent, but also to people of African descent around the world. The ANC inspired the emergence of national movements in the neighbouring countries, helped to organise them and our fighters shared the trenches with all the other liberation movements (with the possible exception of Swapo) in the region. Our own experience in South Africa instructed our movement in non-racialism, while association with international progressive movements taught us internationalism.

In his address from the dock during the Rivonia Trial in 1964, Cde Nelson Mandela summed up the ANC's experience and the evolution of its political identity as a modern national liberation movement in the following terms:

'The Magna Carta, the Petition of Rights, and the Bill of Rights are documents which are held in veneration by democrats throughout the world.

'I have great respect for British political institutions, and for the country's system of justice. I regard the British Parliament as the most democratic institution in the world, and the independence and impartiality of its judiciary never fail to arouse my admiration.

'The American Congress, that country's doctrine of separation of powers, as well as the independence of its judiciary, arouses in me similar sentiments.

'I have been influenced in my thinking by both West and East. All this has led me to feel that in my search for a political formula, I should be absolutely impartial and objective. I should tie myself to no particular system of society other than of socialism. I must leave myself free to borrow the best from the West and from the East.'

With these words Cde Mandela was aligning the ANC with specific political traditions and doctrines, which in broad terms are referred to as democratic. These are traditions rooted in the revolutionary movements that unfolded in the Atlantic region of the world between the 17th and 19th centuries, beginning with the English Revolution of 1640.

In both the great revolutions of that era, in order to establish a democratic order or representative government, the institution of monarchy was overthrown and kings were executed. The American Revolution (1776), by politically seceding from British rule, repudiated the institution of monarchy in favour of a republic. Though the monarchy was permanently restored in Britain, and temporarily in France (between 1815 and 1871), by the end that era, the emperors, kings and other monarchs exercised extremely diminished powers usually defined in a negotiated constitution.

The 1969 *Strategy and Tactics* adopted at Morogoro spells out the ANC's understanding of the liberation struggle:

'The struggle of the oppressed people of South Africa is taking place within an international context of transition to the Socialist system, of the breakdown of the colonial system as a result of national liberation and socialist revolutions, and the fight for social and economic progress by the people of the whole world.

'We in South Africa are part of the zone in which national liberation is the chief content of the struggle. On our continent sweeping advances have been registered which have resulted in the emergence to independent statehood of 41 states. Thus the first formal step of independence has been largely won in Africa and this fact exercises a big influence on the developments in our country.'

The Morogoro document goes further to describe the character of our liberation struggle itself:

'The national character of the struggle must therefore dominate our approach. But it is a national struggle which is taking place in a different era and in a different context from those which characterised the early struggles against colonialism. It is happening in a new kind of world – a world which is no longer monopolised by the imperialist world system; a world in which the existence of the powerful socialist system and a significant sector of newly liberated areas has altered the balance of forces; a world in which the horizons liberated from foreign oppression extend beyond mere formal political control and encompass the element which makes such control meaningful - economic emancipation. It is also happening in a new kind of South Africa; a South Africa in which there is a large and well-developed working class whose class consciousness and in which the independent expressions of the working people - their political organs and trade unions - are very much part of the liberation front. Thus, our nationalism must not be confused with chauvinism or narrow nationalism of a previous epoch. It must not be confused with the classical drive by an elitist group among the oppressed people to gain ascendancy so that they can replace the oppressor in the exploitation of the mass.'

THE INSTITUTION OF MONARCHY

In both our movement and in South African society in general we employ the term 'traditional leaders' rather than the more accurate 'monarchs'. Throughout this paper I will use the term monarch/s, firstly because it is historically more accurate and, secondly, because 'traditional leader' somehow suggests that tradition can endow a person with the right to lead. 'Traditional leader' is a euphemism that conceals the historical reality that many who are so described in fact could not justify that title in terms of tradition (as we shall demonstrate further on). The term itself is ideologically rooted in the monarchist assumptions this paper seeks to debunk. Monarchy is a form of government in which one person – a chief, prince, king, emperor – is the head of state. The word, derived from Greek, literally means one person (mono-) rule (archy). With the exception of hunter-gatherer societies, some of which still survive marginally, the institution of monarchy, in one form or another, has characterised all societies as they develop in size and complexity. Monarchy as an institution is based on the premise of inequality among people. It assumes that some people, by virtue of their birth, are entitled to rule, while others, for the same reason, are born to be ruled by others. Intrinsically, the institution is undemocratic, if not anti-democratic.

The historic origins of the institution are lost in the mists of time, but the careers of a number of historical figures offer a few hints about how monarchies came into being. They also reveal how it has been exploited, utilized and manipulated for both political and economic objectives unrelated to the institution itself.

For example, Napoleon Bonaparte was neither related to the royal family (the Bourbons) of France nor did he claim to be. But, by dint of a distinguished military career he was able to make himself emperor of France in 1803. In South Africa, Shaka, descended from a relatively obscure clan among the Nguni of Natal, performed a similar feat and died as a king. The status of his formerly obscure clan rose with him to become dominant within the kingdom he built, which also took on its name.

History abounds with other examples. The Claudio-Julian clan (gens) in ancient Rome, thanks to Julius Caesar's military career, gave birth to the first five emperors after the fall of the republic. Caesar's name also became synonymous with emperor and all Roman emperors were called 'Caesar', though all those who came after Nero (ruled 55–68 A.D) were not related to the original Caesar. The title Caesar was later Germanized as 'Kaiser' meaning emperor, and as 'Czar' in Russian, also meaning emperor.

In China, two of the famous dynasties that ruled pre-modern China were not even ethnic Chinese. The Yuans (1271 to 1368) of Genghis Khan were Mongols, the Chings or Manchus (1644 to 1911), the last dynasty to rule China, were Manchurians. After defeating the enfeebled indigenously ruled empire's armies in battle, both the Mongols and Manchurians had imposed themselves as rulers.

Monarchy has been manipulated for a range of political and social reasons. Thus, for example, the incumbent royal family of Great Britain are descended from the German House of Hanover, who reigned from 1714 until the death of Victoria in 1901. The Hanovers had been made kings of Britain for a fee. George I, the first Hanoverian king, could not even speak a word of English when he ascended the British throne! The family changed their name from Saxe-Coburg to Windsor under political pressure during the First World War. Battenberg, their original German surname, also became Mountbatten.

The Bernadottes, the royal family of Sweden, are the descendants of a French general, Jean Baptiste Bernadotte, who had risen through the ranks of the Napoleon's army from the rank of a common soldier (a private) to Marshall. Napoleon rewarded him by making him crown prince of Sweden. By 1815 he had become the king of Sweden.

Historically, monarchs have claimed to rule by divine right. Even today monarchs claim they rule by divine grace, hence the titles of Queen Elizabeth II of Britain, are 'Queen Elizabeth II, by the Grace of God, Defender of the Faith, Queen of Britain'. Her father, George VI, was titled 'George VI, by the Grace of God, Defender of the Faith, Emperor of India, King of Great Brtain and Colonies'. The full official titles of the former Emperor of Ethiopia were: 'His Imperial Majesty Haile Selassie I, King of Kings, Lord of Lords, Conquering Lion of the Tribe of Judah, and Elect of God' The Roman Caesars claimed to be descended from the gods. The Egyptian Pharaohs claimed they were themselves Gods! The Emperor of China was called 'the Son of Heaven' and the Emperor of Japan also claims to be descended from divinity. Even the former republican consul of France, Napoleon Bonaparte, funded research he hoped might link him to divinity through the fabled 'Black Madonna'.

Kings, chiefs and princes in Africa also claim/ed to be the representatives of the clan, tribe or nation's founding ancestral spirits on earth. The emperors and kings of Ethiopia claimed descent from the biblical union between King Solomon and Sheba. While the kings of Morocco claim descent from Fatima, a daughter of the prophet Muhammad.

In virtually all monarchies this 'divine spark' was said to be passed down through the eldest or senior male child of the royal family. Consequently male primogeniture (descent through the senior male) is a feature of almost all monarchies. Women could only succeed in the instance that no male heir was available. Consequently, while emperors, kings, chiefs are plentiful, empresses, queens and chieftainesses are few and far between. There are a few instances, like the Lobedu of the Limpopo province, where divinity is said to be passed down through the female descendants of the rain-queen. But that is exceptional.

Whatever its claims were in the past or might be in the present, history demonstrates that monarchy is a political institution created by and manipulated by ruling groups/classes as they deem expedient.

And, though rooted in inequality, monarchy has repeatedly taken account of merit. But, in order to maintain some ideological consistency, such recognition was later rationalised by fabricated 'divine right' (as in the case of Julius Caesar.)

There are many who seem to think that monarchy is a uniquely African institution. Proceeding from that premise they argue that as a system of government indigenous to the continent, monarchy deserves to be upheld and preserved as an aspect of pre-colonial African culture. Parliamentary government, it is argued, is an import from Europe which has its virtues, but these virtues should be assimilated into African political traditions, amongst which is the institution of monarchy.

Firstly, these extravagant claims are completely untrue. Today, after three centuries of political upheavals in Europe, there are monarchies in Sweden, Norway, Denmark, Netherlands, Belgium, United Kingdom, and Spain. Japan, the economic powerhouse of Asia, is a monarchy as are a number of the states in western Asia, Saudi Arabia, Jordan, and the Gulf states.

Monarchy is neither peculiarly African nor is republicanism peculiarly European. A number of African states, ancient, mediaeval and modern, including South Africa itself, are republics .The majority of member states of the African Union are republics. Some accommodate monarchy, others do not. Most 20th century African Nationalists regarded the institution of monarchy as divisive, undermining the effort to build a common allegiance to the nation, by diverting loyalties to ethnic fractions. They saw it as archaic and something to be phased out or completely abolished.

SOUTHERN AFRICAN MONARCHIES IN HISTORICAL PERSPECTIVE

The territories that were finally brought under white control and domination at the end of the Anglo-Boer War had formerly been divided amongst at least nine different African political communities. The political units that existed during the 19th century were the result of centuries of political evolution and a few decades of rapid political change, the Mfecane/Difaqane, characterised by wars and the coalescence of new political units and kingdoms.

By the mid 19th century there were in the southeast the kingdoms of the Xhosa, sub-divided into a number of principalities (or paramountcies as the colonialists preferred to call them); in the north-east, the Zulu kingdom, the Swazi kingdom, the Tsonga kingdom, and the Venda kingdom. On the highveld were the baPedi kingdom, the Tswana and southern Sotho kingdoms. In addition to these there were the independent coloured principalities of the Gri(qua),the Koranas, the Philanders and Nama(qua), under the leadership of their Kapteins (Chiefs).

The Mfecane and its outcome suggest that prior to the late 18th century, most of the African kingdoms in South Africa were decentralised, extended units. A number of relatively autonomous consanguinal clans (persons who are blood relations) clustered around the most powerful amongst them, to which they all ceded senior status. Territorial and political expansion was achieved by the assimilation and incorporation of weaker and dependent neighbours and through alliances sealed through marriages. An example of such expansion was the incorporation and assimilation of Khoikhoi tribes by the Xho-sa. Two large Xhosa clans, amaSukwini and amaGqunukwebe, trace their origins to such incorporation. Within the relatively decentralised kingdom led by the amaGcaleka clan, these assimilated groups retained a large measure of autonomy provided they recognised that they were vassals of amaGcaleka.

Clan heads were usually recognised as chiefs or princes. The power of the state was vested in the chief and his council, usually the oldest male members of the clan, who exercised both law making and judicial powers. They exercised their powers through the lekgotla/inkundla or community forum, which all adult males were free to attend and participate in. All able-bodied adult men were expected to have mastered certain military skills and in times of war served as the community under arms. A clan chief would send a substantial number of his fighters to serve under the king's command in time of war but such warriors owed their primary allegiance to their clan chief.

Historians speculate that the penetration of maize as a grain among the coastal kingdoms led to a population explosion among the northern

Nguni, east of the Drakensberg. As a hardier grain than sorghum, maize soon replaced the former as the staple food though sorghum retained its centrality in ritual. In addition to a higher yield, maize was also less labour intensive and thus indirectly producing more leisure time.

The second external economic factor usually mentioned is the lucrative ivory trade with the Portuguese in Maputo. The clans and kingdoms of the northern Nguni wrestled each other to control this trade leading to wars amongst them. The competition among kingdoms and clans that had recently experienced unprecedented population growth eventuated in a situation of regular military clashes.

It was in this environment that innovative military leaders like Dingiswayo and Shaka rose, from relative obscurity, to forge powerful armies that became highly effective political instruments to create centralised kingdoms.

The kingdoms pioneered by Dingiswayo and Shaka differed from previous political arrangements in that power was centralised in the monarch and the autonomy of the clans was radically reduced. Senior clan heads recognised the need for a new political structure. A centralised state enhanced unity, making possible the maximisation of resources and the end of internecine conflict among the clans.

The centralised state also had a standing army, organised into regiments under the direct control of the monarch, replacing the people under arms in times of war. The enhanced military capacity of these new kingdoms produced a domino effect. To fend off the power of the Zulu kingdom, others emulated it, in the belief that this new model had demonstrated its efficacy. The remnants of other clans and kingdoms, fleeing the heat generated by this competition for the ivory trade, attacked others in their path. Three decades of profound instability that spilled over the Drakensberg into the highveld, into the Eastern Cape, into Mozambique, into Zimbabwe and beyond as far north as Tanzania, ensued. By the time of Shaka's assassination (circa 1828), Dingiswayo and his military exploits had transformed the political landscape of southern Africa.

Shaka established an empire whose boundaries were present day Swaziland in the northeast, the Drakensberg in the west, and the Mzimkhulu River in the south. Diverse and otherwise unrelated clans had been incorporated through conquest. The regiments of the standing army and those for young women served as the primary institution for integrating these previously separate elements into a single kingdom, in the process, also undermining the individuality of the distinct clans. The name of what had been a small, rather insignificant clan, became the name of the kingdom.

Other northern Nguni communities tried to resist Shaka's expansionism. Those whose armies could not hold out against Shaka's well drilled regiments were defeated and their young people were incorporated. Matiwane led his amaNgwane south of the Mzimkhulu, cutting a bloody swathe through the tribes in his path, only to be stopped by British troops of the line on the banks of the Mthatha. The Xhosa king, Hintsa, fearful of the disruptions already caused by the advance of Matiwane, invited the British into his kingdom to halt it. The remnants of the amaNgwane subsequently submitted to Shaka's successor, Dingane.

Mzilkazi kaMashobane, after collaborating with Shaka, fled his authority. Leading his clan, among whom was a body of warriors who had passed through Shaka's regiments, he applied Shaka's battle tactics to great effect against the peoples of the highveld. He established himself as king of a relatively small kingdom in the district of Madikwe, dominating his Tswana neighbours from whom he exacted tribute. Ten years after Shaka's assassination, the horse-riding Boer trekkers broke his power and forced him and his people to retreat across the Limpopo into Zimbabwe where by dint of their military prowess they succeeded to carve out a new kingdom.

In response to the upheavals precipitated by events east of the Drakensberg, another young chief, Lepoqo of the baKwena clan assembled the remnants of other tribes under his leadership. By retreating onto an easily defended mountain plateau, Lepoqo was able to offer those who swore allegiance to him security. In this manner he built around the baKwena an expanding kingdom that assimilated a large number of previously unrelated clans. He soon earned the title Moshoeshoe, for his capacity to 'shave the beard' – defeat in battle – of many of his rivals. The heads of other clans recognised him as king and paid a regular tribute in goods and a number of services.

As in other parts of the world, once these African societies began to grow as a result of internal evolution, conquest or trade, the style of life of the ruling group became noticeably different from the rest. They consumed the most and the best that the society offered. Yet, they were least directly involved in the production of wealth by farming, cattle herding, etc. The kings in particular had the right to call upon the labour of the common man for certain projects and for a given number of days per year. While these were at first regarded as socially significant projects, this was a power that was easily abused and evolved into an aspect of the tribute 'commoners' paid to their monarchs. The construction of the Queen mother's house by the maidens participating in the reed dance is a remnant of this practice. That it could swiftly become a form of forced labour, like the corvée of pre-revolutionary France, should be self-evident. It was into the midst of these relatively new political arrangements that the Boers trekked between 1836 and 1838, becoming a factor for even greater instability and finally the destruction of African independence.

THE SOUTH AFRICAN CONTEXT

As has been noted, many of the 'royal' families of our country, within historical memory, had been persons of no particular status. A brilliant military career had opened the path to kingship in the case of Shaka. In the case of Moshoeshoe his strategic vision and his political skills, had achieved the same. With Mswati I, defensive and offensive alliances amongst clans had also resulted in one chief being elevated above the others, as king.

During the latter part of 18th century and early 19th century, a number of pre-existing kingdoms, chieftaincies and clans disappeared in wars of conquest or self-defence. Some were dismembered and absorbed into Shaka's empire; others had disintegrated and their members were dispersed as refugees; others coalesced with neighbours and fugitive remnants to form new kingdoms; yet others were forged as clans fled before more powerful adversaries - like Shaka or the Trekker Boers; the history of the Khumalo clan, who constituted the core of the migrant Ndebele kingdom led by Mzilikazi, being a case in point.

The nine political units were the outcome of this process that had witnessed formerly powerful rulers reduced to fugitives, while minor chiefs and even 'commoners' had risen to declare themselves or be embraced as kings. What these events demonstrate is the absolute hollowness of the claims made for monarchy! If there is/was 'divine right', it could be earned by brilliant soldiering; by diplomacy and statecraft; and sometimes by default – circumstances foisting it upon a reluctant candidate. Social stratification came into being with the rise of the state, as outlined previously. Thus there emerged royal lineages (or houses) and commoner clans. Though they had not congealed into classes, there were real and recognised distinctions between the families of chiefs, princes and kings, and the rest of the society.

The pre-colonial African monarchs in Southern Africa were the political leaders of agrarian societies based on mixed farming in which land was collectively owned. The monarchs were regarded as custodians of the land on behalf of their kingdom. They had the power to distribute it to families on a usufructuary basis – a family could use the land, but it did not become their private property. Cattle and other livestock were privately owned by and within families, with the most senior male recognised as the decisive voice in their utilization. In most communities there was a gender-defined division of labour, with males responsible for the livestock, while women tended the household and the fields. Tilling in certain cases was also a responsibility men undertook, but livestock was the preserve of men reinforced by a number of taboos that excluded women from the cattle byre and rituals associated with it.

As the ANC's Strategy and Tactics Document of 1969 states:

'From the time alien rule was imposed there has been – historically speaking – unbroken resistance to this domination. It has taken different forms at different times but it has never been abandoned. For the first 250 years there were regular armed clashes, battles and wars. The superior material resources of the enemy, the divided and often fragmented nature of the resistance, the unchallenged ascendancy of imperialism as a world system up to the beginning of the 20th century, the historically understandable absence of political cohesion and leadership in the people's camp; these and other factors combined to end the first phase of resistance against alien domination. But the protracted character of this resistance unequalled anywhere else in Africa is underlined by the fact that the armed subjugation of the indigenous people was only really accomplished by the beginning of this century.'

Monarchs in the wars of resistance

The first war of resistance to colonial expansion occurred within the first decade of the Dutch occupation of the Cape, in 1658. From that date until 1898 there were regular clashes and wars between one or other European colonial authority or its advanced guard in the shape of settler farmers, like the Voortrekkers. African interactions with white governments on and off the battlefield, in their turn, also impacted on the political institutions of African societies, not least the monarchy.

As the embodiment of the state in the African communities, kings, chiefs and headmen were the leaders in all interactions with the colonial powers – Boer and Brit. As in all interactions between separate political communities, such interactions were informed by the past and the present. Both sides to such interactions hoped to maximize their respective positions – employing persuasion where they could, but resorting to force when it was necessary.

As was often the case when dealing with other peoples, the European colonial authorities assumed that political power in the indigenous societies was exercised in the same manner as in Europe. Rather than recognise that the powers of monarchs were often limited and proscribed by convention, colonial officials insisted that they act on their own. Monarchs whose territories were annexed or ceded to a colonial power by treaty saw themselves granted far greater powers over their subjects than they conventionally enjoyed under African customary law, though they were subservient to the colonial power.

Though we tend to emphasise the record of heroic resistance, the performance of African monarchs during the wars of resistance is rather checkered – with some consistently resisting the encroachments of the Europeans, while others resisted inconsistently, others oscillating between resistance and collaboration, and yet others collaborating.

The options chosen by these monarchs were informed by a number of considerations. In certain instances, calculation of the possibility of victory against an enemy equipped with firearms, horses, wagons and even small cannon, persuaded a monarch that it was wiser to pursue accommodation with the Europeans rather than risk annihilation.

After nearly 100 years of resistance, the Khoikhoi chieftaincies were severely weakened. To survive, some chiefs allied with the colonial forces. At the battle in Grahamstown in 1818, for example, it was the arrival of Khoikhoi hunters, under the leadership of Chief Boesak that gave the British garrison the respite it needed to turn its cannon on the advancing Xhosa armies. Grapeshot – ammunition consisting of small iron balls fired together from a cannon – broke the attack Makhanda was leading and was the key factor in his defeat. It was from the remnants of the Khoikhoi tribes of the Eastern Cape that the British created, first the Cape Mounted Rifles, and later the Cape Corps. These Khoikhoi troops became the effective imperial army in the Cape, used against rebellious Boers and other Africans.

After the war of 1835, led by their respective chiefs, the refugee Mfengu communities swore allegiance to the British crown at Peddie (eNgqushwa) and became the principal auxiliaries of the British in all the wars waged in the Cape after that date. A contingent drawn from amongst them, the so-called 'Cape Fingo Boys Column', accompanied Rhodes' invasion of Zimbabwe.

In other instances, as on the highveld, the white newcomers were considered a useful counterweight to more powerful enemies. Thus for example, Moroka, chief of the baRolong of Thaba Nchu, felt it wiser to seek an alliance with the Trekkers against Mzilikazi's Ndebele.

At Vegkop, where the trekkers broke the power of the Ndebele, it was the arrival of Moroka's troops that turned the battle.

Lerothodi, Moshoeshoe's son and successor, first helped the British suppress Moorosi's rebellion in 1880 only to find himself at war with this erstwhile ally a year later, during Ntwa yaDithunya of 1881-2. By contrast, Mhlontlo, king of the Mpondomise, preferred to defy the British when they invited him to join them in an invasion of Lesotho in 1881. He sought an alliance with Lerothodi and was subsequently arrested and sent to Robben Island for his pains.

After defeating the armies of King Cetshwayo in 1879, the British authorities broke up his kingdom by establishing eleven other kinglets, who became their allies. Two of these, Hamu and Zibhebhu, distinguished themselves as pro-British collaborators who harassed and attacked Cetshwayo after he was returned to Natal when he was released from imprisonment.

Resistance consequently was not highly coordinated until the second half of the 19th century when some monarchs succeeded in creating alliances that proved invaluable in times of war. The coloured settlement at Kat River, originally set up as a buffer and as frontier guards for the British-governed Cape Colony, rose in rebellion and allied with the Xhosa under Sandile in 1851. Moshoeshoe too was able to build alliances with the coloured chieftaincies of the Bergenaars and Griqua when he fought the Free State Boers in 1858.

In most instances, however, the African kingdoms and chieftaincies were picked off one by one and had to fight virtually alone. In addition to the disparity in arms, these isolated efforts at resistance were doomed, over time, to fail.

The independence and freedom of the African people was lost on the battlefield, leading to the disintegration of the indigenous social formations. But what is often under-rated are the internal dynamics of these societies themselves, especially as they sought to adjust to the European presence in their midst.

The peoples of Southern Africa had traded among themselves and with other parts of the world for centuries. But in general terms each of the kingdoms were self-sufficient economic units that met most of their needs by what the community itself produced. There was a degree of regional specialisation attributable to the availability of raw materials, climatic and other factors. Trade was incidental to these societies until the mid 17th century, when the presence of the Dutch settlement at the Cape and the Portuguese in Maputo stimulated trade as never before.

African communities traded their surplus goods with Europeans but in return often received necessities for their agrarian life. The economic impact was sometimes disastrous. The Khoikhoi tribes in the Western

Cape lost much of their cattle in trade with the Dutch settlers. Soon, all that many Khoikhoi had to trade was their ability to work. As they became poorer, so the numbers of Khoikhoi servants on white farms and in white homes increased.

The wares Africans bought from the Europeans included iron and steel tools, pots, blankets and cloth. All these became more plentiful after the 18th century, when manufactured goods arrived with the industrial revolution. What was produced by indigenous crafts and smiths could not compete with European goods either in quantity or in quality. Africans became more dependent on trade to meet old and new needs, and thus did increasing numbers of them become detached from African economies to be integrated into the colonial economy, linked to Europe. Like the tribes of the Western Cape, others that became embroiled with the colonial economy sold first their livestock, but eventually their labour power.

The indigenous African societies coexisted side by side with the colonial outposts for close to two centuries. Increasing interaction between more or less self sufficient economic systems evolved into mutual dependence, but it did not however compromise the integrity of either system. Wars of aggression had weakened African societies as they lost more and more land to the expansionist white colonialists. By the mid 19th century this relationship had become unequal. The white trader and his wares had been completely integrated into the lives of African communities. The colourful baSotho blanket and the Ndebele 'kumbesi' were invariably purchased from a trader who could trace these commodities back to a factory in Britain, Holland, Germany or France. The three-legged cast iron pot, glass beads and a host of fabrics, all came from the trader's wagon or his store.

The societies of Southern Africa were prosperous enough to sustain close to two centuries of wars of primary resistance to colonialism. For example, at the height of its power the Zulu kingdom was able to maintain a standing army of 30,000 fighting men and regiments of young women of about the same number. It equipped each warrior with a variety of iron weapons and a full-length war-shield, and put into the field hundreds of young boys who acted as auxiliaries. In the Cape alone between 1779 and 1878 at intervals of approximately ten years, nine successive wars were waged on the frontier. By the second half of the 19th century – the disparity in weaponry being well understood – African kingdoms adopted a common tactic to acquire firearms.

After the opening of the Kimberley mines (1870), a three month contract on the diamond fields could earn a migrant worker a firearm. Moshoeshoe's Sotho kingdom, situated close to the diamond fields, employed this method to build up a formidable arsenal of guns. Fire-arms became more easily available in all colonial countries when the armies of Europe and North America re-equipped after the Crimean War (1851-4).The only problem was that they were obsolete, having been overtaken by the more efficient Martini-Henry, the Winchester, the Schneider, the Mauser and Springfield. Virtually all the kingdoms of Southern Africa were a ready market for firearms, which could only be acquired through legal or illicit trade with Europeans.

Ironically it was the demand for a mass, cheap labour force after the opening of the mines that created the opportunity for African kingdoms to arm temselves for the wars of secondary resistance that ensued all over the Southern Africa after 1870.

'British and colonial troops made war on the Hlubi in 1873, the Gcaleka and the Pedi in 1877, the Ngqika, Thembu, Mpondo, Griqua and baRolong in 1878, the Zulu in 1879, the Sotho in 1880, the Ndebele in 1893 and the Afrikaner republics in 1899,' Jack and Ray Simons tell us.

Doubly ironic is that the drive to acquire firearms enmeshed Africans even more decisively in the white dominated colonial economy. It was the ever increasing demands for labour in mining that finally detached the majority of Africans from the pre-industrial, pre-colonial economy of their forebears and drew them into a common society with whites, coloureds and Asians.

Two centuries of wars of colonial conquest culminated in an attack on the baVenda kingdom in 1898. After a brutal campaign, the Boers of the South African Republic defeated the armies of Machado and Ramabulana and seized their lands. The combined impact of the wars of aggression and the opening of the mines led to the collapse of the African economies and the complete absorption of all blacks into the modern capitalist economy, then dominated by mining.

As Jack and Ray Simons put it: 'South Africa's industrial era was baptized in blood and the subjugation of small nations.'

By 1900 pre-colonial African society had effectively ceased to exist as independent formations, though the outer trimmings continued to survive in highly attenuated form. Even Africans living in the rural areas, ostensibly governed by their monarchs, were integrated into the modern capitalist economy and were either directly or indirectly dependent on it for their livelihoods.

The 1905 Commission on Native Affairs, where the colonial status of all black South Africans was confirmed, was the acknowledgement that Africans and the whites, who had seized their land and dismembered their communities, now lived in a common society and worked within the same capitalist political economy. The formerly discrete, but mutually dependent, economic systems had been subsumed within a dominant, modern capitalist system.

The Africans were required to either adapt to this new reality or go under. The struggle against white domination would have to assume new forms, because the contest would no longer be across frontiers separating two societies. It would assume the shape of a political struggle to wrest political control from a white minority and to acquire an equitable share in the economy within a common society.

The ironies of colonialism

As they were forced to turn away from the familiar symbolic universe of the family, the clan and the ethnic group, the most advanced elements among the Black intelligentsia adopted the more inclusive concepts of the nation, the African continent, and that continent as part of an international community. They also embraced as worthy compatriots others drawn from the most recent immigrant communities from Europe and Asia, who identified with Africa's struggles and the aspirations of her people.

But theirs would be an Odyssey characterised by an agonising existential dilemma: either to confidently confront the uncertainties of progress and the future, or cling to the dubious comfort of a disintegrating past. African writers, poets and leaders of thought experienced the modern era as highly ambiguous, combining extremely destructive aspects with constructive elements.

Their dilemma was brilliantly captured in the epic (misnamed 'Praise poem') Samuel Mqhayi composed to honour the Prince of Wales (later the Duke of Windsor) when he visited South Africa.

Mqhayi personifies modernity as Britain herself, of whom he then says:

'Ah, Britain! Ah Great Britain!
Great Britain on which the sun never sets!
She hath conquered the oceans and laid them low;
She hath drained the little rivers and lapped them dry;
She hath swept away little nations and wiped them away;
And today she lusts even for the open skies.
She sent us the preacher; she sent us the bottle;
She sent us the Bible, and barrels of brandy;
She sent us the breechloader, she sent us cannon;
O, Roaring Britain! Which shall we embrace?
You sent us truth, yet denied us the truth;
You sent us ubuntu, yet took away our ubuntu;
You sent us light, yet we sit in darkness,
Shivering and benighted in the bright noonday sun!
Nay, this mighty Britain is confusing the peoples;
Harsh, hard and cold is she, even unto her womb,
What then shall we say of her offspring?!
And, worse yet, what can be said of her father!'

These excruciating ambiguities of modern times grew as urbanisation accelerated.

In their distress, many intellectuals were tempted to lend an ear to the siren songs of a backward-looking nativism, which its adherents frequently presented as 'authenticity.' The colonial intelligentsia in Africa (as well as in Asia) often portrayed the dilemma posed by modernity as tragic. The national liberation movement's response was that rather than wallowing in their alienation or seeking refuge in the past, the intellectuals should reintegrate themselves with the common people by active engagement in the political and social struggles for freedom, independence and progress.

The most progressive among the Black intelligentsia consequently evolved an inclusive vision of South Africa, embodied in Rev Z R Mahabane's invocation of: 'The common fatherhood of God, and the brotherhood of man.' From its inception, African nationalism in South Africa has preferred inclusivity to ethnicity, and has eschewed racism and tribal particularism. The non-racial national ethos, expressed in the preamble of the Freedom Charter as:

'South Africa belongs to all who live in it. ...' is the legacy they left us.

In 1924, the left wing of the then predominantly white labour movement, organised as the Communist Party of South Africa (CPSA), was the first among whites to accept the notion of a non-racial society. Liberals among the dominant capitalist classes began to see it as the inevitable result of the changes wrought by World War II. White liberalism made its last ambivalent attempt to force this recognition on the rest of white South Africa through the 1946 (Fagan) Commission on Native Laws. The fate of Fagan's recommendations testify to the option the majority of white South Africans chose: excluding Blacks from common citizenship.

Colonialism of a Special Type (CST) thus carried within it two contradictory tendencies – the one, segregationist; the other a countervailing, integrationist thrust. But the empirical fact of institutionalised racism rested like an ominous shadow on the consciousness of all South Africans, in instances shaping it to a greater extent than objective socio-economic forces.

CST AS A PATH OF CAPITALIST DEVELOPMENT

South African capitalist development, unfolding in a colonial setting, acquired a number of features peculiar to itself. The 1905 Commission on Native Affairs symbolised the victory of British imperialism over the Boer republics as well as the incorporation of the former enemy elite into the dominant ruling bloc. Both the victorious Brits and the defeated

Boers regarded all Africans, irrespective of their ethnic affiliation or origin, as a conquered and subject people. Coloureds and Asians though treated marginally better than Africans, shared the same colonial status.

The tenor of and the evidence led at the 1905 Commission made it clear that its purpose was to devise policy for the purposes of laying out an efficient and effective path of capital accumulation for the now dominant Randlords.

The commission recommended that the numerous existing instruments of coercion derived from the previous century, including racism, be harnessed for this purpose. Africans, coloureds and Indians would not be allowed a say in the manner the country was governed, except for a handful that would be permitted to buy their way out of their helot status by ownership of property of a certain value. These were the 'exempted Natives', who had the vote in the former Cape Colony and Natal. The Commission thus cobbled together a system of colonialism, but with distinctive characteristics – the colonial power (the white minority) and the colonised people (the Black majority) lived in the same territory. Our movement has referred to this as a Colonialism of a Special Type (CST)'.

CST was the institutional expression of the economic evolution of South Africa after the opening of the mines. As we have seen, during the 1870s many African kingdoms thought they might more effectively resist conquest and domination by acquiring firearms. That option had however entangled them in the white controlled colonial economy. The indigenous pre-capitalist economic systems thus began articulating with the emergent capitalist economy to their own detriment. African economic independence was more radically compromised when kingdoms were incorporated into either the Boer Republics or the two British colonies of the Cape and Natal. Taxation was the means both systems then employed to compel Africans to make themselves more readily available as a source of cheap labour power. Thousands of African tillers were literally impressed into the modern economy in this fashion, undermining the agrarian economy, leaving it as a subordinate periphery reproducing cheap labour power for mining capital.

CST carried within it two contradictory tendencies – the one, segregationist; the other, its countervailing trend, an integrating impulse. Mining capital and CST more generally were central to driving both tendencies simultaneously. A modern capitalist economy acted as an integrating factor drawing in large numbers of labourers into the economic heartland. At the same time, pass laws, hostels, the migrant labour system and interventions by different white minority regimes to prop up subsistence activities in the reserves, not out of philanthropy, but to impose the burden of labour reproduction (child rearing, care for the sick, the injured and elderly) on to these marginalized location under the patriarchal domination of colonially sanctioned monarchs.

The principal countervailing tendencies to integration were the economic interests of the dominant white capitalist classes – in mining and agriculture – and the sectional interests of the Afrikaner petty bourgeoisie.

Like any other dominant class, the white oligarchy in mining and commercial agriculture sought to limit access to their economic and social status. Law, inherited custom and the mores of British colonialism in Africa were used to deny Africans access to various forms of productive property. This was first applied in the mines, but was incrementally extended to commercial agriculture, then to various trades and professions, then to a number of commercial activities, culminating in 'Stallardism,' that excluded Africans from the urban areas except when 'ministering to the needs of the whites.' By the 1920s all whites, including the recently landed immigrant and even the beggar, were defined as members of an exclusive community, collectively endowed with certain rights and prerogatives solely on account of their race.

Racial domination – in its various guises of 'white supremacy with justice' as with Smuts' United Party, or the 'apartheid' of the National Party – was also the means of domination employed in the pursuance of particular class interests. By legislative fiat and adminisrative measures, the white autocracy steadily destroyed the property-owning classes among Blacks. Beginning with the Natives Land Act of 1913, these measures were followed up by the Natives Land and Trust Act of 1935, the Asiatic Land Tenure Act of 1946, The Group Areas Act of 1951, the Bantu Authorities Act of the same year and a host of others that bankrupted the Black property-owning classes by restricting their rights to own property and engage in commerce. Policies such as the white labour policy instituted by the Nat-Labour Pact government after 1924, then further elaborated in the Job Reservation Act of 1954, also made certain forms of skilled work the exclusive preserve of whites. State policy thus created a racial hierarchy graded by skin colour, with whites at the top and Africans at the bottom.

An intricate dialectic of race and class thus evolved, resulting in a class stratification coinciding in large measure with a racial hierarchy, so that in general terms the overwhelming majority of Blacks were propertyless working people, while the propertied classes were virtually lily white. The ANC's policy thrust of tilting in favour of the working class and its mass organisations is grounded in this reality. It is this same historical experience that is the basis of the alliance with the Communist Party and Cosatu (Congress of South African Trade Unions).

These racial exclusions were institutionalised in the 1909 Act of Union, then by extension differentially applied to the other Blacks. Indians, as a numerically weak minority of recent immigrants, were the easiest victims. Coloureds, the majority of whom were the descendants of propertyless servants and former bonded persons, were to witness steady encroachments on their rights well into the 1970s.

The second powerful reinforcement of racism came from the sectional interests of the Afrikaner petty bourgeoisie and intelligentsia. British victory in the Anglo-Boer War destroyed Afrikaner independence and plunged the Afrikaner people into a cosmopolitan, industrialising society dominated by British monopoly capital. The impoverished Afrikaner ex-farmer of the early 1900s, like his African and coloured counterparts, entered the job market as the least skilled and least acculturated to urban life. All three of these groups of former peasants now had to re-invent and restructure their identities as new persons living in a common society. From the perspective of the Afrikaner petty bourgeois intelligentsia – whose domain was the Dutch reformed churches and its educational institutions – this process held out the prospect of the urbanising Afrikaner community drifting away from the church, the 'volk' and other institutions dominated by themselves.

Consequently, the bearers of Afrikaner nationalist ideology were the small property owners and related strata amongst the Afrikaners, whose livelihood depended on the preservation and elevation of that community's distinct language, the preservation of its churches and exclusive schools, as well as other institutions. They manipulated the totems and symbols of the Afrikaner's recent past – defeat in war, the destruction of their republics, suffering at the hands of the British occupation forces etc. – to cocoon their community against the influences of the cosmopolitan environment. An ethnic nationalism, which alleviated the pain of the Afrikaner working people's alienation, but could not redress their political and economic subordination, was the result. Afrikaner ethnic nationalism defined an ethnic 'home' for a people who had been rudely torn from their pre-industrial life by war and bankruptcy and placed them under the ideological domination of the Afrikaner propertied classes who thenceforth employed ethnic mobilisation as the means to carve out a niche for themselves in South Africa's developing capitalist economy.

The Afrikaner nationalists found ready helpers among the right wing of the white labour movement, led by the South African Labour Party. An electoral pact between the two in 1924, defeated Smuts' South African Party and began an inexorable reinforcement of racism through law. The white labourites hoped to promote the claims of white workers to certain rights by an appeal to their status as whites in a colonial society. White labourism's alliance with the racists was sealed at the expense of the Black people in general, but the Black working class in particular. As the majority of white workers embraced racism, so too did they drift away from the Labour Party, which virtually disappeared from white South African politics by the outbreak of World War II. This led to the coalescence of a racial bloc – whites as a dominant racial group – led by the capitalist classes, who projected the particular interests of the white propertied classes as the general interest of all whites.

The third, but no less important countervailing trend was white racist state policy. Once institutionalised, racial domination and its twin, racism, infected every pore of society. The compound labour system, originally designed to give mining employers greater control over their work force, was extended to virtually every section of African workers. After the Report of the Stallard Commission in 1923, Africans were arbitrarily defined as aliens in all the urban areas of the country. They were residentially segregated to improve control over their movements and residential segregation quickly became the norm in urban areas outside a few areas of the Cape, Natal and some freehold locations in Johannesburg.

The National Liberation Movement and African Monarchies

When the ANC was founded, its founders conceived the movement as something akin to the British parliament. There was a 'House of Commons', which was the dominant part of the movement, but also a 'House of Chiefs', into which all chiefs, kings, headmen and others considered royalty were invited. The Sotho monarch, Letsie, was made head of this house. In his absence the Swazi Queen also was given a special place in this house and she made a substantial monetary contribution to the ANC to enable it to set up a newspaper, Abantu/Batho.

The special status accorded to royals was repeated when the National Liberation League was established in Cape Town in 1935.

The attitude of the movement to African royalty was determined by two considerations. One was the role that a number of African kings and chiefs had played in the struggle to resist conquest. King Dinizulu, for example, was unable to attend the inaugural conference of the ANC because he was still in detention on St. Helena for his alleged role during the Anti-Poll Tax (Bambatha) Rebellion of 1906.

The second was the understanding that many, if not the majority, of ordinary Africans respected royalty and treated them as such. A movement that did not enjoy at least their tacit support was unlikely to be successful.

For the first decade that they participated in the House of Chiefs, there were no serious differences between that house and the rest of the ANC. Strains and stresses began to emerge during the 1920s.

After the passage of the Native Laws and Administration Act of 1927, which made all African monarchs and chiefs the vassals of the

'Supreme Chief of all Natives' in the person of the Governor-General (very much as the King of Britain was by law Emperor of India), reduced all African women to the status of legal minors, and assigned every African, irrespective of choice or preference to a chief, headman or king as a subject. That law reduced the institution of monarch in South Africa to that of employee of the white racist state. Virtually all the hereditary kings, chiefs and headmen withdrew from the ANC and the House of Chiefs fell into disuse. Some elected chiefs, like Chief Albert Luthuli, retained their membership and participated in the movement. When President Dr A B Xuma revised the constitution of the ANC to create a more efficient and effective movement in 1943, he abolished the House of Chiefs.

The ANC's approach to the institution of monarchy has been governed more by tactical considerations than by principles. Though the principles that undergird the political tradition the ANC belongs to and has always identified with are intrinsically opposed to monarchy, the movement has preferred not to oppose the institution per se for the tactical consideration that it was essential to isolate the apartheid regime and its most consistent supporters amongst African monarchs.

As part of that broad strategy, when the mass democratic movement inspired by the ANC reached its height in the mid-1980s, the ANC mobilized the anti-regime monarchs and chiefs into the Congress of Traditional Leaders of South Africa (Contralesa). It is unclear the extent to which by creating such a body the ANC has committed itself to not merely acceptance of the reality of monarchy, but also its perpetuation. What was clear from the outset, though, is that Contralesa was not intended to become a monarchist lobby in the ANC.

Drawing together the threads of argument in this paper, we can summarise them as follows:

- Monarchy, or what we euphemistically refer to as' traditional leadership', is not a uniquely African institution but rather a universal one which all human societies at a certain point in their evolution adopted.
- Monarchy does not derive from any pre-ordained, let alone divinely inspired, source. It has historically been an extremely utilitarian

institution either imposed by successful generals/military leaders or embraced by ruling classes in pursuance of their own political agendas.

• Monarchy is based on the fundamentally anti-democratic notion that some humans are born to rule, while others are born to be ruled.

• The ANC is a democratic national liberation movement inspired by democratic traditions associated with the revolutionary movements that have shaped the modern world since 1789. That tradition established the principles of 'government of the people, by the people, for the people' and equality among all humans.

• For a number of tactical considerations, during the course of the struggle for freedom, the ANC has not addressed the institution of monarchy per se.

What needs to be discussed in the movement is how we proceed beyond the tactical considerations to the issues of principle, recognizing that tactical allies often can transmute into opponents because they are located in political spaces whose fundamental interests run counter to the objectives of the liberation movement.

We need also revisit our own self-definition as set out in a number of historic documents, like the Morogoro *Strategy and Tactics* and subsequent ones, as a struggle that, as was mentioned earlier and is worth repeating:

> '...is taking place in a different era and in a different context from those which characterised the early struggles against colonialism. It is happening in a new kind of world – a world which is no longer monopolised by the imperialist world system; a world in which the existence of the powerful socialist system and a significant sector of newly liberated areas has altered the balance of forces; a world in which the horizons liberated from foreign oppression extend beyond mere formal political control and encompass the element which makes such control meaningful - economic emancipation. It is also happening in a new kind of South Africa; a South Africa in which there is a large and well-developed working class whose class consciousness and in which the independent expressions of

the working people - their political organs and trade unions - are very much part of the liberation front. Thus, our nationalism must not be confused with chauvinism or narrow nationalism of a previous epoch. It must not be confused with the classical drive by an elitist group among the oppressed people to gain ascendancy so that they can replace the oppressor in the exploitation of the mass.'

In the instance that the terrain on which we have been forced to manoeuvre has compelled us to embrace tactical allies who have their own sectional agendas, how much flexibility can we extract from such allies and how flexible are we prepared to be in accommodating them? Would, for example, constitutional monarchy be an acceptable option for us as the ANC? Should we opt for a constitutional monarchy, given that the monarchs are numerous and are found in every province? How many will be recognized? What would such recognition entail? Would this apply only to African monarchs to the exclusion of the coloured/ Khoikhoi monarchs?

If, on the other hand, the ANC is of the view that its strategic objective of attaining maximum unity amongst the African people, in the first instance, is likely to be undermined by the perpetuation of monarchy, how would we as a movement persuade the country and the people to abandon monarchy in preference for an unfettered republic?